ENVIRONMENTAL TOXICOLOGY IN SOUTH EAST ASIA

Environmental Toxicology in South East Asia

B. WIDIANARKO, K. VINK &
N.M. VAN STRAALEN

editors

VU University Press
Amsterdam 1994

VU University Press is an imprint of:
VU Boekhandel/Uitgeverij bv
De Boelelaan 1105
1081 HV Amsterdam
The Netherlands

tel.   +31(0)20 6444355
fax   +31(0)20 6462719

isbn   90-5383-287-4
nugi   825

Layout: Sjoukje Rienks, Amsterdam
Cover design: Neroc Special Services, Amsterdam
Photo on the cover: Karen Vink
Printed by: Wilco, Amersfoort

Table of contents

Part 3
Trace metal studies

Preface

The international conference on Environmental Toxicology in South East Asia was held at Satya Wacana Christian University, Salatiga, Indonesia, in August 1992, in cooperation with the Vrije Universiteit, Amsterdam. The conference was attended by about 200 participants from six countries in the region (Australia, Brunei Darussalam, India, Indonesia, Malaysia, Philippines) and some delegates from the Netherlands. The two organizing universities would like to emphasize the importance of the development and application of studies on environmental toxicology in South East Asia. With the conference, an attempt was made to increase the awareness of the various environmental problems in the region and to emphasize the need for exchange of experience among institutions and scientists. The meeting, under the chairmanship of the editors of this book, was very successful. This proceedings volume contains a selection from the papers presented and illustrates the variety of environmental issues that were discussed. As the conference was the first initiative, we hope that there will be a follow-up of similar meetings, to further develop the science of environmental toxicology in South East Asia.

K.H. Timotius

Dean of the Faculty of Science and Mathematics
Satya Wacana Christian University, Salatiga
Chairman of the steering committee of the Conference

Acknowledgements

The editors wish to acknowledge gratefully all colleagues, secretarial assistents and students who contributed to the preparation of this proceedings volume. In alphabetical order, thanks are due to Dr. M. Ahsanullah, Dr. J.H. Ali, Prof.Dr. S. Bhattacharya, Dr. I.M. Dutton MSc., Dr. P.C. Farley, Drs. M.J. Heijkoop MSc., Dr. D.T. Jones, Drs. A.S. Krave MSc., Prof.Dr. A.C. Posthumus, Dr. A. Tejada and Dr. C.A.M. van Gestel for the scientific reviewing. Furthermore, Dr. I.M. Dutton MSc., Dr. P.C. Farley, Mrs. S.E. Hall, R.S. Kameo MA., Dr. M.S. Prince and Dr. C.E. Prince did a great job in making English style corrections. During the final editing the help obtained from Miranda Aldham-Breary M.Sc. was greatly appreciated. We also thank Mr. S. Basuki for typing the manuscripts and Mr. Luigi Sanna for preparing the drawings. Finally to the students: U. Aryani, N. Budiriyanti, L. Dewi, D. Indriatmoko, Th.A. Kurniawati, B. Pranoto, A.S. Prasojo and W. Wiharti, who took part in the lengthy typing process, we also say thank you.

The editors of this book would like to express their appreciation for the efforts of all members of the organizing committee (staff and students of Satya Wacana) who made the conference possible. We also acknowledge the support obtained from UNESCO/ROSTSEA and IDP (Australia), as well as contributors from several local companies.

The publication of this book is jointly supported by the Faculty of Biology of the Vrije Universiteit, Amsterdam, the Faculty of Biology of the Universitas Kristen Satya Wacana, Salatiga, and the VU, UKSW co-operation project (BFSD).

B. WIDIANARKO
K. VINK
N.M. VAN STRAALEN

Introduction

This volume is an outgrowth of the first ever scientific meeting on Environmental Toxicology in South East Asia. The conference has succesfully brought together delegates from most countries of the region to share their findings and experiences. Although Environmental Toxicology is still a relatively new scientific discipline, considerable efforts have already been made in the region. As a result, in this volume we will find an interesting state of the art in the field, as reflected by the selected papers appearing in this book. Contributions from outside the region have also found a place in this volume.

In the last decade, countries in South East Asia have experienced a substantial economic development which has contributed to an upswing in industrial activities. This condition, combined with the ever increasing population burden, has created environmental problems, which could not have been predicted.

Besides industrial development, almost all countries in the region have put their emphasis on self-reliance with respect to food production. As a consequence, intensive agricultural practices have been chosen and accordingly a massive use of agrochemicals could not be avoided. This particular phenomenon has elicited many studies, as can be seen from the papers dealing with pesticides (and other agrochemicals) in part 2 of this volume.

A considerable amount of work on trace metal contamination, has also been done (part 3). These studies show a broad diversity of approaches, ranging from biochemical studies on the mode of action of metals to residue analysis in food products.

On the more fundamental aspects, it is obvious that there is an urgent need to develop methods which are relevant to the region. It seems that environmental test systems based on indigenous species are highly favoured (part 4). In this respect, papers on methods available or developed in Europe and Australia have enriched the discussion and provide good references.

A special space has been provided for contributions which address the scientific field in general (part 1 and 5). The idea behind this is that, in this very first conference, we tried to accomodate all contributions in the broadest sense of Environmental Toxicology. The leading chapter of the book discusses the challenges that face the development of environmental science, and its implementation in pollution control measures, while the closing chapter presents a series of case-studies in which certain techniques were applied to assess environmental impact of local emissions.

In the years to come another development which can be seen as a potential source of environmental problems is industrial relocation. The latest trend in the region shows that companies are relocating some of their activities from Europe and North-America into the South East Asia region. There is an indication that industrial relocation is not driven simply by classical factors such as cheap labor costs, but also by the more stringent environmental regulations in advanced industrial countries. This means that industry in the region will rely, mostly, on 'second hand' technology from the more advanced countries. There is a potential risk that South East Asia will face the same environmental problems that other countries are now struggling to overcome. This is, of course, a new challenge for environmental toxicologists in South East Asia.

BUDI WIDIANARKO

Part 1

Challenges of environmental toxicology in South East Asia

1.1

Pollution control in Indonesia: Present strategies and future outlooks

N. MAKARIM

Abstract

Indonesia is accellerating its development towards becoming an industrialized country, shifting from a natural resource-based economy to an industry-based economy. This trend, combined with the population growth (approx. 2% per annum), has substantial environmental implications, especially with regard to pollution. To anticipate this problem, in 1990 the Indonesian government established the Environmental Impact Management Agency (BAPEDAL). In this paper, present and future strategies for pollution control by BAPEDAL are described.

1.   The background

Since the opening up of the economy in 1967, Indonesia has experienced three stages of development. The first was during the seventies when oil and gas dominated the economy. This period was marked by investment in primarily import substitution manufacturing industries and the development of infrastructure. Secondly, with the fall of the price of oil early in the eighties, restructuring of the economy began. The economy shifted slowly from oil based to a more mixed one. Thus natural resource based industries flourished in the eighties. It seems that the progress towards a more export-oriented economy will continue in the third stage, in the nineties and beyond. If economic growth can be maintained at the present level of about 6% per annum, by the year 2000 Indonesia's status will be upgraded to that of a middle income country.

Indonesia's population is about 180 million at present. At 2% growth, by 2020 the population will be 267 millions before it levels off. Fifty percent of the population will then live in urban areas. With increased income, it is expected that the population will have a better level of education, higher skill level, and higher mobility with a different pattern of consumption. More globalization of the world economy and the Asean Free Trade Area will push Indonesia into competitive behaviour where efficiency considerations in decision making will be more dominant.

These trends will put more pressures on the environment. Increased levels of urbanization means problems of sanitation, solid wastes and availability of drinking water in urban areas. Higher rate of investment in resource based industries means more pressures on the environment's carrying capacity. Intensification of agriculture in Java (the location of 80% of the industry) means more agricultural chemicals spilled into the environments. Thus it is expected that the major environmental problems in the future will be land use, pollution, degradation of the environment, forest, and urban living. These trends therefore become the main consideration in Indonesia's environmental management planning.

2. Environmental qualities

In 1926, the Dutch colonial government enacted the 'Hinder Ordonantie' (Disturbance Act) to prevent minor disturbances originating from trade and industries. The act continued to be used with various additions as a legal base until 1984 when the act for Environmental Management was enacted. Pollution problems were limited to local problems until the mid seventies when pollution started to become a national concern. With intensification of industrial development, urbanization and population growth, the problem grew. Ten years of water quality monitoring showed deteriorating water quality in some areas:

- pH of Musi River in Palembang, South Sumatra decreased at a rate of 0.16 per year, Ciliwung River in Jakarta at a rate of 0.13 per year and Surabaya River in East Java at a rate of 0.02 per year.
- BOD in Banjir Channel, Jakarta increased at a rate of 3.24 mg/L, in Citarum River at Nanjung, West Java at a rate of 2.70 mg/L per year.
- Segments of certain rivers experience gross pollution; one example is BOD of the water in a segment of the Seputih River at Lampung: 600 mg/L.

Table 1 *Air quality of selected areas in Jakarta (Dec. 1991- Feb. 1992)*

Location	NOx (ppm, 8 h mean)		Particulate matter (ppm, 8 h mean)	
	Readings	Standard	Readings	Standard
Sudirman	0.125	0.05	556.31	260
G. Subroto	0.058	0.05	384.54	260
S. Parman	0.056	0.05	581.42	260
Kramat Raya	0.061	0.05	951.06	260
Casablanca	0.053	0.05	259.07	260

Source: BAPEDAL, KP2L DKI Jakarta.

Air quality in metropolitan areas (Jakarta, Bandung, and Surabaya) and certain industrial concentration areas (Cibinong in West Java and Pulogadung in Jakarta) also shows a trend toward higher levels of pollution. Table 1 shows some spot readings for selected areas in Jakarta.

In addition, the problem of environmental degradation due to sand and gravel quarrying is prevalent in areas of West Java, Central Java, Bali and other areas. The problem of hazardous waste from agriculture and industrial sectors is increasing.

3.   Institutions

Prior to 1978, environmental problems were were solved by ad-hoc interdepartmental teams. With the increase in intensity and frequency of environmental problems, the office of the Minister of State for Development Supervision and the Environment (PPLH) was created in 1978. It later became the office of the Minister of State for Population and the Environment (KLH). The function of KLH is to coordinate environmental management nationwide and thus to prepare environmental policies. Implementation of these policies is in the hands of sectorial departments and provincial governments.

The Environmental Impact Management Agency (BAPEDAL) was created in 1990 by presidential decree with the charge of pollution control. Its scope covers pollution control, management of hazardous wastes, implementation of environmental impact assessments and the development of public participation in environmental impact management. At the end of this year (1992), BAPEDAL will have representative offices in 12 provinces and 12 municipals districts. BAPEDAL's strategies for controlling pollution are described below.

4.   Strategies: present and future

Factors that will determine the success of BAPEDAL in its first years are commitment to environmental management from higher level decision makers, level of public participation, institutional strength, public confidence in BAPEDAL-designed and implemented programs that can deliver results in the shortest possible period but in the medium term may be building blocks for institutional development. The programs have been designed to start in a focused way and expand as institutions are strengthened. Later, the programs may converge and with fine tuning create a more comprehensive management system. Programs being implemented at the moment mare the Clean Water Program (PROKASIH), the Clean City Program (ADIPURA), AMDAL (Environmental Impact Assessment), and the Clean Air Program (Langit Biru or Blue Sky). Four other programs presently being prepared are Coastal and Marine Pollution Control, Control of Environmental Degradation from Mining and Quarrying, Hazardous Waste Management Program, and management of Environmental Impact from Small Scale Activities.

The strategies named above will be implemented from 1990 to 1994. With a changing working environment BAPEDAL must also make adjustments to these strategies. At present, the direction for the rest of the nineties are:

1. Further development of the institutions: division of authority, environmental quality standard methods, administrative procedures.
2. Implemention of a strong professional marketing program to develop further the commitment of decision makers and the public. NGO development, particularly in technical skills, organizational and management are also included in this category.
3. To focus on expanding programs that can then be used to give a system for the development of an infrastructure to deal with various problems, for example hazardous waste disposal sites, urban living quality. Also a full scale environmental quality monitoring program must be implemented.
4. Research, particularly in technical fields (e.g. carrying capacity), public policies, and urban sewage treatment systems.
5. Activities seeking a bigger budget from national and international sources.

Beyond 2000, it is expected that political strengths and institutions for pollution control will be relatively adequate. Thus the emphasis on management will be on strengthening external factors (control NGO and public), developing infrastructures, implementing market mechanisms, and research:

1. Development on a wider scale for the external control system (rewards, procedures, skills, information disseminations etc.).
2. Implementation of policy tools:
    - market mechanism for more efficient use of natural resources,
    - public pressures (green consumerism) for environmental protection,
    - maintaining legal approaches,
    - creative public policies (e.g. disclosure requirements),
    - investment policies.
3. Development and operation of infrastructures:
    - sewage systems for cities with a population of more than 1 million,
    - facilities for disposal and recycling (waste trade etc.).
4. Scientific research: toxic waste in the environment, future public policies etc. for sectorial departments and provincial governments.

1.2

Ecotoxicological approaches to environmental standards, with special reference to soil quality

B. WIDIANARKO, K.H. TIMOTIUS & K. VINK

Abstract

Ecotoxicology is aimed at analysis of impacts induced by toxic substances already present in an ecosystem and the prediction of future impacts of new chemical releases into the environment. Ecotoxicology, although still in its infancy, may provide a foundation for environmental decisions in relation to the presence of pollutants. The feasibility of approaching the problem of establishing measures of environmental quality through ecotoxicology is discussed in this context. Special attention is given to soil quality which has been largely neglected to date. Ecotoxicological risk assessment (ERA) has emerged as a promising field. This new field seeks to protect the environment by considering probabilities of ecological damage occurring. To arrive at standards for protection of environmental quality, empirical results from ecotoxicity tests are combined with extrapolation methodologies. Some technical and methodological insights into several types of ecotoxicity tests have been introduced, including microecosystem (MES) tests as a novel approach in soil ecotoxicology studies. A review of existing extrapolation methodologies is also given.

1. Introduction

In accordance with the framework of the sustainable development concept, the environment as a living support system should be managed in such a way that it can be handed over to the next generations without losing its quality (WCED 1987). When discussing environmental management, we face the problem of defining the changes in ecosystem quality due to the presence of any kind of disturbances. All decisions concerning the quality status of the environment involve political rather than scientific considerations, as value judgments are involved in all decision making processes (Stephan 1986), however, the fundamental position of environmental research cannot be neglected. It should be made clear that basic research is the foundation on which environmental decisions must rely.

In this contribution, we seek to focus on the feasibility of approaching the problem of establishing standards for environmental quality through a newly developed field: ecotoxicology. Ecotoxicology is aimed at the analysis of impacts induced by toxic substances already present in the ecosystem and the prediction of future impacts of new chemical releases into the environment. In our view, ecotoxicology, although still in its infancy, may provide a foundation for environmental decisions in relation to the presence of pollutants.

2. The need for environmental quality standards

Pollution, as one of environmental disturbances generated by the release of toxic compounds into the environment, has been shown to be a major cause of ecological damage. It is not easy to know whether the quality of an ecosystem has been changed due to the presence of pollutants if we do not have reference data on ambient environmental quality. Environmental quality standards are normative statements describing a 'desired' state of some parts of the environment (Vegter et al. 1988). Environmental quality standards are usually expressed as a list of 'safe' concentrations of hazardous chemicals which can be regarded as a lower bound for the concentration that can be expected to be harmful for a given community.

From the above definition, it is easy to understand the meaning of environmental quality standards, but it has to be realized that the derivation of these standards implies the choice of acceptable and unacceptable levels of ecological changes. The decision concerning what is an acceptable or unacceptable level involves not only ecological considerations but also economic arguments.

Soil ecotoxicology is a new field compared to aquatic toxicology and accordingly, environmental regulation concerning soil quality lags behind the application of regulations for water and even atmospheric quality protection. At present quality standards for water and air have been developed by many countries in the world, but this is not the case for soil. Only a few countries have established soil quality standards, the reason being that, relative to air and water pollution, soil pollution has been largely underestimated for a long period (Eijsackers 1991).

Soil quality standards should assure the maintenance of soil condition in relation to considerations such as: (1) the potential for harm to any use by humans, plants or animals, (2) functioning without restriction in natural cycles, and (3) contamination of other parts of the environment (Moen et al. 1986). Furthermore, analogous to water quality standards, soil quality standards should be derived with regard to land-use. For different land uses, different quality standards are required.

As the chemical properties of soil are more complex than those of water, effect-oriented ecotoxicological research will not, on its own, be sufficient. The impact of pollutants on terrestrial ecosystems depends on the distribution of the pollutant in the soil. The irregular spatial distribution of pollution allows soil biota to avoid contact with pollutants. So, the transport, fate and accordingly the bioavailability of pollutants in soil should be incorporated in risk estimation and the derivation of environmental quality standards. This is a challenge for soil ecotoxicology.

3. The role of ecotoxicology in establishing standards

3.1 What is ecotoxicology?

Ecotoxicology or Environmental Toxicology, is the science concerned with the toxic effects of pollutants, chemical or physical, on our living environment, especially on organisms, at individual, population, or community levels. It is also concerned with the effect of toxic substances on interactions within an ecosystem, effects on distribution and abundance of organisms and on important processes within an ecosystem. Ecotoxicology is a relatively new science which covers a broad interdisciplinary field of which ecology and toxicology are the best known disciplines (Moriarty 1988, Koeman 1989).

Pollutants in ecotoxicology are defined as those substances which occur in the environment at least in part, as a result of man's activities, and which have a deleterious effect on living organisms (Moriarty 1988). A pollutant can alter the physical and chemical environment (for example CO_2 in relation to the greenhouse effect, eutrophication of lakes) and may affect the ability of species to survive. Substances such as pesticides and heavy metals have variable toxic effects which depend on dose and exposure time. The toxic effects can be acute or chronic. Acute effects are easy to recognize. Often they can be measured simply by observing survivorship in a population. Chronic effects take time to recognize. Low concentrations of pollutants introduced over a long period may be more harmful for the environment because changes in the ecosystem caused by these low concentrations are slow and not easy to recognize. They could cause changes in community structure as well as genetic changes within the species (Sheehan *et al.* 1984).

While we do not want to go into great detail about the history of ecotoxicology, it is clear that it is a rather new science in which a lot still has to be done, not only in western countries but also in tropical countries such as the South East Asian countries. It is a science in which from a biological point of view, ecology has its importance. The ecological input is: 1. to identify test and indicator species and to study their life cycles and roles in the community; 2. to implement field studies on structure and functioning of an ecosystem; 3. to study environmental variables (Sheehan *et al.* 1984).

Indicator species may be particularly useful for ecotoxicological research. These species, which are commonly important species in the ecosystem structure or in important processes which take place in the ecosystem (Rand & Petrocelli 1985, Kelly & Harwell 1989), can be used in ecotoxicological tests to establish standards. It is clear that, especially for chronic effects, we should know the life cycle of these species to be able to detect the chronic effect of a toxic substance.

The indicator species should be chosen for its sensitivity and abundance (Rand & Petrocelli 1985, Moriarty 1988) or, maybe more important in the tropics, because of its representativeness for a group of species important in a certain stage of a process. The choice of an indicator species depends also on the situation and condition of the ecosystem (Kelly & Harwell 1989). For example, to choose a species because of its abundance is easier in temporal systems than in tropical systems. From ecological research, we know which environmental factors are more or less important for the organism, or process within the system or the system itself. It is also important to know those factors, such as temperature, light, humidity, pH, *etc.*, that affect systems and species functioning. To design a good working test which is also as realistic as possible these factors should be controlled carefully in laboratory tests.

One of the aims of ecotoxicology is to predict the effects of pollutants/toxic substances in the future and to establish standards which can prevent environmental degradation. Establishing standards and predicting effects can only be based on relevant information about the organism, the substance and the effect of the substance on the environment. Not all the information needed for this purpose can be found in the field or by doing ecological or toxicological research. Additional information can be obtained from ecotoxicological experiments in the laboratory. This can be done in several ways. A new experiment can be designed each time a new substance is tested, or the same experiment can be used each time and the pollutant only changed. Some of the standard laboratory tests used in Western countries are described below.

3.2   Types of tests used in ecotoxicology

Toxicity tests commonly used in ecotoxicology can be categorized into single species tests, multispecies tests and field experiments. Single species tests can be subdivided into those which show an acute response and those which show effects after a longer exposure time (Sheehan *et al.* 1984). These last effects are considered to be chronic. Acute toxic effects are recognized as death within a short time after exposure. The concentration which causes 50% mortality is called the LC_{50} concentration. LC_{50} values give information about how harmful the substance could be for organisms just after exposure. This does not mean that if the LC_{50} concentration found is higher than the exposure concentration the substance will not be harmful for the organism. Substances may have effects on organisms after a longer period of exposure as a result of persistent exposure to the substance. These effects can be studied in long term experiments in which effects on growth or reproduction are observed. From the results of these experiments we can estimate NOEC (No Observed Effect Concentration) values.

As the effect of a substance on organisms is not always acute but often chronic, effects on growth and/or reproduction are usually more relevant in determining environmental quality. These effects of pollutants are reflected in population growth and population dynamics. As pollutants often affect more than one species and because of existing interactions between species (such as predator-prey relations) it is possible to speculate about effects at the community level. How these effects will influence population dynamics and population growth and the importance of measuring these effects is explained in Van Straalen (1994).

No sophisticated equipment is needed to measure the LC_{50} for mortality or the NOEC for growth or reproduction. A concentration range of the toxic substance which can be mixed through the food or substrate, small culture boxes (made of PVC for example) and a number of representatives of the test species (at least 25 individuals of the chosen species per concentration) is all that is needed. For NOEC experiments the concentration range should be below the LC_{50} with one above this concentration. For soil ecotoxicity tests it is important to have five or more concentrations and several replicates per concentration, because of the variation in responses of animals, especially in terms of growth and reproduction. The duration of LC_{50} experiments is typically between 48 hours and 2 weeks. The duration of NOEC experiments is at least 6 weeks but it is advisable to take a longer period (Roghair 1989, OESO 1984, Rand & Petrocelli 1985).

By knowing the LC_{50} and NOEC concentrations for several organisms it is possible to make decisions about the acceptable concentration for the tested substance, however, it is then necessary to work with indicator species, or species which are important for certain processes, communities etc. (Gelber et al. 1985). Because LC_{50} and NOEC experiments are done with single species, they give information about effects on the species tested but no information about effects on interactions with other organisms or important processes in an ecosystem. It is clear that the effect will be different from species to species, but still it is important to have these values, as will be explained later. Relying only on single species tests makes it very difficult to regulate or manage the chemical input into the environment and to protect the environment, multispecies experiments are needed for this.

Model ecosystems or microcosms (MES) provide a practical approach to assessing complex interactions and ecological chemodynamic processes. Terrestrial microcosms are useful for observing chemical fate and distribution simultaneously with effects on species and processes. Microcosms can be seen as an intermediate link between the laboratory and the field. In microcosms it is possible to study a specific processes or a specific interaction between two species, by simulating a part of the ecosystem (Van Wensem 1989, Vink 1994). Microcosms are controlled reproduceable laboratory systems which attempt to simulate processes and interactions of components in a portion of the real ecosystem. In MES water input as well as light, temperature and humidity can be controlled (Gillet 1989). The means of control depend on available laboratory conditions, such as climate rooms. There is an enormous variety of types of MES described in the literature, varying from very simple designs up to sophisticated and complex ones (Baath et al. 1978, Baath et al. 1981, Anderson & Ineson 1982, Teuben & Roelofsma 1991, Van Wensem 1989). To set up a useful MES experiment at least some knowledge of the substances and the components used in the experiment is required to interpret the results.

In MES studies it is necessary to know something about the chemical and physical aspects of the toxic substance and to have some information about the life cycle and function of the organism used in the system. It could also be necessary to do some field experiments as well, to calibrate the results found in the laboratory. Field experiments are not so common as laboratory experiments because they are difficult to undertake and interpret. Conditions in the field are much more complex compared with the lab systems.

3.3 Advantages and disadvantages of MES

Microcosms, depending on their design, are inexpensive, do not consume space and are very practical. These attributes make them appropriate at particular stages of research. For example in assessing the effects of pesticides, heavy metals, or other substances or processes on the ecosystem or on species which are active in the processes studied. Many abiotic factors can be controlled (such as temperature, light, and humidity) and there is a great freedom for simple variation in experimental conditions.

Microcosms can be seen as the lowest level of ecological organization for which many processes and interactions between components can be observed. Due to their size, we are not able to investigate complex systems and because of this reduction in complexity care must be taken when extrapolating the results to field situations. Because MES are the lowest unit of ecological organization we can study, it is very tempting to extrapolate results of these experiments immediately to field situations. Care must be taken when doing this, as it must be remembered that the MES only represents a small part of fate and effects in ecosystems. Outcomes observed may be only applicable to that context. Whenever possible the MES conditions should be compared with the field conditions and where necessary field observations should be made to assist the extrapolation of the results of the MES studies. It is even better to evaluate the results of MES using the results of equivalent field observations (Gillet 1989).

Another problem with MES studies is that they are short lived systems in which it is not possible to demonstrate ecological processes as a whole. Although it is often not possible to do equivalent field experiments, MES studies are still very appropriate for investigating fate and effects of substances on processes and interactions in a short period as long as the focus is restricted to those interactions and processes or parts of processes which are realistic enough for this type of research such as microbiological processes (Anderson & Ineson 1982). Microcosm studies which are sufficiently realistic to be extrapolated to field situations are restricted to microbial-invertebrate interactions. Such studies enable us to investigate the effects of invertebrates on that part of the process in which they are active and responsive.

We support the methods used in Western countries for extablishing standards, even though these methods are still in a preliminary stage of development, especially those for terrestrial systems, they are, however, good enough to start with. With LC_{50} and NOEC experiments effects on single species are known; but what to do with this information, how to use this information to establish standards, to protect the environment? Is it a real problem if one or two species are lost due to the toxic substance? Do we need to protect all the species in an ecosystem? It is not that easy to give an answer on these and many other questions. A lot of information about the ecosystem (structure, function, processes, interactions, relations) and about the organisms used as test organisms is necessary before it is possible to answer these questions. It is impossible to know everything but we have to start somewhere. Ecotoxicology is only one of the sciences needed to collect the necessary information.

Just as it is impossible to propose standards based on LC_{50} and NOEC experiments done with one or two species it is also impossible to use microcosm experiments at the single species level. Ecological processes such as nutrient cycling and soil/litter respiration can be studied in these systems as well as interactions between fungi and fauna, or between two fauna species and the effect of these interactions on the processes.

4.   Establishment of soil quality standards

As mentioned in the previous section, as a result of progress in ecotoxicology, a scientific basis for the establishment of environmental quality standards has been provided. If the setting-up of environmental quality standards is aimed at the protection of ecosystems, a standard should allow for the protection of all components of this ecosystem including all interactions and processes which take place within it. To succeed with this sacred task one should take into account the ecological consequences of the discharges of toxic substances into the environment. Ecological arguments have been disregarded for a quite a long time. Too much attention and effort has been devoted to monitoring environmental quality, based mainly on the measurement of chemical concentrations in water, soil and air, without the involvement of biological aspects (Rosemarin 1988). However, the situation is improving now, and there is an increasing demand for the protection of the biological and ecological components of the environment.

Recently, ecotoxicological risk assessment (ERA) has emerged as a promising field. This new field seeks to protect the environment by considering probabilities of ecological damage occurring (Van Straalen 1990). To arrive at so called 'safe' concentrations for the community (*i.e.* standards), in this assessment empirical results from ecotoxicity tests are combined with extrapolation methodologies.

4.1   The ecotoxicity test

In evaluating the impact of toxic substances, the position of laboratory ecotoxicity tests (previously known as environmental bioassays) is central (see Herricks *et al.* 1989, for definitions). However, the body of data from soil ecotoxicity tests is still very limited. Aquatic ecotoxicology has proved its contribution to the improvement of water quality in industrialized countries (see *e.g.* Van der Gaag

1991), but this is not the case for soil, where much needs to be done to reach the same level. Ecotoxicological studies on soil fauna community as well as some selected species of soil fauna have been started by many institutions. In Indonesia, UKSW (Salatiga) and ITB (Bandung) have done some investigations in this field. Adianto (1994) has proposed a standard technique of bioassay employing a number of species of soil invertebrates. At a higher level of integration, Vink (1994) has developed a standard ecotoxicity tests using MES which emphasize the decomposition process.

Following the argument that field tests are not feasible for assessing the impact of all toxic substances (see *e.g.* Cairns 1986, in Van Leeuwen 1990) the derivation of soil quality standards will at best be based on simple ecotoxicity tests followed by an extrapolation step.

4.2 Extrapolation methodologies

The next step after impact evaluation from toxicity tests is risk assessment which is defined as the process of obtaining quantitative or qualitative measures of risk levels, including estimates of possible effects and other consequences as well as the degree of uncertainty in those estimates (Fiksel & Covello 1986). In short, the ecotoxicological process of setting environmental quality standards is composed of two steps, *i.e.* impact evaluation and risk assessment.

Several extrapolation methods have been proposed ranging from simple ones to more complicated methods incorporating complex mathematical formulas. The US-EPA has derived criteria for aquatic species from the extrapolation of toxicity data. This approach is often called triple tens approach (10*10*10). In this extrapolation method a safety factor of 1000 is used if only one acute toxicity test is available for setting the criterion. If three LC_{50}s are available from three different taxonomic groups (algae, crustaceans and fish) a safety factor of 100 is used. The safety factor of 10 can be used only if there is a chronic NOEC value from the most sensitive species. A similar procedure has also been implemented in the German 'Qualitätsziele' recently introduced by the Bundes-Länder Arbeitskreis (Dinkloh 1990, after Van der Gaag *et al.* 1991). In this approach bacteria are introduced as the fourth taxonomic group. This method is also completed by the application of an extra factor of 10 if a compound is persistent or if toxic metabolites can be produced in the environment.

Another method is based on comparison of LC_{50}/NOEC values obtained from different species using log-log regressions taking into account errors of estimation *e.g.* from rainbow trout to fish, from LC_{50} to NOEC, from single species to microcosm (Blanck 1984, Suter *et al.* 1985, Slooff *et al.* 1986). Application of this method in soil ecotoxicology may not be feasible due to the lack of an adequate data base. The other reason for not using this method is an absence of underlying theory to support the log-log regression.

More recently, extrapolations methods based on variation in sensitivity among species have been proposed by Stephan *et al.* (1985), Kooijman (1987) and by Van Straalen & Denneman (1989). Extrapolation methodologies of this kind rely on probabilistic models with a major emphasis on statistical distributions. As with intraspecies variation in sensitivity, it is usually assumed that inter-species variation in sensitivity follows a symmetrical distribution such as the normal distribution, the logistic distribution (Kooijman 1987, Van Straalen & Denneman 1989) or the triangular distribution (Stephan *et al.* 1985). Outcomes of these approaches only differ in the safety margin. The choice of distribution in these approaches is arbitrary, but the logistic distribution is generally preferred over the normal distribution due to its mathematical simplicity. The triangular distribution has a substantially different underlying assumption compared to the other two distributions. By following a triangular distribution it is assumed that there is a threshold value below which effects would not occur. As a consequence, this method offers a possibility of deriving a 100% protection level which is often regarded as unrealistic.

The method introduced by Kooijman (1987) takes into account differences between species exposed to a single toxicant and also allows for uncertainty due to the extrapolation being based on a restricted number of test species. In this method the estimation is directed to a safety factor such that only the most sensitive species in a community will suffer from the lethal effects of a chemical. Later, Van Straalen & Denneman (1989) proposed a more permissive modification of Kooijman's method in the light of the proportion of a community's species to be protected (95% protection level). The argument used to support the chosen protection level is that, taking into account the resilience and the regulatory capacity of ecosystems, to protect an ecosystem it is not necessary to protect the most sensitive species. Small effects may be considered acceptable.

The inter-species variation in sensitivity can be expressed in terms of LC/EC_{50} or preferably the NOEC values for both test species and species in the community. These toxicity criteria for different species are assumed to be independent random samples from the particular distribution. After defining the distribution of the LC_{50}/NOEC values of species in the community it is then possible to establish a concentration value which can protect a designated proportion of the species present in the community. At the decision making level, the maximum acceptable protected proportion of the community is usually the most important topic to be considered.

4.3   Field validation

Due to the presence of a degree of uncertainty associated with risk assessment a validation step is required to test the proposed value. Standard values derived from extrapolation of the results of ecotoxicity tests should, preferably, be validated before being implemented in regulations.

Validation can be obtained by using a type of ecotoxicity test called bioassessment. Bioassessment is a field based analysis which usually focuses on the structure of a community (Herricks *et al.* 1989). The effect of toxic substances in a safe concentration (below the standard) can be measured via bioassessment to see whether it is really safe or not. If some effects are found, then an iterative process of standard derivation and revalidation should be conducted.

5.   Final remarks

As stated earlier in this contribution, soil ecotoxicology is still in its infancy. Much needs to be done to achieve the goal of protecting soil quality. It is not possible, however, to wait until all the theories are established, we should start somewhere.

It is necessary to build a body of data on soil ecotoxicity collected from ecotoxicity tests on various soil biota. There are two priority tasks *i.e.* choosing soil representative species and establishing standardized culture systems for them, and conducting ecotoxicity tests on these species or MES.

Presently available extrapolation methodologies are mainly effect-oriented. We need to develop a more realistic methodology that covers the transport (including the distribution), fate and bioavailability of chemicals in soil, in close relation with the physicochemical properties of the soil. This is not to say that it is useless to apply the methodologies discussed above. The iterative application of available extrapolation methodologies and field-validation will give 'tentative' quality standards which should be adequate to fulfill present needs. In this contribution the focus has been on single compound toxicity which may only occur rarely in the real world situation. Although mixture toxicity has recently become an active research field, none of the available extrapolation methodologies incorporate mixture toxicity. An attempt to tackle the problem of mixture toxicity has, however, been made. Based on findings from preliminary studies, it is usually assumed that additivity of related (structural and mode of action similarities) toxic compounds is the most common interaction, from which it is possible to apply the toxic unit (TU) principle. But, of course, additivity is not the only interaction in a mixture of chemicals. Again, this is a challenge for ecotoxicology.

Finally, it is recommended that the establishment of soil quality standards should run in a parallel and in an iterative way, with the ecotoxicological efforts (tests and extrapolations and validations). One should not wait for the other, because the progress in one component will enhance the development of the two other components.

6.   Acknowledgements

The authors wish to thank Prof.Dr. N.M. van Straalen for his stimulating comments on the manuscript.

7. References

Adianto (1994) The Use of Soil Invertebrates as Test Organisms in Bioassays, in: Widianarko, B., Vink, K. & Van Straalen, N.M. (eds.) *Environmental Toxicology in South East Asia*, VU University Press, Amsterdam, pp. 233-242.

Anderson, J.M. & Ineson, P. (1982) A Soil Microcosm System and Its Application to Measurements of Respiration and Nutrient Leaching, *Soil Biol. Biochem.* 14: 415-416.

Baath, E., Lohm, U., Lundgren, B., Rosswall, T., Soderstrom, B., Sohlenius, B. & Wiren, A. (1978) The Effect of Nitrogen and Carbon Supply on the Development of Soil Organism Populations and Pine Seedlings: A Microcosm Experiment, *Oikos* 31: 153-163.

Baath, E., Lohm, U., Lundgren, B., Rosswall, T., Soderstrom, B., Sohlenius, B. (1981) Impact of Microbial Feeding Animals on Total Soil Activity and Nitrogen Dynamics: A Soil Microcosm Experiment, *Oikos* 37: 257-264.

Blanck, H. (1984) Species Dependent Variation among Aquatic Organisms in Their Sensitivity to Chemicals, *Ecol. Bull.* 36: 107-119.

Eijsackers, H. (1991) Introduction to Soil Ecotoxicology. The Third Advanced Course on Ecotoxicology, April 16-19, Texel.

Fiksel, J. & Covello, V.T. (1986) The Suitability and Applicability of Risk Assessment Methods for Environmental Application of Biotechnology, in: Fiksel, J. & Covello, V.T. (eds.) *Biotechnology Risk Assessment, Issues and Methods for Environmental Introductions*, Pergamon Press, New York.

Gelber, G.D., Lavin, P.T., Mehta, C.R. & Schoenfeld, D.A. (1985) Statistical Analysis, in: Rand, G.M. & Petrocelli, S.R. (eds.) *Fundamentals of Aquatic Toxicology*, Hemisphere Publishing Corporation, Washington.

Gillett, J.W. (1989) The Role of Terrestrial Microcosms and Mesocosms in Ecotoxicological Research, in: Levin, S.A., Harwell, M.A., Kelly, J.R. & Kimball, K.D. (eds.) *Ecotoxicology: Problems and Approaches*, Springer Verlag, New York, pp. 367-410.

Herricks, E.E., Schaeffer, D.J. & Perry, J.A. (1989) Biomonitoring: Closing the Loop in the Environmental Sciences, in: Levin, S.A., Harwell, M.A., Kelly, J.R. & Kimball, K.D. (eds.) *Ecotoxicology: Problems and Approaches*, Springer Verlag, New York.

Kelly, J.R. & Harwell, M.A. (1988) Indicators of Ecosystem Response and Recovery, in: Levin, S.A., Harwell, M.A., Kelly, J.R. & Kimball, K.D. (eds.) *Ecotoxicology: Problems and Approaches*, Springer Verlag, New York.

Koeman (1989) Ecotoxicology: Present Status, in: Løkke, H. & Bro-Rasmussen, F. (eds.) *Proc. 1st European Conf. Ecotoxicology*, DIS Congress Service, Vanløse, pp. 5-20.

Kooijman, S.A.L.M. (1987) A Safety Factor for LC_{50} Values Allowing for Differences in Sensitivity among Species, *Wat. Res.* 21: 269-276.

Moen, J.E.T., Cornet, J.P. & Evers, C.W.A (1986) Soil Protection and Remedial Actions: Criteria for Decision Making and Standardization of Requirements, in: Assink, J.W. & Van den Brink, W.J. (eds.) *Contaminated Soil*, Martinus Nijhoff Publ., Dordrecht.

Moriarty, F. (1988) *Ecotoxicology, the Study of Pollutants in Ecosystems*, Second Edition, Academic Press, London.

OESO (1984) *Guidelines for Testing of Chemicals*, OECD, Paris.

Rand, G.M. & Petrocelli, S.R. (1985) *Fundamentals of Aquatic Toxicology*, Hemisphere Publishing Corporation, Washington.

Roghair, C. (1989) Toetssystemen in de ecotoxicologie, in: Toxicologie College syllabus.

Rosemarin, A. (1988) Ecotoxicology on the Up-swing - But Where are The Ecologists?, *Ambio* 17: 359.

Sheehan, P.J., Miller, D.R., Butler, G.C. & Bourdeau, P. (1984) *Effects of Pollutants at the Ecosystem Level*, John Wiley and Sons, Chichester, New York.

Slooff, W., Van Oers, J.A.M., De Zwart, D. (1986) Margins of Uncertainty in Ecotoxicological Hazard Assessment, *Environ. Toxicol. Chem.* 5: 841-852.

Stephan, C.E. (1986) Proposed Goal of Applied Aquatic Toxicology, in: Preston, T.M. & Prudy, R. (eds.) *Aquatic Toxicology and Environmental Fate: Ninth Volume*, ASTM, Philadelphia, pp. 3-10.

Stephan, C.E., Mount, D.I., Hansen, D.J., Gentile, J.H., Chapman, G.A. & Brungs, W.A. (1985) *Guidelines for Deriving Numerical National Water Quality Criteria for the Protection of Aquatic Organisms and Their Uses*, US Environmental Protection Agency, PB85-227049, Springfield, V.A.

Suter, G.W.I., Barnthouse, L.W., Breck, J.E., Gardner, R.H. & O'Neil, R.V. (1985) Extrapolating from the Laboratory to the Field: How Uncertain are You?, in: Cardwell, R.D., Purdy, R. & Bahner, R.C. (eds.) *Aquatic Toxicology and Hazard Assessment*, ASTM, Philadelphia.

Teuben, A. & Roelofsma, T.P.A.J. (1991) The Role of *Tomocerus minor* (Collembola) and *Philoscia muscorum* (Isopoda) in Decomposition of Black Pine Litter: A Microcosm Study, in: Veeresh, G.K., Rajagopal, D. & Viraktamath, C.A. (eds.) *Advances in Management and Conservation of Soil Fauna*, Oxford & IBH Publ. Co. PVT Ltd., New Delhi, pp. 91-98.

Van der Gaag, M.A. (1991) *Ecotoxicology, an Effective Instrument for Water Quality Management*, Institute for Inland Water Management and Waste Water Treatment RIZA, Lelystad.

Van der Gaag, M.A., Stortelder, P.B.M., Van der Kooij, L.A. & Bruggeman, W.A. (1991) *Setting Environmental Quality Criteria for Water and Sediment in the Netherlands: A Pragmatic Ecotoxicological Approach*, Institute for Inland Water Management and Waste Water Treatment RIZA, Lelystad.

Van Leeuwen, K. (1990) Ecotoxicological Effects Assessment in the Netherlands: Recent Developments, *Environ. Manage.* 14: 779-792.

Van Straalen, N.M. (1990) New Methodologies for Estimating the Ecological Risk of Chemicals in the Environment, in: Price, D.G. (ed.) *Proceedings Sixth International Congress International Association of Engineering Geology*, August, 6-10, Amsterdam, pp. 165-173.

Van Straalen, N.M. & Denneman, C.A.J. (1989) Ecotoxicological Evaluation of Soil Quality Criteria, *Ecotox. Environ. Saf.* 18: 241-251.

Van Straalen, N.M. (1994) Ecotoxicological Responses at the Population Level, in: Widianarko, B., Vink, K. & Van Straalen, N.M. (eds.) *Environmental Toxicology in South East Asia*, VU University Press, Amsterdam, pp. 33-47.

Van Wensem, J. (1989) A Terrestrial Micro-ecosystem for Measuring Effects of Pollutants on Isopod-mediated Litter Decomposition, *Hydrobiologia* 188/189: 509-516.

Vegter, J.J., Roels, J.M. & Bavinck, H.F. (1988) Soil Quality Standards: Science or Science Fiction, in: Wolf, K., Van den Brink, J.W. & Colon, F.J. (eds.) *Contaminated Soil*, Kluwer Acad. Publ., Dordrecht, pp. 309-316.

Vink, K. (1994) A Laboratory Method to Test Side-Effects of Pesticides on Tropical Litter Decomposition, in: Widianarko, B., Vink, K. & Van Straalen, N.M. (eds.) *Environmental Toxicology in South East Asia*, VU University Press, Amsterdam, pp. 223-234.

WCED (1987) *Our Common Future*, Oxford University Press, Oxford.

1.3

Impact of pesticides on tropical ecosystems with emphasis on rice production in the ASEAN countries

E.D. MAGALLONA[*]

1. Introduction

Rice is one of the most important crops in the tropics. About 144.1 million hectares are devoted to its production worldwide and 50% of the global population are rice eaters.

Unfortunately, just as with any other crop, the rice production system is affected by a host of pests: insects, weeds, diseases, rodents, etc. They exact a heavy toll on crop production yields. In the Philippines, Sanchez (1983) estimated that this amounts to 8.4 million tons. In Indonesia, the yield loss due to pests was estimated to be 20-30% up to 50-60% during epidemics.

To solve these pest problems, pesticides have been resorted to. In the Philippines Magallona & Mercado (1978) pointed out that 30% of the area devoted to rice was treated with insecticides. Subsequently, Antazo & Magallona (1982) reported that in a government survey of five major rice-producing areas, there was 100% use of pesticides in farming. Most farmers apply pesticides twice during the cropping season while others use them three times or more. In 1984, 39% of the pesticide volume in the Philippines went to rice production.

In 1985, the pesticide market for the ASEAN countries was about $ 498 millions. Indonesia and the Philippines posted the highest growth rate in pesticide usage from 1980 to 1985 with increases at 30% and 16%, respectively. In Indonesia, about 52% of the total pesticide usage is devoted to rice which accounts for about 45% of the total cultivated hectareage.

In Malaysia, 90% of the pesticides are consumed in the production of three major crops: rubber, oil palm and rice. Of these, about 75% are herbicides used in rubber and oil palm plantation. Most of the insecticides are used for vegetables, rice and tobacco. In Thailand, insecticides are mainly used for vegetables and rice, accounting for 48% of the total insecticides used.

---

[*] Dr. E.D. Magallona, Professor of Pesticide Chemistry and Toxicology, was the driving force behind pesticide regulation and pesticide residue awareness in the Philippines. He met his untimely death on June 21, 1992, while on a trip implementing his project 'Integrated Pest Management on Wheels'.

Given this widespread insecticide utilization in rice production and considering that pesticides are largely misunderstood, the inevitable question is, 'What are the biological effects of these compounds on components of the ecosystem?'

It should be pointed out, however, that there are very many instances in which pesticide use is not needed or advisable. In such situations, pesticides should not be used. One of the biggest problems faced is that unwise/unnecessary use could not only engender false dependence on these chemicals but could also create a situation where rather than being just one of the options in pest management, pesticides become the first choice.

2. Pesticide usage

2.1 Evolution

Insecticide use in rice production essentially followed the general trend for other crops, which was from organochlorines to organophosphates to carbamates to pyrethroids. Currently, insect growth regulators (IGRs), which exert an insecticidal activity via the inhibition of chitin synthesis, are a very promising group of compounds.

Among the herbicides, 2,4-D and butachlor show the most predominant increase among small farmers. As a post-emergent herbicide 2,4-D is used against broad-leaved weeds while butachlor is a preemergent herbicide used against grasses.

Rodenticide use also followed international trends, starting with the acute toxicants such as zinc phosphide to the anticoagulants such as brodifacoum. The acute toxicants are now used mainly in community-wide quick reaction programs to take care of infestations. On the other hand, the anticoagulants are best used as part of an area-wide sustained baiting program.

At present, there is what amounts to a frantic search for molluscicides effective against the golden snail, *Pomacea caniculata*. This snail attacks the rice seedlings and could cause 100% damage if left unchecked. Initially, the organotins were used but they were discontinued on the grounds of fish toxicity and hazards to humans. At present, bayluscide, metaldehyde and miral are promising from a biological efficacy standpoint.

2.2 Rice production and use of pesticides

To better understand the biological effects of pesticides, it is very important to look at when and how these compounds are applied in rice production. Insecticide application against specific pests is carried out at the following general interval before harvest: Seedling pest—100 days, Whorl maggot—75 days, Stemborer—15-100 days, Hoppers—15-100 days, Rice bug—15-100 days.

During the interval between application and drainage, the insecticide is subject to dilution, degradation transfer, and other factors. The small amounts that may be left at the time of draining the paddy could be transported to other bodies of water (rivers, lakes) where they could be taken up by flora and/or fauna or could settle in mud.

Herbicides are applied either before transplanting or in the first three weeks thereafter. This means at least a 50 day interval between application and drainage.

Rodenticides are currently applied as baits, preferably towards the reproduction stage. Continuous baiting may also be used. The baiting stations are usually shielded from rainfall; at least, this is what is recommended. Thus, there is a very small likelihood of mixing with the paddy water.

3. Fate of pesticides

Pesticides could be transferred from the application site to other substrates by rain, wind, evaporation, and other agents. It appears that the ultimate sink is the soil. Degradation may occur during this transfer (Figure 1).

Most of the binding occurs in the soil and the residues are known as 'bound residues'. These bound residues cannot be detected using analytical procedures suited for the parent compound. Therefore, while they may be present, they are recorded as 'lost' when the substrate is analyzed. With the proper treatment, however, these bound residues can become available; uptake by plants has been demonstrated (Magallona *et al.* 1985, Raghu & Drego 1985).

3.1 The tropical ecosystem

There are four basic elements which are important in pesticide degradation/loss especially when one compares temperate and tropical agroecosystems. These are rainfall, temperature, sunlight, and microorganisms. Rainfall washes off pesticides from the application surfaces, mainly leaves and stems. These pesticides fall onto the soil from where they may be transferred by erosion, carried off with the rain water, leach downward, or later evaporate.

The warmer climate is expected to result in faster breakdown, higher microbial activity, and also higher vaporization rates of pesticides. Sunlight is more intense in the tropics. This results in greater photolytic degradation as well as volatilization or codistillation from such substrates as soil and paddy water.

3.2 The paddy rice ecosystem

In the tropical ecosystem, the rice paddy may be considered unique. The main reason for this is the containment of water during certain stages of the rice plant's growth and the soil being dry the rest of the time. As a consequence of this unique situation, the following observations may be made.

a. There is breakup of soil structural aggregates.
b. Water loss by percolation is reduced.

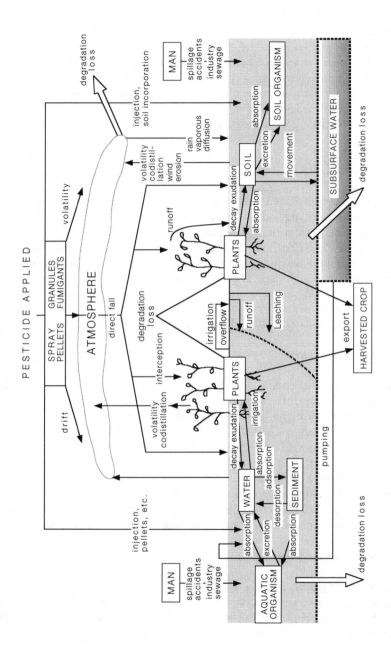

Figure 1 *Fate of pesticides in the environment*
Adapted from Crawford & Donigran (1973)

c. In the flooded state, exchange of gases between the atmosphere and the soil is impeded. Thus, only anaerobic organisms can survive.

d. Two distinct soil layers are formed: the thin upper layer (1-10 mm) thick in an oxidized state and a lower layer in a reduced state.

e. There is a change in the pH of the paddy water depending on the time of day. An increase is noted from slightly acidic in the early morning to basic pH peaking at about 14.00 h and then reverting back to neutral thereafter.

f. Practices such as liming and fertilization as well as decomposition of organic matter (*e.g.* rice stubble) will affect the chemistry of the soil and water.

g. When the water is drained, aerobic organisms begin to proliferate and predominate.

h. When the paddy water is drained, part of the pesticide dissolved therein or absorbed by soil colloids in the mud fraction will move out of the paddy.

Systematic incorporation of fish during the growing season for rice has been introduced. This calls for digging trenches across the paddy fields. These trenches are intended as a refuge for fish during pesticide application; at this time, the paddy is drained of water but the trench has enough water for the fish. This arrangement minimizes fish toxicity due to pesticide application. After a few days, the paddy is again flooded.

3.3   *Effects of pesticides*

The biological effect is a function of concentration, inherent susceptibility of the species, and intensity of factors which favor such effects. Immediately after application, the concentration of a pesticide is high and so this may be considered a very dangerous time for target and several non-target species. As the concentration is reduced with time or is diluted, the impact on the species is reduced; a point will be reached when the level does not cause perceptible effects.

To illustrate the above, let us consider a rice-fish system (Figures 2, 3). As already mentioned, the reason for the trench is to provide a refuge for the fish while the pesticide, mainly an insecticide, is applied or while it is still present at a toxic concentration. Almost all insecticides applied directly into the rice field while the fish are swimming freely in the paddy water, cause fish mortality. So, prior to spraying, the fish are 'herded' to the trench by slowly releasing the paddy water. Pesticide application is then made. It is only after 4-7 days that water is reintroduced. This allows for degradation of pesticides.

Effects are usually measured in terms of toxicity, expressed as LC_{50} (concentration lethal to 50% of a test population) or reduction in population relative to an unexposed population. Bioaccumulation is also considered an adverse effect, although its interpretation is much more difficult than acute effects. It is only in very few species that bioaccumulation levels have been correlated with adverse effects. One of the examples is the level of DDT or DDE that causes egg-shell thinning among predatory birds.

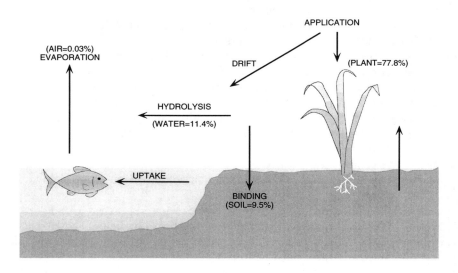

Figure 2 *Transfer processes of pesticides in the rice ecosystem*

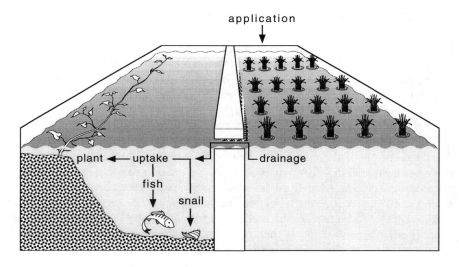

Figure 3 *Schematic drawing of the rice-fish culture*

While it is also convenient to consider the impact of a pesticide inside the paddy system, the chemical applied actually finds its way outside the paddy system. This occurs mainly as the paddy water is drained. Volatilization and leaching also contribute to this movement. Thus organisms outside of the paddy itself may be affected.

3.4   Pests

Toxicity is an expected effect of pesticides on the target pests. Of concern are (a) development of resistance, and (b) resurgence, in the case of the brown plant-hopper (BPH), *Nilaparvata lugens*. Both may be viewed as undesirable effects.

There have been numerous reports of insects becoming resistant to insecticides, and paddy insects are no exception. The Annual Reports of the International Rice Research Institute at Los Banos, Philippines, continually refer to the development of resistance in the most important rice pests, either through comparison with greenhouse strains which have not been exposed to pesticides or to loss of effectiveness by compounds previously known to be effective. Resurgence is the other problem associated with pesticides, notably with the BPH. It is the phenomenon whereby the use of a pesticide results in a population increase over that of untreated controls.

At the International Rice Research Institute, sixteen insecticides used for rice control in Asia were found to cause resurgence. On the other hand, carbofuran, flowable ethylan (perthane), technical BHC (20 EC), BPMC (50 EC), carbophenothion (48 EC), MTMC (30 EC), and chlorpyrifos (40 EC) significantly reduced resurgence. Thus, TN1 rice plants treated with decamethrin (now deltamethrin), a resurgence-inducing insecticide, had significantly higher levels of BPH. Insecticide application did not affect levels of starch, sugar, and total nitrogen in the plants.

3.5   Parasitoids and predators

This aspect of pesticide use has been studied quite extensively for the BPH, a more recent major pest of rice. Among the more important of these beneficial organisms are the spiders, *Lycosa pseudoannulata* and *Collitrichia formosana*, the mirid bug *Cyrtorhinus lividipennis*, and the small water strider, *Microbelia doughlasi atrolineata*. To some extent, one may also consider the fungus, *Metarrhizium anisopliae*.

Toxicity of some insecticides to these beneficial organisms is to be expected because of their biological affinity to the target pest as well as their inevitable contact with the applied chemical.

The botanical insecticides appear to have a better selective toxicity to the predators than the conventional pesticides. Neem and Chinaberry oils were slightly toxic to the mirid but at an LD_{50} of 50 µg/insect, while Custardapple oil was moderately to highly toxic at 10-50 µg/insect. All three oils were essentially nontoxic to *L. pseudoannulata* (IRRI 1983).

3.6   Insect pathogens

Some of the insecticides have also been shown to inhibit insect pathogens. For example, when mixed with culture media of *Metarrhizium anisopliae* and *Beauveria bassiana*, monocrotophos, BPMC, carbofuran, and azinphos-ethyl + BPMC reduced spore germination considerably (IRRI 1984)

3.7 Larger animals

Of interest here are fish, edible snails, toads, frogs, and ostracods. The importance of fish as a food source as well as components of the ecosystem is well recognized so that fish toxicity data is a requirement for registration. The organisms used, however, are mainly temperate fishes, and while the data thereby obtained could be a useful guide, for our purposes they cannot take the place of toxicity data obtained with tropical fishes, especially those that could be integrated with rice production. Rainbow trout or zebra fish are the recommended fishes on which to determine 96-hour LC_{50} for registration purposes (FAO 1981), while *Tilapia* sp. is the fish of interest to us, as it has been found suited for rice-fish culture, being edible and a fast weight gainer. Of course, it is recognized that pesticide manufacturers in general have easier access to the two temperate fishes than to *Tilapia*, and the data generated can already be good indicators of the toxicity potential of a compound. As Nebeker *et al.* (1983) pointed out with endosulfan, sensitivity may vary among species over as much as three orders of magnitude.

Sinhaseni & Tansakul (1987) recommend the minnow, carp, *Esomus metallichus* for toxicological testing of chemicals. This fish was found to be easily reared and more sensitive than the silver carp (*Puntius gonionotus*) and the guppy (*Poecilia reticulata*). Our own preliminary results seem to indicate that *Tilapia* is a more sensitive test species compared to the guppy.

When using pesticides for paddy rice crop protection in the presence of fish, trenches are constructed in the middle of the paddy (Figure 3). One day before spray application, the paddy water is drained and the fishes are confined to the trench, which still contains some water. After several days, water is reintroduced to a depth of 7-11 cm, hopefully avoiding toxicity to the fish by giving adequate time for insecticide degradation. Using this method, *Bacillus thuringiensis*, BPMC + chlorpyrifos, carbaryl, cypermethrin, isoprocarb, monocrotophos and parathion-methyl have acceptable fish recoveries, whereas azinphos-ethyl remains very toxic (CLSU FAC 1978, 1981a, 1981b). In persistence tests, the fish can be introduced safely by reflooding the paddy within one week after the application of monocrotophos, BPMC + chlorpyrifos (as spray) isoprocarb, permethrin and carbaryl (CLSU-FAC 1980, 1981b).

It should be pointed out, however, that in considering the use of these fishes for food, one should be concerned not only with acute toxicity but also with bioaccumulation. Unfortunately, there is a paucity of data in this respect, however, with BPMC, carbaryl, carbofuran, chlorpyrifos, endosulfan, γ-HCH, isoprocarb, siothioate and XMC, this does not appear to be a problem (Bajet & Magallona 1982, Gorbach *et al.* 1971a, 1971b, Zulkifli *et al.* 1983, Argente *et al.* 1977, Tsuge 1980). On the other hand, with lindane significant amounts accumulate in fertilized first eggs (Ramamoorthy 1985). Apparently, bioconcentration potential is related to water solubility and partitioning coefficient (Kanzawa 1981). Similarly, large animals can take in residues of pesticides if fed with contaminated feeds. This could be distributed in different parts of the tissues (Table 1).

Table 1 *Residues of carbofuran in different tissues of lactating goat (average values from two individuals)*

Tissue	Concentration (mg/kg)	
	dosed 0.5 mg/kg/day	dosed 10 mg/kg/day
Blood	0.08	0.07
Liver	0.55	0.69
Omental fat	0.84	1.42
Subcutaneous fat	0.23	0.41
Kidney	0.26	0.43
Brain	0.27	0.34
Heart	0.17	0.33
Muscle (biceps femoris)	0.19	0.34
Muscle (longissimus dorsi)	0.02	0.06

3.8 Microorganisms (including algae)

A detailed review of the relationship between pesticide and soil microorganisms in the rice paddy was presented by Roger *et al.* (1990). It discussed the effects of pesticides on microorganisms as well as those of microorganisms on pesticides. In general, the conclusion was that pesticides at recommended rates and intervals essentially do not have effects on soil microorganisms and their activities.

The preliminary results of Habito (1990) point to the recovery of zooplankton after pesticide application in farmer's fields and using farmer practices. This recovery followed an initial inhibitory effect. Similarly, Martinez *et al.* (1990) found that BPMC + chlorpyrifos, methyl-parathion + machete, aquatin, bayluscide + machete, chlorpyrifos and carbofuran + urea caused an immediate initial inhibition of algae populations in a paddy field. These populations recovered after about four days.

Prot & Matias (1990), in a study using eleven insecticides, three herbicides and two molluscicides on 33 irrigated rice fields, noted that only monocrotophos and ethofonpros reduced the population of the rice root nematode, *Hirschmanniella oryzae*. Muralikrishna & Venkateswarlu (1984) showed that 5-10 mg/kg of carbaryl, endosulfan and parathion in the soil were not harmful to the soil algal population in both flooded and unflooded soils.

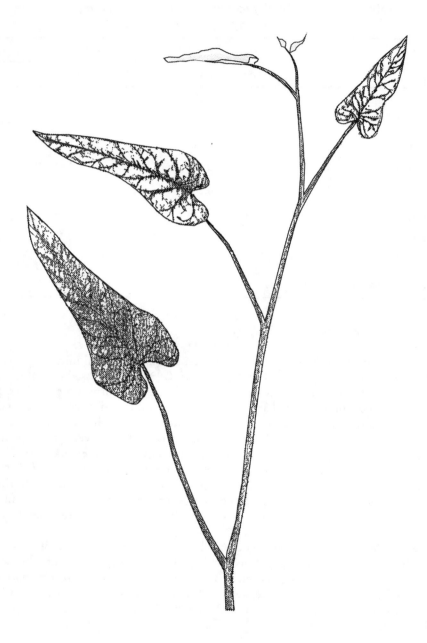

Figure 4 *Distribution of* ^{14}C-*isoprocarb in edible kangkong,* Ipomoea aquatica
Adapted from Bajet & Magallona (1982)

3.9   Uptake by and effects on plants

Of the many species in paddy system, uptake of pesticides is of interest only in the rice plant and edible plants such as *Ipomoea aquatica* (Figure 4). With rice, our interest is in pesticide residues and it has been shown that normal application of carbofuran, lindane, endosulfan, BPMC and carbofuran did not result in residues in grains. This is primarily due to the long interval normally observed between insecticide application and harvest.

3.10   Pesticides in well water

Consciousness of this problem was raised when aldicarb residues were found in well waters in the USA as a result of its use in corn production. This is also a theoretical possibility with pesticides used in rice production, especially in the presence of water which may reduce the absorptive capacity of soils. The problem is considered most acute with the more water soluble compounds.

Table 2 *Insecticide residues (µg/L) of commonly used insecticides in well water near rice paddies in the wet season, 1989-90, at Calauan and Calamba, Laguna*

Artesian well	Endosulfan	Monocrotophos	Chlorpyrifos	Diazinon	BPMC
Calauan					
Well 1	0.03 ± 0.001	1.84 ± 0.064	0.032 ± 0.006	NDR	NDR
Well 2	NDR	NDR	NDR	NDR	NDR
Well 3	0.011 ± 0.003	NDR	NDR	NDR	NDR
Well 4	0.011 ± 0.001	NDR	NDR	NDR	NDR
Well 5	0.002 ± 0.000	NDR	NDR	NDR	NDR
Calamba					
Well 1	NDR	0.22 ± 0.027	NDR	NDR	NDR
Well 2	NDR	0.10 ± 0.009	NDR	NDR	NDR

The detection limit (µg/L) was derived from a 5:1 signal to noise ratio.
NDR = No Detectable Residues.

The presence of a hard pan about 15 cm below the surface may mitigate this effect. This is because the hard pan may impede the downward flux of water to less than 0.5 cm per day. Nevertheless, Medina *et al.* (1990), in a study of artesian wells in farmers fields in two towns of Laguna, were unable to detect residues of endosulfan, monocrotophos, chlorpyrifos, BPMC, and diazinon during the dry season but during the wet season traces of monocrotophos, endosulfan and chlor-pyrifos were detected (Table 2).

The significance of these findings remains to be seen, especially when viewed against the rapid degradation of these pesticides in the rice paddy.

4. Conclusions

The environment, while far from being fragile, must be protected for our continued existence. Pesticides used in rice production are bound to have an impact. What is important is to minimize such impact, at the same time ensuring long and short-term productivity.

5. References

Antazo, T.A. & Magallona, E.D. (1982) Pesticide Use and Specificity on Rice: The Philippine Experience, Country paper presented during the Working Group Meeting on Pesticide Use and Specificity, FAO, Bangkok, Thailand, Nov. 23-26.

Argente, A.M., Seiber, J.M. & Magallona, E.D. (1977) Residues of Carbofuran in Paddy-reared Fish (*Tilapia mossambica*) Resulting from Treatment of Rice Paddies with Furadan Insecticide, Paper presented at the 8th Annual Convention of the Pest Control Council of the Philippines, Bacolod City, Philippines.

Bajet, C.M. & Magallona, E.D. (1982) Chemodynamics of Isoprocarb in the Rice Paddy Environment, *Phil. Entomol.* 5: 335-371.

CLSU-FAC (1978) *Technical Report No. 13*, Freshwater Aquaculture Center, Central Luzon, State University, Munoz, Nueva Ecija, Philippines.

CLSU-FAC (1980) *Technical Report No. 17*, Freshwater Aquaculture Center, Central Luzon, State University, Munoz Nueva, Ecija, Philippines.

CLSU-FAC (1981a) *Technical Report No. 19*, Freshwater Aquaculture Center, Central Luzon, State University, Munoz, Nueva Ecija, Philippines.

CLSU-FAC (1981b) *Technical Report No. 20*, Freshwater Aquaculture Center, Central Luzon, State University, Munoz, Nueva Ecija, Philippines.

Crawford, N.H & Donigran Jr, A.S. (1973) *Pesticide Transport and Runoff Model for Agricultural Lands. Environmental Protection Technology Series*, Office of Research and Development U.S. Environmental Protection Agency, Washington, D.C.

FAO (1981) *Proc. Second Experts Consultation on Environmental Criteria for Registration of Pesticides.* FAO, Plant Production and Protection Paper No. 28.

Gorbach, S., Haaring, R., Knauf, W. & Werner, H.J. (1971a) Residue Analysis in the Water System of East Java (River Brantas, Ponds, Sea-water) after Continued Large-scale Application of Thiodan in Rice, *Bull. Env. Contam. Toxicol.* 6: 40-47.

Gorbach, S., Haaring, R., Knauf, W. & Werner, H.J. (1971b) Residue Analysis and Biotests in Rice Fields of East-Java Treated with Thiodan, *Bull. Env. Contam. Toxicol.* 6: 163-199.

Habito, C.D.L. (1990) Effect of Pesticide Use on the Zooplankton Populations in a Rice Field Ecosystem, in: *Proc. Workshop on Environmental and Health Impacts of Pesticides Use in Rice Culture*, 28-30 March, International Rice Research Institute, Los Banos, Philippines.

IRRI (1983) *Annual Report for 1982*, International Rice Research Institute, Los Banos, Laguna, Philippines.

IRRI (1984) *Annual Report for 1983*, International Rice Research Institute, Los Banos, Laguna, Philippines.

Kanazawa, J. (1975) Concentration ratio of diazinon by freshwater fish and snail, *Bull. Environ. Contam. Toxicol.* 20: 613-617.

Magallona, E.D., Bajet, C.M. & Barredo, M.J.V. (1985) Bound Residues of Isoprocarb in Some Compounds of the Rice Paddy Ecosystem, in: *Quantification Nature and Bio-availability of Bound ^{14}C-Pesticide Residues in Soils, Plants and Food*, International Atomic Agency, Vienna.

Magallona, E.D. & Mercado, B.L. (1978) Pesticide Use in the Philippines, in: *Pesticide Management Southeast Asia*, Proc. of the Southeast Asian Workshop in Pesticide Management, *BIOTROP Special Publication* 7: 71-77.

Martinez, M., Guevarra, H., Palacpac, N. & Leysa, M. (1990) Impact of Pesticides on the Algae in the Floodwater of Wetland Rice Field. *Proc. Workshop on the Environmental and Health Impacts of Pesticide Use in Rice Culture*, 28-30 March, 1990, International Rice Research Institute, Los Banos, Philippines.

Medina, J.R., Calumpang, S.M.F. & Barred-Medina, M.J.V. (1990) Insecticide Residues in Selected Well Waters, *Proc. Workshop on Environmental and Health Impacts of Pesticide Use in Rice Culture*, 28-30 March, 1990, International Rice Research Institute, Los Banos, Philippines.

Muralikrishna, P.V.G. & Venkateswalu, K. (1984) Effect of Insecticides on Soil Algae Population, *Bull. Environ. Contam. Toxicol.* 33: 241-245.

Nebeker, A.V., McCrady, J.K., Shar, R.M. & McAulife, C.R. (1983) Relative Sensitivity of *Daphnia magna*, Rainbow Trout and Fathead Minnow to Endosulfan, *Environ. Toxicol. Chem.* 1: 69-72.

Prot, J.C. & Matias, D.M. (1990) Impact of Pesticide on *Hirschmanniella oryzae* and *Hirschmanniella sucronata* in Rice Field in Laguna Province, Philippines, *Proc. Workshop on Environmental and Health Impacts of Pesticide Use in Rice Culture*, 28-30 March, 1990, International Rice Research Institute, Los Banos, Philippines.

Raghu, K. & Drego, J. (1985) Bound Residues of Lindane: Magnitude, Microbial Release, Plant Uptake and Effects on Microbial Activities, Paper presented at the 3rd Research Coordination Meeting on Isotopic Tracer-aided Studies on Bound Residues in Soils, Plants and Foods, Gainesville, Florida, USA, March 25-29.

Ramamoorthy, S. (1985) Competition of Fate Processes in the Bioconcentration of Lindane, *Bull. Env. Contam., Toxicol.* 54: 349-356.

Roger, P.A., Jimenez, R., Official, B., Santiago-Andales, S. & Simpson, I. (1990) Survey of Microbial Biomass, Blue-green Algae, and Tubificid Populations in Rice Fields of the Laguna Region (Philippines) with Regard to Pesticide Utilization, in: *Proc. Workshop on Environmental and Health Impacts of Pesticide Use in Rice Culture*, 28-30 March, 1990, International Rice Research Institute, Los Banos, Laguna, Philippines.

Sanchez, F.F. (1983) Pest Management: Status and Potential Contribution to Philippine Agriculture, *Phil. Entomol.* 6: 595-606.

Sinhaseni, P. (1987) Applied Metcalf Model: Rating of Insecticides in Thailand Regarding Environmental Hazard Potential, in: *11th Int. Congress Plant Protection*, Manila, Philippines, Oct. 5-9, 1987, pp. 69-70.

Sinhaseni, P. & Tansakul, V. (1987) Pesticide Toxicity Testing Using Minnow Carp, in: *11th Congress Plant Protection*, Manila, Philippines, Oct. 5-0, 1987, p. 68.

Tejada, A.W., Calumpang, S.M.F. & Magallona, E.D. (1990) The Fate of Carbofuran in Rice-fish and Livestock Farming, *Trop. Pest. Mgt.* 36: 237-243.

Tsuge, S., Nishimura, T., Kazano, H. & Tomizawa, C. (1980) Uptake of Pesticides from Aquarium Tank Water by Aquatic Organisms, *J. Pestic. Sci.* 5: 585-593.

Zulkifli, M.A.W., Tejada, A.W. & Magallona, E.D. (1983) The Fate of BPMC and Chlorpyrifos in Some Components of the Rice Paddy Ecosystem, *Phil. Entomol.* 6: 555-565.

1.4

Ecotoxicological responses at the population level

N.M. VAN STRAALEN

Abstract

Ecotoxicology aims to recognize, analyse and predict effects of potentially toxic chemicals at higher levels of biological organization, such as the population level. This paper reviews various theoretical approaches that have been undertaken to relate properties of individual organisms (age, body size, fertility) to properties of populations (age-distribution, growth rate, biomass turnover). Population analysis may then be used to answer the question whether populations may respond more sensitively to toxicants than individual organisms. An example of the theory is given using data obtained from life-cycle toxicity experiments on springtails (Collembola) and mites (Oribatida). Two species representing different life-styles accumulate cadmium from food in different ways: the mite Platynothrus peltifer *excretes Cd very slowly while the springtail* Orchesella cincta *is able to excrete cadmium rapidly. The species with the higher equilibrium body burden (P. peltifer), however, is more resistant in terms of the LC_{50}, although it is more sensitive in terms of effects on reproduction, compared to O. cincta. Population responses are determined mainly by effects on reproduction. It is argued that the classification of life-forms of Collembola, which joins morphology with life-history strategies, forms a good basis for classifying ecotoxicological responses of soil invertebrate populations.*

1. Introduction

The aim in environmental toxicology is to recognize, analyse and predict possible negative effects of man's activities on the environment, especially in relation to the release of toxic substances and in relation to the increase of availability of mineral nutrients in one place or their decrease in another place. This chemical alteration of the environment is associated with various human activities such as crop production, industry, housing, traffic and the like. Above all, these activities have important socio-economic dimensions. It has been a great achievement of the World Commision on Environment and Development to analyse the link between economics and environment using the concept of Sustainable Development (WCED 1987). In this book, we discuss a much more narrow issue, but we are all aware of the fact that our relatively small-scaled research has important socio-economic implications.

In this contribution, I would like to analyse one of the very small steps that has to be taken to fulfill the aims of environmental toxicology: the relationship between toxic effects on individuals of a certain species, and the response of a population, inhabiting a certain area, of the same species. This small step is essential to understand any further steps in the extrapolation to ecosystem disturbances by toxic chemicals.

At the level of populations, we have to deal with several important characteristics that cannot be measured on individuals. In population ecology, several approaches have been laid out to find the relationships between individual characteristics and population characteristics (Kooijman 1985). In doing so, population ecology has developed into a rigorous discipline, often using mathematical models to predict population responses. In my opinion, this mathematical, quantitative approach is also needed in ecotoxicology.

2.   Population performance indices

Population characteristics are called 'emergent' when they are typical for the population level and cannot be seen as properties of lower levels. Table 1 lists several of these emergent properties of populations. Three of them: the intrinsic rate of increase, the intrinsic rate of biomass turnover, and the carrying capacity, are also used in ecotoxicology. This paper will review their theoretical basis and then discuss some applications.

Table 1 *Emergent properties of populations*

Density	Number of individuals per unit habitat
Sex ratio	Ratio of males to females
Age-structure	Frequencies of juveniles and adults
Intrinsic rate of increase	Capacity to grow under non-limiting conditions
Carrying capacity	Maximum density achieved under limiting conditions
Biomass	Amount of living organic matter per unit habitat
Production	Amount of biomass added to the population through body-growth and reproduction, per time unit
Biomass turnover	Ratio of production to biomass
Genetic variation	Variability due to inter-individual differences in the genome

The use of the intrinsic rate of increase as a measure of population performance under toxic stress is motivated by the fact that, according to Fisher's fundamental theorem of natural selection, it is a measure of Darwinian fitness for age-structured populations. Euler's equation gives the relationship between survival as a function of age (l_x), fertility as a function of age (m_x), and the intrinsic rate of increase (r):

(1)
$$\sum_{x=0}^{\infty} l_x m_x e^{-rx} = 1$$

The usefulness of this expression in ecotoxicology has been demonstrated by various authors (Day & Kaushik 1987, Meyer *et al.* 1987, Seitz & Ratte 1991). The equation may be used to integrate the effects of a chemical on survival and mortality, in an ecologically relevant way, into a single measure. It is ecologically relevant because it takes account of the life-cycle peculiarities of the species under study. There are however two drawbacks to using only the intrinsic rate of increase r and I will demonstrate these using two of the other measures pointed out in Table 1.

Using the same life-table approach, it is possible to estimate the intrinsic biomass turnover of a population. When an age-structured population has achieved a stable age distribution, the total production of the population, that is the amount of biomass produced per time unit through growth and reproduction, will increase at the same rate as the total population abundance. Consequently, the ratio of production to biomass (abbreviated to P/B) will be constant. This ratio is called the intrinsic biomass turnover rate. It is possible to predict the biomass turnover rate, if the survival function, the body-growth function, and the fertility schedule are known, using equation (2):

(2)
$$\frac{P}{B} = \frac{\sum_{x=0}^{\infty} (l_x - l_{x+1}) w_x e^{-rx}}{\sum_{x=0}^{\infty} l_x w_x e^{-rx}} + r$$

where:
l_x = survival from birth to age x
w_x = body-weight at age x,
and r is calculated using equation (1).

Biomass turover depends on three variables: l_x, m_x and w_x, instead of two, because it also takes account of the weight of the animals as a function of age. The derivation of the expression is given in Van Straalen & De Goede (1987). It may be seen from equation (2) that the biomass turnover rate is always greater than r, because it equals a positive quantity plus r. This is easy to understand, because even if r is zero, the population does not grow at all and the biomass is constant, there will always be some production: organisms will take up food, grow, reproduce and eventually die. Even a stationary population has a certain production of biomass, which is removed by death at the same rate as it is produced by growth and reproduction.

The use of the biomass turnover rate is not so common in ecotoxicology, partly because the theory is not in the textbooks, but has been developed by Aldenberg (1986) and Van Straalen & De Goede (1987). It may be relevant though, because in toxicity tests there is often a negative relationship between growth and reproduction. For example, Van Gestel *et al.* (1992) have shown that, using toxicity tests with earthworms, in experiments where the worms produced cocoons at a high rate, they did not grow so well, while in other experiments, when reproduction was not so high, the worms increased in body size considerably. If a chemical inhibits reproduction, growth might be stimulated, and vice-versa. Equation (2) shows how all these factors might be considered in an ecologically relevant way. Biomass production, especially for earthworms, is very relevant, because these animals are eaten by many surface-active birds, such as thrushes.

The third population measure to be discussed is carrying capacity, often denoted by K. Equation (3) represents the logistic equation for population growth:

$$(3) \qquad N(t) = \frac{K}{1 + \left[\dfrac{K - N_0}{N_0}\right] e^{-r_m t}}$$

where:
$N(t)$ = population size at time t,
N_0 = initial population size,
K = carrying capacity,
r_m = maximal population growth rate.

Of course no one population will grow exponentially forever. After some time the food supply will be limiting, growth will be stopped and the population size will be more or less in equilibrium with the environment. The carrying capacity, which is then achieved, will measure the ability of a population to maintain itself in a situation where there is shortage of food, intense competition, and selection pressure for efficiency, rather than for high production.

The intrinsic rate of increase is actually relevant only at low densities, when there is plenty of food, and there are no restrictions to high productivity. In equation (3) the rate of increase depends on density; its maximum value r_m is achieved when N approaches zero.

The theory of the logistic equation is not so well developed, because it is not so clear what exactly is the relationship between the individual measures mortality, fertility and body-growth, and the carrying capacity K. Nevertheless it has been applied in several examples in ecotoxicology, mainly in aquatic studies (Halbach *et al.* 1983, Van Leeuwen *et al.* 1987).

One of the questions which has been posed by ecotoxicologists is whether it is possible that populations respond more sensitively to toxicants than individual organisms? The issue was raised in an article by Halbach *et al.* (1983), who maintained that population measures may act as a magnifying glass; some very subtle effects cannot be observed in individual organisms, but on the level of the population they will appear because this is composed of many individuals. In this way toxic levels may be exaggerated by populations. If this is true then it will seriously invalidate any predictions made on the basis of single species tests, looking only at mortality and reproduction, because in this way we cannot predict effects on the level of populations from simple laboratory experiments.

3.   Soil invertebrates

The soil community is very diverse and it holds many species. Even more important-antly, it covers species with a great variety of life-cycles. Some of them have a very rapid turnover, high fertility and short life-time, while others may live for more than a year with a low turnover. The soil community provides us with an excellent opportunity to test the theory on the influence of life-tables and the importance of population level effects, by comparing the effects in different spe-cies. For the purpose of this contribution, I will present the results for only two species which I chose more or less at random out of the community of inverte-brates: a springtail, *Orchesella cincta*, and an oribatid mite, *Platynothrus peltifer*.

Springtails or Collembola are primitive insects which are abundant in forest soils, especially when there is a good cover of litter. The density of the total springtail fauna may vary between 5,000 and 50,000 per square meter in forest soils of the temperate zone, but their density seems to be lower in tropical ecosys-tems. Usually there are some 20 to 30 species within a single research plot, and several thousands of species have been described for Europe and America. Ori-batid mites are also a very numerous group of soil arthropods. Total Oribatida may amount to 100,000 animals per square meter, while there are several thou-sands of species.

The great variety of the arthropods in organic soils has been a drawback for their study, because many of them are not so easy to identify. The taxonomical problems in the tropics are still considerable and it takes a specialist to make reli-able identifications.

Table 2 *Contrasting life-histories of two forest floor arthropod species*

	Orchesella cincta	Platynothrus peltifer
Average life-time (months)	0.5 - 1.0	7.8
Survival to reproduction	0.02 - 0.04	0.3
Fertility (eggs/female/month)	33 - 46	1 - 3

The two species chosen represent two different life-styles, which actually form a continuum ranging over all the species. Table 2 presents an overview of the life-histories of the two contrasting species. Under natural conditions, *Orchesella cinc-ta* has an average life-time of only a few weeks, up to one month, while *Platyno-thrus peltifer* may live on average for 7 to 8 months, and some of them may live for more than a year. It is extraordinary that a small animal like *Platynothrus peltifer* which is only 1 mm long, lives for such a long time. Usually one would expect that the smaller a species is, the shorter it will live. This trend is certainly not true for soil microarthropods.

There is also a great difference with respect to the survival probability to reproduction. Only 2 to 4 percent of *Orchesella cincta* hatchlings will reach the adult stage, while for *Platynothrus*, this is 30%. With respect to fertility, expressed as the number of eggs per female per month, the opposite is true: *Orchesella* females may produce as many as 48 eggs, while *Platynothrus* lays only 2 eggs at a time during one month.

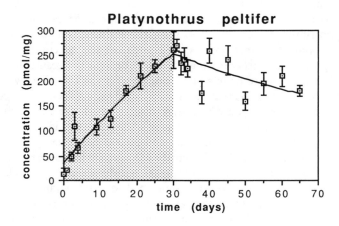

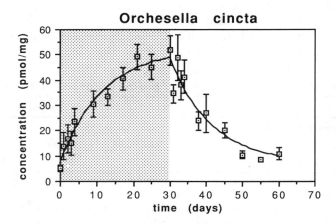

Figure 1 *Accumulation and elimination of cadmium by two species of soil arthropods, when exposed to cadmium contaminated food (± 20 μg/g) during the shaded period, followed by clean food*
Adapted from Janssen *et al.* (1991)

These species thus really represent two different life-styles, varying from very fertile, short-lived species to longer living species producing not so many eggs. These different life-styles are correlated with various physiological characters, one of the most important being the metabolic rate. Using the Cartesian diver respirometer, it is possible to measure the metabolic rate of these animals, expressed as mL of oxygen consumed per gram of body-weight per hour. In a study conducted by Janssen & Bergema (1991), the metabolic rate was 542 mL/g/h for *O. cincta* and 405 mL/g/h for *P. peltifer*, both at 20°C.

These two species were used in chronic toxicity tests using cadmium as the toxic compound. Cadmium, belonging to the heavy metals, is emitted into the environment by various human activities, most notably the smelting of zinc ore. All over the world there are foundaries which emit this toxic element into the air.

When heavy metals are deposited from air pollution onto the ground they tend to be bound by the upper organic layers of the soil. This is because dead organic matter has a great capacity to bind divalent ions, due to various functional groups in humus molecules. Unfortunately, saprotrophic invertebrates have to eat this material and by doing so, they are exposed to high doses of metals.

4.   Kinetics of cadmium

Figure 1 shows the results of experiments conducted by Janssen *et al.* (1991), designed to quantitatively estimate the uptake and elimination of cadmium by the two selected invertebrates. During the shaded period, the animals were exposed to cadmium-contaminated food for 30 days. In the rest of experiment, the animals were given clean food, for another 30 days. Obviously, the cadmium concentration increases when the food is contaminated, while it decreases again when the food is clean. The solid line represents a curve fit based on a one compartment model.

Table 3 *Summary of cadmium kinetic parameters, estimated from uptake-elimination experiments (Figure 1), using a one-compartment model*

Parameter	Orchesella cincta	Platynothrus peltifer
Cadmium assimilation from ingested food (%)	9.4	17.2
Cadmium excretion rate relative to body burden (d^{-1})	0.087	0.013
Equilibrium concentration relative to food (BMF)	0.22	3.4

After Janssen *et al.* (1991).

From these experiments we may estimate some parameters characterizing the uptake and elimination of cadmium in these two species. These are summarized in Table 3. *Orchesella* will assimilate 9.4% of the cadmium consumed, while the corresponding figure for *Platynothrus* is 17.2%. Both figures are significantly higher in comparison to humans, who will assimilate 4.8% of the cadmium consumed with the food (Nordberg & Kjellstrom 1979).

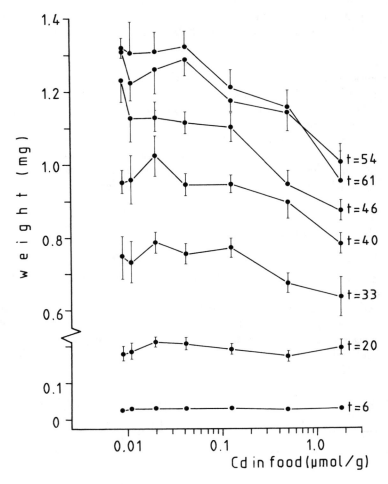

Figure 2 *Growth of female springtails,* Orchesella cincta, *exposed to various levels of cadmium contaminated food for a period of 61 days. Means are given with their standard errors*
Adapted from Van Straalen et al. (1989)

Excretion is 0.087 d⁻¹ for *Orchesella* and 0.013 d⁻¹ for *Platynothrus*, so the second species not only assimilates cadmium more efficiently, it also excretes the material less efficiently. This will cause a higher body burden: the equilibrium concentration is 3.4 times the concentration in the food for *P. peltifer*, while *O. cincta* keeps its body concentration almost 5 times below the food concentration (Table 3).

Summarizing, there is a clear difference between the species in kinetics, which of course relates to a difference in physiology. Care should be taken, however, in not to base the conclusions only on kinetics. A species having a higher body burden is not necessarily more sensitive to the metal, it might even be more resistant. Next to the kinetic experiments we thus also have to consider toxicity experiments to analyse the relationship between external concentration, internal concentration and toxicity.

5.   Toxicity of cadmium

Figure 2 gives a series of dose-effect curves for growth of *Orchesella cincta*, obtained for various levels of Cd in the food, after increasing exposure times. The curves are all on top of each other because the animals increased in weight during the experiment. It may be seen from the graph that after 33 days there is an effect of cadmium on the growth of those animals at the two highest cadmium concentrations, and further on in the experiment, the effect also becomes visible at lower concentrations.

From a graph like this, one may estimate the lowest concentration causing a negative effect on growth, as well as the highest concentration causing no effect. The latter is called the NOEC, no observed effect concentration. Using appropriate statistical methods (Williams 1971) the NOEC is estimated as 4.7 μg/g.

In a similar way, one may analyse the effects of cadmium on reproduction. It appears that cadmium does not have very drastic effects on the reproduction of *Orchesella*, it has a slight effect because of the decreased body-size. This is because smalller animals lay smaller clutches; the primary effect, however, is on growth.

Figure 3 gives a response curve for fertility of *Platynothrus peltifer*, expressed as the number of eggs per female over 9 weeks. This species shows a rather strong effect of cadmium: at the highest concentration, no eggs at all were laid during the whole experiment, however, at the 3rd concentration, there is a significant decrease of egg production. The NOEC is estimated as 2.9 μg/g. The toxicity of Cd in *P. peltifer* may be be related to a disturbance of the Zn metabolism. This species has a very high Zn concentration and under Cd exposure Zn is lost from the body (Van Straalen *et al.* 1989).

The data obtained from these life-cycle toxicity experiments can now be used for calculating population parameters. As a good ecological background knowledge exists for these species, it is possible to include mortality data from field studies to arrive at realistic estimates for the population growth rate.

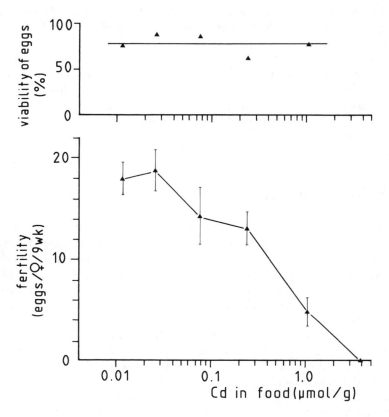

Figure 3 *Reproduction of oribatid mites,* Platynothrus peltifer, *exposed to various levels of cadmium contaminated food for a period of 9 weeks. Means are given with their standard errors*
After Van Straalen *et al.* (1989)

6. Population responses

Figure 4 provides a dose-response curve for the population growth rate r. When these is little Cd in the food the population growth rate is close to zero, because in the field these animals will have more or less stable populations from year to year. When we add cadmium, the population growth of *Orchesella* remains positive up to a rather high concentration. However, the population growth of *Platynothrus* is already negative at the 3rd concentration level.

These responses may be relevant when extrapolating to the field situation. At contaminated sites, *Platynothrus* will be in danger because it is not able to maintain its population due to a negative population growth, while *Orchesella* may still be present.

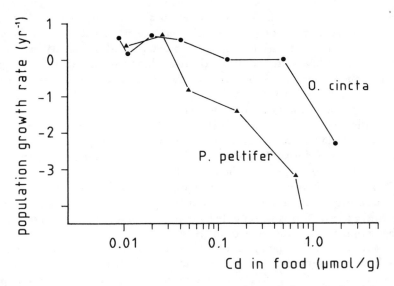

Figure 4 *Population growth rate of* O. cincta *and* P. peltifer, *calculated from toxicity data combined with life-history data from the field, as a function of cadmium in the food*
Source: Van Straalen *et al.* (1989).

Table 4 summarizes the results of the toxicity experiments. When comparing the two species, it appears that *Platynothrus* has the highest LC_{50}. Despite the fact that it accumulates Cd to a higher degree (Table 3), it is actually more resistant, in the sense that it takes a rather high concentration in the food to induce mortality.

Considering the NOEC for the sublethal parameters growth and reproduction, these are much lower than the LC_{50} and they do not show such a large difference between the species. But we have seen that in *Orchesella*, the effect is primarily on growth, and in *Platynothrus* it is primarily on reproduction. The NOEC for population growth of *Platynothrus* clearly is more sensitive than for *Orchesella*.

Table 4 *Comparison of criteria obtained from cadmium toxicity experiments, combined with life-history information to estimate the population growth rate*

Critical level of cadmium in food (μg/g)	Orchesella cincta	Platynothrus peltifer
LC_{50} (9 weeks)	180	817
NOEC (growth, reproduction)	4.7	2.9
NOEC (population growth)	56	2.9

After Van Straalen *et al.* (1989).

This comparison leads to the clear conclusion that the LC_{50} may give a totally wrong indication of the differences between species in their susceptibility to toxicants. Of course, population growth is the most relevant criterion for the prediction of effects in the field. The LC_{50} is often determined in toxicity experiments, but it does not allow a straightforward extrapolation to the field. In the present example, conclusions on the differences between species are the opposite to what would be expected on the basis of the LC_{50}.

The response of the population growth rate reflects a difference in strategy between the two species. When *Orchesella* is confronted with cadmium in the food, it tries to lay as many eggs as possible, until it dies. Protection of egg production is its top priority. However, by doing this, *Orchesella* is not able to prevent cadmium intoxication, and the LC_{50} is low.

When *Platynothrus* is confronted with cadmium in the food, it first stops producing new eggs, because this costs too much energy. Survival is top priority. By doing this, *Platynothrus* is better able to resist cadmium, but the loss of reproduction has a drastic effect on population growth.

These two strategies are typical for these two species. It would be interesting to see how representative such a trend may be for the soil invertebrate community as a whole. This is a difficult question, but there are some interesting patterns among Collembola especially, that may be relevant.

7.   Ecological classifications

Figure 5 shows six species of springtails, which are classified according to three categories; epigeon, hemiedaphon, euedaphon. This classification refers to the average position of the species in the soil profile: the epigeon lives on the soil, the hemiedaphon lives 'halfway' in the soil, and the euedaphon lives deeper in the soil (Christiansen 1964). The upper group has colour patterns, long legs, and a well developed furca, while the lower species are white, they have no eyes and often no furca. The groups are called life-forms.

This classification of the springtails is dated, but in the light of ecotoxicology it may be relevant, because life-history patterns are correlated with life-forms. The surface-active species have higher metabolism, higher fertility and higher population turnover. *Orchesella cincta* clearly belongs to the upper group. The lower group, the true soil inhabitants, have lower fertility, lower metabolism and low population turnover. *Platynothrus*, although it is not a springtail, resembles this group.

If we apply this ecological classification system to ecotoxicology, we may expect that the upper group will be relatively indifferent to persistent toxicants, while the lower group will be more susceptible. Whether this is actually true or not cannot be confirmed on the basis of present evidence. Extrapolation to the field situation has to deal not only with effects at the population level but also with effects due to interactions between species. Vink (1994) has shown that interactions between soil invertebrates and soil microflora may indeed be important for effects of toxicants under more natural conditions.

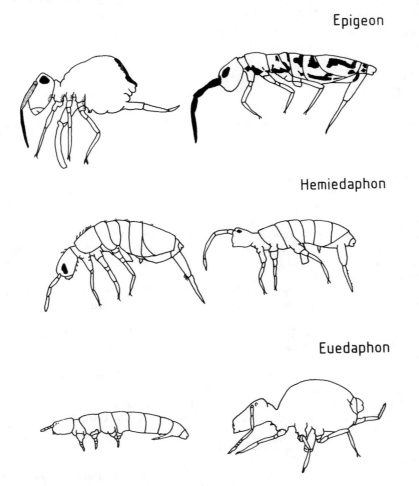

Epigeon

Hemiedaphon

Euedaphon

Figure 5 *Some examples of life-forms of Collembola*
After Gisin (1960)

The above arguments lead to three main conclusions. In the first place, life-history information is vitally important for the evaluation of the population consequences of toxic effects. If we use only the LC_{50}, we may arrive at wrong conclusions. Secondly, to obtain bioindicators for soil pollution, the best way to do this will be to classify species according to life-forms, because these seem to be correlated with susceptibility patterns. In the third place, soil contamination will favour opportunistic species with a high reproductive output, even if these are more sensitive in terms of their LC_{50}.

A more extensive comparison of species is needed before these conclusions may be fully validated. There is a great need for more information on toxicity of chemicals in soil, in order to achieve better soil quality criteria (Widianarko *et al.* 1994). Unfortunately, the data base for soil ecotoxicology is not very large, although the community of invertebrates provides an excellent opportunity to study questions of ecotoxicological responses at the population level.

8. References

Aldenberg, T. (1986) Structured Population Models and Methods of Calculating Secondary Production, in: J.A.J. Metz & O. Diekmann (eds.) *The Dynamics of Physiologically Structured Populations, Lecture Notes in Biomathematics* 68, Springer Verlag, Berlin, pp. 409-428.

Christiansen, K. (1964) Bionomics of Collembola, *Ann. Rev. Entom.* 9: 147-178.

Day. K., & Kaushik, N.K. (1987) An Assessment of the Chronic Toxicity of the Synthetic Pyrethroid, Fenvalerate to *Daphnia galeata mendotae*, Using Life Tables, *Environ. Poll.* 44: 13-26.

Gisin, H. (1960) *Collembolenfauna Europas*, Musée d'Histoire Naturelle, Geneve.

Halbach, U., Siebert, M., Westermayer, M. & Wissel, C. (1983) Population Ecology of Rotifers as a Bioassay Tool for Ecotoxicological Tests in Aquatic Environments, *Ecotox. Environ. Saf.* 7: 484-513.

Janssen, M.P.M. & Bergema, W.F. (1991) The Effect of Temperature on Cadmium Kinetics and Oxygen Consumption in Soil Arthropods, *Environ. Toxicol. Chem.* 10: 1493-1501.

Janssen, M.P.M., Bruins, A., De Vries, T.H. & Van Straalen, N.M. (1991) Comparison of Cadmium Kinetics in Four Soil Arthropod Species, *Arch. Environ. Contam. Toxicol.* 20: 305-312.

Kooijman, S.A.L.M. (1985) Toxicity at Population Level. in: J. Cairns Jr. (ed.) *Multispecies Toxicity Testing*, Pergamon Press, New York, pp. 143-164.

Meyer, J.S., Ingersoll, C.G. & McDonald, L.L. (1987) Sensitivity Analysis of Population Growth Rates Estimated from Cladoceran Chronic Toxicity Tests, *Environ. Toxicol. Chem.* 6: 115-126.

Nordberg, G.F. & Kjellstrom, T. (1979) Metabolic Model for Cadmium in Man, *Env. Health Perspect.* 28: 211-217.

Seitz, A. & Ratte, H.T. (1991) Aquatic Ecotoxicology: On the Problems of Extrapolation from Laboratory Experiments With Individuals and Populations to Community Effects in the Field, *Comp. Biochem. Physiol.* 100C: 301-304.

Van Gestel, C.A.M., Dirven-Van Breemen, E.M. & Baerselman, R. (1992) Influence of Environmental Conditions on the Growth and Reproduction of the Earthworm *Eisenia andrei* in an Artifical Soil Substrate, *Pedobiologia* 36: 109-120.

Van Leeuwen, C.J., Niebeek, G. & Rijkeboer, M. (1987). Effects of Chemical Stress on the Population Dynamics of *Daphnia magna*: A Comparison of Two Test Procedures. *Ecotox. Environ. Saf.* 14: 1-11.

Van Straalen, N.M & De Goede, R.G.M. (1987) Productivity as a Population Performance Index in Life-cycle Toxicity Tests, *Wat. Sci. Tech.* 19: 13-20.

Van Straalen, N.M., Schobben, J.H.M. & De Goede, R.G.M. (1989) Population consequences of Cadmium Toxicity in Soil Microarthropods, *Ecotox. Environ. Saf.* 17: 190-
204.

Vink, K. (1994) A Laboratory Method to Test Side Effects of Pesticides on Tropical Litter
Decomposition, in: Widianarko, B., Vink, K. & Van Straalen, N.M. (eds.) *Environmental Toxicology in South East Asia*, VU University Press, Amsterdam, pp. 223-234.

WCED (World Commision on Environment and Development) (1987) *Our Common
Future*, Oxford University Press, Oxford.

Widianarko, B., Timotius, K.H. & Vink, K. (1994) Ecotoxicological Approaches to Environmental Standards, with Special Reference to Soil Quality, in: Widianarko, B., Vink,
K. & Van Straalen, N.M. (eds.) *Environmental Toxicology in South East Asia*, VU University Press, Amsterdam, pp. 7-18.

Williams, D.A. (1971) A Test for Differences between Treatment Means When Several
Dose Levels Are Compared with a Zero Dose Control, *Biometrics* 27: 103-117.

1.5

Biochemical effects of industrial pollutants in animals

S. BHATTACHARYA

Abstract

With the increase in industrialization, a variety of chemicals are being added to the environment, posing a serious threat to animals. Among the major components of industrial effluents are heavy metals, ammonia, phenol and sulfide. As fish are the most helpless when it comes to aquatic pollution, toxic responses have been studied in fish in great detail. Biochemical lesions are found to occur in brain, kidney, liver and blood. As is the case with the anticholinesterase pesticides, fish brain cholinesterase activity is equally inhibited by industrial pollutants such as phenol, ammonia, sulfide and copper. Moreover, the fish suffer from depressed thyroid function, which is probably mediated both by inhibition of thyroxine synthesis and its release. Blood characteristics such as glucose and cholesterol profiles were found to be disturbed as evidenced by depletion of cholesterol and hyperglycemia in short term exposures. The situation is reversed in a long term treatment. However, the hepatic glycogen profile remained unchanged under both exposure regimes while the hepatic cholesterol profile demonstrated an increase. Similarly, the hepatopancreatic α-amylase and cardiac diaphorase activity was at first inhibited, recovering only at a later period of exposure. In mammals during an acute exposure, various homeostatic controls are switched on which are more or less nonspecific. Immune response has been found to be affected by a number of metals including cadmium and mercury. Mercury is also known to block the synaptic and the neuromuscular transmission and is obviously more hazardous to the thyroid than organic mercury leading to the reduction of serum thyroxine levels, antibody response and albuminuria. Although there are deleterious consequences of xenobiotic exposure, detoxication mechanisms help the animals to survive the stress. The most significant of these mechanisms is the glutathione-S-transferase system. Recently it has been revealed that the C-reactive protein (CRP) sequesters heavy metals with a consequent high rate of clearance of the toxicants, thus being another candidate for a detoxication pathway. It is noteworthy that, although fish and mammals are under continuous exposure to environmental pollutants, they have developed a means of survival by counteracting toxication processes. Nevertheless, the extent and magnitude of biochemical lesions point to the danger of the incessant exposure to low doses of toxicants, not causing death but seriously compromising the physiological well-being of the animals.

1.   Introduction

In the present century, we are face to face with a condition of environmental deterioration for which we ourselves have to bear the blame. Nonetheless, we must have a straightforward database which will not unduly alarm us. Quite naturally, we find that research in environmental toxicology has gained momentum over the last two decades. In the present review, attention will be paid to the biochemical effects of industrial pollutants in vertebrates, namely fish and mammals.

2.   Response to industrial pollutants

Metals are the major components of industrial effluents which are discharged untreated in the environment in many circumstances. Thus heavy metals have assumed greater toxicological significance in the environment. Besides heavy metals, ammonia, phenol and sulfide are also discharged in the aquatic resources where fish are the most vulnerable animals. The responses can be categorized in the following manner.

3.   Toxic responses

Striking biochemical lesions have been found in fish brain as evidenced by depressed cholinesterase activity (Mukherjee & Bhattacharya 1974). Physiological dysfunctions were demonstrated in the form of thyroxine deficiency (Mukherjee & Bhattacharya 1975) and altered thyroid function (Bhattacharya et al. 1989). The dysfunctions were identified at three locations. In the first place, iodide peroxidase, the key enzyme in thyroid hormone biosynthesis exhibited significant inhibition; secondly, this can be correlated with a depleted titer of the serum thyroxine (Table 1). Thirdly, lysosomal protease of thyroidal tissue in the fish head kidney was grossly inhibited. These results indicate that industrial pollutants such as sodium sulphide, phenol, ammonia, $HgCl_2$ and $CdCl_2$ have their effect on thyroid function mediated via two pathways; one via the thyroxine synthesis pathway of iodide peroxidation and the other via the lysosomal pathway of thyroxine release.

Other biochemical parameters studied were blood characteristics (Christensen et al. 1972). Chavin (1973) suggested that among all biochemical parameters, blood glucose and hepatic glycogen can be utilized as a rapid, practicable and quantitative parameter of stress. Various authors (Hanke et al. 1982a,b, Gluth & Hanke 1983) have shown that increased glucose titer in the blood is a typical response of carp to industrial pollutants. Cadmium induced hyperglycemia was reported in catfish (Sastry & Subhadra 1982) and hepatic glycogen depletion in Channa punctatus (Dubale & Shah 1981). Mercury produced similar effects in Sarotherodon mossambica (Das et al. 1980, Srivastava 1982). On the other hand, Bhattacharya et *al.* (1987) showed that in short term tests, hyperglycemia occurred, which became hypoglycemic with long term exposure to industrial pollutants. Interestingly, there was not much difference in the hepatic glycogen profile under both exposure regimes.

Table 1 *Influences of industrial pollutants on the thyroid function in fish and mammals* (all values are means ± S.E.)

System	Thyroxine (ng/mL serum)	Lysosomal protease (μg tyr/mg protein)	Lysosomal acid phosphatase (nmol n-nitro-phenol/ min/mg protein)	Kidney iodide peroxidase (OD/ min/mg protein)
a. *Channa punctatus*				
Control	2.75 ± 0.15	171 ± 1.76	127 ± 2.25	1.71 ± 0.09
Phenol	2.26 ± 0.21	69 ± 2.85	94 ± 5.21	0.60 ± 0.09
Ammonia	1.90 ± 0.20	52 ± 3.00	175 ± 5.70	1.89 ± 0.20
Mercuric chloride	1.35 ± 0.12	76 ± 3.0	160 ± 4.99	1.09 ± 0.04
Cadmium chloride	0.57 ± 0.16	59 ± 4.0	141 ± 5.80	1.26 ± 0.08
b. *Anabas testudineus*				
Control	2.60 ± 0.17	-	-	26 ± 5.20
Phenol	1.11 ± 0.04	-	-	23 ± 3.95
Ammonia	1.48 ± 0.02	-	-	13 ± 2.01
Mercuric chloride	3.50 ± 0.26	-	-	34 ± 3.65
Cadmium chloride	2.73 ± 0.03	-	-	21 ± 2.00

System	Triiodothyronine (μg/mL serum)	Thyroxine (μg/mL serum)	Thyroid peroxidase activity (OD/min/mg protein)
c. Rabbit			
Control	2.4 ± 0.07	2.2 ± 0.08	0.40 ± 0.02
Cadmium	3.3 ± 0.10	1.6 ± 0.07	0.68 ± 0.03
Mercury	4.2 ± 0.13	0.7 ± 0.07	1.10 ± 0.04

Cholesterol is another important biomolecule whose profile may be disturbed under xenobiotic stress. Dubale & Shah (1981) have demonstrated an alteration in the hepatic cholesterol level while Bhattacharya *et al.* (1984) clearly gave evidence that at first the industrial pollutants impose depletory action on the blood and hepatic cholesterol profile, later being replaced by a stimulatory effect. Two other enzymes which are significantly affected in fish are hepatopancreatic α-amylase and cardiac diaphorase activity in *C. punctatus* and *Clarias batrachus*. The response of these enzymes is similar to the cholesterol response, *i.e.* inhibition of the enzymes is somewhat recovered at certain time periods (Mukherjee & Bhattacharya 1977, 1978).

The biochemical effects of pollutants in mammals have also been studied from various viewpoints of which only a few will be discussed here. The maintenance of physiologic homeostasis during the normal stress of daily living is assured by various physiological mechanisms. Bornstein & Walsh (1978) through their studies have implicated certain biologically active substances as inducers of the acute phase response. Finch (1977) demonstrated that there is an increase in the granulocyte count in blood during acute phase reaction. Crosby (1971) indicated that after surgery and in some inflammatory states, blood platelet count also increases. This response includes a variety of cellular, neurological, biochemical, endocrine and other metabolic changes such as leucocytosis, fever, decreased or increased serum zinc and iron concentration, increased serum copper concentration, increased protein catabolism and gluconeogenesis, and negative nitrogen balance despite increased total protein synthesis (Kushner *et al.* 1982). Among endocrine changes are increased rates of synthesis of a number of hormones: glucagon, insulin, adrenocorticotropic hormone, cortisol, catecholamines, growth hormone, thyroid stimulating hormone, thyroxine, aldosterone and vasopressin (Beisel 1977, Egdahl *et al.* 1977). On the other hand, a variable picture has been provided by changes in lipid metabolism during acute response.

A number of metals or metal compounds have been shown to affect immune response or host defense mechanisms. Low level exposure to cadmium enhanced antibody responses (Jones *et al.* 1977). Exposure of mice to cadmium has been reported to suppress the ability of B-cells to form erythrocyte-antibody-complement rosettes (Koller & Braune 1977). In addition to affecting humoral immunity, cadmium has been shown to modulate cellular immunity. Cadmium has also been shown to have direct effects *in vitro* on lymphocyte function causing suppression of mitogen responsiveness (Gaworski & Sharma 1977, Shenker *et al.* 1977). Finally, mice chronically exposed to cadmium were shown to have enhanced activity of peritoneal macrophages (Koller 1973).

Being highly toxic, mercury can cause serious environmental problems. Mercury is present both in organic and inorganic forms. Inorganic mercury has been found to accumulate in the tissue of animals exposed to methylmercury compounds (Magos & Butler 1976, Evans *et al.* 1977). Accumulation of inorganic mercury suggests an *in vivo* biotransformation mechanism which helps in the release of inorganic mercury by cleavage of the carbon mercury bond as reported by Norseth & Clarkson (1970). Several physiological disturbances caused by mercury are on record. It has been found that mercury blocks synaptic and neuromuscular transmission. Kobayashi *et al.* (1979) described that methylmercury chloride potently inhibited the choline-acetyltransferase activity and also the high affinity uptake of choline into the brain synaptosomes. But according to Hrdina *et al.* (1976), acetylcholine content in cerebral cortex of rats decreased when methylmercury was administrated for a prolonged time.

Kawada *et al.* (1980) found that mercuric chloride created more hazards to the thyroid than methylmercury at lower concentration. The intrathyroidal radioiodide distribution revealed significant reduction of thyroxine and triiodothyronine fractions. The serum thyroxine level was affected more than of triiodothyronine by intraperitoneal administration of mercury. Hilmy *et al.* (1982) showed that exposure to a sublethal concentration of mercury impaired liver function due to increased plasma Na, K, Ca and Mg concentrations. Exposure of rabbits (Koller 1973) to inorganic mercury has been reported to suppress antibody responses. Prolonged exposure of rabbits to methylmercury suppresses antibody responses to influenza virus (Koller & Exon 1977).

Albumin appears to be the major carrier of metals in plasma (Smith *et al.* 1977). The albumin-bound metals are referred to as the 'loosely bound pool'. There are plasma low molecular weight ligands such as histidine and cystein in this pool (Henkin 1974, Prasad & Oberleas 1970). Determination of total serum protein is an important clinical test. Serum protein analysis can diagnose liver disorders, nutritional protein deficiency, renal failure and lymphoproliferative disorders. From the data profile of albumin in cadmium and mercury-treated rabbits (Ghosh 1990), rats and mice, significant albuminuria is evident (unpublished observation).

It is known that environmental factors and chemical compounds alter thyroid function in animals. Cold exposure induces thyroid hypertrophy via the thyrotropin releasing hormone - thyroid stimulating hormone pathway associated with increased circulating thyroid hormones (Hefco *et al.* 1975, Honma 1976) where increased peripheral monodeiodination of thyroxine to triiodothyronine probably plays a contributory role (Bernal & Escobar del Roy 1975).

A similar trend of reduced thyroxine fractions were noted not only in rabbits (Ghosh 1990) but also by various authors in Hg-treated mice (Kawada *et al.* 1980, Nishida *et al.* 1986). In rabbit, mercury and cadmium treatments lead to increased thyroid peroxidase activity and triiodothyronine titre within 24 hours of administration, suggesting a stimulatory effect of group II-B metals on both thyroid peroxidase and deiodinase as a compensatory mechanism to survive the toxic metal stress (Table 1).

4.   Detoxication mechanisms

It is now amply clear that fish do show some sort of resilience to survive the xenobiotic onslaught. It is obvious that fish have a strong detoxication mechanism as evidenced by the reduced glutathione-S-transferase system (Nimmo *et al.* 1979,

Chatterjee & Bhattacharya, 1984). Reduced glutathione also plays a similar role in rabbits (Ghosh 1990), rats and mice. The other detoxication pathway known is significant induction of metallothionein by industrial pollutants both in fish (Marafante 1976, Overnell *et al.* 1977, Beattie & Pascoe 1979, Bouquegneau 1979, McCarter *et al.* 1982, Kito *et al.* 1983, Chatterjee & Bhattacharya 1986, Dalal & Bhattacharya 1991) and mammals (Margoshes & Vallee 1957, Piotrowski *et al.* 1974, Winge *et al.* 1975, Oh *et al.* 1978, Scheuhammer *et al.* 1985, Ghosh 1990).

It has only been recently demonstrated that the acute phase protein (CRP) can also be considered as a metal sequestering protein. It possibly serves a major role in detoxication of industrial pollutants in rats (Agrawal & Bhattacharya 1989a, b) and fish (Ghosh & Bhattacharya 1992). However, further research is warranted to establish the role of CRP in detoxication.

5. Conclusion

The review shows that a multiple array of biochemical responses are elicited by animals exposed to industrial pollutants which follow a more or less similar pattern in the vertebrates. What is noteworthy is that the biochemical alterations sometimes act as a tool to overcome the xenobiotic stress imposed upon the animals. This biochemical compensation may be visualized as a means of adaptive survival of animals in a permanently contaminated environment.

6. References

Agrawal, A. & Bhattacharya, S. (1989a) Appearances of C-reactive Protein (CRP) in Serum and Liver Cytosol of Cadmium-treated Rats, *Indian J. Exp. Biol.* 27: 1024-1027.

Agrawala, A. & Bhattacharya, S. (1989b) Binding Property of Rats and *Limulus* C-reactive Proteins (CRP) to Mercury, *Experientia* 45: 567-570.

Beattie, A. & Pascoe, D. (1970) A Cadmium Binding Protein in Rainbow Trout, *Toxicol. Letters* 4: 241-246.

Beisel, W.R. (1977) Metabolic Response to Infection, *Annu. J. Clin. Nutr.* 30: 1236-1247.

Bernal, J. & Escobar del Roy, F. (1975) Effect of the Exposure to Cold or Extra Thyroidal Conversion of T4 to T3, *Acta. Endocrinol.* 78: 481-492.

Bhattacharya, T., Ray, A.K. & Bhattacharya, S. (1984) Response of *Channa punctatus* (Bloch) under Short and Long Term Exposures to Industrial Pollutants, *Comp. Physiol. Ecolo.* 9: 435-438.

Bhattacharya, T., Ray, A.K. & Bhattacharya, S. (1987) Blood Glucose and Hepatic Glycogen Interrelatonship in *Channa punctatus* (Bloch): A Parameter of Nonlethal Toxicity Bioassay with Industrial Pollutants, *Ind. J. Exp. Biol.* 25: 539-541.

Bhattacharya, T., Ray, A.K. & Bhattacharya, S. (1989) Influence of Industrial Pollutants on Thyroid Function in *Channa punctatus* (Bloch), *Ind. J. Exp. Biol.* 27: 65-68.

Bornstein, D.L. & Walsh, E.C. (1978) Endogenous Mediators of the Acute Phase Reaction in Rabbit Granulocyte Pyrogen and Its Chromatographic Subfractions, *J. Lab. Clin. Med.* 91: 236-245.

Bouqueqneau, J.M. (1979) Evidence for Protective Effect of Metallothioneins againsts Mercury Injuries to Fish, *Bull. Environ. Contam. Toxicol.* 23: 218-219.

Chatterjee, S. & Bhattacharya, S. (1984) Detoxication of Industrial Pollutants by the Glutathione, Glutathione-S-transferase System in the Liver of *Anabas testudineus* (Bloch), *Toxicol. Letters* 22: 187-198.

Chatterjee, S. & Bhattacharya, S. (1986) Inductive Changes in Hepatic Metallothionein Profile in the Climbing Perch *Anabas testudineus* (Bloch) by Industrial Pollutants, *Ind. J. Exp. Biol.* 24: 455-457.

Chavin, W. (1973) in: Chavin, W. (ed.) *Response of Fish to Environmental Changes*, Springfield, Illinois, pp. 199-239.

Christensen, G.M., Mckim, J.M., Brungs, W.A. & Hunt, E.P. (1972) Changes in the Blood of Brown Bullhead (*Ictalurus nebulosus*) Following Short and Long Term Exposure to Copper, *Toxicol. Appl. Pharmacol.* 23: 417-427.

Crosby, W.H. (1971) in: Brinkhous, K.M., Shermer, R.W. & Mostofi, F.K. (eds.) *The Platelet*, Williams and Wilkins, Baltimore, Md, pp. 309-314.

Dalal, R. & Bhattacharya, S. (1991) Effect of Chronic Non-lethal Doses of Non-metals and Metals on Hepatic Metallothionein in *Channa punctatus* (Bloch), *Ind. J. Exp. Biol.* 29: 693-694.

Das, K.K., Dastidar, S.G., Chakraborty, S. & Banerjee, S.K. (1980) Toxicity of Mercury: A Comparative Study in Air Breathing and Non Air Breathing Fish, *Hydrobiologia* 68: 225-229.

Dubale, M.S. & Shah, P. (1981) Biochemical Alterations Induced by Cadmium in the Liver of *Channa punctatus*, *Environ. Res.* 26: 110-118.

Egdahl, R.H., Meguid, M.M. & Aun, F. (1977) *Crit. Care Med.* 5: 257-263, cited by Kushner, I. (1982) The Phenomenon of the Acute Phase Response, *Annals N.Y. Acad. Sci.* 389: 39-48.

Evans, H.L., Garman, R.H. & Weiss, B. (1977) Methylmercury: Exposure Duration and Regional Distribution as Determinants of Neurotoxicity in Nonhuman Primates, *Toxicol. Appl. Pharmacol.* 41: 15-33.

Finch, S.C. (1977) in: Williams, W.J., Buetler, E., Erslev, A.J. & Rundles, R.W. (eds.) *Hematology*, 2nd edition, Mc Graw-Hill, New York, pp. 7646-7775.

Gaworski, C.L. & Sharma, R.P. (1977) Heavy Metals and Lymphocytes: A Possible Site of Immunosuppression by Chemicals, *Toxicol. Appl. Pharmacol.* 41: 149.

Ghosh, N. (1990) *Acute Phase Response to Tissue Injury of Rabbit under Metal Stress*, Ph.D. dissertation, Visva-Bharati University, Santiniketan, India.

Ghosh, S. & Bhattacharya, S. (1992) Elevation of C-reactive Protein in Serum of *Channa punctatus* as an Indicator of Water Pollution, *Indian J. Exp. Biol.* 30: 736-737.

Gluth, G. & Hanke, W. (1983) The Effect of Temperature on Physiological Changes in Carp *Cyprinus carpio* L. Induced by Phenol, *Ecotox. Environ. Saf.* 7: 373-389.

Hanke, W., Bittner, A., Horn, G., Muller, R. & Keppler, R. (1982a) Untersuchungen der physiologischen Wirkungen von Schadstoffen bei Karpfen, *Jul-Spez.* 163: 42-63.

Hanke, W., Gluth, G., Bubel, H. & Muller, R. (1982b) Physiological Changes in Carp Induced by Pollution, *Ecotox. Environ. Saf.* 7: 229-241.

Hefco, E., Krulich, L., Illner, P. & Larsen, P.R (1975) Effect of Acute Exposure to Cold on the Activity of the Hypothalamic Pituitary Thyroid System, *Endocrinol.* 97: 1185-1195.

Henkin, R.I. (1974) Metal-albumin-amino Acid Interaction: Chemical and Physiological Relationships, in: Friedman, M. (ed.) *Protein-Metal Interactions*, Plenum, New York, pp. 299-328.

56 - S. BHATTACHARYA

Hilmy, A.M., Shabana, M.B. & Saied, M.M. (1982) Ionic Regulation of the Blood in the Cyprinodont *Aphanius diapas* Rupp. under the Effect of Experimental Mercury Pollution, *Wat. Air Soil Poll.* 18: 467-473.

Honma, K. (1976) Role of Thyroid Hormone in Cold Adaptation 2. Increase in Food Consumption and fecal excretion of thyroxine during cold exposure, *Hokkaido. Iquaku. zasshi.* 50: 393-396.

Hrdina, P.D., Peters, D.A.V. & Singhal, R.L. (1976) Effects of Chronic Exposure to Cadmium, Lead and Mercury on Brain Biogenic Amines in the Rat, *Res. Commun. Pathol. Pharmacol.* 16: 483-493.

Jones, R.H., Williams, R.L. & Jones, A.M. (1977) Effects of Heavy Metals on the Immune Response, Preliminary Findings for Cadmium in Rats, *Proc. Soc. Exp. Biol. Med.* 137: 1231.

Kawada, J., Nishida, M., Yoshimura, Y. & Yamamota, T. (1980) Comparative Studies on Acute and Subacute Effects of Organic and Inorganic Mercury on Thyroidal Functions, *Environ. Poll. Kobe.* S-71.

Kito, H., Ose, Y., Yonezawa, S., Satoh, T., Ishikawa, T., Kinoshita, M. & Kondo, K. (1983) Amino Acid Composition of Carp Kidney Metallothionein, *J. Pharm. Dyn.* 6: 17.

Kobayashi, H., Yuyuma, A., Matsusaka, N., Takeno, K. & Yanagiya, I. (1979) Effects of Methylmercury Chloride on Various Cholinergic Parameters in Vitro, *J. Toxicol. Sci.* 4: 351-362.

Koller, L.D. (1973) Immunosuppression Produced by Lead, Cadmium and Mercury, *Am. J. Vet. Res.* 34: 1457.

Koller, L.D. & Braune, J.A. (1977) Decreased Lymphocyte Response after Exposure to Lead and Cadmium, *Toxicol. Appl. Pharmacol.* 43: 621.

Koller, L.D. & Exon, J.H. (1977) Methylmercury: Effect on Serum Enzymes and Humoral Antibody, *J. Toxicol. Environ. Health.* 2: 1115.

Kushner, I., Volanakis, J.E. & Gewurz, H. (1982) C-reactive Protein and the Plasma Protein Response to Tissue Injury, *Ann. N.Y. Acad. Sci.* 389: 1-482.

Magos, L. & Butler, W.H. (1976) The Kinetics of Methylmercury Administered Repeatedly to Rats, *Arch. Toxicol.* 35: 25-39.

Marafante, E. (1976) Binding of Mercury and Zinc to Cadmium Binding Protein in Liver and Kidney of Goldfish *Carassius auratus, Experientia* 32: 149-150.

Margoshes, M. & Vallee, B.L. (1957) A Cadmium Protein from Equine Kidney Cortex. *J. Am. Chem. Soc.* 79: 4813-4814.

McCarter, J.A., Matheson, A.T., Roch, M., Olafson, R.W. & Buckley, J.T. (1982) Chronic Exposure of Coho Salmon to Sublethal Concentrations of Copper II. Distribution of Copper between High and Low-molecular Weight Proteins in Liver Cytosol and the Possible Role of Metallothionein in Detoxification, *Comp. Biochem. Physiol.* 72: 21-26.

Mukherjee, S. & Bhattacharya, S. (1974) Effects of Some Industrial Pollutants on Fish Brain Cholinesterase Activity, *Environ. Physiol. Biochem.* 4: 226-231.

Mukherjee, S. & Bhattacharya, S. (1975) Changes in the Kidney Peroxidase Activity in Fish Exposed to Some Industrial Pollutants, *Environ. Physiol. Biochem.* 5: 300-307.

Mukherjee, S. & Bhattacharya, S. (1977) Variations in the Hepatopancreatic α-amylase Activity in Fishes Exposed to Some Industrial Pollutants, *Water Research* 11: 71-74.

Mukherjee, S. & Bhattacharya, S. (1978) Localisation of Cardiac Diaphorase in Fish and Effects of Some Industrial Pollutants Thereon, *Comp. Physiol. Ecol.* 3: 143-148.

Nimmo, I.A., Clapp, J.B. & Strange, R.C. (1979) A Comparison of Glutathione-S-transferase of Trout and Rat Liver, *Comp. Biochem. Physiol.* 63: 423-427.

Nishida, M., Yamamoto, T., Yoshimura, Y. & Kawada, J. (1986) Subacute Toxicity of Methylmercuric Chloride and Mercuric Chloride on Mouse Thyroid, *J. Pharmacobio. Dyn.* 9: 331-338.

Norseth, T. & Clarkson, T.W. (1970) Biotransformation of Methylmercury Salts in the Rat by Specific Determination of Inorganic Mercury, *Biochem. Pharmacol.* 19: 2775-2783.

Oh, S.H., Deagen, J.T., Whanger, P.D. & Weswig, P.H. (1978) Biological Function of Metallothionein. V. Its Induction in Rats by Various Stresses, *Am. J. Physiol.* 234: 282-285.

Overnell, J., Davidson, I.A. & Coombs, T.L. (1977) A Cadmium-binding Glycoprotein from the Liver of the Plaice (*Pleuronectes platessa*), *Trans. Biochem. Soc.* 5: 267-269.

Piotrowski, J.K., Trojanowska, B., Wisniewska-Knypl, J.M. & Bolanowska, W. (1974) Mercury Binding in the Kidney and Liver of Rats Repeatedly Exposed to Mercuric Chloride: Induction of Metallothionein by Mercury and Cadmium, *Toxicol. Appl. Pharmacol.* 27: 11-19.

Prasad, A.S. & Oberleas, D. (1970) Binding of Zinc to Amino Acids and Proteins in Vitro, *J. Lab. Clin. Med.* 76: 416-425.

Sastry, K.V. & Subhadra, K. (1982) Effect of Cadmium on Some Aspects of Carbohydrate Metabolism in a Freshwater Catfish *Heteropneustes fossilis*, *Toxicol. Letters* 14: 45-56.

Scheuhammer, A.M., Onosaka, S., Rodgers, K. & Cherian, M.G. (1985) The Interaction of Zinc and Cadmium in the Synthesis of Hepatic Metallothionein in Rats, *Toxicology* 36: 101-108.

Shenker, B.J., Matarozzo, W.J., Hirsch, R.L. & Gray, I. (1977) Trace Metal Modification of Immunocompetence. I. Effect of Trace Metal in the Cultures on in Vitro Transformation of β-lymphocyte, *Cell. Immunol.* 34: 19.

Smith, G.J., Ohl, V.S. & Litwack, G. (1977) Ligandin, the Glutathione-S-transferase and Chemically Induced *Hepatocarcinogenesis*: A Review, *Cancer Res.* 37: 8-14.

Srivastava, D.K. (1982) Comparative Effects of Copper, Cadmium and Mercury on Tissue Glycogen of the Catfish *Heteropneustes fossilis*, *Toxicol. Letters* 11: 135-140.

Winge, D., Premakumar, R. & Rajagopalan, K,V. (1975) Metal-induced Formation of Metallothionein Rat Liver, *Arch. Biochem. Biophys.* 170: 242-252.

1.6

Ecotoxicology and marine environmental monitoring: emerging research needs and opportunities

I.M. DUTTON & M. CULLEN

Abstract

Ecotoxicology has traditionally played a significant, but limited role in understanding the functioning of marine environments. It is suggested that this role could be greatly expanded, and made more relevant to emerging management needs throughout the Asia-Pacific region by broadening the focus of ecotoxicological research, particularly in the area of marine environmental monitoring. While various ecotoxicological methods are widely used or potentially applicable to marine monitoring, there appears to be numerous conceptual and practical difficulties in meshing these approaches more effectively with monitoring programs. Such problems can be resolved by both careful specification of monitoring requirements and by aggregation of single parameter tests to develop broader indices of environmental change.

1.   Introduction

Ecotoxicology has been characterised as a reductionist discipline (Dickson 1982; White & Champ, 1983), pre-occupied with increasingly detailed understanding of pollutant effects at the elemental or individual level of ecosystem studies. Such characterisation derives largely from the medical science base of the discipline in which it is essential in research design to exclude as many sources of variance as possible under highly controlled experimental conditions. The consequent effect on the discipline at large has been that ecotoxicological approaches and models are often not readily extrapolated to other, more general, levels of ecosystem understanding. Unfortunately, however, such extrapolation is increasingly being demanded by management institutions seeking unequivocal advice on appropriate control measures for pollution and/or better understanding of the nature of change in marine environments.

In this paper, we will examine the difficulties involved in ensuring that the principles inherent in ecotoxicological procedures remain relevant to emerging social needs. In particular, the paper explores the growing potential of ecotoxicology in the domain of marine environmental monitoring.

Marine monitoring is fast becoming a major industry throughout Asia and the Pacific with numerous agencies (*e.g.* Lassig *et al.* 1988, Sindermann 1988, Brock & Dorsey 1991, VIMS 1992) now actively promoting monitoring as a key supplement to traditional research and management programmes. While many ecotoxicological methods are routinely used in marine monitoring, the context of their use and the application of results to address social concerns remains poorly developed and often leads to inefficient use of typically limited management resources (Segar & Stamman 1986, Cairns 1990).

2.   Attributes of the marine environment of significance

Before examining how ecotoxicology can contribute to a more systematic understanding of the functioning of marine environments, it is useful to briefly review key attributes of marine environments. As Figure 1 indicates, marine ecosystems are 'driven' by dynamic transport and mixing processes.

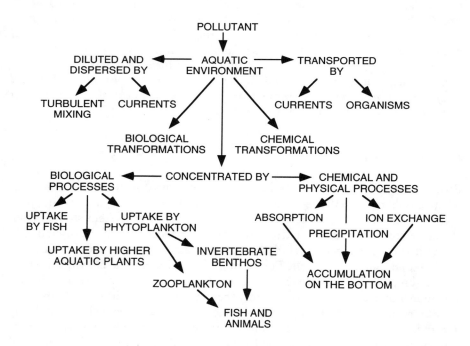

Figure 1 *General environmental distribution processes in marine systems*
Adapted from Dawson *et al.* (1970)

Ray & Grassle (1991) note that the spectrum of environmental variation is also fundamentally different in marine and terrestrial ecosystems. They observe that:

a. Marine environments have a 'spectral shift' toward longer wavelengths;
b. Variations in marine ecosystems may be chaotic;
c. Physical extremes are less in some marine systems (than terrestrial systems); and
d. Major perturbations on geologic time scales may be less frequent in marine systems.

A key implication of these differences is that persistent dissolved contaminants may impact on a much broader range of ecosystems components, and over a much larger scale than comparable inputs to terrestrial systems. This conclusion is supported by evidence, for example, of PCB contamination of Great Barrier Reef waters from northern hemisphere sources (Dutton 1985) which although considered novel at that time, is now recognised as indicative of the significance of met-ocean contaminant pathways (GESAMP 1990 estimate that 80 to 90 percent of PCBs, DDT, HCB and HCH found in open ocean water are derived from atmospheric input).

Such differences are significant both in terms of how they relate to our understanding of change in marine ecosystems, and in terms of the types of issues and approaches which researchers must address in order to ensure the social relevance and statistical rigour of environmental investigations (Burns & Smith 1981).

3.   Present ecotoxicological applications

3.1   General role

Ecotoxicological approaches are currently used for a range of pollutant testing, impact estimation/risk assessment and ecosystem process studies in marine environments. As a result of ecotoxicological studies, marine management agencies now have a defensible basis to, for example:

a. regulate the use of hazardous substances such as tributyltin (TBT) which was previously in wide use for the control of fouling organisms, but which are now being phased out due to growing evidence of adverse toxic effects (Ward 1987, McMahon 1989).
b. establish discharge and receiving water standards for sewage discharges (Limburg et al. 1986, Grimes & Colwell 1989).
c. assist in determining criteria for the introduction of control substances such as oil spill dispersants (Harrisson et al. 1990) and for assessment of oil spill impact/resource sensitivity (e.g. Knap 1987); and
d. assist in the establishment of 'safe' levels of human and biotic exposure to bacteriological infection (Fattal et al. 1986, Boyle et al. 1991) and organochlorine compounds and trace metals (Lincoln Smith & Mann 1989).

These applications have shown the social relevance of ecotoxicological studies to aspects of the marine environment, especially in relation to understanding the consequences or likely effects of various types of resource use - environmental impact interactions.

3.2 Limitations of present approaches

White & Champ (1982) observe that because of the complexity of behavioural, physiological and genetic processes in living organisms, toxicity determinations are not usually repeatable except in highly controlled laboratory situations. They argue that the ecological consequences of bioassay predictions are frequently obscure as a result of this variability. Laboratory modelling does not take into account long term ecosystem responses to perturbation. For example, changes in reproduction, mortality rates and behaviour can greatly modify population dynamics. Changes in species diversity and nutrient cycling can lead to changes in ecosystem structure and functioning. Despite these concerns, much remains to be learnt about the sub-lethal or synergistic effects of chemical stressors. Perhaps even more importantly, there is little evidence that either present ecotoxicological research or most marine pollution monitoring programmes are adequately seeking to address these needs.

After an extensive analysis of ecotoxicological studies, White & Champ (1982), propose that any study to assess the impact of a specific pollutant must be viewed as a model of that environment, and that the model must meet three fundamental test criteria:

Test 1:   Do experimental manipulations of the model constitute sound science?
Test 2:   Do the model's responses bear some relationship (preferably quantified) to responses of the natural system being modelled?
Test 3:   Do the effects measured by the model bear a (quantified) relationship to the broad-scale, important ecosystem processes, effects on commercially important species, or effects on human health?

While there is little debate as to whether most ecotoxicological studies meet the first test to varying degrees, the level of satisfaction of tests 2 and 3 is questionable. This is largely because of the difficulties in comprehending multivariate environmental processes, and because of the socio-political and economic difficulties inherent in meeting the last test. For example, Loya & Rinkevich (1980) observed that even when meso-scale toxicity tests of oil dispersed in water have assisted in understanding the ecosystem level effects of oil spills, little extrapolation was made to field-based studies of actual incidents. Such extrapolation is vital for estimating sub-lethal residual effects of spills and determining management policy in the vital clean-up phase of spill response (Dutton & Holmes 1990).

4. Emerging requirements and opportunities

Dickson (1982) proposes five key areas for ecotoxicological research which appear equally relevant, and opportune at present, particularly in view of the recent growth in marine environmental management regimes throughout Asia and the Pacific:

a. determining the ecological significance of laboratory-derived aquatic toxicity data;
b. assessing and understanding the biological availability of toxic substances;
c. assessing the impact on ecosystem functions;
d. understanding modes of action and mechanisms (processes); and
e. validation of environmental fate models.

To this list should be added assessment of the impact and behaviour of pollutants on local biota under local conditions; much research conducted in temperate regions is of questionable relevance to tropical conditions, particularly in view of the differences in ecosystem functioning in the tropics (Saenger & Holmes 1992). A further need is to expand the understanding of impacts on marine systems of terrestrial activities, such as outlined by Olafsen (1978) in a pioneering study of terrestrial-marine system coupling.

Such basic research is an essential precursor to the incorporation of ecotoxicological research and methods in broader environmental monitoring programs. Without such understanding, much of the information derived from monitoring studies (*e.g.* as described by Limburg *et al.* 1986, Lassig *et al.* 1988) cannot be fully interpreted. Indeed, as Segar & Stamman (1986) imply, it is unlikely, in the absence of more complete understanding of ecosystem processes, that any program to detect change in marine systems can be properly designed. This view is also supported by Underwood (1990) in a review of experimental design requirements.

GESAMP (1980) recognise these problems, and propose a set of principles which should be taken into account in the selection of variables for biological monitoring. These principles (Table 1), and the corollary requirements for more complete understanding of ecosystem processes outlined in Figure 1 serve as potentially important research foci for future marine ecotoxicological studies.

While each of the areas outlined in Table 1 are of growing research significance, there are also a number of related considerations which serve to reinforce the need to resolve the emerging dichotomy between typically narrow scientific interests and broader social interests. Specifically, O'Connor & Dewling (1986) observe that agreement on the social importance of marine pollution is only possible if scientific information is collected and presented to the public in a manner which is consistent with their interests and decision-making needs.

Table 1 *Summary of principles for selecting biological monitoring variables*

Area	Summary of considerations
Ecological significance	Can effect be shown at individual and/or system level?
Specificity	How specific is effect in relation to causative agent?
Reversibility	To what degree can variable/system return to original condition once agent removed?
Range of taxa	Is the effect specific to a particular taxa?
Sensivity	What intensity of stressor is required to elicit an effect?
Response rate	How quickly is there an observable effect?
Application	To what extent is the variable useful in a field monitoring program ?
Precision and cost-effectiveness	Can the effect be measured accurately and at what cost?

To meet these needs, O'Connor & Dewling (1986) propose an integrative approach to monitoring and research design which allows qualitative judgments for the incorporation of quantitative data so as to address often poorly defined social concerns. For example, they note that terms used in national environmental legislation such as 'unreasonable degradation' (of coastal water quality) can only be interpreted by a mixture of scientifically-derived information and socio-political assessment. In addressing the scientific component of this 'mixture', they argue that the focus of monitoring should be expanded from simple species level tests or routine chemical surveillance to broader 'indices' of degradation, as outlined in Table 2.

Table 2 *Proposed indices of coastal degradation*

Dietary risks from toxicants in marine food
Pollutant stress in sediments
Pollutant stress in the water column
Human pathogen risks
Benthic species composition and abundance
Fish and shellfish diseases
Fecundity in fish and shellfish
Mortality in eggs and larvae of fish and shellfish - field measurements
Mortality in eggs and larvae of fish and shellfish - laboratory measurements
Reproductive success in marine birds
Oxygen depletion effects

From O'Connor & Dewling (1986)

While such approaches have been at least partially attempted previously (*e.g.* Burns & Smith 1991, Cairns 1990, Jeffrey *et al.* 1991), O'Connor & Dewling (1986) suggest that eleven such indices (presented in Table 2) would serve a multitude of social needs and provide an adequate integrative framework for linking ecotoxicology and environmental monitoring. These indices thus address the general recommendations of Dickson (1982) and the more specific guidelines proposed in Table 1.

The above indices could be readily supplemented as proposed by VIMS (1992) to develop more regionally appropriate measures. They could also (as suggested by Segar & Stamman 1986) be developed as the basis for more sophisticated hypothesis-testing studies to enable MAELs (maximum acceptable effect levels) to be developed and applied to the regulation of coastal water quality.

5. Conclusion

Ecotoxicology has played an important role in developing our understanding of marine environmental processes, particularly in relation to our knowledge of the impacts of specific types of change. Unfortunately, such understanding is largely incomplete, particularly at the meso and macro system levels.

With growing interest in the global status of marine environments and the consequent emphasis on environmental monitoring, ecotoxicological approaches could serve a vital role in contributing to a more complete understanding of the dynamic nature of marine systems. To fulfil that role will, however, require a considerable broadening of current research horizons and a greater responsiveness on the part of scientists to the changing information needs of decision-makers and society at large.

6. Acknowledgements

We would like to thank Dr. Nick Holmes (UNE-NR) for comments on a draft of this paper, and the International Development Program of Australian Universities and College (IDP) for supporting attendance at the Conference by ID whilst on secondment to the Indonesian Marine Science Education Project at the University of Diponegoro, Semarang.

7. References

Boyle, O.C., Masterson, B.F. & Stapleton, L. (1991) The Use of Indicator Organisms for the Protection of Recreational Users of Estuarine and Coastal Waters from Risks to Health, in: Jeffrey, D.W. & Madden, B. (eds.) *Bioindicators and Environmental Management*, Academic Press, London, pp. 37-54.

Brock, B.B. & Dorsey, J. (1991) Marine Monitoring in Heterogeneous Environments, *J. Environ. Manage.* 32: 227-240.

Burns, K.A. & Smith, J.L. (1981) Biological Monitoring of Ambient Water Quality: The Case for Using Bivalves as Sentinel Organisms for Monitoring Petroleum Pollution in Coastal Waters, *Estuarine, Coast and Shelf Science* 12: 433-443.

Cairns, J.J. Jr. (1990) The Genesis of Biomonitoring in Aquatic Ecosystems, *Environmental Proffessional* 12: 169-176.

Dawson, G.W., Shuckrow, A.J. & Swift, W.H. (1970) *Control of Spillage of Hazardous Polluting Substances*, U.S. Federal Water Quality Administration, Washington D.C. p. 55.

Dickson, K.L. (1982) Research Needs in Aquatic Toxicology and Hazard Assessment: A Sojourner's Perspective, in: Pearson, J.G., Foster, R.B. & Bishop, W.E. (eds.) *Aquatic Toxicology and Hazard Assessment - Proceedings 5th Conference ASTM, STP 766,* Washington D.C., pp. 9-14.

Dutton, I.M. (1985) *Contaminants in Waters of the Great Barrier Reef*, GBRMPA, Townsville.

Dutton, I.M. & Holmes, N. (1990) *Scientific Input to Oil Spill Response*, Proceedings of 2nd National Workshop on Role of Scientific Support Co-ordinator, Dept. Transport and DASETT, Canberra.

Fattal, B., Peleg-Olevsky, E., Yoshe-Purer, Y. & Shuval, H.I. (1986) The Association between Morbidity Amongst Bathers and Microbial Quality, *Wat. Sci. Tech.* 18 (11): 59-69.

GESAMP (1980) *Monitoring Biological Variables Related to Marine Pollution*, IMCO/FAO/UNESCO/WMO/IAEA/UNEP, Report Studies GESAMP 11, Paris.

GESAMP (1990) The State of the Marine Environment, IMCO/FAO/UNESCO/WMO/IAEA/UNEP, Regional Seas Report No. 115, Nairobi.

Grimes, D.J. & Colwell, J. (1989) Ocean Discharge of Industrial and Domestic Wastewater at Barceloneta, Puerto Rico: Bacteriological Considerations, in: Wood, D.W., Schoener, A. & Park, P.K. (eds.) *Oceanic Processes in Marine Pollution*, Vol. 4, Krieger Publishing, Fl.

Harrison, P.L., Collins, J.C., Alexander, C.G. & Harrison, B.A. (1990) The Effects of Fuel Oil and Dispersant on the Tissues of a Staghorn Coral (*Acropora formosa*): A Pilot Study, in: Dutton, I.M. & Holmes, N. (eds.) Scientific Input to Oil Spill Response, *Proceedings of 2nd National Workshop on Role of Scientific Support Co-ordinator*, Dept. Transport and DASETT, Canberra, pp. 51-61.

Jeffrey, D.W., Madden, B., Rafferty, B., Dwyer, R. & Wilson, J.G. (1991) Indicator Organisms as a Guide to Estuarine Management, in: Jeffrey, D.W. & Madden, B. (eds.) *Bioindicators and Environmental Management*, Academic Press, London, pp. 55-64.

Knap, A.H. (1987) Effects of Chemically Dispersed Oil in the Brain Coral, *Diploria Strigosa, Mar. Poll. Bull.* 18: 119-122.

Lassig, B.R., Baldwin, C.L., Craik, W., Hillman, S., Zann, L.P. & Otteson, P. (1988) Monitoring the Great Barrier Reef, *Proc. 6th Int. Coral Reef Symposium*, Townsville, Vol. 2, pp. 313-318.

Limburg, K.E., Levin, S.A. & Harwell, C.C. (1986) Ecology and Estuarine Impact Assessment: Lessons Learned from the Hudson River (USA) and Other Estuarine Experiences, *J. Env. Man.* 22: 255-280.

Lincoln Smith, M.P. & Mann, R.A. (1989) *Bioaccumulation in Nearshore Marine Organisms II: Organochlorine Compounds in the Red Morwong (Cheilodactylus fuscus) around Sydney's Three Sewage Ocean Outfalls*, SPCC, Sydney.

Loya, Y. & Rinkevich, B. (1980) Effects of Oil Pollution on Coral Reef Communities, *Mar. Ecol. Prog. Ser.* 3: 167-180.

McMahon, P.J.T. (1989) The Impact of Marinas on Water Quality, *Wat. Sci. Tech.* 21: 39-43.

O'Connor, J.S. & Dewling, T.T. (1986) Indices of Marine Degradation: Their Utility, *Environ. Manage.* 10: 335-343.

Olafsen, R.W. (1978) Effects of Agricultural Activities on Levels of Organochlorine Pesticides in Hard Corals, Fish and Molluscs from the Great Barrier Reef, *Mar. Env. Res.* 1: 87-107.

Ray, G.C. & Grassle, J.F. (1991) *Marine Biology Diversity*, Dept. Environmental Sciences, University of Virginia.

Saenger, P. & Holmes, N. (1992) Physiological, Temperature Tolerance and Behavioural Differences between Tropical and Temperate Organisms, in: Connell, D.W. & Hawker, D.W. (eds.) *Pollution in Tropical Aquatic Systems*, CRC Press, Florida, pp. 69-95.

Segar, D.A. & Stamman, E. (1986) Fundamentals of Marine Pollution Monitoring Design, *Mar. Poll. Bull.* 17: 194-200.

Sindermann, C.J. (1988) Biological Indicators and Biological Effects of Estuarine/Coastal Pollution, *Wat. Res. Bull.* 24: 931-939.

Underwood, A.J. (1990) Experiments in Ecology and Management: Their Logic, Functions and Interpretations, *Aust. J. Ecol.* 15: 365-389.

VIMS (Victorian Institute of Marine Science) (1992) *Indicator for Victoria's Marine and Coastal Environments*, Office of the Commissioner for the Environment, Melbourne.

Ward, T. (1987) TBT - A New Environmental Hazard, *ALS Bull.* 10: 6-7.

White, H.H. & Champ, M.A. (1983) The Great Bioassay Hoax and Alternatives, in: Conway, R.A. & Gulledge (eds.) *Hazardous and Industrial Solid Waste Testing*, Proceedings 2nd Symposium ASTM, STP 805, Lake Buena Fl., pp. 299-312.

1.7

Carbon dioxide and other greenhouse gases, climate changes and the importance of biodiversity: Our options for climate stabilization

K.W. Sorensen

Abstract

At present atmospheric CO_2 content is rising faster than at any time in the past 500 million years. The present sharp rise in CO_2 levels is expected to have profound effects on the global climate, sea level rise, as well as on natural ecosystems, their associated biodiversity and current patterns of agricultural production. Since pre-industrialization (1750) atmospheric CO_2 levels have risen from ca. 270 ppmv to 350 ppmv in 1989-1990 and are presently rising at 0.4-0.48% annually, or approximately 3 Gt/yr (3,000,000,000 tons) which corresponds to 1.2-1.5 ppmv/yr (Mitchel 1989, Mooney 1990, Harger 1991, Keir 1991, Siegenthaler 1990). It should be noted however, that some researchers are more pessimistic and quote figures as high as 2-3% annual increase (Grubb et al. 1991, Hall & Rosillo-Calle 1989). A doubling of atmospheric CO_2 is expected to occur between year 2025 and 2050 if no immediate counter-actions are taken. Present anthropogenic actions have now overtaken the biosphere's and ocean's natural capacity to absorb excess carbon. Other greenhouse gases exist and are all on the increase, changing the chemistry of the atmosphere. This is expected to effect all ecosystems on the planet and will have serious consequences for all of humanity. Toxicology in the broadest use of the term would involve such chemical changes that ultimately change species composition and reduce diversity. To avoid possible global biotic reductions of near catastrophic proportions, mankind has found himself in the position where we must reverse the present development of deliberately changing the chemistry of the atmosphere.

1. Atmospheric chemistry changes

The burning of fossil fuels is both the largest contributor of atmospheric CO_2 as well as having the sharpest rate of increase of between 2 and 4.3% per year (Chen & Drake 1986, Harger 1991). According to some authors, the rate of increase of fossil fuel burning may possibly be on the decline, from 4% per year in the early 1970s to 2% per year in the 1980s (Mitchel 1989), but obviously this will not be sustained as developing countries industrialise. Other sources of anthropogenic CO_2 are, forest clearing and other vegetation changes associated with land use, *e.g.* increased oxidation of organic material in soils and fire (see Table 1). Carbon is partly reabsorbed by the oceans, coral reefs, peat and wetlands and by vegetation (Table 2).

Table 1 *Net sources of carbon (Gt/year)*

Source	Range	Median	%	Reference
Fossil	5.3-5.9*	5.6	52	Schlesinger (1990), *Post *et al.* (1990)
Biosphere (fire)	1.8-4.7	3.25	30	Crutzen & Andreae (1990)
Deforestation alone	1.0-2.0			Crutzen & Andreae (1990)
Tropical def. alone	0.5-2.1			Dixon *et al.* (1991)
Land use	0.6-2.6	1.60	15	Post *et al.* (1990)
Soil alone	0.1-4.6	2.35		Maltby & Immiziri (1991) (quoting various sources)
Volcanic	0.2 -< 0.5*	0.35	3	Gerlach (1991), *Malling, pers. comm.
Total (approx.)	7.9-13.7	10.80	100	(1989 data)

The total annual anthropogenic input of CO_2 to the atmosphere is 10-11 Gt C/yr. There would however, be a certain amount of double accounting between landuse, soils, deforestation alone, and biosphere burning owing to difficulties in obtaining exact data and therefore uncertainties are involved in calculating individual figures. The true figures for some sources could possibly be higher, others may be lower.

Table 2 *Net sinks of carbon (Gt/year)*

Sink	Range	Median	Reference
Oceans (surface waters)	1.6-3.0	2.3	Post *et al.* (1990), Kerr (1992b), Dixon *et al.* (1991)
Coral reefs	0.11	0.11	Kinsey (1991)
Other oceanic carbonates	1.5-6.7	4.1	Sundquist (1985)
Peat & wetlands (total)	< 0.08	0.08	Schlesinger (1990)
Soil (potential)	< 0.4	0.4	Schlesinger (1990)
Flux from rivers	0.51-0.63	0.57	Sundquist (1985)
Total	4.2-10.92	7.77	
Approximate net increase	10.8 - 7.77 = 3.03 Gt C/yr		

Peat and wetlands in the tropics are, in their original state, net carbon sinks, taking carbon out of the system by organic burial during peat formation. However, large areas have now been cleared or drained especially for rice production and these areas have now become net carbon producers of especially methane. In measuring oceanic fluxes, there is also some double accounting. The difference in the measured annual increase and the calculated increase could be possibly be found in terrestrial primary production (tempory carbon stores) or faulty measurements of either sources or sinks.

Present uncertainties with estimating carbon flows result primarily from the disputed contribution of deforestation, the level of increased plant productivity and carbon storage due to CO_2 fertilization and problems with estimating net primary production.

Carbon dioxide presently makes up approximately only 0.035% of the composition of the atmosphere. Nevertheless it is one of the most important gases for conserving radiated heat as glass does in a greenhouse. Hence the name greenhouse gas. There are other greenhouse gases, *i.e.* water vapour, N_2O, CFCs, CH_4 and O_3, to name the most important (see Table 3). Combined, the effect of these gases is now the same as that of CO_2 (Houghton & Woodwell 1989).

1.1 Ozone

Ozone is important for the earth as it protects against ultraviolet radiation. This protective layer is presently being severely threatened by ozone depleting chemicals, such as CFCs. The concentration of ODCs (ozone depleting chemicals) in the atmosphere earlier this year, were high enough over Canada, United States and Europe to destroy the ozone at the rate of 1-2% per day for brief late-winter periods.

Table 3 *Selected greenhouse gases and their relative contribution to the greenhouse effect*

	CO_2	CH_4	N_2O	CFCs
Pre-industrial concentration (ppmv)	270-280	0.65	0.28	0
Present concentration (ppmv)	350	1.7	0.31	$3\text{-}4 \cdot 10^{-4}$
Present rate of increase (% p.a.)	0.4	0.9	0.25	4
Atmospheric residence time (years)	50-230	10	150	63-130
Molecular radiative effect	1	20-30	200	> 11,000

Based on Ashmore (1990).

According to a recent study the effect of ozone reduction can already be seen in the Antarctic region, where the reproduction rate of phytoplankton has been reduced by as much as 12% during maximum thinning of the ozone layer which has occasionally been measured at as low as 50% of normal (Smith *et al.* 1992). Each year, the ozone is further depleted. According to the same study, the primary production of phytoplankton in the Antarctic has also been reduced by a minimum of 6-12% in association with ozone depletion. The ecological consequence of this effect reduces significantly the CO_2 absorbing capacity of these waters and may ultimately result in massive die-back of phytoplankton. In turn this will release large quantities of CO_2 as the plankton decomposes which will considerably shorten the doubling time of atmospheric CO_2.

1.2 Methane

Methane increases by between 0.8% per year (IGBP 1992) and 1% per year (Ashmore 1990, Hogan *et al.* 1991) of which more than 60% is directly associated with human activities especially biomass burning, rice production and animal husbandry (see Figure 1). Within the next century CH_4 could be just as important if not more so than CO_2 as a greenhouse gas. The radiation absorbance per molecule of CH_4 is 20 times more effective than CO_2 (Table 3), and in the last 300 years, the atmospheric content has more than doubled (Houghton & Woodwell 1989). Eventually, methane is oxidized to carbon dioxide.

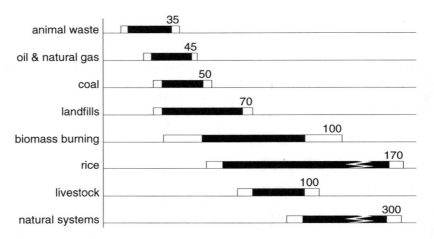

Figure 1 *Estimates for methane production by different sources (10^6 tons per year). The black bars indicate the ranges of production and the white bars the associated uncertainty margins*
Data obtained from Hogan *et al.* (1991), Cicerone & Ormland (in TIME International, April 20, 1992, No. 16) and Neue, IRRI (1992, pers. comm.)

1.3 Carbon dioxide

As CO_2 is at present the largest single contributor to the greenhouse effect, this paper will concentrate primarily on this gas.

CO_2, like other greenhouse gases, and climate are closely interlinked and a doubling of CO_2 levels in the atmosphere is expected to induce a rise in average global temperature of between 3-4°C. Initially, this does not sound like much, but during the last glacial period, the global temperature was only 4-5°C lower than today (Lorius *et al.* 1990) when large parts of Northern Europe and America was under 2-3 kilometers of ice. Obviously such an increase in temperature will have serious effects on present ecosystems and agriculture. However, the exact nature of these changes are unknown as we know little about changes in oceanic currents and also cannot predict the effect of changes in cloud cover.

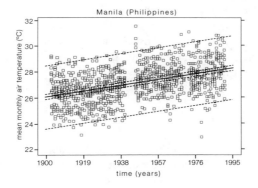

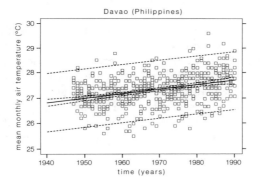

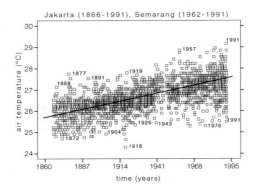

Figure 2 *Air temperature trends in three cities in the South East Asia region: Manila (top), Davao (middle) and Jakarta plus Semarang (below). The solid lines indicate linear regression fits*

Adapted from Harger (1992).

Note: In the lower figure data for Jakarta (8.8 million inhabitants) have been pooled with those for Semarang (1.1 million inhabitants). The Semarang data run from 1982 to 1991 and are not significantly different from those in the Jakarta data set over the same time period. Therefore, the overall trend does not depend on the 'heat island' effect of Jakarta alone.

Additionally we also have large gaps in our knowledge of atmospheric-ocean CO_2 exchange mechanisms which may be crucial to climate dynamics. There may be an unknown factor which we have overlooked as were the holes in the ozone layer over the Antarctic which no-one predicted and which may now also threaten the Northern hemisphere.

2.   Present climate trends

Climate change is almost certainly here. Globally, the mean annual temperature has increased in the last 100 years by about 0.5-0.7°C (Sass 1991, Houghton & Woodwell 1989) and the sea level has as a result risen by possibly 10-15 cm, 2-5 cm of which can be contributed to thermal expansion (Hall & Rosillo-Calle 1989).

However, this temperature increase has not been evenly distributed. Jakarta and Semarang have experienced a steady rise in temperature of almost 2°C over 1865 to 1990 (Harger 1992). Manila has experienced a steady temperature rise of approximately 1°C since 1903 and in Davao, also in the Philippines, since 1947, the temperature has risen slightly less than 1°C (Figure 2). Simultaneously, the length of the dry season is steadily becoming longer on Java, Indonesia (Harger 1992, Figure 3). North-central United States and southern Africa have experienced temperature increases of 0.5-2°C during the past century (Sass 1991) (see also Figures 2, 3).

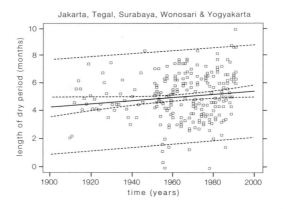

Figure 3 *Length of the dry season in five selected cities on Java, Indonesia. Jakarta, Tebal and Surabaya are on the North coast of Java, while Wonosari and Yogyakarta are in Central Java. The length of the dry season is defined as the number of consecutive months with less than 100 mm rain fall. The solid line was obtained by linear regression where y = -18.90 + 0.0122 x*
Adapted from Harger (1992).

The Japanese magazine, Mainichi News, 29 March 1992, reported in an article, that in the last 10 years the annual mean temperature near the soil surface in the tundra regions of Alaska was 2-4°C higher than the mean for the past century and that sea-ice cover in the region decreased significantly, by 2.1%, during the 80s (Gloersen & Campbell 1991, Walsh 1991). This temperature increase has also had the consequence of an increased thawing of the tundra soil, which in turn releases CO_2 through oxidation of soil organic matter.

The global climate changes occurring presently correspond well with prediction models, albeit to a somewhat lesser degree than anticipated. This 'less than anticipated' increase is expected to be caused by other pollutants such as SO_2 and microscopic dust in the upper atmosphere - so called aerosol particles, that reflect radiant energy (Kerr 1992a). In fact, the cooling effect caused by aerosols has been calculated to be almost equal to half the radiative energy trapped by all greenhouse gases combined, resulting in the observation that the global temperature rise is only half of what is expected. Kerr (1992a) also reports on records of three countries (USA, the former Soviet Union and the People's Republic of China) on minimum and maximum temperatures from the past 40 years. For all three countries, the mean maximum temperatures (daytime) remained unchanged or only rose insignificantly. However, the minimum temperatures (mostly nighttime) have risen significantly. This is explained by aerosol particles reflecting incoming solar energy back into space before it reaches the earth during the day, thus holding the greenhouse effect in check. At night however, these particles have no effect when the greenhouse gases continue to trap heat. But this is probably only part of a more complex explanation, another factor being increased cloudiness in certain regions, a mechanism which is incompletely understood. As, however, most aerosols are very short-lived, $i.e.$ weeks (Kerr 1992a), and CO_2 is long lived, up to 200 years or longer (Maltby & Immiziri 1991, Ashmore 1990), it is believed that the greenhouse effect will eventually prevail.

3.   The geological record

At present the earth is in a relatively cool period. During the past 500 million years, more than 400 million have been hotter and with considerably more atmospheric CO_2 than today (Spicer 1991). Atmospheric CO_2 has been perhaps up to 7-16 times the present concentration within the last 120 million years and global sea level changes have, as a result, exceeded 200 m (Arthur $et\ al.$ 1985, 1991).

During different climatic regimes, the major carbon sequestering systems thrived at different latitudes, $i.e.$ during high CO_2 and increased temperature, these systems were found mainly in latitudes between 30-60°L, whereas in cooler regimes, with low atmospheric CO_2, these systems were found mainly near the equator, such as the present Indonesian peat swamp forests (Spicer 1992 pers. comm.).

The geological record also indicates that during periods with the highest CO_2, the areas of high biological productivity shifted from low latitudes to 50-60°L.

The areas where we now find the 'humid tropics', were then drier and were occupied by quite different plant communities than today (Ziegler et al. 1987, Spicer & Chapman 1990). Many marine and terrestrial species that presently occur in restricted areas were much more common under environments of the past and some biotops and species associations have become extinct, presumably due to environmental change. Previous biodiversity distributions are thus expected to have been adapted to the prevailing conditions and as the environment changed, so did the biotic communities. Not only has adjustment of the biosphere taken place on a passive basis but it is probable, indeed highly likely that the biosphere itself has influenced the climate by directly sequestering carbon in the vast fossil deposits known today, so reducing atmospheric CO_2.

Where there has been rapid climatic change in the past it has always been associated with higher rates of extinction, community and biosphere restructuring, and has 'required' prolonged recovery lasting more than a million years (Wolfe & Upchuch 1986, DeMichelle & Phillips, in press). Studies of biotic interchange occurring within the last 20 million years, show that large-scale extinction of species before the onset of interchange renders biotas especially prone to invasion (Vermeij 1991).

The best documented discontinuity of this type, which may be termed a global catastrophy, was at the end of Cretaceous, 65 million years ago. According to one prominent theory, the discontinuity was due to the impact of a meteorite, resulting in a significant change in global climate, long term vegetation restructuring, and a major change in especially the Northern hemisphere biota (Wolfe & Upchurch 1986).

Fossil records indicate that the carbon sequestering systems of the past (e.g. coal-forming mires) were susceptible to climate change and that change produced community structure collapse when relatively few (possibly < 20% of species in the system) were lost (DeMichelle & Phillips, in press, Spicer, pers. comm.).

This situation will also affect present day carbon sequestering systems such as peat swamp forests. The degree of inter-species competition is greatest in high diversity forests with associated complex pollination and dispersal strategies, thus making them more vulnerable to the effects of change outside the range of normal experience. As a consequence of this intensive organization, high diversity forests may also be expected to collapse towards species poor associations when faced with the effects of rapid global climatic change. What effect this may have on these systems future abilities to sequester carbon is unknown.

4.   Links between climate and biodiversity

That vegetation is indicative of climate is understood and is reflected in the various biomes. Desert vegetation looks the same the world over regardless of the constituent species. The same is true for very diverse types of vegetation such as rain forests. All such different and characteristic vegetation systems represent inherited biological 'solutions' to particular environmental conditions, especially precipitation and temperature.

High biomass ecosystems such as rain forests act as buffers against droughts through evapotranspiration. In Amazonia for example, more than half of the region's rainfall is generated from evapotranspiration (Lovejoy & Salati 1982). To what extent natural forests and plantation forests contribute to precipitation patterns in the South East Asian region is less well understood. However, it has been shown that the normal seasonal dry periods have become increasingly longer over the past decades, with progressively restricted rainfall in parts of Indonesia (Figure 3). Changes of this nature when translated from an essentially maritime situation into a continental regime such as Amazonia, are likely to become even more severe as larger areas of forest are converted into lower biomass systems for agriculture.

Plants are the only organisms capable of removing significant amounts of CO_2 from the atmosphere through various photosynthetic processes. In the growth phase, there is a net absorption of carbon which eventually becomes equilibrium between absorption and liberation as the plants and their associated ecosystems approach climax communities. Through these photosynthetic processes, vegetation may thus have acted as a 'climate-buffer' by storing carbon in their woody tissues and by actively sequestering carbon in peat and coal formations. High biomass forest especially would act as an effective buffer against higher temperatures caused by elevated CO_2.

On the other hand, an increase in CO_2 availability through a doubling of atmospheric CO_2, will theoretically result in an increase in net photosynthesis of 30% in C_3 plants (including most trees) and of about 10% in C_4 plants (mostly grasses) (Sombroek 1991). Some researchers speculate that this may reduce the greenhouse effect.

5.   Problem statement

The amount of terrestrial biomass has been reduced in the past 3000 years to roughly half of the original stock (from 1080 Gt C to 500 Gt) (Sundquist 1985). This is due primarily to deforestation and other vegetation change for agriculture, which in the past mostly occurred in the temperate regions and now occurs in the tropics. The present rate of species and biomass loss due to vegetation change exceeds anything we have evidence for in the geological record (Harger *et al.* 1992). The present change is even greater than that recorded from the meteorite impact catastrophy at the Cretaceous/Tertiary boundary, where the most severe ecological damage was primarily restricted to North America (Spicer 1989). The present situation is not only unique as regards the rate of environmental change, but also in that biomass loss (read: reduction of photosynthetic capacity) and extinction rates have been enhanced before the full impact of climate change has been felt and not as a consequence of climate change.

It is also now certain that natural responses for sequestering carbon will be outstripped if present development does not change radically, and that action must be taken now. If we fail to react accordingly, major irreversible climatic and further biotic changes will occur that will effect all remaining life on earth.

It is the rate of climate change, rather than the eventual magnitude of the total anthropogenically induced change, that will be the most troublesome. Warming of the earth by a few degrees over the course of several millenia has happened many times in the earth's history without serious consequences, as biodiversity has had ample time to adapt. Currently, changes in the chemical composition of the atmosphere and climate changes are occurring within a time-frame that is shorter than an average tree's lifetime. Biological diversity (species and ecosystems) no longer have the necessary time to move or adapt naturally. In the next 50-100 years, temperature change (and associated change in precipitation) is projected to happen 10-50 times faster than the changes seen in the last 12,000-15,000 years - since the latest ice-age (White 1990).

Furthermore if significant global warming is allowed to happen, then the effect alone will lead to the permanent loss of the current rain forest environment due to increased equatorial aridity (Spicer & Chapman 1990). The tendency for a hotter and drier South East Asia with less biomass and higher atmospheric CO_2, shown in Figures 2 and 3 is exactly what can be expected from the geological record. However, our level of understanding of what is a significant warming and exactly what will happen is still very limited.

Palaeological records and present trends strongly suggest that our most effective and manageable multi-story carbon sequestering system, the tropical rain forests, will be lost forever or significantly species impoverished under warmer, high CO_2 regimes. No other biome stores/sequesters as much as carbon as forest ecosystems, especially tropical rain forests and peat swamp forests (Brown & Lugo 1990) (see also Tables 4 and 5).

With no actions taken against present developments, both in the developed world and the developing world, ecosystems will be forced back into the CO_2 dominated mode of earlier times and in addition, will also be forced to function with a much lower biodiversity than might otherwise have occurred naturally. This will significantly limit possibilities for active recovery.

As mentioned earlier, many researchers have speculated that a CO_2 enriched atmosphere will enhance plant growth as C_3-plants are stimulated by higher CO_2 levels. Most field fertilization studies, however, have shown little response as primary production is usually quickly limited by low supply of nutrients in soils (Schlesinger 1990) and, according to Kerr (1992b), most researchers view such salvation as speculative and there is much ongoing research trying to understand ecosystem response to elevated CO_2.

Table 4 *Monoculture forests as carbon storage systems (selected species)*

Species	Rotation length ('maturity') (years)	Specific gravity (g/cc)	Height (m)	Wood production (m³/ha/yr)	Storage capacity (wood=45% C) (tonnes C/ha/yr)	Area required in order to store 3 Gt (million ha)
Acacia auriculiformis	10-20 (15)	0.6-0.75 (0.68)	30	10-15 (12.55)	8.50	352.9
Acacia mangium	12-20 (16)	0.5-0.6 (0.55)	35	20-30 (25)	13.75	218.2
Albizia falcataria	8-15 (11.5)	0.24-0.44 (0.34)	45	20-50 (35)	11.90	252.1
Albizia procera	10-15	0.6-0.65	40	8-12	6.30	476.2
Casaurina litoralis	7-10 (8.5)	0.8-1.2 (1.0)	30	3-25 (14)	14.00	214.3
Dalbergia sissoo	10-15 (12.5)	0.64-0.8 (0.72)	30	9-15 (12)	8.64	347.2
Eucalyptus brassiana	5-10 (7.5)	0.5-0.8 (0.65)	40	10-30 (20)	6.30	476.2
Eucalyptus citridora	5-25	0.7-1.1	40	10-20	13.50	222.2
Eucalyptus tereticornis	5-10 (7.5)	0.66-1.05 (0.86)	45	15-30 (22.5)	19.35	155.0
Gmelina arborea	10-20 (15)	0.42-0.64 (0.53)	30	10-25 (17.5)	9.28	323.3
Leucaena leucocephala	5-10 (?) (7.5)	0.5-0.7 (0.6)	20	10-25 (17.5)	10.50	285.7
Samanea saman	5-15 (10)	0.6-0.7 (0.65)	20	5-12 (8.5)	5.53	542.5
Sesbania grandiflora	2-4 (3)	0.4-0.5 (0.45)	10	20-25 (22.5)	10.13	296.2
Median	10.9	0.66			11.11	270.0

Adapted from Davidson (1985). The trees have been selected on the basis of wood production, length of harvest cycle and availability ('commonness'). The table does not include leaves, twigs and below-ground biomass. For total biomass, add 20-40% (Whitmore 1984). Total biomass of tropical forest plantations are estimated to be approx. 100 t/ha (Palm et al. 1986), which seems somewhat low. Dixon et al. (1991) quote figures as high as 100 t C/ha for agroforestry systems. The figures in this table on wood production are their absolute potential, this is only achieveable in relatively small areas of optimal conditions. Also not included in the table is the carbon which must be substracted as the considerable energy costs in planting the vast areas required. (Note: for comparison, Indonesia is 1.19 million km²)

Other speculations on biotic reactions include increased plant respiration due to increased temperature. If respiration exceeds photosynthesis, then the plants produce more CO_2 than they absorb and will eventually die (Postel 1988). The rate of photosynthesis is most importantly affected by light, water, nutrients and CO_2, it is not however, very much affected by temperature. What is affected by temperature, is respiration rates, a one-degree temperature change in either direction often alters rates of respiration by 10-30% (Houghton & Woodwell 1989).

Table 5 *Natural forests as carbon storage systems*

Forest type	Biomass (t/ha)	Biomass (t/ha)	Capacity (t/ha)
Tropical rain forest:			
Pasoh, W. Malaysia*	475-664	467-655	256 (252)
San Carlos, Venezuela**	391-441		187
Manaus, Brazil*	473		213
Ivory Coast**	425-465		200
Median			214
Semi evergreen rain forest:			
Khao Chong, China*	331	(323)	149 (145
*Temperate coniferous rain forest***	400		180
*Temperate broad-leaved deciduous mixed forest***	170		77

* Whitmore (1984); ** Hall & Rosillo-Calle (1989); *** Adams *et al.* (1990).
Note: An average specific gravity of 0.66 g/cc was used to calculate storage. The results correspond well with Dixon *et al.* (1991), who report 220 t C/ha for tropical forests. Maximum productivity however, for tropical rainforest is found in stands of pole size trees, of lesser height and lower biomass, and in areas of secondary forest regrowing in the larger clearings (Whitmore 1984).

Finally, with our scantly knowledge of how global ecosystem and climate interlinkages work, some scientists fear that the earth system may have some unpleasant surprises in store for us with the climate changing even more rapidly after reaching some (unknown) threshold level (Broeker 1987, after Mooney 1990).

6.   Conclusion

Climate changes occurring now will have profound negative impacts on all biota. The change is caused primarily by anthropogenic actions and is not sustainable. We have three possible actions to take which must all occur now:

1. Make significant emission cuts
2. Preserve biological diversity
3. Increase biological productivity of forests

Ad 1.
Carbon emissions must be cut, primarily by reducing the burning of fossil fuels, but also by changing land-use patterns and present animal husbandry systems.

These actions encompass change in the lifestyles of the developed countries and change in the course of present development patterns in the developing countries, as basically every anthropogenic action has an energy cost based on carbon. One action may include carbon benefits/penalties according to a system based on 'transferrable carbon equivalent' depending on the net absorption or production of carbon. Such measures will however be extremely difficult to enforce and their implementation would involve stringent international regulations and cooperation. Theoretically speaking, it would probably be easier to prohibit private cars which, according to the automobile magazine 'Wheels' in 1992, are the largest single contributor of carbon equaling approximately 2 Gt C/yr; others, however, estimate much lower contributions for private cars (0.5-5% of anthropogenic contributions).

Ad 2.
One of the recommendations from the Regional Workshop on the Carbon Cycle and Global Climate Change, 24-26 October, 1991 in Kuala Lumpur, Malaysia, stated:

> 'The workshop concluded from the evidence presented, that climate change is now inevitable and in order that the natural systems can remain sufficiently resilent to survive that change we must retain present biodiversity. Any reduction in biodiversity increases the risk of biosphere collapse.'

Presently we do not know enough about different species reactions or limits to changes in atmospheric chemistry and climate change, including elevated CO_2, ozone reductions, temperature increase and precipitation patterns. Estimating all the species on earth to be 30 million, we have described only a small fragment (1.7 million) and some are, we may presume, presently living at their limits regarding these parameters. Others will undoubtedly benefit and proliferate under high CO_2 regimes owing to genetic 'memory' of past experiences. However, the potentially proliferating species are not neccesarily the ones we want and may need in the future. It is thus of prime importance that a large genetic range, interspecific as well as intraspecific is maintained to ensure as far as possible, the means to find the plant communities best adapted to climate change. Thus it follows that:

Ad 3.
'Mankind is forced to accelerate the biosphere adjustment processes, *i.e.* massive reforestation programmes in order to buffer atmospheric CO_2' (UNESCO/ROSTSEA 1992).

From a meeting held in Jakarta, 25-26 February, 1992 with KLH, LIPI and UNESCO, it was concluded that simple plantation forests are no longer adequate to buffer or absorb anthropogenic atmospheric carbon. Their carbon storage capacity is not high enough and will demand more arable land to do the job. It was agreed that, based on the pressure on land due to overconsumption and overpopulation and the geological evidence on the fragility of the global ecosystem, it has become necessary to seek biosphere solutions other than simple plantations. Tropical rain forests due to their high biomass, which in part is due to high species diversity and the associated multi-tier structure of the forests, have the highest productivity and storage capacity. This must be imitated by using selected (and probably poorly known) species and possibly enhancing the growth rates of individual species through genetical engineering, *i.e.*, 'designed ecosystems'.

Absorbing an annual atmospheric input of 3 Gt carbon (1989), requires approx. 270 million ha of plantation forest (see Table 4). Planting conventional plantation forest will however not solve the problem, it only buys a little time - 11 years. After the forests are mature, more forests would have to be planted (11 year after 1992) and what shall we do with the wood if we harvest the original planting ? Finding 303 million ha (3.37 Gt atmospheric C in 1992) that are suitable for forestry and not already in use for agriculture is difficult enough, finding an additional 466 million ha in 2003 will be impossible (5.18 Gt).

To reabsorb the total amount of CO_2 already emitted, 80 ppmv (350 ppmv-270 ppmv) is not possible by conventional methods. As 1.2 ppmv atmospheric carbon equals 3 Gt C globally, it follows that 80 ppmv corresponds to approximately 200 Gt additional carbon in the atmosphere, compared to pre-industrial times. To reabsorb this thus requires an area equal to a staggering 180 million km^2 or an area 94 times the size of Indonesia or six times the African continent if the carbon were to be stored by conventional monoculture plantation forests. It can not be done. There is not that much land on earth.

With proper funding and research, the area required may be reduced to perhaps half that size, possibly a quarter, if high-storage ecosystems 'designed' to imitate the complex systems of a multi-tiered, high species diverse, tropical rainforest are planted.

Of the original global forest cover, only half is left and the remaining world's forests are rapidly shrinking. The genetic memory of a multitude of species is disappearing with the forest. Reducing deforestation alone has the potential to conserve 1.5 Gt C/year (Dixon *et al.* 1991). It will also preserve species which we may need under elevated CO_2 regimes. Proper management in forestry practices and agriculture could conserve upto 10.1 Gt C/year with a potential 6.8 Gt/year in the tropics alone (Dixon *et al.* 1991). It is thus much cheaper in the long run and makes more sense to manage and conserve present land resources as this includes other value added benefits, than to continue with present practices. We have no choice.

7.   References

Adams, J.M., Faure, L., Faurre-Denard, L., McGlade, M. & Woodward, F.I. (1990) Increases in Terrestrial Carbon Storage from the Last Glacial Maximum to the Present, *Nature* 328: 711-719.

Arthur, M.A., Dean, W.E. & Schlanger, S.O. (1985) Variations in the Global Carbon Cycle During the Cretaceous Related to Climate, Volcanism and Changes in Atmospheric CO_2, in: Sunquist, E.T. & Broeker, W.S. (eds.) *The Carbon Cycle and Atmospheric CO_2: Natural Variations Archean to Present, Geophysical Monograph* 32: 504-529.

Arthur, M.A., Allard, D., Minga, K.R. (1991) Cretaceous and Cenozoic Atmospheric Carbon Dioxide Variations and Past Global Climate Change, *Geophysical Society of America* (Abstract with program) 23A: 127.

Ashmore, M. (1990) The Greenhouse Gases. *Trends Ecol. Evol.* 5: 296-297.

Brown, S. & Lugo, A.E. (1990) The Storage and Production of Organic Matter in Tropical Forests and Their Role in the Global Carbon Cycle, *Biotropica* 14: 161-187.

Chen, C-T., A. & Drake, E.T. (1986) Carbon Dioxide Increase in the Atmosphere and Oceans and Possible Effect on Climate, *Ann. Rev. Earth Planet Sci.* 14: 210-235.

Crutzen, P.J. & Andreae, M.O. (1990) Biomass Burning in the Tropics: Impact on Atmospheric Chemistry and Biochemical Cycle, *Science* 250: 1678-1699.

Davidson, J. (1985) *Trees: Species and Sites. Assistance to the Forestry Sector of Bangladesh*, FAO Field Document No. 5, April.

DeMichelle, W.A. & Phillips, T.L. (in press) The Response of Hierarchically-structured Ecosystems to Long-term Climatic Change: A Case Study Using Tropical Peat Swamps of Pennsylvanian Age.

Dixon, R.K., Schroeder, P.E. & Winjum, J.K. (1991) *Assessment of Promising Forest Management Practices and Technologies for Enhancing the Conservation and Sequestering of Atmospheric Carbon and Their Costs at the Site Level*, US Environmental Protection Agency, Environmental Research Laboratory, Office of Research and Development, Washington DC, Oct., 138 pp.

Gerlach, T.M. (1991) Present Day CO_2 Emissions from Volcanoes. *EOS, Trans. American Geophysical Union* 72: 23.

Gloersen, P. & Campbell, W. (1991) Recent Variations in Arctic and Antartic Sea-ice Covers, *Nature* 352: 33-36.

Grubb, M.J., Victor, D.G. & Hope, C.W. (1991) Pragmatics in the Greenhouse, *Nature* 354: 348-350.

Hall, D.O. & Rosillo-Calle, F. (1989) CO_2 Cycling by Biomass: Global Bioproductivity and Problems of Deforestation, paper presented at the conference 'Amazonia: Facts, Problems and Solutions', July 31-August 2, 1989, University of Sao Paulo, Sao Paulo, Brazil.

Harger, J.R.E. (1991) Potential Limits of Human Dominated Fossil Energy Based Global Ecosystems, in: *UNESCO/UNEP/Dept. of Environment, Malaysia*, Regional Workshop on the Carbon Cycle and Global Climate Change. Kuala Lumpur, Malaysia, October 24-26, 1991.

Harger, J.R.E. (1992) 'Environment Trends and Reef Monitoring Strategies', paper presented at the 7th International Coral Reef Symposium, Guam, 22-26 June 1992.

Harger, J.R.E., Sorensen, K.W., Spicer, R.A., Malling, S.T. & Wasser, H.J. (1992) *Contending with Global Change*, Study No. 5., Human action to control global climate through designed ecosystems, UNESCO/ROSTSEA, 1992.

Hogan, K.B., Hoffman, J.S. & Thomson, A.M. (1991) Methane on the Greenhouse Agenda, *Nature* 354: 181-182.

Houghton, R.A. & Woodwell, G.A. (1989) Global Climate Change, *Sci. Amer.* 260: 18-26.

IGBP (1992) *Global Change: Reducing Uncertainties*, The Royal Swedish Academy of Sciences, 40 pp.

Keir, R.S. (1991) Ironing out Greenhouse Effects, *Nature* 255: 682-683.

Kerr, R.A. (1992a) Pollutant Haze Cools the Greenhouse, *Science* 256: 1138-1140.

Kerr, R.A. (1992b) Fugitive Carbon Dioxide: It's Not Hiding in the Ocean, *Science* 256: 35-36.

Kinsey, P.W. (1991) The Greenhouse Effect and Coral Reefs. XVII Pacific Science Symposium, Honolulu, Hawaii, May 27-June 3, 1991, *Coral Reefs and Environmental Change: The next 100 years.*

Lovejoy, T. & Salati, E. (1982) Precipitation Change in Amazonia, in: Moran, E. (ed.) *The Dilemma of Amazonian Development,* Westerly Press.

Maltby, E. & Immiziri, P. (1991) Carbon Dynamics in Peatlands and Other Wetland Soils. Regional and Global Perspectives, in: *UNESCO/UNEP/Dept. of Environment, Malaysia. Regional Workshop on the Carbon Cycle and Global Climate Change,* Kuala Lumpur, Malaysia, October 24-26, 1991.

Mitchell, J.F.B. (1989) The Greenhouse Effect and Climate Change, *Rev. Geophys.* 27: 115-139.

Mooney, J.F.B. (1990) Address of the Past President: Toward the Study of the Earth's Metabolism, *Bull. Ecol. Soc. Am.* 71: 221-228.

Lorius, C., Jouzel, J., Raynaud, D., Hansen, J. & Le Treut, H. (1990) The Ice-core Record: Climate Sensitivity and Future Greenhouse Warming, *Nature* 347: 139-145.

Palm, C.A., Houghton, R.A., Melillo, J.M. & Skole, D.L. (1986) Atmospheric Carbon-dioxide from Deforestation in South East Asia, *Biotropica* 18: 177-188.

Post, W.M., Peng, T.-H., Emanuel, W.R., King, A.W., Dale, V.H. & DeAngelis, D.L. (1990) The Global Carbon Cycle, *American Scientist* 78.

Postel, S. (1988) A Green Fix to the Global Warm-up, *Reforestation,* September-October 1988, Worldwatch Institute, pp. 29-36.

Sass, J. (1991) Climate Plumbs the Depths, *Nature* 349: 458.

Schlesinger, W.H. (1990) Vegetation Unlikely Answer, *Nature* 348: 679.

Siegenthaler, U. (1990) El Nino and Atmospheric CO_2, *Nature* 345: 295-296.

Smith, R.C., Prezelin, B.B., Baker, K.S., Bidigare, R.R., Boucher, N.P., Coley, T., Karentz, D., MacIntyre, S., Matlick, H.A., Menzies, D., Ondrusek, M., Wan, Z., Waters, K.J. (1992) Ozone Depletion: Ultraviolet Radiation and Phytoplankton Biology in Antarctic Waters, *Science* 255: 952-958.

Sombroek, W.G. (1991) The Greenhouse Effect, Plant Growth and Soils. Summary of talk at the annual meeting of the Österreichische Bodenkundliche Gesselschaft, Wien, January 23, 1991. International Soil Reference and Informations Centre ISRIC.

Spicer, R.A. & Chapman, J.L. (1990) Climate Change and the Evolution of High Latitude Terrestrial Vegetation and Floras, *Trends Ecol. Evol.* 5: 279-284.

Spicer, R.A. (1989) Plants at the Cretaceous-Tertiary Boundary, in: Chaloner, W.G. & Hallam, A. (eds.) *Evolution and Extinction,* Proceedings of a joint symposium of the Royal Society and the Linnean Society held on 9 and 10 November 1989.

Spicer, R.A. (1991) Palaecology, Past Climate Systems and C3/C4 Photosynthesis, in: *UNESCO/UNEP/Dept. of Environment, Malaysia. Regional Workshop on the Carbon Cycle and Global Climate Change.* Kuala Lumpur, Malaysia, October 24-26, 1991.

Sundquist, E.T. (1985) Geological Perspective on Carbon Dioxide and the Carbon Cycle, in: Sundquist, E.T. & Broeker, W.S. (eds.) *The Carbon Cycle and Atmospheric CO_2: Natural Variations Archaen to Present, Geophysical Monograph* 32. American Geophysical Union, Washington DC, pp. 5-60.

UNESCO/ROSTSEA (Regional Office for Science and Technology for South East Asia), KLH (State Ministry of Population and Environment, Indonesia) & LIPI (Indonesian Institute of Sciences) (1992) *Contending with Global Change,* Study No. 5, Human action to control global climate through designed ecosystems, UNESCO/ROTSEA, Jakarta, Indonesia.

Vermeij, G.J. (1991) When Biotas Meet: Understanding Biotic Interchange, *Science* 253: 1099-1104.

Walsh, J.E. (1991) The arctic as a Bellwether, *Nature* 352: 19.

White, R.M. (1990) The Great Climate Debate, *Sci. Amer.* 263: 36-43.

Whitmore, T.C. (1984) *Tropical Rainforests of the Far East*, 2nd Edition, Clarendon Press, Oxford.

Wolfe, J.A. & Upchurch, G.R. (1986) Vegetation, Climatic and Floral Changes at the Cretaceous-Tertiary Boundary, *Nature* 324: 148-152.

Ziegler, A.M., Raymond, A.L., Gierlowski, T.C., Horrel, M.A., Rowley, D.B. & Lottes, A.L. (1987) Coal, Climate, and Terrestrial Productivity: The Present and Early Creatceous Compared, in: Scot, A.C. (ed.) Coal and Coal Bearing Strata: Recent Advances. *Geol. Soc. Special Publ.* 32: 25-49.

Part 2

Pesticide studies

2.1

Toxicity of pesticides to target and non-target fauna of the lowland rice ecosystem

A.W. Tejada, C.M. Bajet, M.G. Magbauna,
N.B. Gambalan, L.C. Araez & E.D. Magallona

Abstract

The toxicity of some commonly used pesticides in rice culture, expressed as median lethal concentration (LC$_{50}$), was determined in the target pests, brown planthopper (Nilaparvata lugens) *and the striped stemborer* (Chilo suppressalis) *and in non-targets organisms such as Nile tilapia* (Oreochromis niloticus), *guppy fish* (Poecilia reticulata), *snails (hybrid of* Pila luzonica *and* Pomacea canaliculata) *and tadpoles* (Bufo marinus). *The majority of the pesticides used in rice paddies were extremely toxic to fish with LC$_{50}$ values < 0.5 mg/L. Toxicity indices of insecticides were calculated as the ratio of the toxicity to target organisms against toxicity to fish. The decreasing order of toxicity indices is as follows: azinphos-ethyl > endosulfan > BPMC + cypermethrin > cypermethrin > chlorpyrifos > BPMC + chlorpyrifos > triazophos > BPMC > etofenprox > carbosulfan > methyl-parathion > monocrotophos. Paddy water collected just after spraying insecticides 40 days after transplanting was bioassayed using tilapia. For fish, 100% survival was observed for monocrotophos and complete mortality for azinphos-ethyl and endosulfan.*

1. Introduction

Pesticides are still widely used to control insect pests, weeds and diseases and are a vital part of Integrated Pest Management, especially in lowland rice production. Considering that these compounds are never fully selective, they could also affect organisms present in the paddy water other than the target pest species. This could result in unintended effects such as pest resurgence, emergence of new pest species, depletion of natural enemies and beneficials, among others. These adverse effects are never completely addressed during the registration of pesticides.

Of major interest are the effects of pesticides on large animals found in the paddies such as fish, edible snails, toads and frogs. The importance of fish as food is recognized so that fish toxicity data is a requirement for registration. However, the data are usually based on temperate species such as rainbow trout, carp or zebra fish. These may be useful guides but cannot replace the toxicity data obtained using tropical fish such as tilapia that are recommended for use in rice fish culture. In addition, the toxicity information on temperate species is only of marginal use, if at all, for extrapolating the adverse effects of pesticides on a tropical ecosystem. Fish toxicity reported by Cagauan (1990) using Nile tilapia, Java tilapia and Crucian carp indicated the possibility of fish kills due to insecticide application, however, tests were done under various conditions to make comparisons between pesticides.

Much less is known about the effect of pesticides on other organisms, probably because of the difficulties involved in the assay, as well as in the interpretation of its importance. *Pila luzonica* Reeve, an edible freshwater snail which is considered a delicacy in some parts of the Philippines, has been studied in detail. Guerrero & Guerrero (1980) found an LC_{50} value for γ-HCH at 2.8 and 4.5 mg/L for this organism and *Vivipara angularis* Muller (another edible snail), respectively, when these were cultured in rice paddies. This could indicate a capacity for pesticide uptake and possibly, bioaccumulation. A low level of uptake was likewise observed with isoprocarb BPMC and carbofuran/carbosulfan (Bajet & Magallona 1982, Varca & Magallona 1987, Tejada & Magallona 1985). Bajet & Magallona (1982) reported an LC_{50} of 25.3 mg/L isoprocarb for this snail.

The golden apple snail (*Pomacea canaliculata*) is considered a pest of rice but at the same time may be used as food and feed. Since organotin compounds necessary for the control of snails were banned because of toxic side effects, other effective chemicals have been found. However, residues of these molluscicides have not been studied extensively elsewhere. They may remain in snails for a long period of time and may pose a hazard to man and wildlife when used as food.

This study was, therefore, undertaken to determine the toxicity levels of several pesticides used in lowland rice production to some target and non-target fauna and to express the toxicity levels as toxicity indices, which may be a basis for rapid assessment of safe but effective pesticides. This study will give an indication of the impact of these pesticides on the lowland rice ecosystem.

2. Materials and methods

2.1 Laboratory tests

The toxicity of pesticides was evaluated by determining the median lethal concentration (LC_{50}) on target and non-target fauna of the lowland rice paddy. The organisms studied were: (a) brown planthoppers (BPH), *Nilaparvata lugens*, (b) striped rice stemborer (RSB), *Chilo suppressalis*, (c) Nile tilapia, *Oreochromis niloticus*, (d) guppy fish, *Poecilia reticulata*, (e) tadpoles, *Bufo marinus* and (f) golden apple snails, hybrid of *Pila luzonica* x *Pomacea canaliculata*. The formulations of pesticides used are listed in Appendix 1.

2.1.1 Toxicity to brown planthoppers (target organism)

Brown planthoppers (*Nilaparvata lugens*, Homoptera; Delphacidae) were reared on 50-70 day old rice seedlings (variety TN1) inside rearing cages. Rice seedlings, about 30-50 days old, planted in pots, were trimmed to about three to four tillers.

Bracketing range finding tests were done to establish a mortality range of 10 to 90% suitable for calculating LC_{50} values. Five graded concentrations of pesticides in 10% aqueous acetone were prepared ranging from 10 to 200 mg/L. The insecticides were applied to rice seedlings using a De Vilbiss hand sprayer until just before runoff. Each pot was considered a treatment and there were two replicates per dosage level.

The control was sprayed with 10% aqueous acetone. After one hour, 20 brown planthoppers (BPH) (3 days old) were introduced per pot and then encased in a cage. Mortality counts were made after 24 and 48 hours.

After the dosages to be used in the test were established, five dosages, which at first estimate should give at least 10% mortality for the lowest dose and at most 90% mortality for the highest dose were selected. The testing procedure was similar to the bracketing test except that three replications were used. The results were analyzed statistically by probit analysis to estimate the LC_{50} values. The LC_{50} values were expressed as mg/L of spray solution, based on the active ingredient of the formulation.

2.1.2 Toxicity to rice stemborer (RSB)

Rice stemborers (*Chilo suppressalis*) were reared on rice stems, cut to about 4 inches long. The rice was cultivated without the use of any pesticide. Feeds were changed as often as needed. The pupae were collected and placed in petri dishes inside cages containing potted rice plants where the emerging adults were allowed to lay their eggs. Mature eggs were collected and allowed to hatch in rice stems.

For the toxicity test, third instar larvae were used and insecticide application was directed to the cut stems. The other end of the stem was plugged with wax to allow the borer to remain inside the stem. Each treatment consisted of 20 larvae each placed in an individual rice stem in separate test tubes. Mortality was observed after 24 hours.

2.1.3 Toxicity to fish (non-target organism)

About one-inch Nile tilapia fingerlings and guppy fish were used for the test. Nile tilapia were obtained from the Bureau of Fisheries and Aquatic Resources and from nearby fish nurseries at Bay, Laguna. The two week old fingerlings were acclimatized in the laboratory and fed with rice bran for at least three days in a large aerated aquarium before toxicity tests were conducted.

The guppy fish were collected from a ditch in Makati, Metro Manila, Philippines, and were assumed pesticide free due to the absence of agricultural or pesticide formulation activity within the surrounding area.

The fish were starved for 24 hours prior to, and until the completion of the test. The procedures for bracketing and determination were similar to those of the brown planthopper as far as dosage selection was concerned. The procedures inherent in fish toxicity testing were observed.

The acetone solution of insecticides was added to 750 mL of aged tap water. The aging of water was achieved by allowing tap water to stand overnight. The water was contained in two liter capacity aquaria and five fish were introduced per treatment. The weight of all the fish in a test container did not exceed 1 gram per liter of the liquid medium being tested. Moribund fish were counted as dead.

The pesticides were ranked based on the standard set by Nishiuchi (1974) for fish toxicity. The ranking standards were determined as follows:

Rank	Carp (mg/L)	Daphnids (mg/L)	Remarks
A	> 10	> 0.5	Low toxicity: can be used practically without any special precaution.
B	0.5-10	< 0.5	These chemicals will not constitute a hazard unless a large amount of them contaminate the waters.
C	< 0.5		These chemicals have a high change of injuring aquatic organisms even when a slight amount contaminates the waters.

2.1.4 Toxicity to field-collected tadpoles
The same procedure for toxicity testing of fish was used for the tadpoles. Tadpoles of the same size were tested as soon as they were collected from the field.

2.1.5 Toxicity to snails (target organism)
Golden snails reared in a fish pond were collected and allowed to acclimatize in an aquarium for 3-5 days. A toxicity test was conducted in a similar manner as for fish. The snails were considered dead when they floated on the water surface or when there was no movement after gently tapping the shell.

2.2 Field tests

Selected commercial formulations of monocrotophos, azinphos-ethyl, endosulfan, cyfluthrin, chlorpyrifos and cypermethrin (Annex 1) were sprayed separately in a farmer's field 40 days after transplanting the rice (DAT), using the recommended rate of application. Paddy water was collected just after spraying and was bioassayed using Nile tilapia in a manner similar to that used in toxicity testing. Mortality readings were done after 24 and 48 hours.

The concentration of these insecticides in paddy water was analyzed by partitioning with methylene chloride for azinphos-ethyl and monocrotophos or 15% methylene chloride in hexane for endosulfan. The water layer was re-extracted with solvent and the pooled organic layer was dried using anhydrous sodium chloride, concentrated to almost dryness by a rotary evaporator, taken up in 5 mL methanol and analyzed by Gas Liquid Chromatography.

A Tracor Model 560 Gas Chromatograph equipped with a ^{63}Ni Electron Capture detector was used under the following conditions:

Column: 6 ft x 2 mm packed with 2.5% DC-200 + 2.5% QF-1 on 100/120 Aeropak 300
Column temperature: 170 °C
Injector temperature: 200 °C
Detector temperature: 300 °C
Nitrogen flow rate: 60 mL/min
Nitrogen purge gas: 15 mL/min

A Hewlett Packard 5840A Gas Chromatograph with N-P Detector was also used under the following conditions:

Column: 6 ft x 1.5 mm packed with 3% SE-30 on chromosorb WHP 80/100
Column temperature: 200 °C
Injector temperature: 215 °C
Detector temperature: 300 °C
Nitrogen: 30 mL/min
Hydrogen: 3 mL/min
Air: 50 mL/min

Table 1 *LC$_{50}$ of some insecticides used on brown planthopper* (Nilaparvata lugens)

Insecticide	LC$_{50}$ (mg/L) 48 hrs
Carbosulfan	3.0
Triazophos	8.4
Chlorpyrifos	10.4
Cypermethrin	10.9
Endosulfan	14.4
Etofenprox	11.0
Monocrotophos	21.5
Methyl-parathion	28.3
Azinphos-ethyl	56.6
BPMC + chlorpyrifos	79.6
BPMC + cypermethrin	92.7
BPMC	102.4

3. Results and discussion

Carbosulfan was the most toxic insecticide tested on brown planthoppers (BPH). This is shown in Table 1, where the insecticides are given, BPMC being the least toxic. Fabellar (1983) also reported carbosulfan was most toxic to BPH by foliar and Potter spray application with an LC_{50} of 0.018 and 0.034 mg/L respectively.

For stemborers, triazophos was the most toxic, followed by monocrotophos, chlorpyrifos + BPMC, diazinon, chlorpyrifos, etofenprox, endosulfan, azinphos-ethyl, phosphamidon, cypermethrin + BPMC and BPMC (Table 2). The toxicity of the mixtures of BPMC with chlorpyrifos and cypermethrin was improved over pure BPMC.

Table 2 *Toxicity of insecticides to rice stemborer* (Chilo suppressalis)

Insecticide	LC_{50} (mg/L) 48 hrs
Triazophos	16.9
Monocrotophos	18.4
Chlorpyrifos + BPMC	21.8
Diazinon	25.3
Chlorpyrifos	46.6
Etofenprox	> 75
Endosulfan	83.8
Azinphos-ethyl	99.0
Phosphamidon	105.0
Alpha cypermethrin + BPMC	118.6
BPMC	3438.1

The majority of the insecticides tested were ranked as highly toxic to Nile tilapia with LC_{50} values less than 0.5 mg/L (Table 3). The decreasing order of toxicity is as follows: azinphos-ethyl > endosulfan > cyfluthrin > chlorpyrifos > fenvalerate > cypermethrin > triazophos > etofenprox > thiodicarb > carbosulfan > alpha cypermethrin + BPMC > monocrotophos + fenvalerate > BPMC + chlorpyrifos > fenitrothion > BPMC. These insecticides have a high chance of injuring organisms even when there is slight contamination of the water (Nishiuchi 1974).

Azinphos-ethyl was more toxic to Nile tilapia than to goldfish with an LC_{50} value of 0.1 mg/L (Bayer Technical Product Information) but cyfluthrin was more toxic to carp, rainbow trout and golden orfe with LC_{50} values of < 0.01, 0.0006 and 0.0032 mg/L, respectively at 96 h exposure time (Bayer Technical Product Information). On the other hand, BPMC was less toxic to carp with an LC_{50} of 4.2 mg/L (Bayer Technical Product Information), compared to tilapia with a value of 0.64 mg/L. The toxicity data of Webbe (1961) for tilapia using

methyl-parathion with LC_{50} of 1-5 mg/L (48 h) is comparable to our results, *i.e.*
3.5 mg/L.

All the insecticides tested had lower LC_{50} to fish than to BPH. Monocrotophos
(Rank A) may be the most promising insecticide tested since it was least toxic to
tilapia, and effective against BPH. Nishiuchi (1974) likewise placed monocrotophos under Category A. Azinphos-ethyl may be the least preferred insecticide
because it is extremely toxic to tilapia and the least effective to BPH, among the
insecticides tested.

Table 3 *Toxicity of insecticides to Nile tilapia* (Oreochromis niloticus)

Insecticide	LC_{50} (mg/L) 48 hrs	Rank
Azinphos-ethyl	1.0×10^{-6}	C
Endosulfan	6.9×10^{-4}	C
Cyfluthrin	1.6×10^{-2}	C
Chlorpyrifos	3.0×10^{-2}	C
Fenvalerate	3.0×10^{-2}	C
Cypermethrin	3.1×10^{-2}	C
Triazophos	3.5×10^{-2}	C
Etofenprox	9.1×10^{-2}	C
Thiodicarb	0.12	C
Carbosulfan	0.17	C
Alpha cypermethrin + BPMC	0.22	C
Monocrotophos + fenvalerate	0.25	C
BPMC + chlorpyrifos	0.28	C
Fenitrothion	0.49	C
BPMC	0.64	C
Malathion	1.48	B
Methamidophos	2.96	B
Methyl-parathion	3.50	B
Carbaryl	3.52	B
Monocrotophos	13.80	A

Ranking was adapted from Nishiuchi (1974), see the classification given above.

Paddy water collected at the farmer's field just after spraying monocrotophos 40
days after transplanting and bioassayed using tilapia showed no fish mortality.
The concentration in the paddy water was 0.58 mg/L and this is lower than the
LC_{50} value which was 13.8 mg/L. Likewise Wang *et al.* (1988) found a maximum
concentration of 0.882 mg/L using radiochemical techniques which was below the
reported LC_{50}.

Azinphos-ethyl and endosulfan treated paddy water both resulted in 100% fish mortality at 24 and 48 h after exposure of the fish. The concentration of azinphos-ethyl in paddy water was 0.068 mg/L and this exceeded the LC_{50} in fish which is 0.001 mg/L. Cagauan (1990) reported the concentration of azinphos-ethyl to be 0.132 to 0.271 $\mu g/L$ when it is sprayed at 14 DAT. At this time the canopy of the rice plant is not so dense, resulting in a higher concentration of insecticide in the paddy water. For endosulfan, Medina *et al.* (1993) observed 100% mortality in tilapia when endosulfan was sprayed at 30 DAT. At 10 days after spraying, the residue level in water was 0.12 $\mu g/L$ and fish mortality decreased to 44%. The endosulfan concentration just after spraying at 40 DAT was 0.75 $\mu g/L$. This exceeds the LC_{50} value obtained in the laboratory which explained the observed fish mortality. Jarayman (1988) reported that endosulfan concentration in paddy water was 0.995 $\mu g/L$ at 3 days after seeding (DAS) and 0.503 $\mu g/L$ at 15 DAS, and this indicates that fish mortality may be possible within 15 days because the LC_{50} value obtained in the laboratory was 0.69 $\mu g/L$ (Table 3). Observed fish mortality for cypermethrin, cyfluthrin and chlorpyrifos were 25, 50 and 50%, respectively after 48 h. This emphasizes the importance of driving the fish into the trench or always keeping the fish in the trench to lessen the effect of insecticide application. Cagauan (1990) found that the concentration of cypermethrin and cyfluthrin in paddy water when applied at 14 DAT were 0.025 and 0.022 mg/L, respectively. These are within the LC_{50} values obtained in the laboratory which are 0.031 and 0.016 mg/L, for cypermethrin and cyfluthrin, respectively (Table 3). Under the farmer's field conditions, no fish mortality was observed using cypermethrin. Therefore, the correct management of the rice-fish culture is very important to minimize fish kills during insecticide application (Tejada & Bajet 1990).

To reconcile pesticide use for rice with the presence of fish, the freshwater Aquaculture Center recommended that fish are driven the trench one day before pesticide application to avoid toxicity and to allow time for degradation. After one week, water is reintroduced to a depth of 7-11 cm. With this practice, BPMC, BPMC + chlorpyrifos, carbaryl, cypermethrin, isoprocarb, monocrotophos and methyl-parathion have acceptable fish recovery rates, whereas azinphos-ethyl is still very toxic (CLSU-FAC 1978, 1981a, 1981b).

In the case of mixtures of insecticides, the toxicities for tilapia were midway between the toxicity of both pure insecticides (Table 3). This is true in the case of cypermethrin + BPMC, monocrotophos + fenvalerate and BPMC + chlorpyrifos. The rank of the mixture is determined by the more toxic ingredient in the formulation (Nishiuchi 1974).

Some of the insecticides tested belong to the Rank B category and are classified as moderately toxic with a LC_{50} ranging from 0.5 mg/L to 10 mg/L: malathion, methamidophos, methyl-parathion, and carbaryl. These pesticides will not contribute a hazard unless an abnormally large amount contaminates the water (Nishiuchi 1974).

The index of toxicity was derived by taking the LC_{50} of the target organism, BPH, over that of the non-target organism, tilapia. This could be a basis of selecting pesticides suitable for rice-fish culture or areas near natural waters. Most of the insecticides tested had low LC_{50} values which indicated high toxicity to fish. The index of toxicity (Table 4) indicated that monocrotophos may be the most suitable for rice-fish culture, among the insecticides tested, because it was the least toxic to tilapia and the most effective against the target organism. Nishiuchi (1974) likewise placed monocrotophos in Category A, least toxic to fish. Similarly, the Freshwater Aquaculture Center reported a LC_{50} of 70 mg/L formulated product for monocrotophos, equivalent to 21 mg/L active ingredient for tilapia (Magallona 1989).

Table 4 *Toxicity index of common pesticides used in lowland rice protection*

Pesticide	Toxicity index*
Azinphos-ethyl	5,660,00
Endosulfan	20,870
BPMC + cypermethrin	421
Cypermethrin	352
Chlorpyrifos	347
BPMC + chlorpyrifos	284
Triazophos	240
BPMC	160
Etofenprox	121
Carbosulfan	17.6
Methyl-parathion	8.1
Monocrotophos	1.6

* Toxicity index is the ratio of LC_{50} for BPH (a target species) to LC_{50} for tilapia (a non-target species).

Table 5 *Toxicity of some herbicides and a fungicide to Nile tilapia (O. niloticus)*

Pesticide	LC_{50} (mg/L) 48 hrs	Rank
Herbicides		
Pretilachlor	2×10^{-3}	C
Piperophos + 2,4-D	9×10^{-3}	C
2,4-D	1.4×10^{-2}	C
MCPA	2.2×10^{-2}	C
Butachlor	1.5×10^{-1}	C
Fluazipof-butyl	2.9×10^{-1}	C
Thiobencarb	1.135	B
Oxadiazon	60.49	A
Fungicide		
Mancozeb	16.30	A

Ranking was adapted from Nishiuchi (1974), see the classification system given above.

Table 5 shows the decreasing order of toxicity of herbicides for tilapia fingerlings: piperophos + 2,4-D > MCPA > butachlor > fluazipof-butyl > thiobencarb > oxadiazon. These data may be useful to rice-fish farmers who stock their fish long before planting or leave the fish in the trench after rice harvest to provide ample time for the fish to grow. Since herbicide application is usually done before planting, runoff due to heavy rains after application could be lethal to the fish, especially if the active ingredient is water soluble. The herbicide oxadiazon was found to have low toxicity to tilapia with LC_{50} = 60.49 mg/L (Table 5).

Table 6 *Toxicity of insecticides to guppy fish* (Poecilia reticulata)

Pesticide	LC_{50} (mg/L)		Rank
	24 hrs	48 hrs	
Endosulfan		> 0.007	C
Cyfluthrin		> 0.02	C
Azinphos-ethyl		0.02	C
Methomyl		0.04	C
Chlorpyrifos		0.067	C
Carbofuran		0.09	C
Cypermethrin		0.104	C
Thiobencarb	0.61	-	B
BPMC + alpha cypermethrin	0.81	1.2	B
Isoprocarb		1.6	B
Carbaryl		2.3	B
Thiodicarb	2.60	-	B
Diazinon	5.1	1.4	B
Permethrin	3.2	2.3	B
BPMC	1.85	0.8	B
		0.96	B
MTMC		9.5	B
Oxadiazon	> 20		A

Ranking was adapted from Nishiuchi (1974), see the classification given above.

The toxicity of pesticides tested vary with species of fish. Generally, all pesticides tested were more toxic to tilapia than guppy fish (Table 6). For example, Nile tilapia was more sensitive to azinphos-ethyl than guppy fish (*Poecilia reticulata*) with LC_{50} values of 1.0×10^{-6} (Table 3) and 0.02 mg/L, respectively (Table 4).

The ranking of guppy fish can be compared with the daphnids (*Daphnia magna*). It can be a good indicator of the pollution potential of a pesticide comparable to mosquito fish. Azinphos-ethyl and methomyl were highly toxic to guppy while oxadiazon was the least toxic (Table 6).

Table 7 shows the toxicity of insecticides to field-collected tadpoles. These insecticides were more toxic to tilapia than to tadpoles with the exception of carbaryl and thiodicarb.

Table 7 *Toxicity of some pesticides to field-collected tadpoles*

Pesticide	LC_{50} (mg/L)		Rank
	48 hrs	96 hrs	
BPMC + chlorpyrifos	10.5		A
Monocrotophos	60.7		A
Methyl-parathion	5.0		B
Malathion	> 5.0	1.5	B
Carbaryl	> 5	2.1	B
Mancozeb	> 5	0.12	C
Thiodicarb	> 5	0.04	C

Ranking adapted from Nishiuchi (1974)

Table 8 *Toxicity of some pesticides to snails* (Pomacea caniculata)

Pesticide	Type	LC_{50} (mg/L) 48 hrs	Rank
Piperophos + 2,4-D	H	4.8×10^{-2}	C
Endosulfan	I	0.675	B
Chlorpyrifos	I	0.978*	B
Butachlor	H	1.005	B
Thiobencarb	H	2.20	B
Thiodicarb	I	2.595	B
Azinphos-ethyl	I	3.082	B
2,4-D	H	5.08	B
Malathion	I	18.68	A
Oxadiazon	H	> 20*	A
Monocrotophos	I	53.79	A

* 24 hrs - LC_{50}; H = herbicide, I = insecticide
Ranking adapted from Nishiuchi (1974)

The most toxic pesticide tested for golden snails was piperophos + 2,4-D (Rank C), followed by endosulfan, chlorpyrifos, butachlor, thiobencarb, thiodicarb, azinphos-ethyl, 2,4-D, malathion (Rank B), and mancozeb, oxadiazon and mono-crotophos (Rank A) (Table 8). The snails were more resistant to herbicides than fish except for piperophos + 2,4-D, and this may be partly due to their hard shell which may protect the snails from the effect of the herbicide. Nevertheless, the residues of these pesticides may be bioconcentrated in the flesh which could pose a hazard if consumed by animals or humans (Tejada & Magallona 1985).

A summary ranking of all pesticides used is shown in Table 9. The majority of the pesticides used were extremely toxic to fish (Rank C) with LC_{50} less than 0.5 mg/L. Pesticide application techniques in rice-fish culture may be manipulated using these results to minimize fish toxicity (Tejada & Bajet 1990).

Table 9 *Summary ranking of pesticides based on fish toxicity*

Rank C Extremely toxic	Rank B Moderately toxic	Rank A Low toxicity
Insecticides		
Azinphos-ethyl	Malathion	
Endosulfan	Methyl-parathion	
Cypermethrin	Methamidophos	
Etofenprox	Carbaryl	
Thiodicarb		
Carbosulfan		
BPMC + chlorpyrifos		
Alpha cypermethrin + BPMC		
Triazophos		
BPMC		
Fenitrothion		
Cyfluthrin		
Chlorpyrifos		
Fenvalerate		
Monocrotophos + fenvalerate		
Herbicides		
Pretilachlor	Thiobencarb	Oxadiazon
Piperophos + 2,4-D		
2,4-D		
MCPA		
Butachlor		
Fluazipof-butyl		
Fungicide		Mancozeb

4.   Conclusion

The toxicity index of pesticides might be used as a basis for determining the suitability of a compound in an environment consisting of target and non-target organisms. This can be derived by taking the ratio of the LC_{50} of the target and the non-target organisms.

The decreasing order of toxicity index for pesticides commonly used in rice paddies is as follows: azinphos-ethyl > endosulfan > BPMC + cypermethrin > cypermethrin > chlorpyrifos > BPMC + chlorpyrifos > triazophos > BPMC > etofenprox > carbosulfan > methyl-parathion > monocrotophos.

Monocrotophos appears to be suitable for the rice-fish paddy ecosystem or within the vicinity of natural waters containing fish because it has the lowest toxicity index. Sensitivity of aquatic organisms to pesticides varies with species.

5.   Acknowledgement

This project was funded by the U.P. Los Banos Research Trust Fund, a part of U.P. Basic Research Project No. 88-931-21.

6.   References

Bajet, C.M & Magallona, E.D. (1982) Chemodynamics of Isoprocarb in the Rice Paddy Environment, *Phil. Entomol.* 5: 355-371.

Cagauan, A.G. (1990) Fish Toxicity, Degradation Period and Residues of Selected Pesticides in Rice Fish Culture, paper presented at the Workshop on Environmental and Health Impact of Pesticide Use in Rice Culture, March 28-30, 1990. IRRI, Los Banos, Laguna, Philippines.

CLSU-FAC (1978) *Tech. Report No. 13*, Freshwater Aquaculture Center, Central Luzon State University, Nueva Ecija, Philippines.

CLSU-FAC (1981a) *Tech. Report No. 19*, Freshwater Aquaculture Center, Central Luzon State University, Nueva Ecija, Philippines.

CLSU-FAC (1981b) *Tech. Report No. 20*, Freshwater Aquaculture Center, Central Luzon State University, Nueva Ecija, Philippines.

Guerrero, L.A. & Guerrero, R.D. III (1980) Preliminary Studies on the Culture of Edible Freshwater Snails in Central Luzon, Philippines, *CLSU Sci. J.* 1: 11-14.

Fabellar, L.T. (1983) *The Selective Toxicity of Insecticides to BPH Nilaparvata lugens Stal. (Homop. Delphacidae) Predator*, M.Sc. Thesis, University of the Philippines at Los Banos.

Jarayman, J. (1988) Chemodynamics of Pesticides - Studies Using Simulated Rice-fish Ecosystem, *Proc. 2nd IAEA/FAO Research Coordination Meeting in Rice-Fish Ecosystems*, Schezuan, China.

Magallona, E.D. (1989) Effects of Insecticides in Rice Ecosystems in Southeast Asia, in: Bourdeau, P., Haines, J.A., Klein, W. & Krishna Murti, C.R. (eds.) *Ecotoxicology and Climate*, John Wiley and Sons, pp. 265-297.

Medina, M.J.B., Calumpang, S.M.F., Tejada, A.W., Medina, J.R. & Magallona, E.D. (1993) *Fate of Endosulfan in Rice Fish Ecosystem*, International Atomic Energy Agency Tech. Document 695, Vienna, Austria, pp. 33-45.

Nishiuchi, Y. (1974) Testing Methods for the Toxicity of Agricultural Chemicals, *Japan. Pestic. Info.* 19: 16-19.

Tejada, A.W. (1990) *Final Report on the Training Course on Pesticide Management*, Jakarta, Indonesia, 43 pp.

Tejada, A.W. & Bajet, C.M. (1990) Fate of Pesticides in Rice Fish Ecosystem, *Phil. Agric.* 73: 153-163.

Tejada, A.W. & Magallona, E.D. (1985) Fate of Carbosulfan in the Rice Paddy Environment, *Phil. Entomol.* 6: 255-279.

Varca, L.M. & Magallona, E.D. (1987) Residues of BPMC in Some Components of the Rice Paddy Ecosystem, *Phil. Entomol.* 7: 177-189.

Wang, H, Zhang, Z., Ren, G., Guo, D., Wu, S. & Chen, Z. (1988) Residues of ^{14}C Monocrotophos in Rice Fish Ecosystem, *Proc. 2nd IAFA/FAO Research Coordination Meeting in Rice-Fish Ecosystems*, Schezuan, China.

Webbe, G. (1981) Field Trials of Phosphoric Acid Esters as Larvicides and Their Toxicity to Fish, *Ann. Trop. Med. Parasit.* 55: 187-191.

Appendix Table 1
Formulations used in the study

Common name	Trade name	Type
Insecticides		
Monocrotophos	Azodrin	OD
Methyl-parathion	Folidol	OP
Endosulfan	Thiodan	OCl
Carbofuran	Marshall	C
BPMC + chlorpyrifos	Brodan	C + OP
Chlorpyrifos	Lorsban 20% EC	OP
Cypermethrin	Cymbush	Py
Etofenprox	Trebon	IGR
Thiodicarb	Larvin 375F	C
Methamidophos	Tamaron	OP
Malathion	Malathion	OP
Azinphos-ethyl	Gustahion A	OP
Triazophos	Hostathion	OP
Alpha cypermethrin + BPMC	Fastac	Py + C
Fenvalerate	Sumicidin	Py
Cyfluthrin	Baythroid	
Monocrotophos + fenvalerate	Azocidin	OP + Py
Fenitrothion	Sumithion	Py
BPMC	Baycarb	C
Carbaryl	Sevin	C
Herbicides		
Pretilachlor	Sofit EC	
Pretilachlor	Rilof - H	
Piperophos + 2,4-D	2,4-D	
2,4-D	Agroxone EC	
MCPA	Machete	
Butachlor	Fucilade EC	
Fluazipof-butyl	Saturn	
Thiobencarb	Ronstar 25 EC	
Oxadiazon		
Fungicide	Dithane M-45	
Mancozeb		

OP = organophosphate; OCl = organochlorine; C = carbamate; Py = pyrethroid;
IGR = insect growth regulator

2.2

The influence of food (algae) concentration on the NaPCP toxicity for *Brachionus calyciflorus* based on its life table

H.K. SURTIKANTI

Abstract

A life table approach was developed to assess the chronic toxicity of chemicals for the freshwater rotifer, Brachionus calyciflorus. *The four parameters studied for* Brachionus calyciflorus *were: intrinsic rate of natural increase, mean fecundity, mean survivorship and mean lifespan. These parameters were evaluated in combination with the concentration of algae in the test medium (no. cells/mL) and the concentration of natriumpentachlorophenol (NaPCP). This combination was used as a medium for culturing* Brachionus calyciflorus *(one rotifer per mL). The medium was renewed daily. Number of offspring and mortality were evaluated daily. At the highest food concentration (10^6 cells/mL) natural increase of* Brachionus calyciflorus *there is a clear influence of the food concentration on these parameters (for all NaPCP concentrations). At the lowest food concentration ($5 \cdot 10^4$ cells/mL), however we observed a clear decrease in population growth at 0.4 mg/L NaPCP. The negative effect of NaPCP on fecundity was clearly visible also at 0.4 mg/L NaPCP and $5 \cdot 10^4$ cells/mL algae concentration. Both mean lifespan and mean survivorship of* Brachionus calyciflorus *revealed similar trends. At the highest toxicant concentration a dramatic decrease in mean lifespan and mean survivorship was observed at the lowest food concentration.*

1. Introduction

Technological progress, especially in developing countries is characterized by a rapid growth in industrial development. This is caused by increasing demands for improvement in the quality of life, often resulting in adverse environmental impacts (Soemarwoto 1991). At first people did not pay attention to the negative effects caused by the accompanying discharge of industrial waste. However, increased pollution has become a serious problem. Mainly in the developing countries, many people are still using river water for their daily life. Chemical substances, which are present in discharged water are harmful, not only for human beings, but also for aquatic organisms.

In aquatic toxicology, the quantification of toxicant stress on biota has relied principally on traditional acute and chronic test methods (Rand & Petrocelli 1985). These acute tests have become the major tool in ecotoxicological investigations largely because these tests have a simple design, short duration and low cost. Unfortunately, in evaluating the effects of chemicals on the organism, population or ecosystems, the threshold level for chronic effects which are measured in longer 'chronic tests' are generally of more crucial value than the median lethal concentration (LC_{50}) measured in short term 'acute tests'. This study focuses on a chronic life table test using the freshwater rotifer, *Brachionus calyciflorus*. Besides the toxicant stress, the influence of food concentration on the demographic parameters of the test organism was also evaluated.

2.   Literature review

Toxicity tests are used to evaluate the adverse effect of chemicals on living organisms. Most chemicals can have undesirable or distinctly harmful effects when the compound comes into contact with a biological system and the concentration of the toxicant is high enough.

In evaluating the hazard of chemicals in effluents, to protect the ecosystem, selecting the most sensitive organism in the ecosystem is the most important rule in single species toxicity test (Cairns & Niederlehner 1987). However, the sensitivity of different organisms can vary by several orders of magnitude. The aquatic organisms which have been used in acute tests are: *Artemia, Daphnia,* fishes, rotifers and bacteria (Tapaneeyakul 1990) We selected the freshwater rotifer (*Brachionus calyciflorus*) as a suitable test organism for the following reasons (Janssen & Persoone 1989):

1. They are easy to rear under laboratory conditions.
2. They reproduce quickly and have a short generation time.
3. The constancy of cell numbers (which is a consequence of the lack of mitoses after the embryological period), results in a extremely constant life history.
4. They can produce resting eggs (cysts) which can be stored for long periods of time and used as starting material for the bioassay, thus eliminating the need for stock-culturing of the test organisms.
5. Their cosmopolitan distribution and their importance in freshwater communities make their selection ecologically relevant.

3.   Materials and method

3.1   *Material preparation*

3.1.1   *Preparation of* Brachionus calyciflorus
This experimental work used neonates hatched from *Brachionus calyciflorus* cysts (resting eggs). These resting eggs were obtained from Prof.Dr. T.W. Snell (Uni-

versity of Tampa, Florida, USA). Cyst hatching is initiated by transferring them into a 5 mL petri dish containing EPA medium (see below) and incubating at 25°C in light. After 23-24 h, hatching begins and proceeds rapidly. The neonates are transferred into the test solution using a micropipet. Test animals need to be less than 3 h old, so neonates collection should be carried out within 3 h after hatching (Snell & Persoone 1989).

3.1.2 Preparation of EPA (Environmental Protection Agency) medium
EPA medium is a synthetic freshwater which is prepared from reagent grade chemicals and is composed of 96 mg NaHCO$_3$, 60 mg CaSO$_4$·2H$_2$O, 60 mg MgSO$_4$ and 4 mg KCl in 1 L deionized water. This medium was used for culturing the test animals.

3.1.3 Algae used
The microalga used as a rotifer food was *Nannochloris oculata*. This species should be prepared during experimental work.

3.1.4 Chemical preparation
The chemical used in this study was NaPCP. The concentrations tested of NaPCP were 0.05 mg/L, 0.1 mg/L, 0.2 mg/L and 0.4 mg/L. These concentrations were derived using EPA medium for dilution. All dilutions were made using standard laboratory glassware.

3.2 Experimental method

The test method used was a life table test. This test is able to evaluate chronic toxicity, by examining the demographic characteristics of *Brachionus calyciflorus* under toxicant stress.

The test consisted of 12 replicates for each treatment. In the experiments the 2-3 h old neonates were placed individually in 1 mL of medium of a multiwell plate, and incubated at 25°C in darkness. For each toxicity test, four toxicant concentrations and a control were used.

In the life table test, the number of attached eggs, offspring and mortality were recorded daily. At the beginning of the experiment (first two days), the number of offspring were counted every 24 h. To avoid possible confusion between maternal rotifers and offspring, the offspring were discarded after counting. The maternal rotifers were transferred daily to fresh medium (toxicity concentration and the appropriate food concentration). The life table test was terminated when the last rotifer had died. The data obtained were used to calculate and evaluate the following demographic parameters: intrinsic rate of natural increase, mean fecundity, mean survivorship and mean lifespan.

4.   Results

For the intrinsic rate of natural increase of *Brachionus calyciflorus*, there was a clear influence of food concentration on this parameter (for all NaPCP concentrations). At a food concentration of 10^6 cells/mL, the *Brachionus calyciflorus* population rate increased two times faster than at 10^5 cells/mL. At the two highest food concentrations, the NaPCP did not have a clear negative effect. At the lowest food concentration, however, we saw a clear decrease in population growth at 0.4 mg/L NaPCP (see Figure 1)

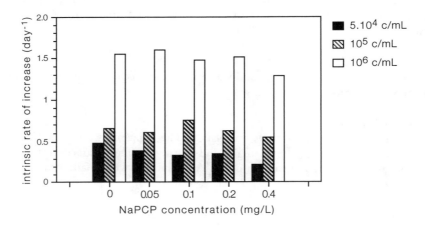

Figure 1 *The intrinsic rate of increase of* Brachionus calyciflorus *populations at different food densities (expressed as the number of algal cells per mL), in relation to the concentration of NaPCP*

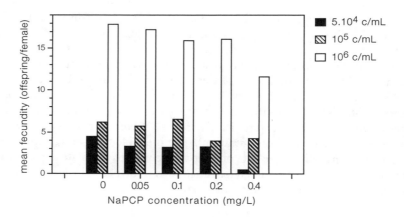

Figure 2 *Fecundity of* Brachionus calyciflorus *at different food densities (no. algal cells per mL) in relation to the concentration of NaPCP*

Mean fecundity was clearly influenced by food level (Figure 2). Mean fecundity at high food level (10^6 cells/mL), for all NaPCP concentrations (0, 0.05, 0.1, 0.2, 0.4 mg/L) was much higher than mean fecundity at moderate and low food level. At low food concentration ($5 \cdot 10^4$ cells/mL), the negative effect of NaPCP on fecundity was clearly visible at the 0.4 mg/L concentration. It seemed that there was a decrease in fecundity with increasing concentrations of NaPCP only at low food levels. A NaPCP concentration of 0.2 mg/L did not seem to have an effect at both high and low food concentrations, but it did have a detrimental effect on mean fecundity at the medium food level.

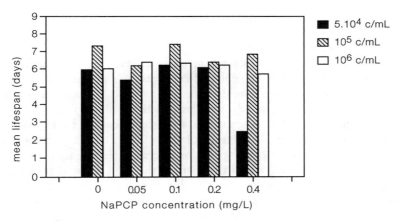

Figure 3 *Mean lifespan of* Brachionus calyciflorus *at different food densities (no. algal cells per mL) in relation to the concentration of NaPCP*

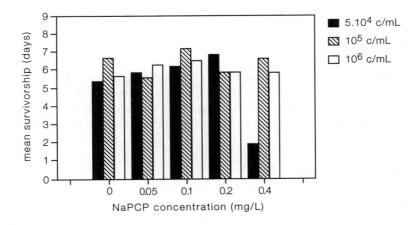

Figure 4 *Mean survivorship of* Brachionus calyciflorus *at different food densities (no. algal cells per mL) in relation to the concentration of NaPCP*

Both mean lifespan (Figure 3) and mean survivorship (Figure 4) of *Brachionus calyciflorus* revealed similar trends. When mean lifespan of the rotifers cultured at the different food levels (in the controls) are compared, it can be seen that the food level did not influence mean lifespan much. The same phenomenon could be observed for the mean survivorship. At the NaPCP concentration of 0.2 mg/L and lower no adverse effects of the toxicant on mean lifespan and mean survivorship (at all food levels) were observed. At the highest toxicant concentration, however, a dramatic decrease of mean lifespan and mean survivorship was observed at the lowest food concentration.

5.   Discussion

A decline in the rate of natural increase, mean fecundity, mean lifespan and mean survivorship with the increasing sublethal concentration of NaPCP occurred at a low food concentration. The combination of low food concentration and the high toxicity of NaPCP gave an adverse effect on the demographic status of *Brachionus calyciflorus*. This phenomenon has also been recorded by Halbach *et al.* (1983), who found detrimental effects of 0.2 and 0.15 mg/L NaPCP on the population dynamics of *B. rubens* at $2\text{-}7 \cdot 10^6$ of Chlorococcales green algae.

Kooijman & Metz (1984) stated that part of the food ingested by an animal will be digested and can therefore by regarded as assimilation energy. A certain amount of this energy has to be spent on maintenance, growth and reproduction. When food is abundant, the animals store a large amount of energy. The stored energy may be consumed when there is less food and it may be spent to compensate reduction in environmental quality. From this it was obvious that poorly fed animals will not have an available store of energy and therefore will not be able to compensate for environmental stress.

6.   Conclusion

From this study, it can be concluded that reduced food levels will increase the adverse effect of a toxicant. The demographic parameters of *Brachionus calyciflorus* will thus be sensitive under conditions of reduced food supply. This information is important for further development of chronic toxicity testing methods.

7.   Acknowledgments

This work was part of my thesis work for a Masters degree. I am grateful to Prof.Dr. G. Persoone, Director of the Laboratory for Biological Research in Aquatic Pollution RUG Belgium, for his permission to use the facilities and to Lic. C. Janssen, for his supervision and for his suggestions on parts of the manuscript.

8. Reference

Cairns Jr., J. & Niederlehner, B.R. (1987) Problems Associated with Selecting the Most Sensitive Species for Toxicity Testing, *Hydrobiologia* 153: 87-94.

Halbach, U., Siebert, M., Westermayer, M. & Wissel, C. (1983) Population Ecology of Rotifers as a Bioassay Tool for Ecotoxicological Tests in Aquatic Environments, *Ecotox. Environ. Saf.* 7: 484-513.

Janssen, C. & Persoone, G. (1989) *Development of Methodologies for Chronic Toxicity Tests with the Rotifer Brachionus calyciflorus*, EEC Contract EV4-0110-UK (BA), 32 p.

Kooijman, S.A.L.M. & Metz, J.A.J. (1984) On the Dynamics of Chemically Stressed Populations: The Deduction of Population Consequences from Effects on Individuals, *Ecotox. Environ. Saf.* 8: 225-274.

Rand, G.M. & Petrocelli, S.R. (1985) *Fundamentals of Aquatic Toxicology. Methods and Applications*, Hemisphere Publ. Co., Washington.

Snell, T.W. & Persoone, G. (1989) Acute Toxicity Bioassays Using Rotifers II-A: Freshwater Test with *Brachionus rubens, Aquat. Toxicol.* 14: 81-82.

Soemarwoto, O. (1991) *Ecology in Environmentally Sound and Sustainable Development*, Committee in Commemorating Professor Otto Soemarwoto Retirement, Bandung.

Tapaneeyakul, N. (1990) *Determination of Toxicity of Effluents and Solid Waste Leachates Using a Battery of Cost-effective Tests*, Thesis for Masters degree, University of Groningen, Netherlands.

2.3

The effect of pentachlorophenol (PCP) on *Lemna minor*

S.B. Sembiring, G. Merlin & G. Blake

Abstract

Pentachlorophenol (PCP) is a pesticide belonging to the organochlorine group. This pesticide has a wide spectrum of toxicity for organisms and is used, particularly in industries, for the protection of wood and in agriculture. A study of low concentrations of PCP (0.05, 0.1, 0.2, 0.3 and 0.5 mg/L) was carried out on the growth, respiration and photosynthesis of the floating macrophyte Lemna minor *using an oxygen electrode and by estimating the number of fronds. Results of this study showed that the growth of* Lemna minor *was inhibited by 8-42% in the first four days at all concentrations of PCP, but from the 7th day until the 21st day growth was stimulated by 0.2-15% at concentrations less than 0.2 mg/L and was inhibited by 14-33% at concentrations more than 0.3 mg/L. Respiration activity was stimulated significantly for concentrations higher than 0.3 mg/L and photosynthesis activity decreased significantly at the same concentration after two days contamination.*

1. Introduction

Pentachlorophenol (PCP), a pesticide, can be included in the organochlorine group. This pesticide is used widely (50,000 tons in 1981) in industries and agriculture because of its high toxicity and relatively low price, particularly for wood preservation (Crosby 1981). The production of paint, textiles and oil drilling also uses PCP. In agriculture this toxine can be used as an insecticide, herbicide, molluscide, bactericide, and algicide. Tests undertaken by Crossland & Wolf (1985) gave the following results. Lethal concentrations (LC_{50}) of PCP during a four day study on goldfish, *Daphnia*, and *Scenedesmus capricornutum* were 0.22 mg/L, 0.60 mg/L and 0.08 mg/L respectively. The high toxicity of PCP can be dangerous to organisms and to the environment.

Since 1986, the US Environmental Protection Agency (EPA) and the European Economic Community have given special attention to this substance along with another 123 pollutants (Merlin 1988). The objective of this study was to investigate the effect of PCP on the growth, respiration and photosynthesis of *Lemna minor*.

2. Materials and methods

2.1 Culture of Lemna minor

An aseptic *Lemna minor* culture was obtained from the Laboratory of Physiology of the University of Grenoble. The plants were exposed under light at Grolux 4500 Lux for 8 h at 25°C in Erlenmeyer flasks with Hutner's modified medium with pH = 7. Each flask contained two colonies (10-12 leaves = 1 frond) of *Lemna minor* and after 10 days of incubation, the plants (70-80 fronds) were contaminated by PCP concentrations of 0.05 mg/L, 1.0 mg/L, 0.2 mg/L, 0.3 mg/L and 0.5 mg/L. Growth was measured each day by counting the number of leaves.

2.2 Effect of PCP on growth

The percentage of growth of *Lemna minor* was calculated by the formula:

(1)
$$P = \frac{N_t - N_o}{N_o} \times 100\%$$

P = Percentage of growth in each concentration and in the control
N_t = Number of fronds at time t
N_o = Number of fronds at time zero

The percentage of growth inhibition was calculated by application of the following formula:

(2)
$$I = \frac{P_c - P_x}{P_c} \times 100\%$$

I = Growth Inhibition (%)
P_c = Percentage growth of control plants
P_x = Percentage growth of contaminated plants

2.3 Respiration and photosynthesis

Respiration and photosynthesis were measured by determination of O_2 consumption or O_2 production using an oxygen electrode (Delieu & Walker 1972)

2.4 Statistics

Experiments were repeated four times and results were compared with the control value represented as a percentage.

3. Results

3.1 Growth

The application of formulas (1) and (2) for the growth of *Lemna minor* indicated that growth was inhibited in the first four days of exposure at all concentrations. After seven days, the growth of *Lemna minor* was different at concentrations less than 0.2 mg/L and more than 0.3 mg/L. At concentrations less than 0.2 mg/L, growth was higher when compared to the control plants after seven days of contamination. The growth of *Lemna minor* in experiments at concentrations of 0.05 mg/L, 0.1 mg/L and 0.2 mg/L was stimulated by 15%, 12% and 8%, but at concentrations more than 3 mg/L the growth of *Lemna minor* was inhibited by 18% to 35%. At the end of the experiments (21 days) growth was decreased by 16% for the concentration of 0.5 mg/L, 14% for 0.3 mg/L, while for the concentrations of 0.05 mg/L, 0.1 mg/L, and 0.2 mg/L, growth was stimulated by 4.6%, 11% and 3.8% (see Figure 1 and Table 1).

Table 1 *Percentage growth of* Lemna minor *in various concentrations of pentachlorophenol*

Time (days)	Control	0.05 mg/L	0.1 mg/L	0.2 mg/L	0.3 mg/L	0.5 mg/L
1	100	31 (i)	36 (i)	37 (i)	42 (i)	27 (i)
2	100	21 (i)	8 (i)	8 (i)	26 (i)	26 (i)
4	100	20 (i)	6 (i)	7 (i)	28 (i)	35 (i)
7	100	6 (i)	0.2 (s)	0.2 (s)	26 (i)	33 (i)
10	100	14.7 (s)	12.2 (s)	8 (s)	18 (i)	33 (i)
14	100	5 (s)	3 (s)	2.6 (s)	17 (i)	28 (i)
21	100	4.6 (s)	11 (s)	3.8 (s)	14 (i)	16 (i)

(i) = inhibition, (s) = stimulation

3.2 Respiration

Figure 2 shows that PCP stimulates the respiration activity of *Lemna minor*. Optimum stimulation occurred on day 4 and it started to decrease on day 7 at concentrations of 0.3 mg/L and 0.5 mg/L. Although stimulation of respiration decreased on day 7, the PCP effect remained significant ($P < 0.05$) until day 10. For concentrations of 0.05 mg/L, 0.1 mg/L and 0.2 mg/L optimum stimulation occurred on the second day after contamination, but was not significant ($P < 0.05$).

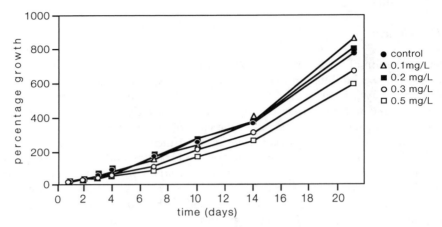

Figure 1 *Growth of* Lemna minor *at different concentrations of pentachlorophenol. Each point indicates the mean of 4 to 5 replicated experimental units (Erlenmeyer flasks)*

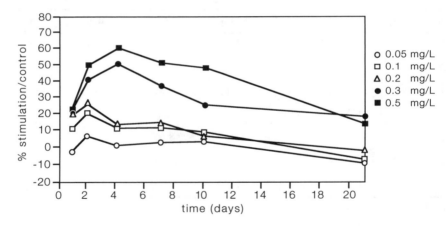

Figure 2 *Changes in the respiration activity of* Lemna minor *at different concentrations of pentachlorophenol. Respiration is expressed as the percentage increase relative to the control, which had a mean respiratory activity of 1733 ± 329 nmol O_2 per g dw per min. Each point indicates the mean of 4 replicate experiments; coefficient of variation is 10 to 30% of the mean*

3.3   Photosynthesis

Contrary to the effect on respiration, PCP did inhibit the *Lemna minor* photosynthetic activity (Figure 3). Maximum inhibition of the real photosynthetic activity occurred on day 4 at a concentration higher than 0.2 mg/L and decreased on day

7. Decrease of photosynthetic inhibition occurred after day 7 at concentrations of 0.2 mg/L, 0.3 mg/L and 0.5 mg/L. The inhibition was significant ($P < 0.05$) until day 10 of the experiment, with the exception of the concentration of 0.2 mg/L. At a concentration lower than 0.2 mg/L, inhibition of photosynthesis was not significant ($P < 0.05$) during the experiments.

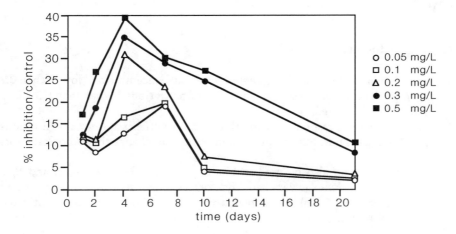

Figure 3 *Effect of pentachlorophenol on photosynthetic activity of* Lemna minor. *Activity is expressed as percentage inhibition relative to the control, which had a mean photosynthetic activity of 7186 ± 639 nmol O_2 per g dw per min; the coefficient of variation is 20 to 30% of the mean*

4.   Discussion

Stimulation of the growth of *Lemna minor* in concentrations lower than 0.2 mg/L is probably due to a phytohormone, formed from the decomposition or degradation of PCP, whereas in concentrations higher than 0.3 mg/L the inhibitory effect predominates. According to Doberski (1986), quoting Kafelei & Dashek (1981), the degradation product of PCP is the indole-acetic-ethonic-acid forming phytohormone. Results of this experiment showed that PCP in low concentrations will stimulate respiration because PCP has the ability to act as an agent to uncouple oxidative phosphorylation in the mitochondria. PCP will also hamper the transport of electrons in the mitochondria structure without producing ATP (Ravanel & Tissut 1986). The increase of respiration up to day 4 and the decrease on day 5 is due mainly to the decrease of PCP toxicity caused by *Lemna minor* which has the ability to degrade PCP, producing a less toxic compound. According to Engelhard (1986), paddy rice and soybeans can decompose PCP and produce 1-pentadichlorophenyl-gluropyranocide, a nontoxic compound. PCP is also decomposed by the irradiation used in the test.

The decrease of real photosynthetic activity is caused mainly by the interference in chlorophyll decomposition. Sembiring (1987) stated that 0.5 mg/L PCP can decrease 70% of the chlorophyll after a four day contact. This decrease is caused mainly by the blockage of electrons in the thylakoid membrane (Tissut 1987) and the dying-out of cells. PCP also destroys or hampers the synthesis of 5-aminolevulinic-acid, a compound which is essential for the formation of chlorophyll (Senger & Ruhl 1981).

5.   Conclusions

1. PCP stimulates the growth of *Lemna minor* at concentrations lower than 0.2 mg/L after seven days contact, but for concentrations higher than 0.3 mg/L growth was inhibited.
2. PCP can stimulate respiration and inhibit photosynthesis at low concentrations (> 0.3 mg/L). Thus, PCP in aquatic conditions can change the ecological structure.
3. *Lemna minor* can also be used in bioassays as can *Daphnia*, algae, and fish, because *Lemna minor* is very sensitive for pesticides. Its leaves are very small in diameter (0.5-0.8 cm). These plants are easy to obtain and easily cultivated in the laboratory.

6.   References

Crosby, G. (1981) Environmental Chemistry of Pentachlorophenol, *Pure Appl. Chem.* 53: 1051-1080.

Crossland. N.O. & Wolf, C.J.M. (1985) Fate and Biological Effect of PCP in Outdoor Ponds, *Env. Toxicol. Chem.* 4: 73-86.

Delieu, T. & Walker, D.A. (1972) An Improved Cathode for the Measurement of Photosynthetic Oxygen Evolution by Isolated Chloroplast, *New Phytol.* 71: 201-225.

Doberski, J. (1986) Simple Phenolic Compound and the Growth of Plants: A Short Review, *J. Biol. Education* 20: 96-98.

Engelhardt, G. (1986) Transformation of Pentachlorophenol part II Transformation under Environmental Condition, *Toxicol. Env. Chem.* 11: 233-255.

Merlin, G. (1988) *Contamination par le PCP d'Ecosystems Aquatiques Reconstitutes Degradation et Effects sur les Vegetaux*, Doctoral Thesis, Université de Grenoble, France.

Ravanel, P. & Tissut, M. (1986) Toxicity of Pentacholorophenol on Isolated Plant Mitochondria, *Phytochemistry* 25: 557-583.

Sembiring, S.B. (1987) *Perturbation de la Physiologie et la Croissance de Lentille d'Eau par Pentachlorophenol*, DEA Thesis, Université de Metz, France.

Senger, H. & Ruhl, D. (1981) The Influence of PCP on the Biosynthesis of 5 Amino Levuline Acid and Chlorophyll, *Int. J. Biochem.* 12: 1045-1048.

Tissut, M. (1987) Effect of Chlorophenols on Isolated Class a Chloroplast and Thylakoid: A QSAR Study, *Ecotox. Environ. Saf.* 13: 32-42.

2.4

Evaluation of controlled release formulations of thiobencarb in rice-fish ecosystems using radiochemical techniques

C.M. BAJET, L.C. ARAEZ & E.D. MAGALLONA

Abstract

The corncob-based formulation of the herbicide thiobencarb released the maximum concentration in water at 7 days after application (DAA) and sustained the release up to 56 DAA as compared to the alginate-based formulation which slowly released the active ingredient and attained maximum release at 56 DAA. The corncob formulation was more useful since maximum release coincided with the critical period for weed competition in rice. The LC_{50} of thiobencarb to tilapia (Oreochromis niloticus) was found to be 0.234 mg/L. Bioaccumulation of fast (TA1) and slow (TA2) corncob-based formulations at 0.2 µg/mL maximum concentration and 7 days exposure time were 0.256 and 0.285 µg/g in the fillet, respectively. Average concentrations of thiobencarb in dead fish fillet were 0.312 and 0.332 µg/g, respectively for TA1 and TA2. Low level of thiobencarb uptake of by young and old leaves of kangkong, Ipomoea aquatica, was found for TA1 and TA2. The stalk absorbed most of the ^{14}C-thiobencarb and no visible signs of phytotoxicity was observed at 1 µg/g exposure level. Efficacy evaluation against the barnyard grass, Echinocloa crus-galli showed no significant weed control and yield difference between commercial and controlled release formulations when applied at 0.75 and 1.5 kg a.i./ha. The cost effective rate was 0.75 kg a.i./ha indicating that half the recommended dose could be effective when using controlled release formulations.

1. Introduction

When pesticides are applied by conventional spraying, about 60-90% of the chemicals fail to reach the target. The available concentration is reduced by drift and by environmental degradation. It is therefore necessary to carry out repeated applications or apply higher dosages to guarantee the effectiveness of these pesticides. However, this becomes a burden to the environment and also results in more pesticide residues in food. Controlled release technology is a new approach to solving these problems by releasing only the necessary amount of pesticide at an appropriate rate at a time interval when the pest is present or most active.

Thiobencarb, s-(4-chlorobenzyl)-N,N-diethylthiocarbamate, is a commonly used herbicide in directly seeded and transplanted rice culture (Ishii 1974). It is effective against the barnyard grass (*Echinocloa crus-galli*) which is a predominant weed problem in the rice paddy. Zimdahl (1980) reported that 40 *E. crus-galli* per m^2 at 7-40 days after emergence reduced yield by 40% whereas Mercado (1979) reported that competition against transplanted rice is greatest when the density is 20 *E. crus-galli* per m^2 with a critical period of 40 days.

The use of a calcium alginate matrix for controlled release formulations (CRF) was investigated by Pfister *et al.* (1986) for the herbicides monolinuron, desmetryn, chloridazon, atrazine, MCPB, simazine, and chloroxuron. Thiobencarb (Hussein *et al.* 1992), butachlor (Hussein & Oh 1991) and dichlobenil (Connick *et al.* 1984) were likewise studied with the use of alginate-based formulations. Biodegradable basic polymeric materials like natural organic macromolecules such as bark, sawdust, lignin, waste paper and plant-derived fibers such as corncob or rice straw may be useful as carriers.

This study therefore aims to evaluate laboratory-prepared alginate and corncob-based CRF of thiobencarb by determining its release rates in distilled and paddy water using radiotracer techniques. Since it is intended to be used in the rice paddy and irrigated rice fields constitute an important inland fishery resource, uptake and bioconcentration studies on *Nile tilapia* were considered very important. Data generated could provide an insight into the usefulness of CRF thiobencarb in rice fish culture. Uptake by the edible plant, kangkong (*Ipomoea aquatica*), usually found in irrigation, drainage canals and water ways and which constitutes farmer's vegetable diet could help to assess environmental contamination and risk due to outflow of paddy water from the fields. The importance of evaluating the effectiveness of these CRFs in rice compared to the commercially available form is necessary so this research will be useful to farmers.

2. Materials and methods

2.1 Release rates in water

The following controlled release formulations (CRF) of thiobencarb were tested using one liter distilled and paddy water. The formulations were provided by the International Atomic Energy Agency.

TH1 - 6.5% ^{14}C-thiobencarb in alginate and kaolin, specific activity = 1.291 µCi/ g, fast release CRF

TH2 - 8.1% ^{14}C-thiobencarb in alginate and kaolin, specific activity = 8.071 µCi/ g, slow release CRF

TA1 - 4% ^{14}C-thiobencarb, 4% PVA, 8% POEG and 84% corncob, specific activity = 5.405 µCi/g, fast release CRF

TA2 - 4% ^{14}C-thiobencarb, 8% PVA, 4% POEG and 84% corncob, specific activity = 5.405 µCi/g, slow release CRF.

The formulations were added to water to give a concentration of 16 mg/L. The flasks were wrapped in aluminium foil to minimize photodegradation and water was sampled at 2, 4, 8, 24, 48 and 96 h and after 1, 2, 3, and 8 weeks for released radioactivity. Analysis was done by adding 15 mL universal cocktail Instagel XF (Packard) before counting the radioactivity by Liquid Scintillation Counter (LSC) [Tricarb 1000, Packard Instrument Co. Downers Grove, Il., USA]. On each sampling occasion, the water was stirred gently and 4 mL water was sampled and was replaced with the same amount of distilled water. For release rates in paddy water, the sample was centrifuged before taking samples for LSC. The paddy water had a pH of 7.4 with 0.059 % total suspended particles. The average water and ambient temperature were 28 and 30°C, respectively.

At the end of the eight week period, pellets were filtered and each flask was rinsed with 100 mL water followed by acetone. The filter paper, water and acetone rinses were analyzed and total radioactivity was accounted for. The filtered formulation was analyzed by combustion using a Biological Material Oxidizer (BMO) [Model OX-400, Harvey Instruments Corp., Hillsdale, NJ. USA]. The released $^{14}CO_2$ was absorbed in a mixture of 10 mL absorbent and 5 mL prepared liquid scintillation cocktail. The absorbent was a solution of 125 mL ethanolamine with 875 mL methanol to make one liter. The cocktail was prepared by dissolving 50 mg POPOP (1,4 bis-5-phenyloxazole-2-yl benzene) and 5.0 g PPO (2,5 diphenyloxazole) in toluene to make one liter. After combustion, 5 mL of the prepared cocktail was further added and radioactivity was measured by LSC.

The water was extracted by partitioning with 100 mL methylene chloride and dried by passing through anhydrous sodium sulphate. The extraction was done three times with 50 mL solvent and the pooled dried extracts were concentrated to almost dryness, taken up in 4 mL methanol and analyzed by Gas Liquid Chromatography (GLC). Extraction recovery was 89-90%.

The Hewlett Packard Gas Chromatograph Model 5840, with a nitrogen phosphorus detector, was operated with the following conditions.

Column:	6 ft x 1.5 mm, glass 3% SE-30 on chromosorb WHP 80/100	
Temperature (°C):	column	- 200
	detector	- 300
	injector	- 220
Gas (mL/min):	hydrogen	- 3
	nitrogen	- 30
	air	- 50

Confirmatory analysis of water extract was done by thin layer chromatography (TLC) using a benzene : ethyl acetate (10:1) mixture as developing solvent (Ishikawa et al. 1976) and the spots were viewed under ultraviolet light.

2.2 Toxicity and uptake of thiobencarb to Oreochromis niloticus fingerlings

Two weeks old Nile tilapia, *Oreochromis niloticus*, fingerlings with a body length of approximately one inch were acclimatized for one week in an aquarium and were given rice bran rations. The fingerlings were starved for 24 hrs prior to and until the completion of the test. The fish were exposed to a series of concentrations and mortality counts were done after 48 hrs. The LC_{50} value was calculated by probit analysis.

Nile tilapia used for rice fish culture with average weight of 30 g were exposed to radiolabeled CRF thiobencarb (TA1 = 2.83% a.i., activity = 11,752 dpm/mg and TA2 = 3.05% a.i., activity = 12,221 dpm/mg) and to a commercial formulation at a maximum release of 0.2 μg/mL. The water level was maintained daily and sampled for 15 days then analyzed by LSC. Dead fish were collected and the concentration of ^{14}C-thiobencarb was analyzed by BMO. The amount bioaccumulated after 7 days was also determined by combustion of the tissues of the surviving fish. A parallel test using a commercial formulation (Saturn 10G) and an untreated control was done to determine the mortality difference due to thiobencarb released from CRF.

2.3 Uptake of thiobencarb by edible kangkong (Ipomoea aquatica)

Radiolabeled corncob-based TA1 and TA2 were applied at the rate of 1 μg/ml at maximum release. One part kangkong to 10 parts water was maintained. Sampling of water was done daily up to 15 days and kangkong was sampled at 1, 3, 5, 7, 10 and 15 days after application. A parallel test was done using a commercial formulation to determine if there were any visible signs of phytotoxicity of thiobencarb with respect to kangkong. The plant was cut up, with the two youngest shoots classified as young leaves, all others as old leaves and the stem. A 0.2 g sample was analyzed by combustion using BMO.

2.4 Herbicidal activity against the grass Echinocloa crus-galli

Maahas clay loam soil was collected at the University of the Philippines at Los Banos Experimental Station and was covered with a fine mesh cloth to prevent contamination by other weed species. The soil was left undisturbed for 2 weeks to ensure the germination of other weed seeds present in the soil. Equal amounts of soil were weighed and put into plastic pots of 14 cm diameter.

Two week old rice seedlings (variety IR66) were transplanted at three seedlings per mound, per pot. Each pot was seeded with eleven *Echinocloa crus-galli* seeds to compensate for the 10% ungerminated seeds as predetermined by a germination test. Four days after transplanting (DAT), the test formulations [TA1 (corncob, fast release), TA2 (corncob, slow release), TAL 2490 (alginate, fast release) and commercial formulation] were applied at the rate of 1.5 and 0.75 kg a.i./ha with 4 replications. Control pots with no herbicide application were included to determine the difference in yield due to weed control.

At 21 and 49 DAT, the number of germinated weeds and plant height of both weed and rice plant were measured. Fertilizer was applied at a rate corresponding to 60 kg N + 14 kg P + 14 kg K per hectare. Nitrogen fertilization was split into three applications: basal, 25 DAT and at panicle initiation whereas the P and K fertilizers were applied basally at last harrowing. Yield was projected on per hectare basis with the assumption of 16,000 mounds/ha.

3.   Results and discussion

3.1   Release rate in distilled water

The release of thiobencarb from CRF alginate in distilled water was relatively slower than the corncob-based formulation (Figure 1). The maximum concentration was released on the 8th week equivalent to 68.50 and 61.56% of the total amount applied for TH1 and TH2, respectively. In contrast, TA1 and TA2 released 50-58% and 45-50%, respectively starting 7 to 56 days after application. Thin layer chromatographic analysis of the methylene chloride extracts produced two distinct spots for the alginate formulation with average Rf values of 0.15 and 0.68. The reported Rf values of the metabolite 4-chlorobenzyl methyl sulfone and thiobencarb are 0.18 and 0.74, respectively (Ishikawa et al. 1976). However, further confirmatory tests should be done.

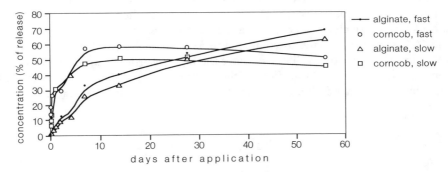

Figure 1 *Release rate of four thiobencarb formulations in distilled water*

Low total recovered radioactivity after the eighth week may be due to the high room temperature (28-34C°) and this may effect covolatilization with water (Table 1). Higher recovered radioactivity was found for the fast release formulations than the slow release formulations, for both alginate and corncob-based CRF.

The corncob-based CRF of thiobencarb may be more efficient since the maximum concentration was attained faster and release was sustained over a longer period of time. The maximum release at 7 days after application is an advantage because keeping the rice weed-free during the 7-40 day period after transplantation is critical for preventing competition (Mercado 1979, Zimdahl 1980). Weeds emerging 40 days after transplanting or later did not affect yield (Zimdahl 1980). In comparison, the alginate-based CRF was just equal to the release concentration of the corncob CRF at approximately 30-40 days after application (Figure 1).

Table 1 *Recovery of ^{14}C-thiobencarb after eight weeks as a percentage of the total amount applied*

	Formulation			
	Alginate		Corncob	
	Fast	Slow	Fast	Slow
Water (%)*	88.50	61.56	53.47	49.68
Beads (%)**	22.28	15.46	17.66	16.48
Degraded (%)***	-	-	7.82	4.51
Total recovered (%)	90.78	77.02	78.95	70.67

* includes correction due to sampling, water and acetone rinses and filter paper counts.
** remaining in granules, as determined by combustion.
*** difference between the maximum concentration released and the concentration at eight weeks.

3.2 *Release rate in paddy water*

The release rate in paddy water indicated that degradation and/or soil adsorption or absorption was faster than the release of thiobencarb (Figure 2). The maximum amount released was 35.78 and 23.66 percent of the applied thiobencarb for TA1 and TA2, respectively. The amount released at 14 days after application was 13.30 and 11.08% in paddy water as compared to 58.23 and 49.05 in distilled water for TA1 and TA2, respectively. This indicates the high adsorption capacity of the suspended soil particles and the effect of the slightly basic pH. The concentration of thiobencarb in water and in the upper soil layer is important for efficacy.

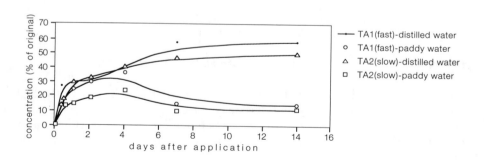

Figure 2 *Release of fast and slow corncob formulations of thiobencarb in distilled water and in paddy water*

3.3 Toxicity of thiobencarb to fish

The LC_{50} of technical thiobencarb to 2 weeks old Nile tilapia fingerlings was found to be 0.234 mg/L. Thiobencarb could be lethal to fish present in the paddy based on the maximum concentration found by Ross & Sava (1986) in paddy water for commercial formulations, which is 0.676 mg/L.

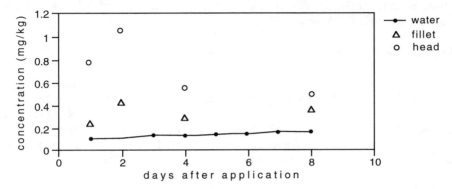

Figure 3 *Concentrations of ^{14}C-thiobencarb in fish (tilapia), exposed to the fast release formulation*

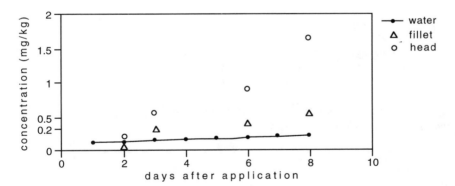

Figure 4 *Concentrations of ^{14}C-thiobencarb in fish (tilapia), exposed to the slow release formulation*

At a maximum concentration of 0.2 mg/L, released thiobencarb in water remains relatively constant for both TA1 and TA2. The concentration in fish was, however, variable and no relation for lethal concentration with time of exposure was noted (Figure 3, 4). This may be due to other factors such as sensitivity as affected by size differences. Average concentrations of thiobencarb in dead fish fillet were 0.312 and 0.332 μg/g respectively for TA1 and TA2. There were no significant differences between the concentration accumulated by surviving fish after 7 days of exposure and concentrations of thiobencarb found in dead fish. The concentrations of thiobencarb in survivors were 0.256 and 0.285 μg/g respectively for TA1 and TA2. This could indicate that with controlled release formulation, the tilapia could survive even if the concentration in water is around the LC$_{50}$ value. More residues were found in the head compared to fish fillet. Tejada & Bajet (1993) reported an LC$_{50}$ value of 1.97 and 1.14 mg/L, respectively at 24 and 48 h, for the commercial formulation. Zhang *et al.* (1991) reported LC$_{50}$s of 3.2, 2.8 and 2.5 mg/L respectively at 24, 48 and 96 h.

3.4 Uptake of thiobencarb by edible kangkong (Ipomoea aquatica)

Low level uptake of thiobencarb from CRF TA1 and TA2 was found for both young and old leaves (Figure 5, 6). However, the stalk absorbed most of the ^{14}C-thiobencarb for both formulations. No visible signs of injury to kangkong such as necrosis or phytotoxicity were observed. This indicates a high tolerance of kangkong to thiobencarb up to the maximum release of 1 μg/ml. The concentration in water remained relatively constant up to 15 days after application.

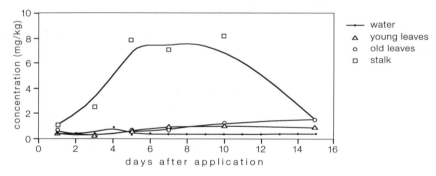

Figure 5 *Concentrations of ^{14}C-thiobencarb in edible kangkong (Ipomoea aquatica) exposed to the fast release formulation*

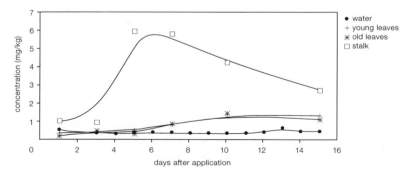

Figure 6 *Concentrations of ^{14}C-thiobencarb in edible kangkong (Ipomoea aquatica) exposed to the slow release formulation*

3.5 *Herbicidal activity to* Echinocloa crus-galli

The pot experiment showed that all treatments had a significantly lower number of weeds than the control at 21 and 49 DAT (Table 2). There were no significant differences between treatments and rates based on weed number data. It appears that the rate of 0.75 kg a.i./ha could be sufficient to control *E. crus-galli*. However, the commercial formulation applied at 0.75 kg a.i./ha resulted in tall weeds comparable to the untreated group at 49 DAT.

Table 2 *Effect of four controlled release formulations of thiobencarb on plant height and number of* Echinocloa crus-galli *seedlings*

Formulation	Rate	Height (cm)		Number	
	(kg a.i./ha)	21 DAT	49 DAT	21 DAT	49 DAT
TA1	0.75	0.0^d	0.0^d	0.0^b	0.0^b
	1.50	0.0^d	8.0^d	0.0^b	0.5^b
TA2	0.75	0.0^d	9.0^d	0.0^b	0.3^b
	1.50	1.1^{cd}	18.3^{cd}	0.5^b	0.8^b
TAL 2490	0.75	3.0^{bc}	27.0^{bc}	1.8^b	1.3^b
	1.50	0.0^d	12.0^{cd}	0.0^b	0.8^b
Saturn G	0.75	4.4^b	39.5^{ab}	1.0^b	1.5^b
	1.50	12^{cd}	0.0^d	0.3^b	0.0^b
Control	-	10.8^a	49.3^a	6.5^a	6.0^a

Means followed by the same superscript (a, b, c, d) are not significantly different at the 5% level.
Note: DAT = days after transplanting.

Table 3 *Effect of four controlled release formulations of thiobencarb on yield, height and tiller number of rice*

Formulation	Rate	Height (cm)		Tiller number		Yield
	(kg a.i./ha)	21 DAT	49 DAT	21 DAT	49 DAT	(tons/ha)
TA1	0.75	18.4^{abc}	54.4^a	4.0^{ab}	28.5^a	4.04^a
	1.50	20.5^{abc}	56.0^a	3.0^b	25.8^a	3.43^a
TA2	0.75	19.8^{abc}	62.8^a	3.0^b	30.5^a	3.75^a
	1.50	18.5^{abc}	61.5^a	4.8^a	26.0^a	4.08^a
TAL 2490	0.75	22.2^{ab}	55.5^a	3.0^b	31.5^a	3.56^a
	1.50	23.2^a	55.8^a	3.0^b	26.8^a	4.02^a
Saturn G	0.75	16.9^{bc}	57.7^a	3.5^b	28.3^a	3.48^a
	1.50	16.0^d	62.0^a	5.0^a	26.0^a	3.77^a
Control	-	22.6^a	57.1^a	3.0^b	21.8^a	1.45^b

Means followed by the same superscript (a, b, c, d) are not significantly different at the 5% level.
Note: DAT = days after transplanting.

No phytotoxicity in rice was observed by visual assessment but there was significant stunting of the rice plants treated with the commercial formulation compared to the control at 21 DAT (Table 3). No significant difference in plant height
and tiller number was observed later at 49 DAT. The low tiller number and plant
height at 21 DAT was due to keeping the plants in the shade for two weeks after
transplanting. This was done to prevent dilution due to heavy rainfall and loss of
weed seeds due to splashing.

The control pots had an average of 6.5 weeds per mound. The low germination of the weeds was enhanced by the environmental condition wherein the soil
was partially or fully submerged most of the time. These conditions were not
conducive to the growth of *E. crus-galli*.

The projected yield of rice variety IR66 treated with CRFs of thiobencarb was
not significantly higher than the yield obtained when using commercial formulations. All treatments had higher yield than the untreated control (Table 3). The
application of thiobencarb at a rate of 0.75 kg a.i./ha was the most cost-effective,
having no significant yield difference over the recommended rate at 1.5 kg a.i./ha.

4.　Conclusions

The corncob formulation of thiobencarb was found to be more useful than the
alginate-based formulation because the maximum release of the active ingredient
in water was sustained from 7-56 days after application. This coincides with the
critical period for weed competition in rice. Yields of rice treated with fast (TA1)
and slow (TA2) release corncob formulations were not significantly different from
those obtained when using the commercial formulation when thiobencarb was
applied at both 1.5 and 0.75 kg a.i./ha. CRFs were shown to be effective against
Echinocloa crus-galli at one half the recommended rate.

Low levels of uptake by young and old leaves of kangkong were observed
with ^{14}C-thiobencarb, the residues being concentrated mostly in the stalk. Fillet
of tilapia accumulated 0.256 and 0.285 μg/g when exposed to a maximum concentration of 0.2 mg/L for 7 days using fast (TA1) and slow (TA2) release formulation
respectively. More residues were accumulated in the head than in the fillet. LC_{50}
for tilapia was 0.234 mg/L using thiobencarb.

5.　Acknowledgements

The authors gratefully acknowledge the assistance and suggestions of Dr. Man-
zoor Hussein of the International Atomic Energy Agency and the suggestions of
Lorenzo E. Fabro, weed scientist of the National Crop Protection Center for improving the efficacy evaluation. This research project was funded by the International Atomic Energy Agency.

6. References

Connick, W.J., Bradow, J.M., Wells, W., Steward, K.K. & Van, T.K. (1984) Preparation and Evaluation of Controlled Release Formulations of 2,4 Dichlorobenzonitrile, *J. Agric. Food Chem.* 32: 1199-1205.

Hussein, M., Gan, J. & Rathor, M.N. (1992) Preparation of Controlled Release Formulations of [14]C Labelled Thiobencarb Herbicide and Study of Their Environmental Behaviour, *Pestic. Sci.* 34: 341-347.

Hussein, M. & Oh, B.Y. (1991) Preparation and Study of Controlled Release Formulations of [14]C Labelled Butachlor, *Toxicol. Environ. Chem.* 35: 101-110.

Ishikawa, K. Nakamura, Y. & Kuwatsuka, K. (1976) Degradation of Benthiocarb Herbicide in Soil, *Pestic. Sci..* 1: 49-57.

Ishii, Y. (1974) Saturn: New Selective Herbicide, *Japan Pestic. Info.* 19: 21-25.

Mercado, B.L. (1979) *Introduction to Weed Science*, South East Asian Regional Center for Graduate Study and Research in Agriculture, College, Laguna, Philippines.

Pfister, G.M., Bahadir, M. & Korte, F. (1986) Release Characteristics of Herbicides from Calcium Alginate Gel Formulation, *J. Controlled Release* 3: 229-233.

Ross, L.J. & Sava, R.J. (1986) Fate of Thiobencarb and Molinate in Rice Fields, *J. Environ. Qual.* 15: 220-225.

Tejada, A.W. & Bajet, C.M. (1993) Toxicity of Some Pesticides Used in Rice, *Phil. Agric.* 76, in press.

Zhang, Q.H., Sun, J.H., Li, X.M. & Chang, D.F. (1991) Research on the Herbicidal Efficacy and Residues of Controlled Release Formulations of Thiobencarb in Rice Fish Ecosystem, *Proceed. 2nd FAO/IAEA Research Coordination Meeting on Controlled Release Formulation*, Beijing Agric. Univ., October 14-18, 1991.

Zimdahl, R.L. (1980) *Weed-Crop Competition: A Review*, International Plant Protection Center, Corvalis, Oregon.

2.5

The effect of organophosphorus insecticide on hematological parameters of carp (*Cyprinus carpio* L.)

D. GOENARSO, O. B. LIANG & S. SASTRODIHARDJO

Abstract

Hematological observations were made on carp (Cyrpinus carpio L.), which had been exposed to trichlorfon. The hematological parameters included the red blood cell (RBC) count, the hemoglobin (Hb) concentration, and the hematocrit (Ht) value. From those parameters, mean cell volume (MCV), mean corpuscular hemoglobin (MCH), and mean corpuscular hemoglobin concentration (MCHC) were calculated. Trichlorfon, an organophosphorus insecticide was used in a sublethal concentration. Trichlorfon in high concentrations decreased the RBC count, the Hb concentration and the Ht value of fish blood. The compound also increased the MCV and decreased the MCH and the MCHC. It seems that trichlorfon in high concentrations hemolyzed the red blood cells of the fish.

1.   Introduction

Toxic substances may be found in air, on land or in surface water. Surface water contaminated with a toxicant may become a hazard to aquatic animals or other organisms that need water for their life. If the toxicant is dissolved in low concentrations (sublethal), physiological changes might occur in the animals which live in or consume such water.

Physiological changes in an organism may indicate the existence of a toxicant that affects water quality. Any symptom of physiological change in a fish could be used as an early warning system of water pollutants (Alabaster & Lloyd 1980, Gluth & Hanke 1985, Goenarso 1984, Larsson *et al.* 1985, Tewari *et al.* 1987).

Much work has been directed towards the use of fish as indicator organisms for the measurement of the effects of environmental pollution. Several variables in the physiological condition of fish affected by toxicants have been investigated, such as oxygen consumption, heart rate activity and hematology (Gluth & Hanke 1985, Goenarso 1984, Tewari *et al.* 1987).

This paper investigates blood parameters of fish influenced by trichlorfon (an organophosphate insecticide). Measurements were made on fish held for a period of time under conditions of exposure to the insecticide. The parameters were red blood cell (RBC) count, hemoglobin (Hb) concentration, hematocrit (Ht) value, mean corpuscular volume (MCV), mean corpuscular hemoglobin (MCH) and mean corpuscular hemoglobin concentration (MCHC).

2.   Materials and methods

Studies were made on carp (*Cyprinus carpio* L.) weighing from 50 g to 100 g, at the age of 2 months. The carp were held individually in 50 L tanks and exposed to certain concentrations of trichlorfon. The exposure times were 24, 48, 72 and 96 hours. The concentrations of trichlorfon used were 50 mg/L, 100 mg/L and 200 mg/L. After each termination of the exposure, the fish were taken out, and the brain was destroyed directly through the skull using a needle. The heart was isolated and the ventral aorta was cut. Blood from the aorta was then collected through heparinized capillary tubes. Using the collected blood, three parameters were determined, red blood cell (RBC) count, hemoglobin (Hb) concentrations, mean corpuscular volume (MCV), mean hemoglobin concentration (MHC), and hematocrit (Ht) value. From those three parameters the mean corpuscular hemoglobin concentration (MCHC) was then calculated using a formula given by Wintrobe (1974). The RBC were counted by means of an improved Neubauer chamber after mixing the blood with Hendrick's solution (Hesser 1960). The Hb concentration and the Ht value were determined respectively by cyanmethemoglobin and microhematocrit methods. The results obtained were then computed and analyzed using regression lines.

3.   Results and discussion

The concentrations of the trichlorfon solution were $C_1 = 50$ mg/L, $C_2 = 100$ mg/L and $C_3 = 200$ mg/L. The computed regression lines showed that the RBC count was not influenced by C_1. Fish exposed to C_2 showed higher RBC count compared with control fish. A higher concentration of the trichlorfon solution (200 mg/L) decreased the fish RBC count. Fish exposed to the solution for 96 hours showed a 9.1% lower RBC count than the corresponding control fish (Figure 1A).

The hemoglobin concentration of the test fish after 96 h exposure to trichlorfon solution was 5.4%, 3.9% and 13.5% lower than the Hb concentration of the control fish (mean = 10.8 g/dL) due to C_1, C_2 and C_3 respectively (Figure 1B).

The Ht value of the test fish exposed to trichlorfon solution was 4.8% and 7.3% higher than the control (mean = 0.41 L/L) due to C_1 and C_2, respectively. The Ht value decreased in the C_3 solution, 2.4% lower than the control after 96 h of exposure (Figure 1C).

It seems that trichlorfon hemolyzed the RBC of test fish. This may increase the release of RBC in the blood circulation and induce the production of new RBC. However, at the severe treatment (C_3), the RBC count and the Hb concentration of the test fish were lower than the control fish. From these three parameters (RBC count, Hb concentration and Ht value), the MCV, the MCH and the MCHC were then calculated.

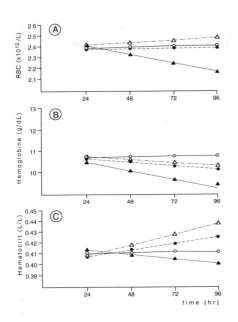

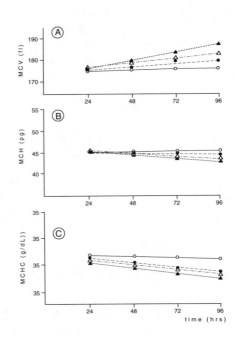

Figure 1 *The RBC count (A), the Hb concentration (B) and the Ht value (C) of carp exposed to trichlorfon*
—— o = control; ---- • = 50 mg/L;
···· △ = 100 mg/L; ····· ▲ = 200 mg/L

Figure 2 *The MCV (A), the MCH (B) and the MCHC (C) of carp exposed to trichlorfon*
—— o = control; ---- • = 50 mg/L;
···· ▲ = 100 mg/L; ····· △ = 200 mg/L

The MCV of control fish was 176.8 fl (standard deviation = 0.74). Fish exposed to trichlorfon showed an enlargement of the RBC. When the fish were exposed to C_1, C_2 and C_3 of trichlorfon solutions, the red cell volumes were respectively 2.1%, 4.3% and 6.6% larger than the MCV of the control fish (Figure 2A).

The mean weight of Hb in each RBC of the control fish was 45.5 pg (standard deviation = 0.23). The MCH of the treated fish decreased due to the exposure to trichlorfon solution. When the test fish were exposed to C_1, C_2 and C_3 solutions, the MCH were respectively 1.8%, 4.0% and 5.3% lower than the MCH of the control fish (Figure 2B).

The mean Hb concentration in each cell (MCHC) of the control fish was 26.6 g/dL (standard deviation = 0.27). The trichlorfon solution decreased the MCHC of the test fish. When the fish were exposed to C_1, C_2 and C_3 solutions the MCHC were respectively 10.6%, 10.8% and 15.3% lower than the control fish (Figure 2C).

The increase of cell volume and Ht value occurred due to the influence of the high concentration of the insecticide on the test fish. However, each RBC of the test fish contained less Hb concentration and weight compared to that of the control fish. It seems that new cells were produced and released for circulation. These were larger in volume compared with the MCV of the control fish.

4.   Conclusions

Blood parameter changes in the fish occurred due to sublethal concentrations of trichlorfon. Trichlorfon decreased the RBC count, the Hb concentration and the Ht value of fish blood. The compound also increased the MCV and decreased the MCH and MCHC. It seems that trichlorfon in high concentrations hemolyzed the red blood cells of the fish.

5.   References

Alabaster, J.S. & Lloyd, R. (1980) *Water Quality Criteria for Freshwater Fish*, Butterworth, London.

Gluth, G. & Hanke, W. (1985) A Comparison of Physiological Changes in Carp, *Cyprinus carpio*, Induced by Several Pollutans at Sublethal Concentrations, I. The Dependency on Exposure Time, *Ecotox. Environ. Saf.* 9: 179-188.

Goenarso, D. (1984) The Effect of Water Temperature on the Respiration Rate of *Cyprinus carpio* L., *Proceedings ITB* 17: 1-10.

Hesser, E.F. (1960) Methods for Routine Fish Hematology, *Progress Fish Culturist.* 22: 164-171.

Larsson, A., Haux, C. & Sjobeck, M.L. (1985) Fish Physiology and Metal Pollution: Results and Experiences from Laboratory and Field Studies, *Ecotox. Environ. Saf.* 9: 250-281.

Tewari, H., Gill, T.S. & Pant, J. (1987) Impact of Chronic Lead Poisoning on the Hematological and Biochemical Profiles of a Fish, *Barbus conchonius* (Ham), *Bull. Environ. Contam. Toxicol.* 38: 748-752.

Wintrobe, M.W. (1974) *Clinical Hematology*, 7th edition, Lea & Febiger, Philadelphia, pp. 80-134.

2.6

Effects of oral uptake of carbofuran on somatic growth and liver degeneration in chicken

S. WULANDARI & WURYADI

Abstract

The objective of this research was to study the negative effects of carbofuran on non-target animals, such as chickens. We used 60 Hubbard strain chickens of the same age (one day) and weight (average 55 g) as samples which were distributed in six boxes of ten chickens each. Dose variations given as treatments were 0, 2, 2.5, 3, 3.5 and 4 mg/kg body weight; these were given as an oral toxicant every two days for 35 days (5 weeks). Liver degeneration was investigated at the end of this experiment. Macroscopically, the livers appeared pale and swollen with blue-black margins in the caudal area. Microscopically, there was cellular swelling and leucocyte infiltration in the liver tissue. This degeneration was shown only at the dose of 3.5 and 4 mg/kg body weight treatment. There were very significant effects of sublethal doses and time-length variation in growth of male chicken.

1. Introduction

Pesticides have been utilized for quite a long time in Indonesia. Since there is no specific and selective utilization, there is a broad spectrum of pesticide use. Due to this condition, an effect on nontarget organisms cannot be avoided (Tarumingkeng 1977) The possible effects of pesticides on non-target organisms are (1) the extinction of non-target organisms; (2) accumulation via the food chain; (3) decreasing potential of reproduction; and (4) stimulation of resistance development.

The possibility of chickens being orally contaminated by pesticides is very high due to their feeding behavior. There will be direct contact with the digestive tract, followed by absorption and distribution to all organs and tissues. The effects depend very much on the characteristics of the pesticides and those of the target organs.

Sublethal effects (chronic effects) of carbofuran may occur in organs other than the nervous system (which is the main target for acute intoxications). Toxic substances absorbed by the digestive tract are transported directly to the liver. The biotransformation of these substances is one of the liver functions. Thus, the liver is the most likely organ to be affected by toxicants. The toxicants can be excreted through the hepatic tissue to the gall duct and bladder, and finally to the intestine (Cassaret & Doull 1975). Biotransformation of toxic substances can occur in the endoplasmatic reticulum and mitochondria of the hepatic cells (Banks 1981).

2. Material and methods

We used healthy Hubbard strain male chickens, aged one day with an average weight of 55 g, as the objects of this study. Carbofuran was used as a granular toxicant. Chickens were fed ad libitum with a standard food, BR-I.

A preliminary study was done to measure the LC_{50} for 96 hours and to decide on the sublethal doses as treatment factors. In the main experiment 60 samples were used, taken randomly from 100 selected chickens, distributed in 6 cages, 10 in each. These chickens were fed normally for five days as they were acclimated in their cages; then two days before being treated with carbofuran, food was not given to them.

In this study, the treatment variables are sublethal dose of carbofuran (0, 0.2, 2.5, 3.0, 3.5, 4.0 mg/kg body weight, given every two days) and time (1, 2, 3, 4, and 5 weeks). The response variables are body weight (g) indicating growth, physical fitness and histological changes in the liver. The experimental design is a factorial design (6 x 5).

Table 1 *General effects of sublethal doses of carbofuran on chicken (Hubbard strain) after 42 days*

Observed variable	Treatments (mg/kg body weight)					
	0	2	2.5	3	3.5	4
Feeding	normal	lower	lower	lower	lower	lower
Growth	normal	slower	slower	slower	slower	slower
Fitness	normal	weaker	weaker	weaker	weaker	weaker
Behaviour	normal	sensitive	sensitive	sensitive	sensitive and aggressive	sensitive and aggressive

3. Results

The 96h oral LC_{50} was determined as 12.04 mg/kg body weight; based on this figure, the upper limit of the sublethal dose series was set at 4 mg/kg body weight. Some symptoms, *i.e.* diarrhoea, vomiting, muscle weakness, and hypersensitivity were observed (Table 1). All these symptoms were related to the chronic effect of this insecticide, and the chickens recovered when the treatment was stopped. These chronic symptoms were followed by general weakness. Death occurred due to the lack of nutrition, and not directly because of the insecticide.

There was a very significant difference in growth among the treated chickens. The interaction showed that the chickens responded differently according to the dose treatment (Table 2).

Table 2 *Analysis of variance for the effect of oral intoxication by carbofuran on growth of male chicken (Hubbard strain)*

Source	SS	df	MS	F	P
Dose treatment	293827.1	5	58765.4	69.0	< 0.01
Time	3970267.2	4	992566.8	1165.4	< 0.01
Interaction	97946.5	20	4897.3	5.7	< 0.01
Error	229942.5	270	851.6		

Table 3 *Macroscopic degeneration effects of oral intoxication by carbofuran on the liver of male chicken (Hubbard strain)*

Treatments	Observed variable			
	Color	Consistency	Volume	Margin of caudal lobe
0 mg/kg	brown-red	solid	normal	brown-red
2 mg/kg	brown-red	solid	normal	brown-red
2.5 mg/kg	brown-red	solid	normal	brown-red
3 mg/kg	brown-red	solid	normal	brown-red
3.5 mg/kg	pale	not solid	swollen	blue-black
4 mg/kg	pale	not solid	swollen	blue-black

Table 4 *Effects of carbofuran on the microscopic structure of the liver cells of male chicken (Hubbard strain)*

Treatment	Observed variable		
	Liver cells	sinusoid	Central vein
0 mg/kg	regular	normal	more red blood cells
2 mg/kg	regular	normal	more red blood cells
2.5 mg/kg	regular	normal	more red blood cells
3 mg/kg	regular	normal	more red blood cells
3.5 mg/kg	swollen, leucocyte infiltration	normal	less red blood cells
4 mg/kg	regular	normal	more red blood cells

Abnormalities of the liver, due to the effect of carbofuran, could be detected when the dose was equal to or more than 3.5 mg/kg body weight. From the histological inspection, it could be concluded that the liver structure was abnormal due to the swelling of cells, with minimal vascularization (Table 3).

The hepatic responses demonstrate that sublethal doses of carbofuran have non-typical chronic effects (Table 4). It is feared that other insecticides at sublethal intoxication levels may have similar effects.

4.   Discussion

Oral intoxication with carbofuran may give rise to effects outside the nervous system, such as the liver and the general metabolic system. The absorption through the tunica mucosa of the intestine has a direct effect on substance translocation to the lymph and portal circulation system around the liver. Since there will be enterohepatic circulation of the pesticides, it will possibly affect liver and the intestine to such an extent that the general metabolism of the chicken is affected.

5.   References

Banks, W.J. (1981) *Applied Veterinary Histology*, William and Wilkins, Baltimore.

Cassarett, D.L. & Doull, J. (1975) *Toxicology, The Basic Science of Poissons*, MacMillan Publishing Co., New York.

Tarumingkeng, R.C. (1976) Side Effects of Insecticides on Birds (in Indonesian), *Media Veteriner*, Tahun I, Biro Dekan Fakultas Kedokteran Hewan, IPB, Bogor.

2.7

Effect of pesticide use on non-target soybean arthropods in Central Lampung, Indonesia

F.X. SUSILO, I.G. SWIBAWA, M. SOLIKHIN & S.W. SUPRIYONO

Abstract

This investigation was aimed at studying the effects of insecticide use on (1) the trophic relationship between pest arthropods or 'other' soybean arthropods and their natural enemies and (2) the competitive relationship between pests and 'other' arthropods. Polycultured and monocultured soybean fields in central Lampung were selected for the study. Two farmer-owned polycultured fields were sprayed excessively with mono-crotophos and phenthoate, two other fields serving as controls. In addition, untreated controls and decamethrin treatments were randomly allocated to six monocultured soybean plots. During the months of May and July of 1992, soybean arthropods were collected in three consecutive weeks prior to harvesting using a 42 cm diameter sweep net. Relationships between groups of soybean arthropods were analyzed by correlation. The variables correlated were abundance of arthropods expressed in numbers caught per field in one sampling occasion. In polycultured soybean there was no relationship between pests or 'other' arthropods and natural enemy groups. Insecticide treatment did not affect this (lack of) trophic relationship. In monocultured soybean, however, the relationship between pests and natural enemies was strengthened and the relationship between 'other' arthropods and natural enemies was weakened by insecticide treat-ment. The competitive interactions between pests and 'other' arthropods were weakened by insecticide treatment in monocultured soybean but were strengthened in polycultured soybean. Pest resurgence probably occurs in monocultured soybean through changes in trophic relationships. Should a pest outbreak occur in polycultured soybean, it might be attributed to the changes in competitive relationships among arthropod groups existing in the agro-ecosystem.

1. Introduction

Farmers in South and Central Lampung have cultivated soybeans for many decades. Relatively easy access to fertilizers and pesticides in the areas has contributed to an extensive use of those agrochemicals. For more than one decade, however, soybean productivity in the areas has declined considerably (Kuwatsuka *et al.* 1985) partly due to the severity of arthropod attacks. Nakasuji *et al.* (1985) suggested that resurgence of some pest arthropods has occurred in Lampung soybean fields and that this was perhaps due to the excessive uses of insecticides. How can one elucidate, in a better ecological sense, the interrelations between insecticides and resurgence taking into account contributions of other determinants to the occurrence (or lack thereof) of pest outbreaks? We argued that crop diversity and abundances of some arthropod groups in soybean fields may also be crucial factors determining the pest outbreaks. Furthermore, levels of relationships between interacting arthropod groups in a soybean ecosystem could explain a potential pest outbreak in the ecosystem. This work tested a prediction that combinations of pesticide use and crop diversity determine the strength of relationships between interacting groups of animals in an agroecosystem. Observations were made to document the effects of insecticide applications on the relationships between pests and their natural enemies, pests and 'other' arthropods, or natural enemies and 'other' arthropod groups in soybean fields that differed in their crop diversity in Central Lampung.

2.   Study sites

Soybean fields in Kalirejo and Trimurjo, Central Lampung, Indonesia, were selected as the study sites. Kalirejo and Trimurjo are respectively located at ca. 50 km Southwest and 40 km Northeast of Bandar Lampung, Indonesia. Four farmer-owned soybean fields in Kalirejo, sized ca. 0.25 ha each, were observed; of these, two had been sprayed heavily with mixtures of monocrotophos and phenthoate, the other two were treated only lightly. In the Trimurjo area the soybean plots were owned by a local agricultural experiment station (headed by S.W. Supriyono). Untreated control and decamethrin treatments were randomly allocated to six of these 5 m x 5 m size plots. The study plots were interspaced with soybean barrier plots of at least the same size as the study plots.

In the Trimurjo area, soybean was grown as a single crop (monoculture). The surrounding area was hectares of rice fields. In contrast, soybean in the Kalirejo area was polycultured with cassava and corn. The soybean fields were located well within villages characterized by their diverse vegetation.

3.   Materials and methods

Arthropod samples were collected using a 42 cm diameter muslin sweep net, swung down the crown 18 times across two rows of soybean stands consisting of 36 mounds per field (plot). Inter-row spacings in Kalirejo and Trimurjo fields were 35 cm and 30 cm, respectively. All arthropods caught were identified 'in situ' and their abundance was recorded in three consecutive weeks prior to harvesting. The specimens were then divided into target pest (herbivores) and non-target arthropod groups. The latter group was further subdivided into natural enemies (parasitoids and predators), and 'other' arthropods (scavengers, etc.). Arthropod abundance was expressed in numbers of arthropods caught per field in one sampling occasion. Relationship between groups of arthropods were analyzed by means of correlation. The variables correlated were abundances of pests versus natural enemies, pests versus 'other' arthropods, and natural enemies versus 'other' arthropods. The concept of pests, natural enemies, and 'other' arthropods was taken from Price & Waldbauer (1982) and Price (1984).

4.   Results

There was strong evidence for a combined effect of insecticide use and crop diversity on the relationship between arthropod groups in soybean fields in Central Lampung. The association (or rather, lack of association) of pests and their natural enemies in polycultured soybean was not affected by insecticide treatment (Table 1). In monocultured soybean, however, the relationship between pests and natural enemies became significantly stronger as insecticide was applied.

Table 1 *Strength of correlations (r values) between the abundance of pest arthropods and their natural enemies in monocultured and polycultured soybean fields exposed to insecticide use*

Insecticide	Crop diversity	
	Monoculture (Trimurjo)	Polyculture (Kalirejo)
Non-intensive	0.427 (ns)	-0.328 (ns)
Intensive	0.800**	0.426 (ns)

(ns) = not significantly different from zero at the 0.05 level; ** = significantly different from zero at the 0.01 level; non-intensive = less than three insecticide applications prior to arthropod sampling in Kalirejo or no applications in Trimurjo; intensive = more than three applications prior to sampling in Kalirejo or three applications in Trimurjo.

Table 2 *Strength of correlations (r values) between the abundance of pest arthropods and 'other' arthropods in monocultured and polycultured soybean fields exposed to insecticide use*

Insecticide	Crop diversity	
	Monoculture (Trimurjo)	Polyculture (Kalirejo)
Non-intensive	0.740**	0.063 (ns)
Intensive	-0.210 (ns)	0.817**

(ns) = not significantly different from zero at the 0.05 level; ** = significantly different from zero at the 0.01 level; non-intensive = less than three insecticide applications prior to arthropod sampling in Kalirejo or no application in Trimurjo; intensive = more than three applications prior to sampling in Kalirejo or three applications in Trimurjo.

Table 2 illustrates an inverse tendency of relationships between pests and 'other' arthropods as a result of combined effects of insecticide and crop diversity. The association between pests and 'other' arthropods was strong in monocultured soybean fields untreated with insecticides or in polycultured soybean fields treated with excessive insecticides. No association between pests and 'other' arthropods was detected in polycultured soybean fields treated with less insecticides. Moreover, insecticide treatment in monocultured soybean fields weakened the association between pests and 'other' arthropods.

Table 3 *Strengths of correlations (r values) between the abundance of natural enemies and 'other' arthropods in monocultured and polycultured soybean fields exposed to insecticide use*

Insecticide	Crop diversity	
	Monoculture (Trimurjo)	Polyculture (Kalirejo)
Non-intensive	0.650*	0.035 (ns)
Intensive	-0.150 (ns)	-0.235 (ns)

(ns) = not significantly different from zero at the 0.05 level; * = significantly different from zero at the 0.05 level; non-intensive = less than three insecticide applications prior to arthropod sampling in Kalirejo or no application in Trimurjo; intensive = more than three applications prior to sampling in Kalirejo or three applications in Trimurjo.

The strength of associations between natural enemies and 'other' arthropods was also affected by combined effects of insecticide treatment and crop diversity (Table 3). The association between natural enemies and 'other' arthropods was strong in monocultured soybean fields untreated with insecticides. The association was weakened by insecticide treatment. No association between natural enemies and 'other' arthropods was detected in polycultured soybean field untreated with insecticides. This lack of association was not changed significantly by insecticide treatment.

5. Discussion

Associations between natural enemies and pests dominated by trophic relationships (Price & Waldbauer 1982, Price 1984, Russell 1989). Relationships between natural enemies and 'other' arthropods may also have a trophic component, as the latter could serve as hosts or prey for the former. It could even be that the 'other' arthropod groups served as the primary source of food for the natural enemy group, while the pest group served as the secondary or alternative food source for the natural enemies. Meanwhile, associations between pests and 'other' arthropods are mainly competitive in nature (Price 1984). This reasoning at least had two implications.

First, natural enemies which include predatory and parasitic arthropods in undisturbed soybean stands monocultured in the Trimurjo area might have consumed mainly 'other' arthropods and therefore a strong correlation between the two groups was shown in Table 3. This strong association was accompanied by a weak association between natural enemies and pests. As the fields were disturbed with insecticide treatments, the association between natural enemies and 'other' arthropods weakened because perhaps insecticides were more suppressive to the 'other' arthropods in the fields. Consequently, natural enemies switched hosts (preys) to pest arthropods leading to a stronger association between the pests and the natural enemies (Table 1).

Second, in undisturbed monoculture soybean stands the 'other' arthropods were allowed to compete strongly for available space with pest arthropods (Table 2). Insecticide treatment in such fields weakened the competitive interactions through its more suppressive effects on the 'other' arthropod groups. This weak, or lacking, competition seemed to expose available pests to predators or parasitoids that had switched their searching mode to the pest groups as a result of, curiously enough, weaker trophic relationships between natural enemies and the suppressed 'other' arthropod groups.

This further implied that, should pest resurgence occur in monocultured soybean fields, the phenomenon can reasonably be attributed to the negative effect of insecticide treatment on natural enemies as the chief pest controlling agent, given that trophic interactions between natural enemies and 'other' arthropods or competitive interactions between pests and 'other' arthropods were lacking because the 'other' arthropods were suppressed by the insecticide in the first place. This finding was rather different from one claimed by Haryanto & Untung (1989) in a resurgence case of jassids (leafhoppers) in monocultured cotton. They found no significant association between jassids and a complex of natural enemies in cotton fields treated with insecticides and argued that negative effects of insecticide treatment on natural enemies did not have any bearing on the occurrence of the outbreak of the cotton jassid. In their study, however, Haryanto & Untung (1989) did not take the role of 'other' cotton arthropods into account.

In polycultured soybean fields treated with less insecticides scramble competition between pests and 'other' arthropods may have occurred leading to random correlations between the two groups. The term 'scramble' competition (Price 1984) was used here in a rather loose concept to include not only intraspecific but also interspecific competition among members of pests and those of 'other' arthropod groups. As stated by Price (1984), the outcome of this type of competition is not complete which could in this study lead to random preferences of the natural enemies to any members of the pest or 'other' arthropod groups. This phenomenon may be illustrated by the lack of trophic relationship between pests or 'other' arthropods and natural enemies (Table 1, 3) and no competitive relationships between pests and 'other' arthropods (Table 2). Excessive use of insecticides in polycultured soybean fields may have changed the nature of competition between pests and 'other' arthropod groups which includes interference competition as defined by Miller (1967) resulting in a stronger competitive relationship between pests and 'other' arthropod groups (Table 2). Nevertheless, this did not change the trophic relationship (or lack thereof) between natural enemies and pests or natural enemies and 'other' arthropods (Table 1, 3). This implied, (1) should a pest outbreak occur in polycultured soybean fields treated with excessive insecticide, this is unlikely to have anything to do with trophic relationships, (2) if Root's (1973) enemies theory is true that predators and parasitoids are more effective in polyculture, then it would be unlikely that pest resurgence would occur in polycultured soybean fields.

6. Acknowledgements

We are very grateful to Subrani B. Widodo, Trikoranto, Zul, Thamrin, Jasmin, and Sarjuni for their kind assistence during the selection of the study sites. We also thank landowners in the Kalirejo area for permitting us observe their soybean fields. This work was done in cooperation with Laboratorium Pengamatan Peramalan Hama dan Penyakit Tanaman Pangan, Trimurjo, Lampung Tengah.

7. References

Haryanto & Untung, K. (1989) Resurgence of *Empoasca* sp. (F.) after Insecticide Treatment on Cotton Plant (*Gossypium* sp.). Berkala Penelitian Pasca Sarjana UGM, *Ser. B: Kelompok Ilmu Pengetahuan Alam dan Teknologi* 2: 1007-1015.

Kuwatsuka, S., Yoshida, K., Mahi, A.K. & Lumbanraja, J. (1985) Relationship between Growth of Soybeans and Characteristics of Soils, in: Yamamoto, I. & Sosromarsono, S. (eds.) *Ecological Impact of Pest Management in Indonesia*, Tokyo Univ. Agric., pp. 49-58.

Miller, R.S. (1967) Pattern and Process in Competition, *Adv. Ecol. Res.* 4: 1-74.

Nakasuji, F., Ichikawa, T. & Susilo, F.X. (1985) Insect Pests and Insect-borne Diseases of Soybean in Lampung, in: Yamamoto, I. & Sosromarsono, S. (eds.) *Ecological Impact of Pest Management in Indonesia*, Tokyo Univ. Agric., pp. 17-36.

Price, P.W. (1984) *Insect Ecology*, 2nd edition, John Wiley & Sons, New York.

Price, P.W. & Waldbauer, G.P. (1982) Ecological Aspects of Pest Management, in: Metcalf, R.L. & Luckmann, W.H. (eds.) *Introduction to Insect Pest Management*, 2nd edition, John Wiley & Sons, New York, pp. 33-68.

Root, R.B. (1973) Organization of a Plant - Arthropod Association in Simple and Diverse Habitats: The Fauna of Collards (*Brassica oleracea*), *Ecol. Monogr.* 43: 95-124.

Russell, E.P. (1989) Enemies Hypothesis: A Review of the Effect of Vegetational Diversity on Predatory Insects and Parasitoids, *Environ. Entomol.* 18: 590-599.

2.8

Fate and residues of pesticides in paddy rice production in the Philippines

A.W. Tejada, L.M. Varca, P. Ocampo, C.M. Bajet & E.D. Magallona

Abstract

The fate and residues of pesticides in a rice paddy ecosystem were monitored because this is thought to contribute more to pesticide pollution of the environment than any agro-ecosystem in the tropics. Twenty nine farmer cooperators were selected in rice growing areas for two cropping seasons, Extensive sampling of rice at harvest from farmer cooperators did not show any detectable residues of any pesticides used in the field. The usual practice of harvesting rice 30 to 40 days after the last application of pesticide may be considered safe from the standpoint of consumption. Parallel to this, intensive sampling (i.e. sampling at 0 to 30 days after last application of pesticides) at farmers fields and supervised trials at the Central Experiment Station, UPLB, was conducted. In chlorpyrifos treated rice fields, residues in soil were detected up to 15 days after application from high pesticide users farms while remaining only up to 5 days in the low pesticide users fields. A similar trend was observed in the supervised trial. Chlorpyrifos residues in the paddy water were detected only from the high pesticide user. On rice plants, chlorpyrifos residues were detected up to 15 days after application in leaves and up to 5 days in the stalk both in high and low pesticide users. The residues did not exceed the Maximum Residue Limit (MRL) set for chlorpyrifos by FAO/WHO which is 2 mg/kg for several agricultural commodities. In monocrotophos treated fields, residues were detected only in rice leaves and stalk up to 7 days after last application but were not detected in paddy water and soil. In the supervised trial, residues remained up to three days in water and three hours in soil. Residues were not detected in grains. Both monocrotophos and chlorpyrifos treated fields had considerable residues in the immediate atmosphere three hours after application of the insecticides but these were reduced greatly after 24h. Concentrations did not exceed the threshold level value (TLV) of 0.2 mg/m^3 of air. A 48h, re-entry period is recommended by US EPA. In endosulfan treated fields, the residues were still detected on soil up to 7 days and up to 9 days in water. Residues were not detected in rice grains. Samples of fish, frogs, ducks and snails collected in the vicinity of the treated fields contained monocrotophos and chlorpyrifos residues at levels within the ADI set by FAO/WHO. In the supervised trial, monocrotophos and chlorpyrifos did not affect fish survival when the paddy water was drained into the trench prior to insecticide treatment. The danger lies in the ability of the organisms to bioconcentrate residues. These may exceed the ADI *which in turn could pose hazards to consumers. Live fish depurate easily when transferred to pesticide-free water.*

1. Introduction

Today there is increasing concern about pollution of the environment by pesticides. In spite of the introduction of Integrated Pest Management to lessen the use of pesticides, many farmers still rely on these compounds.

The rice paddy is thought to be one of the major contributors to pesticide pollution. Farmers still spray pesticides as much as five or six times in one cropping season although two applications may be considered the average. The usual practice of draining the paddy water into irrigation canals could cause the pesticide to eventually find its way to rivers and lakes emptying into the sea. The residues carried by the water can be taken up by other non-target flora and fauna, they can settle in the sediment, or they can leach out of the soil, and contaminate the ground water and possibly the potable water.

A greater problem lies in the bioaccumulation of pesticides in beneficial organisms such as fish. DDT for example has a bioaccumulation factor of 10,000 to 100,000 (Metcalf *et al.* 1971). Residues in food will, in one way or another, pose hazards to consumers if the Maximum Residue Limit (MRL) is exceeded.

There have been several studies undertaken by the Pesticide Toxicology and Chemistry Laboratory of the National Crop Protection Center, the Philippines, to determine the fate of pesticides when applied in a rice paddy ecosystem. This ecosystem was chosen primarily because rice is planted by small farmers who may be at special risk from pesticide use. Among the pesticides so far studied are carbofuran, carbosulfan, isoprocarb, BPMC, endosulfan, lindane, monocrotophos and a formulated mixture of chlorpyrifos and BPMC. Carbosulfan was not detected on almost all components of the rice paddy except in rice leaves where it remained up to seven days. Carbosulfan was rapidly converted to carbofuran. Carbofuran residues were concentrated in the leaves, followed by the stem and the least in the grains. These samplings were carried out during the milking stage (Tejada & Magallona 1985). Celino *et al.* (1988) determined the fate of ^{14}C-carbofuran in a simulated rice-fish ecosystem and she was not able to detect any residue in the rice grains at harvest time. Residues of BPMC were maximal in the leaves, then in the stem and the lowest in the grains (Varca & Magallona 1987). Residues in the grains were concentrated in the husk. Normal application of lindane and endosulfan, BPMC and carbofuran did not result in residues in grains (Medina-Lucero 1980, Varca & Magallona 1987, Celino *et al.* 1988). Monocrotophos sprayed one to three times using the rate recommended by the manufacturer did not result in any detectable residue in the grains at harvest (Tejada & Bajet 1990).

This report will cover our attempt to monitor the impact of pesticides resulting from their use in the rice paddy ecosystem.

2. Materials and methods

A variety of approaches were used. In the first one, high and low pesticide user farmers were identified. The residues in different substrates arising from pesticide use by both farmer types were monitored. Parallel experiments were done at the Central Experiment Station, UPLB, Laguna.

2.1 Pesticide application schedules

The first application of pesticides by low pesticide users was one day after trans-planting rice and the last application was 30-39 days after transplanting, with a total of three applications for the dry season (Table 1). For the high pesticide users, the first application of pesticides was made one day after transplanting and the last application was 76 days after transplanting with a total of ten applications (Table 2).

Table 1 *Schedule of pesticide application by low pesticide users*

Area	Rice variety	Date of trans-planting	Pesticide applied	Quantity per farm	Date of applica-tion
2.8 ha	C-4	July 11, 1989	Machete	1 L	July 12
	IR-10	July 23, 1989	Machete	1 L	July 24
	C-4		Brodan	0.5 L	Aug. 10
	IR-10		Brodan	0.5 L	Aug. 31

For the wet season, the last pesticide application was 75 days after transplanting with a total of nine applications (Table 2) for high pesticide users and a total of three applications for the low pesticide users.

2.1.1 Monitoring of pesticide residues in fields of cooperating farmers

Rice grains at harvest time were sampled from fields of various cooperating farmers in Calauan, Calamba and Binan. Soil samples were also collected prior to the next planting season to determine the presence of pesticides in the field that may contaminate the plant before treatment.

Intensive sampling of some of the components of the rice paddy ecosystem was also done to determine the degradation pattern of pesticides under actual field conditions. Samples were collected from both high and low pesticide users. Rice, soil and water were collected at various intervals: 0 (about 3 h after spraying), 1, 2, 3, 5, 7, 15, 30 and 45 days after the last spray application. Rice leaves and stalk were also sampled.

Samples of fish, snails, shrimps, frogs and chicken were collected from selected paddies and adjacent irrigation canals. Snails were collected at pre-booting and two weeks before harvest. Fish, shrimps and frogs were collected only once during the pre-booting stage because irrigation canals during the pre-harvest period were already drained. Chicken were also collected in the areas were they were available. These chicken are known to forage directly on the rice paddies under observation.

All the samples were weighed and stored frozen until analysis. The chicken were dewinged, debeaked and the entrails were removed before freezing.

Table 2 *Schedule of pesticide application by high pesticide users*

Area	Rice variety	Date of transplanting	Pesticide applied	Quantity per farm	Date of application
4.7 ha	IR-70	June 8	Aquatin	2 L	June 8
	C-1	June 8	Baylucide	2 L	June 9
	Malagkit	June 8	Machete	4 L	June 9
			Lorsban	1 L	June 26
			Lorsban	1 L	June 28
			Furadan	1 bag	July 3
			Lorsban	2 L	July 28
			Hytox	1 kg	July 29
			Furadan	2 bags	Aug. 5
			Lorsban	2 L	Aug. 23, 24

2.1.2 Supervised trial

Three (20 x 25 m) rice paddies located at the Central Experiment Station (CES) of UPLB, Laguna were treated separately with monocrotophos and endosulfan at 15 and 40 days after transplanting using the recommended rate of application; this simulated the practice of a low pesticide user. Samples of water and soil were analyzed at 0 to 30 days after the last spraying of the insecticide. Rice grains were collected at harvest. A trench was constructed on each side of the paddy. This trench served as a refuge and collection point for fish during and immediately after pesticide application. Fish samples were taken at harvest.

Air sampling was carried out by installing a fine nylon cloth treated with ethylene glycol stapled on sticks placed at different distances from the treated plot three hours and one day after application of the insecticide. Sampling was done after 24 hours exposure of the nylon and mesh cloth.

2.2 Extraction and clean-up of samples

2.2.1 Rice grains, stalks, leaves

Following the procedure by Luke *et al.* (1975), the samples were extracted with acetone and the extracts were partitioned in 100 mL of petroleum ether and 100 mL of methylene chloride. The combined organic layer was passed through anhydrous sodium sulphate powder and concentrated to almost dryness in a vacuum. The residue was recovered in methanol for gas chromatographic analysis.

2.2.2   Soil

The procedure of Ambrus *et al.* (1981) was followed. Soil samples were extracted with acetone and 2 N ammonium acetate. The extracts were partitioned into methylene chloride and passed through anhydrous sodium sulphate. It was then evaporated to almost dryness and the residue was dissolved in acetone for gas chromatography.

2.2.3   Water

The procedure followed was that of the U.S. Environmental Protection Agency (1974). Paddy water was extracted with 15% methylene chloride in hexane. The aqueous layer was extracted twice, first with the solvent mixture and then with hexane. The combined extracts were passed through anhydrous sodium sulphate, and concentrated to almost dryness. The residue was dissolved in methanol for gas chromatography.

2.2.4   Animals

The samples were thawed and briefly washed in running water. The shells of shrimps and snails were removed; in the case of fish and frogs, the animals were decapitated and the heads were stored separately. Tissue samples were chopped into small pieces, and 25 g samples were ground with granular sodium sulphate in a mortar. The mixture was extracted in succession with four 100 mL portions of boiling petroleum ether for 10 minutes under reflux. The combined extract was transferred into a small tube after washing with petroleum ether.

The chromatographic tube was filled with 100 mL of petroleum ether, and 25 g of deactivated Florisil was added slowly with 5 g of sodium sulphate powder. This was pre-wetted with 35 mL petroleum ether which was later discarded. The fat extract dissolved in 5 mL of petroleum ether was applied to the column and eluted with 300 mL of 8:2 mL volume with acetone for gas chromatography.

2.3   Gas chromatography

The organophosphate and the carbamate pesticides were analyzed in an Hewlett Packard 5840 gas chromatograph with a nitrogen phosphorus detector. The following parameters were used:

Column:	3% SE-30 on WHP 80/100 mesh	
Gas flows:	nitrogen:	30 (mL/min)
	hydrogen:	3
	air:	50
Temperature:	column:	200 (°C)
	injector:	215
	detector:	300

Endosulfan was analyzed in a Tracor 580 gas chromatograph equipped with a ^{63}Ni electron capture detector with the following parameters:

Column:	10% DC-200 on 80/100 WHP	
Temperature:	column:	168 (°C)
	detector:	298
	injector:	249
Nitrogen flow:	30 mL/min	

3. Results and discussion

3.1 Pesticide residues in fields of cooperating farmers

Random sampling of rice grains at harvest for pesticide residue analysis taken from cooperating farmers showed no detectable levels of chlorpyrifos, BPMC, methyl-parathion, diazinon, monocrotophos and endosulfan both in dehusked and rough rice. This could be expected because of the time interval between the last spray application and harvest which ranged from 30 to 40 days. There was adequate time for degradation due to sunlight and rainfall. Previous studies in the laboratory showed that after five days from application, residues of methyl-parathion, monocrotophos, tetrachlorvinphos and triazophos were not detected on vegetables treated with these chemicals (Tejada et al. 1977). BPMC on rice was lost rapidly, at five days after application only 0.2 and 0.03 mg/kg of the chemical was found on rough and milled rice, respectively (Varca & Magallona 1987). The rapid loss of these pesticides can be attributed to the low vapor pressure of these compounds and the intense heat of the sun.

Soil samples collected prior to the next cropping season for residue analysis did not have any residue of BPMC, chlorpyrifos, monocrotophos, endosulfan and diazinon. This indicates that there is no build-up of pesticide residue in the soil. Similar results were obtained with repeated applications of carbosulfan (Tejada & Magallona 1985) and endosulfan and lindane in lowland rice paddy ecosystems (Medina-Lucero 1980).

3.1.1 Degradation studies of chlorpyrifos in farmer fields

Chlorpyrifos was degraded rapidly in paddy water (sampled at high pesticide users) with detectable residues only up to three days. This agrees with the findings of Zulkifli et al. (1983) and Smith et al. (1966). Coincidentally, this is the time when chlorpyrifos residues were highest in rice stalks. This could be the period when the rice plants absorbed the chemical from the water by capillary action. The residues then started to decline, giving a half-life of 1.87 days (Table 3).

Chlorpyrifos residues on rice leaves were still detected up to the 15th day. Analysis of soil from high pesticide users showed that the levels on day zero were higher than in rice plants i.e. 0.25 mg/kg in soil compared to 0.09 mg/kg in the leaves. This could be due to rainfall after application of the insecticide, washing the residues from the leaves and depositing them on the soil. Rainfall is known to reduce pesticide residues by as much as 90% (Tejada & Magallona 1985). The soil retained the residue longer than any other component of the rice paddy due to absorption and bound residue formation. In addition, the soil is the ultimate sink of pesticide deposition.

Table 3 *Residues of chlorpyrifos in samples from high pesticide and low pesticide user farms (wet season, 1989)*

| DAA[*] | Residues (mg/kg) | | | | | | | |
| | Water | | Rice stalks | | Rice leaves | | Soil | |
	A[1]	B[1]	A	B	A	B	A	B
0	-		0.003	0.09	0.09	0.24	0.25	0.04
1	0.001	<0.001	0.006	0.05	0.12	0.39	0.23	0.15
2	0.001	<0.001	0.009	0.04	0.1	0.21	0.21	0.04
3	0.001	<0.001	0.01	0.03	0.07	0.13	0.11	0.002
5	<0.001	<0.001	0.002	0.03	0.01	0.07	0.06	-
7	<0.001	<0.001	<0.001	-	-	0.05	0.08	-
15	<0.001	<0.001	<0.001	-	0.003	-	0.05	-

[*] DAA: Days after application
[1] A = high pesticide user farm, B = low pesticide user farm

Samples of rice from a low pesticide user showed that leaves had the highest level of residues among the components analyzed (Table 3). The size of the plant per volume of spray solution, affected the distribution of the pesticide in the plants. Again, rice grain taken at harvest time did not have any pesticide residue both on dehusked and rough rice, therefore the usual practice of harvesting rice 40 days after the last application may be considered safe from the consumer's standpoint.

3.1.2 Degradation studies of monocrotophos in farmer fields

Intensive sampling in fields of a high pesticide user and a low pesticide user showed rapid degradation of monocrotophos with no detectable residues in soil and water (Table 4). Monocrotophos was detected in rice leaves up to five days after application. This compliments the findings of Tejada & Bajet (1990) where monocrotophos residues remained in rice plants for up to five days. The residues did not exceed the Maximum Residue Limit of 0.05 mg/kg set by FAO/WHO (1973, 1985, 1989) for some agricultural commodities. A 14 days safety period was recommended by FAO/WHO but a period of 7 days under tropical conditions can already be considered acceptable for monocrotophos. There was not much difference between residue levels in high and low pesticide user fields. Monocrotophos was rapidly degraded in surface soil and in paddy water so that no residue build-up was observed during the entire season.

Table 4 *Residues of monocrotophos in samples from high pesticide and low pesticide user farms (dry season, 1990)*

DAA*	Residues (mg/kg)							
	Water		Soil		Rice stalks		Rice leaves	
	A[1]	B[1]	A	B	A	B	A	B
0	NDR	NDR	NDR	NDR	0.03	0.012	0.01	0.02
1	NDR	NDR	NDR	NDR	0.01	0.028	0.03	0.03
2	NDR	NDR	NDR	NDR	0.002	0.009	0.01	0.02
3	NDR	NDR	NDR	NDR	0.002	0.002	-	0.009
5	NDR	NDR	NDR	NDR	0.001	NDR	0.001	0.005
7	NDR	NDR	NDR	NDR	NDR	NDR	NDR	NDR
15	NDR	NDR	NDR	NDR	NDR	NDR	NDR	NDR

* DAA: Days after application
[1] A = high pesticide user farm, B = low pesticide user farm
NDR = no detectable residue

The results of this study compliment the findings from earlier supervised studies (Tejada & Magallona 1985, Varca & Magallona 1987, Celino *et al.* 1988, Tejada & Bajet 1990). Rice grains at harvest normally would not contain any detectable residues of monocrotophos.

3.2 Supervised trial at the UPLB Central Experiment Station

In the supervised trial, the rates of decline for monocrotophos, chlorpyrifos and endosulfan residues were consistent with those occurring in farmer's fields except for monocrotophos where residues were detected up to 3 days after spray application (Table 5). This could be due to rainfall immediately after spraying which washed the residues on to the paddy water. As expected, residues were not detected in grains.

Residues of monocrotophos and chlorpyrifos in the air ranged from 0.001 to 0.04 mg/m^3 at the time of application (Table 5). Residues detected 3 h after application did not exceed the threshold level value (TLV) of 0.2 mg/m^3 and the residues were reduced greatly after 24 hours.

Table 5 *Residues of monocrotophos, chlorpyrifos and endosulfan in some components of the rice paddy ecosystem*

Days	Soil (mg/kg)	Water (mg/L)	Air (mg/m³)
Monocrotophos			
0	0.002	0.002	0.001
1	ND	0.008	0.004
2	ND	0.003	ND
3	ND	0.0028	-
9	ND	ND	-
Chlorpyrifos			
0	0.59	0.21	0.04
1	0.04	0.35	-
3	0.05	0.42	-
9	-	0.0007	
14	0.004	ND	
23	ND	ND	
Endosulfan			
0	0.51	1.8	
1	0.37	2.6	
3	0.19	0.85	
7	0.11	0.5	
9	0.09	ND	

3.3   Ecological impacts

3.3.1   Effects on fish and other animals

Some samples of fish, snails and frogs contained residues of monocrotophos, iso-procarb and chlorpyrifos at levels within the Maximum Residue Limits (MRL) (Table 6). If we consider further that these edible animals are consumed only sparingly, then there should be no problem from their intake. The daily intake (DI) may be calculated from the following equation:

$$DI = \frac{R \times F}{P}$$

where
R = residue level in fish
F = weight of daily fish consumption
P = average weight of a person

Table 6 *Pesticide residues detected in some aquatic organisms and animals found in the vicinity of the experimental area during the pre-booting stage of rice culture*

Species	Insecticide(s) used	Residue level (mg/kg)
1. Snails	monocrotophos (Azodrin)	trace
	chlorpyrifos + BPMC (Brodan)	NDR
	monocrotophos + fenvalerate (Azocord)	trace
	endosulfan (Thiodan)	NDR
	chlorpyrifos (Lorsban)	NDR
2. Tilapia (*Oreochromis niloticus*)	chlorpyrifos	NDR
	monocrotophos	NDR
Hito (*Chanca batrachus*)	decamethrin	NDR
	chlorpyrifos + BPMC	NDR
Shrimps (*Marabraechium sp.*)	methyl-parathion	NDR
	carbofuran	NDR
	MIPC	NDR
3. Duck: heart	chlorpyrifos (Lorsban)	0.020
muscle		0.027
4. Mudfish (*Ophicephalus striatus*)	chlorpyrifos	NDR
5. Gurami	chlorpyrifos	NDR

NDR = No detectable residues or residues were below the MRL
MRL = maximum residue limits (FAO/WHO 1973, 1985, 1989)
    chlorpyrifos: 0.002 - 0.2 mg/kg
    monocrotophos: 0.005 - 0.02 mg/kg
    BPMC: 0.001 - 1.0 mg/kg
    endosulfan: 0.0001 - 0.2 mg/kg

Assuming that an average person weighing 60 kg consumes 100 g of fish per day containing 0.027 mg chlorpyrifos per kg of fish then $DI = (0.027 \times 0.1)/60 = 0.000045$ mg per kg body-weight. The acceptable daily intake (ADI) for chlorpyrifos is 0.01 mg/kg, therefore the daily intake of 100 g fish containing 0.027 mg/kg chlorpyrifos residues is still below the ADI value set by FAO/WHO (1973, 1985, 1989).

Monocrotophos and chlorpyrifos did not affect fish survival when paddy water was drained and the fish found refuge in a trench. On the other hand, endosulfan was still toxic to tilapia up to 20 days after treatment of the field with about 18% fish mortality (Barredo-Medina *et al.* 1991). The lethal concentration was verified in the laboratory to determine if the concentration in the field directly after spraying exceeded the LC_{50}. The concentration of monocrotophos in paddy water was measured as 0.002 mg/L, and it did not exceed the LC_{50} of fish (13.8 mg/L). Concentrations of chlorpyrifos and endosulfan were 0.21 and 1.8 mg/L, respectively, and exceeded the LC_{50} of fish (Table 7). Monocrotophos was categorized as a low toxic compound while chlorpyrifos and endosulfan were extremely toxic to fish. The reason why chlorpyrifos did not affect fish survival in the field was due to the size of the fish which was three times larger than those tested in the laboratory. While there could be danger from biomagnification, live fish easily depurates if they are transferred to pesticide-free water. Absorption and depuration must occur continuously in the environment.

Table 7 *Toxicity of some insecticides in aquatic organisms at 48 hrs (LC_{50})*

	Tilapia (*Oreochromis niloticus*)	Guppy fish	Snails (*Pomacea caniculata*)
Endosulfan	6.9×10^{-4}	0.007	0.675
Chlorpyrifos	3.0×10^{-2}	0.978	0.067
BPMC	0.64	0.8	-
Carbofuran	-	0.09	-
Monocrotophos	13.8	-	53.8
Isoprocarb	-	1.6	-

Ranking (adapted from Nishiuchi 1974):
$LC_{50} > 10$ mg/L: low toxicity
$LC_{50} = 0.5 - 10$ mg/L: moderately toxic
$LC_{50} < 0.5$ mg/L: extremely toxic

4.   Conclusions

On the basis of these studies, it may be concluded that pesticides used in rice production do not pose grave hazards to the environment if good agricultural practice is followed.

5.   Acknowledgments

This is a part of the program on the 'Environmental and Health Impact of Pesticides' and financial support given by IRRI-ROCKEFELLER through the leadership of Dr. Pengali is greatly appreciated.

6.   References

Ambrus, A., Lantos, J., Visi, E., Csatlos, I. & Sarvari, L. (1981) General Method for the Determination of Pesticide Residues in Samples of Plant Origin, Soil and Water. I. Extraction and Cleanup, *J. Assoc. Off. Anal. Chem.* 64: 733-768.

Barredo-Medina, J., Calumpang, S.M.F., Tejada, A.W., Medina, J.R. & Magallona, E.D. (1991) Paper presented at the Final Research Coordination Meeting on the Use of Isotopes in Studies of Pesticide in Rice Fish Ecosystem, Phase II. November 11-15, 1991. Bangladesh, Thailand.

Celino, L.P., Gambalan, N.P. & Magallona, E.D. (1988) Fate of Carbofuran in a Simulated Rice-fish Ecosystem. Paper presented at the Third FAO/IAEA Meeting on the Use of Isotopes in Studies of Pesticide Residues in Rice/Fish Ecosystem.

Environmental Protection Agency (1974) *Manual for Analytical Methods for Analysis of Pesticides Residues in Human and Environmental Samples*, Revised December 2, 1974.

FAO/WHO (1973) Pesticide Residues in Food. FAO Plant Production and Protection, Paper, Rome.

FAO/WHO (1985) Pesticide Residues in Food. FAO Plant Production and Protection Paper #72/1, Rome.

FAO/WHO (1989) Pesticide Residues in Food. FAO Plant Production and Protection Paper, #99, Rome.

Luke, M.A., Froberg, J. & Masumoto, H.T. (1975) Extraction and Cleanup of Organochlorine, Organophosphate, Organonitrogen and Hydrocarbon Pesticides Products for Determination by Gas Liquid Chromatography, *J. Assoc. Off. Anal. Chem.* 58: 1020-1026.

Medina-Lucero, C. (1980) *The Dynamics of Transport and Distribution of Two Organochlorine Insecticides (Lindane and Endosulfan) in a Lowland Rice Field Ecosystem*, PhD Dissertation in Chemistry, U.P. at Los Banos, College, Laguna.

Metcalf, R.L., Sangha, G.K. & Kapoor, I.P. (1971) Model Ecosystem for the Evaluation of Pesticide Biodegradability and Ecological Magnification, *Env. Sci. Technol.* 5: 709-713.

Nishiuchi, Y. (1974) Testing Methods for the Toxicity of Agricultural Chemicals, *Japan. Pestic. Info.* 19: 16-19.

Smith, G., Betty, N., Watson, S. & Sebold, F.M. (1966) The Metabolism of ^{14}C-O,O-diethyl O-(3, 5, 6-trichloro-2-pyridyl) Phosphorothioate (Dursban) in Fish, *J. Econ. Entomol.* 59: 1464-1475.

Tejada, A.W. & Bajet, C.M. (1990) Fate of Monocrotophos, Methyl Parathion and Cypermethrin in Rice-fish Ecosystem, *Phil. Agric.* 73: 153-163.

Tejada, A.W. & Magallona, E.D. (1985) Fate of Carbosulfan in a Model Ecosystem, *Phil. Entomol.* 6: 275-285.

Tejada, A.W., Varca, L.M. & Magallona, E.D. (1977) Insecticide Residues in Vegetables. II. Effect of Dosage Rates and Pre-harvest Intervals on Residues in and on Green Beans (*Phaseolus vulgaris* L.), *Phil. Entomol.* 3: 273-280.

Varca, L.M. & Magallona, E.D. (1987) Residues of BPMC in Some Components of the Rice Paddy Ecosystem, *Phil. Entomol.* 7: 177-189.

Zulkifli, M., Tejada, A.W., & Magallona, E.D. (1983) The Fate of BPMC and Chlorpyrifos in Some Components of Paddy Rice Ecosystem, *Phil. Entomol.* 6: 555-565.

Part 3

Trace metal studies

3.1

Heavy metal uptake by crops on different soils treated with an industrial sludge

SURYANTO

Abstract

Pot experiments in a glasshouse showed that sludge produced by a waste water treatment plant at the Rungkut Industrial Estate, Surabaya, has a value as an organic fertilizer for crop production. In the pot system, crop biomass increased with increasing rate of sludge application, but heavy metal (Fe, Zn, Cu, Mn, Pb, Ni, and Hg) uptake by some crops also increased. Soil type had an important effect on heavy metal uptake by some crops. On heavy clay soil (vertisol) heavy metal uptake by crops was lower than on light sandy soil (regosol). However, the total metal residue was higher in a heavy clay soil than in a sandy soil. The maximum limit for Pb in food is 2.56 mg/kg, Zn and Cu 50 mg/kg, Hg (alkyl mercury compounds) 0.5 mg/kg, Ni-carbonyl 0.001 mg/kg. In the experiment, the concentration of heavy metals in the edible part of some crops were generally lower than the critical threshold for toxicity, some were higher. Metal accumulation in crops should be taken into account if industrial waste sludge is used as an organic fertilizer for crop production.

1. Introduction

At present, one of the most important problems facing metropolitan areas is the disposal of the large volumes of liquid and solid wastes generated by urban and industrial activities. In Indonesia's 'big city development program', locations have been planned for some industries in special areas called 'Industrial Area'. One of these is the Rungkut Industrial Estate Area, in Surabaya. In this area every industrial plant has a water treatment system for its waste, and the water from all the plants in the area is collected and treated again in a general water treatment system, managed by PT SIER, Surabaya. This process results in dischargeable clean water and a dry sludge residue produced at the rate of about 2 ton/day.

As large amounts of dry sludge are produced in the waste water treatment system PT SIER would like to increase the value of the sludge by recycling it in the farming system. The sludge residue may then be used as a fertilizer, or as a soil treatment, applied directly or indirectly after composting.

This paper is a compilation of some experimental results using sludge from the Rungkut Industrial Estate Area for different crops on different soil types.

2. Materials and methods

2.1 Materials

Dry sludge samples were obtained from the Industrial Estate, Rungkut, Surabaya. They were applied to regosol soil samples from Yogyakarta, and Wonosobo, vertisol soil samples from Sragen, Central Java, and ferralsol soil samples from Karanganyar, Central Java. These soils were sown with seeds of maize (*Zea mays* L. Hybrid variety C-1), peanut (*Arachis hypogaea* L.), spinach (*Amaranthus sp.*), lettuce (*Lactuca sativa* L.), tomato (*Lycopersicum esculentum* Mill.), and stern of sweet potato (*Ipomoea batatas* L.), obtained from Yogyakarta.

2.2 Methods

Soil samples were passed through a 5 mm sieve and put into plastic pots (depending on crops, between 2 - 7.5 kg/pot). Dry sludge was added at various rates, corresponding to 0-32 ton/ha, depending on the surface area of the soil in the pot; water was added until field capacity was reached. Crops were grown as follows: two plants per pot for maize, tomato, sweet potato; ten plants per pot for spinach; one plant per pot for peanut and lettuce. Observations on the plant growth were made every week until harvest. At harvest time all plant parts were cleaned from soil and the fresh weights of shoot, fruit, root, stems of the crops were measured. Plant parts were dried in an oven at 60°C for two days and the dry weight of the material was measured. Wet digestion was carried out using HNO_3 + $HClO_4$ + H_2SO_4 in a ratio of 40:4:1 (Schaumlaffel after Roesmarkam 1982). Heavy metal contents in the digest solutions were determined by Atomic Absorption Spectrophotometry (AAS).

3. Results and discussion

3.1 Characteristics of Rungkut Industrial Estate dry sludge

The sludge from Rungkut has a value as a fertilizer, because the sludge contains a high amount of nitrogen and organic matter (Table 1); however, the heavy metal contents of the dry sludge are also high, and therefore it has the potential to increase the heavy metal content in edible parts of the crop. The effects of sludge on the concentration of heavy metals in crop depends on the nature of the soil where the crops are grown. Table 2 shows the characteristics of the soils which may have an effect on plant growth.

Table 1 *Chemical composition of Rungkut Industrial Estate dry sludge*

Variable	Value	Variable	Value
Clay (%)	14.6	Total Cu (mg/kg)	2092
Silt (%)	18.1	Total Zn (mg/kg)	3602
Sand (%)	67.3	Total Pb (mg/kg)	216
pH H$_2$O	7.65	Total Ni (mg/kg)	2088
pH KCl	6.78	Total Fe (mg/kg)	822
Organic matter (%)	39.73	Total Mn (mg/kg)	248
Total N (%)	4.96	Total Cd (mg/kg)	1.2
Available N (%)	0.44	Total Cr (mg/kg)	10.0
HCl 25% ext. P (%)	1.28	Total Hg (mg/kg)	0.1
Available P (mg/kg)	69.0	Total Al (mg/kg)	10.0
HCl 25% ext. K (%)	0.06	Total Ag (mg/kg)	70.0
Available K (mg/kg)	4.90	Total As (mg/kg)	0.0
HCl 25% ext. S (%)	0.14		
Available S (mg/kg)	408.40		

Source: Notohadiprawiro *et al.* (1991)

Table 2 *Characteristics of soil types used in the experiment*

Variable	Soil type			Variable	Soil type		
	Vert.	Ferr.	Reg.		Vert.	Ferr.	Reg.
Clay (%)	70.5	55.2	10.0	Total Mn (%)	0.7	0.65	0.29
Silt (%)	8.3	39.3	13.8	Av. Mn (mg/kg)	67.5	63.20	24.40
Sand (%)	21.2	5.5	76.2	Total Zn (mg/kg)	49.8	42.70	20.70
pH H$_2$O	7.05	5.65	7.12	Av. Zn (mg/kg)	3.9	1.90	4.40
pH KCl	5.60	4.72	6.10	Total Cu (mg/kg)	27.7	35.40	18.70
CEC cmol/kg	65.59	25.05	10.23	Av. Cu (mg/kg)	2.6	5.60	3.10
OM (%)	1.68	0.89	1.22	Total Pb (mg/kg)	10.5	15.10	5.60
Total N (%)	3.29	0.07	0.09	Av. Pb (mg/kg)	0.5	0.60	0.40
Total Fe (%)	0.11	0.11	0.94	Total Ni (mg/kg)	28.8	14.90	6.40
Av. Fe (mg/kg)	12.5	13.3	12.8	Av. Ni (mg/kg)	1.7	0.90	0.90

Source: Notohadiprawiro *et al.* (1991)
Note: Vert. = vertisol, Ferr. = ferralsol, Reg. = regosol, Av. = available, OM = organic matter

3.2   Crop responses to sludge application

Some crops such as spinach, sweet potatoes, corn, lettuce and tomatoes showed a similar trend in terms of their response to the sludge application. Increasing the rate of sludge increased the growth of crops. A representative example of plant growth affected by the Rungkut sludge is presented in Table 3.

Table 3 shows that the sludge has a high value as an organic fertilizer for all of the soils. The crop's response varies according to soil type.

Table 3 *Effect of dry sludge from Rungkut Industrial Estate Area on dry weight of tomato (g/pot)*

Soil type	Rate of sludge application (ton/ha)					
	0	5	10	15	20	Average
Vertisol	107.5	165.0	217.7	240.1	254.2	196.9
Ferralsol	40.6	88.3	132.3	146.9	167.6	119.2
Regosol	64.0	99.4	168.9	241.5	334.8	181.7
Average	70.7	117.6	173.0	209.5	258.9	

Tabel 4 *Effect of Rungkut dry sludge on concentrations of heavy metals in spinach shoot (µg/g)*

Metal	Soil type and rate of sludge application (ton/ha)														
	Vertisol					Ferralsol					Regosol				
	0	5	10	15	20	0	5	10	15	20	0	5	10	15	20
Pb	0.1	0.1	0.2	0.3	0.3	2.0	2.9	3.8	4.6	6.2	0.8	1.5	3.9	3.6	4.1
Ni	0.0	0.0	0.1	0.3	0.2	1.4	2.2	4.6	6.2	6.6	0.4	0.4	0.9	1.0	1.2
Zn	29.8	33.2	32.7	29.8	35.4	46.8	118.8	156.4	156.7	150.7	22.8	12.8	22.3	22.5	25.4
Cu	0.5	0.7	0.8	0.7	0.9	2.0	1.4	1.9	2.4	2.2	2.5	1.1	1.8	1.2	0.8
Fe	65.2	64.0	44.9	42.2	29.6	144.3	125.4	190.1	193.0	189.0	57.8	83.2	58.6	45.7	29.8
Mn	2.4	6.8	9.0	6.8	5.6	66.3	64.9	77.1	80.5	77.0	4.8	5.0	8.1	6.7	5.4

Source: Notohadiprawiro *et al.* (1991)

3.3 Heavy metals in crop

3.3.1 Heavy metals in spinach

Concentrations of heavy metals in spinach were affected by the industrial sludge from Rungkut. Table 4 shows that in spinach shoots the sequence of concentration of heavy metals is Fe > Zn > Mn > Cu > Pb > Ni. Comparing the sludge-treated soils (5, 10, 15, 20) to the blank soil, it appears that in most cases sludge increased the concentration of heavy metal spinach shoots.

3.3.2 Nickel in peanut

In peanut the application of dry sludge from Rungkut increased the concentration of Ni in all parts of the crop: root, shoot, stem, leaf, and kernel. Table 5 shows that Ni accumulated mostly in root, then kernel, leaf and stem. With increasing rate of sludge application the concentration of Ni in peanut increased.

Table 5 *Effect of Rungkut dry sludge on the concentration of Ni in peanut (μg/g)*

Plant tissue	Rate of sludge application (ton/ha)				
	0	5	10	15	20
Kernels	5.3	32.3	35.7	44.6	44.6
Root	9.6	89.2	129.1	100.0	132.8
Stem	9.6	20.1	21.7	33.3	24.7
Leaf	9.6	39.6	25.2	38.6	33.4

Source: Mulyadi (1988)

Table 6 *Effect of Rungkut sludge on Pb concentrations in various plant parts of maize on regosol and ferralsol soils (μg/g)*

Plant tissue	Rate of sludge application (ton/ha)				
	0	5	10	15	20
Regosol					
Root	0	15.9	16.6	17.9	20.3
Stem	0	11.8	15.3	15.7	16.4
Leaves	0	11.6	12.0	12.0	13.2
Seed	0	37.7	93.4	113.8	124.6
Ferralsol					
Root	0	13.9	15.1	15.5	16.4
Stem	0	10.8	13.9	14.2	15.0
Leaves	0	9.1	9.6	9.9	12.4
Seed	0	14.3	43.4	62.3	78.7

Source: Wardi (1988)

3.3.3 Lead in maize

Sludge from Rungkut increased the Pb concentration in maize plants grown on regosol and ferralsol soils. Table 6 shows that sludge from Rungkut influenced the concentration of Pb in all parts of maize. Increasing the level of application of dry sludge increased the concentration of Pb in the plants. Accumulation of Pb occurred in the following order: seed > root > stem > leaf. Higher concentrations of Pb were found in plants grown on regosols compared to those grown on ferralsols.

3.3.4 Mercury in tomato

Rungkut dry sludge increased the concentration of Hg in the tomato fruits. Table 7 shows that with increasing rate of sludge application the concentration of Hg in fruits of tomato also increased. The increase depended on the soil type. Accumulation of Hg in fruits of tomato was 0.07-2.50% on regosol, 0.01-0.74% on ferralsol and 0.02-0.035% on vertisol soils.

Table 7 *Effect of Rungkut Industrial Estate Area dry sludge on the concentration of Hg in tomato fruit (μg/kg)*

Type of soil	Rate of sludge application (ton/ha)					
	0	5	10	15	20	Average
Regosol	52.1	289	517	783	1019	532
Ferralsol	15.3	370	483	517	547	386
Vertisol	66.0	102	150	238	392	184
Average	44.4	254	383	512	642	

Source: Ashari (1991)

3.4 Effects of soil type

Soil type influences the concentration of heavy metal in crops. With each pot lacking a leaching system, it was observed that in light soils (regosol) the concentration of heavy metal in crops was higher than in heavy clay soils (vertisol). Soils with clay texture have a high cation exchange capacity (CEC), and a high metal absorption capacity, increasing the ability of the soil to adsorb heavy metals and reducing the uptake of heavy metals by plants.

According to Driesbach (1975) the maximum limit for Pb in food is 2.56 mg/kg, Hg (alkyl mercury compounds) 0.5 mg/kg, Ni-carbonyl 0.001 mg/kg. In the experiment, the concentration of heavy metal in the edible parts of some crops were generally lower than the critical threshold for toxicity, but were higher in some cases.

From the above discussions it can be concluded that

1. Dry sludge from Rungkut Industrial Estate area has value as an organic fertilizer for some crops; increasing the level of application of sludge increased crop growth.
2. Application of the sludge increased the concentration of heavy metals in crops. The concentration of the heavy metal depended on the kind of crop, and crop physiology. Concentrations of heavy metals in edible parts of some crops were higher than the maximum permissible limit.
3. The type of soil had a significant effect on the concentration of heavy metals in crop. Pot experiments have shown that sandy soil results in higher concen-

tration of heavy metals than clay soil, while metal concentrations are higher in acidic soils compared to alkaline soils.

4.   References

Adinugroho, V. (1991) *Effect of TSP and Lime on Uptake of Lead (Pb) by Tomato (*Lycopersicum esculentum *Mill.) on Oxic Dystropept Fertilized by Dry Sludge of Rungkut Industrial Estate Area, Surabaya*, Thesis, Faculty of Agriculture, Gadjah Mada University, Yogyakarta (in Indonesian).

Arinto, E.A. (1988) *Rungkut Industrial Estate Dry Sludge as Copper Source for Maize (*Zea mays *L.) on Regosol From Wonosobo*, Thesis, Faculty of Agriculture, Gadjah Mada University, Yogyakarta (in Indonesian).

Ashari, R. (1991) *Impact of Rungkut Industrial Estate Dry Sludge as N Source on Uptake and Distribution of Hg in Tomato* (Lycopersicum esculentum *Mill.) on Entisol, Inceptisol and Vertisol*, Thesis, Faculty of Agriculture, Gadjah Mada University, Yogyakarta (in Indonesian).

Driesbach, R.H. (1975) *Handbook of Poisoning. Prevention Diagnosis and Treatment*, 10th edition, Large Medical Publ. Los Altos, California.

Mulyadi, B. (1988) *Distribution of Nickel (Ni) in Plant's Organ of Peanut (Arachis hypogaea L.) on Oxisol Treated with Dry Sludge of Rungkut Industrial Estate, Surabaya*, Thesis, Faculty of Agriculture, Gadjah Mada University, Yogyakarta (in Indonesian).

Notohadiprawiro, T., Suryanto, Hidayat, M.S. & Asmara, A.A. (1991) The Fertilizer Value of Industrial Estate Sludge and Its Impact Usage on Environment, *Ilmu Pertanian* 4: 361-384.

Sadono, J. (1988) *Dry Sludge of Rungkut Industrial Estate Area as Source of Nitrogen and Its Side Effect for Supplying Zink of Peanut (Arachis hypogaea L.) on Regosol*, Thesis, Faculty of Agriculture, Gadjah Mada University, Yogyakarta (in Indonesian).

Santoso, N.B. (1991) *Effect of Rungkut Industrial Estate Sludge Organic Fertilizer on Uptake of Copper by Lettuce* (Lactuca sativa *L.) on Regosol and Vertisol*, Thesis, Faculty of Agriculture, Gadjah Mada University, Yogyakarta (in Indonesian).

Wardi (1987) *A Comparison of Lead (Pb) Distribution in Maize (*Zea mays *L.) on Regosol and Luvisol Fertilized by Dry Sludge from Rungkut Industrial Estate Area, Surabaya*, Thesis, Faculty of Agriculture, Gadjah Mada University, Yogyakarta (in Indonesian).

3.2

Growth performance of soybean on soils treated with metal based fungicides

M. MISHRA

Abstract

The use of copper oxychloride and mancozeb as fungicides for crop protection in Malwa (India) is thought to have undesirable effects on ecosystem components. To investigate the persistence potential of these two heavy metal based pesticides, since they do not degrade and tend to accumulate in soil and plant systems, effects were assessed employing the most nutritionally important crop, soybean. Pesticides were applied in doses corresponding to one half and two times the average (recommended) field rate. To quantify the likely morphological and biochemical variations under stress, plants were analyzed for growth response, photosynthetic pigment, protein content, quantitative estimation of heavy metals in different plant parts and microbial population by imposing a one week difference in the sowing period. As predicted, however, a dose corresponding to one half of the field rate did not produce drastic effects but double field rates produced detrimental effects. A one week difference and immediate rainfall could help to lessen accumulation of heavy metals in plants.

1. Introduction

Screening of research papers published in the last six years in India indicates the importance of heavy metal research but it further reveals that plant systems remained a low priority test organism with a narrow choice of just a few crop cultivars (Dubey & Mishra 1991). While trace metals play a vital role in the growth and development of plants, there are apprehensions regarding accumulation of these elements in soil and subsequent uptake by crops leasing to risk of toxicity. Intensive studies are therefore needed to evaluate and assess the potential hazard in a country with significant variations in agroclimatic conditions, such as India.

It has been established that in the three soils of Malwa *i.e.* Black Cotton Soil (BCS), Kshipra Alluvial Soil (KAS) and Ujjain Loam (UL), pesticide residues occur and show variations (Rao & Dubey 1980, Shrivastava & Dubey 1983, Sikka & Dubey 1984, Dubey *et al.* 1988, 1989). The available information on microorganisms and heavy metals is scanty and sketchy. The present research described below delineates the toxicity of the heavy metal based fungicides, copper oxy-chloride and mancozeb in block cotton soil planted with soybean.

2. Materials and methods

Two heavy metal based fungicides, copper oxychloride (copper chloride oxide containing 50% copper) and Dithane (Mancozeb 80%: zinc/manganese ethylene-bisthiocarbamate) were used. Black Cotton Soil (BCS) which covers 60% area of the Malwa region, a deep black in colour with rich organic matter and pH 7.8, was sampled from crop fields following Greaves et al. (1978), and soybean (*Glycine max* L., var. Punjab-1), the commonest cultivar was selected for assessment.

3. Experimental design

Earthenware pots were filled with 2 kg of well mixed, air dried and sieved BCS. Both pesticides were applied at Half Field Rate (1/2 FR) and Twice Field Rate (2 FR) to the soils directly using a sprayer. The field rate of copper oxychloride and mancozeb is 2-4 and 1.5-3 kg/ha respectively. Untreated soil kept in a pot served as a control. Two triplicate sets for each pesticide were made. Seeds were sown immediately after treatment in one set and after one week in the other set. Pots received a total of 380 mm natural rainfall. After 30 days of seed germination, the composite sample of three replicates was analyzed for the following parameters.

3.1 *Photosynthetic pigment* (Arnon 1949, Duxbury & Yentsch 1956)

100 mg of fresh leaf sample was cut into fine pieces and extracted with 80% acetone by grinding in a pestle mortar. The extract was centrifuged at 3000 rpm for 10 minutes. The supernatant was diluted to 10 mL of extracting solution (80% acetone) and OD was measured on a spectrophotometer at 480, 510, 645 and 663 nm. The pigment concentrations were calculated from the formula given by the authors.

3.2 *Protein content* (Lowry et al. 1951)

Freshly harvested 100 mg leaf tissue was crushed in 0.05 N NaOH and centrifuged at 3000 rpm for 15 minutes. The supernatant was collected and sediment was washed twice with 0.05 N NaOH. The total volume was made upto 10 mL. Of this 0.2 mL extract was taken and diluted with 1 mL of distilled water. To this was added 1.5 mL of 10% trichloroacetic acid so as to precipitate the protein fraction. The mixture was centrifuged after 30 minutes and the supernatant was discarded. The sediment was dissolved in 0.1 mL of 1 N NaOH. After 30 minutes, when the protein had dissolved, 1 mL of a carbonate copper solution (50 mL of 2.0% sodium carbonate + 1.0 mL 0.05% $CuSO_4 \cdot 5H_2O$) in 1% sodium tartrate was added, followed by addition of 1.0 mL of Folin reagent after 10 minutes. After 30 minutes the absorbance of blue color developed was read at 750 nm.

3.3   Quantitative estimation of heavy metals

Concentrations of copper (Cu) and manganese (Mn) were estimated for different plant parts. For digestion 1 g ground, dried plant tissue was placed in a beaker, 10 mL concentrated HNO_3 was added and allowed to stand overnight. This was then heated on a hot plate until the production of NO_2 fumes ceased. After cooling, 2-3 drops of 70% perchloric acid were added. The extract was allowed to concentrate to a small volume on the hot plate and 10 mL distilled water was added; the mixture was shaken well and filtered using Whatman filter paper No. 42 and diluted to 50 mL with distilled water. The amount of copper was measured at 324.7 nm and manganese at 279.5 nm, using an AAS 2380, Perkin Elmer.

3.4   Microbial population (Johnson & Curl 1972)

1 g of air-dried soil was placed in 99 mL of sterile water and the suspension was shaken for 15 minutes to ensure thorough dispersion of the soil. For fungi the soil suspension was diluted to 10^3 and for bacteria the dilution factor was 10^5. Of the diluted suspension, 1 mL was poured onto sterile petriplates containing a suitable melted medium i.e. peptone dextrose rose bengal agar (PDA) for fungi and soil extract agar (SEA) for bacteria. The plates were then incubated at $30° \pm 2°C$ and after 7 days the colonies were counted.

4.   Results and discussion

Since time of sowing, as well as pesticide persistence in soil, is critical to many production activities (Jadhav & Singh 1991) the present study was carried out by imposing one week difference in sowing i.e sowing immediately after treatment (sowing period A) and sowing after one week of pesticide application (sowing period B).

Following copper oxychloride application a significant difference was apparent from the results of root length, root nodule and protein content. Root length increased by 83% at double field rate (2 FR) which was nearly two times the length of plants of sowing period B, i.e. 60% and 48% respectively. However roots are the most sensitive parts and large amounts of copper always lead to complete inhibition (Blaschke 1977); the observed stimulation was perhaps due to the rainfall after treatment which resulted in leaching. Together with the presence of a lesser amount of copper, this induced growth.

The root nodules appeared to be the most affected parts of the plant. Sowing immediately after treatment resulted in a 17% reduction at half field rate (1/2 FR) whereas 2 FR suppressed nodulation by 50%. Several studies using soluble metal salts of Cd, Cu, Ni and Pb have demonstrated the toxic effects of these metals on nitrogenase activity and nodulation (Vigue *et al.* 1981). Heckman *et al.* (1987) reported that reduction in nodulation could occur as a result of metal toxicity to the microsymbiont *Bradyrhizobium* in soil.

Table 1 *Growth performance of soybean* (Glycine max *L., cv Punjab-1) in relation to pesticide application*

Parameters	Pesticide	Sowing					
		Immediately			After one week		
		Control	1/2 FR	2 FR	Control	1/2 FR	2 FR
Shoot length (cm)	C	22.70	23.70	23.80	23.00	20.20	20.00
	M	18.70	19.50	16.50	19.50	20.30	18.20
Root length (cm)	C	13.00	26.90	20.20	12.50	20.00	18.50
	M	17.60	26.00	19.40	21.00	22.50	18.00
Fresh weight (g)	C	3.20	3.50	2.70	3.20	5.70	2.80
	M	1.40	4.40	1.40	1.70	2.30	2.20
Number of nodules	C	12.00	10.00	6.00	11.00	19.00	10.00
	M	8.00	11.00	6.00	10.00	14.00	12.00
Total chorophyll (mg/g fr wt)	C	1.62	1.66	1.41	1.48	1.64	1.45
	M	1.33	1.75	1.21	1.53	1.86	1.31
Carotenoids (mg/g fr wt)	C	1.18	1.03	1.01	1.03	1.02	0.96
	M	0.85	1.03	0.85	1.02	1.20	0.87
Protein (mg/g fr wt)	C	9.73	8.53	8.06	9.76	9.83	9.21
	M	10.93	12.40	11.46	8.50	8.23	8.90

C = Copper Oxychloride, M = Mancozeb
1/2 FR = Half Field Rate
2 FR = Double Field Rate

In plants from sowing period B, a considerable increase (73%) at 1/2 FR was noted, but at 2 FR, the decrease was not large: 9.1%. Dubey *et al.* (1988) reviewed the stress of different agrochemicals on root nodules and suggested that nodules with their nitrogen fixing bacteria are sensitive to any stress and can serve as a good bioassay tools. Protein content was also affected with the greater reduction confined to the plants of sowing period A (Table 1).

Morphological and biochemical responses do not provide satisfactory evidence, but the quantitative estimation of copper from different parts of the plant illustrates the influence of time of sowing. Results indicated a lower copper concentration in all plant parts (root, shoot and leaf) in set B in comparison to the results for sowing immediately after treatment. The affinity of Cu^{2+} for organic matter may explain the lower copper concentration in plant tissues. Copper accumulated mostly in roots (92%) at 2 FR (Table 2).

Table 2 *Quantitative estimation of copper and manganese in different parts of the soybean* (Glycine max *L., cv Punjab-1) treated with copper oxychloride and mancozeb* (for abbreviations see the legend to Table 1)

Heavy metal (μg/g)	Plant parts	Sowing					
		Immediately			After one week		
		Control	1/2 FR	2 FR	Control	1/2 FR	2 FR
Copper (Cu)	Root	0.211	0.302	0.405	0.188	0.205	0.285
	Stem	0.064	0.093	0.120	0.059	0.069	0.079
	Leaf	0.066	0.091	0.113	0.072	0.081	0.101
Manganese (Mn)	Root	0.424	0.443	0.541	0.427	0.449	0.478
	Stem	0.374	0.394	0.448	0.378	0.436	0.579
	Leaf	0.475	0.543	0.610	0.441	0.457	0.612

Trace metals are well known to be adsorbed to soil surfaces in non-salt extractable forms (Miller *et al.* 1986). Hence toxicity for microorganisms due to greater persistence is not surprising. In the case of BCS, a soil rich in organic matter, it may be alarming because any compound which affects soil microorganisms will certainly influence soil fertility. The results revealed that apart from actinomycetes in both sowing periods (A & B) and treatments (1/2 FR and 2 FR) populations decreased more steeply in sowing period B, a removal of the metals by plants was not apparent. According to Domsch (1980) even a 90% fall in microflora activity may return back to normal in a period of 30 days, but a 43% reduction in fungi and 57% suppression in bacteria suggests that copper oxychloride is highly toxic and a period of 30 days is not sufficient for microflora to return back normal, at least in tropical farming conditions (Table 3). Another finding of interest is the return of normal population size in BCS and KAS soils under controlled conditions without plants (Mishra 1991). This suggests that the plant root exudates, dried leaf decay etc. may release substances which interact synergistically with copper to induce higher toxicity. According to Miller *et al.* (1987), the increased organic matter and manure additions provide conditions favorable for an increase in organically bound Fe - oxide occluded forms of copper.

Under conditions similar to those for copper oxychloride, mancozeb also responded quite similarly; a good performance was observed following lower applied doses while higher applied doses caused a reduction in most of the parameters (Table 1). The stimulation in growth parameters, photosynthetic pigment and protein might be due to the presence of Mn and Zn. Increases in fresh weight by 71% at 1/2 FR in plants of sowing period A were observed but delay in sowing just halved the weight (35%). Likewise, protein contents also increased. A report by Gettier *et al.* (1985) showed that a critical Mn level is required to prevent reduced yield. In fact, Mn is active in various photosynthetic activities, it is a constituent of several enzymes, and also regulates the oxidation of iron. Zn also plays a role in chlorophyll synthesis.

Table 3 *Microbial populations in soil treated with heavy metal based pesticides*
(for abbreviations see the legend to Table 1)

Parameters	Pesticide	Sowing					
		Immediately			After one week		
		Control	1/2 FR	2 FR	Control	1/2 FR	2 FR
Fungi	C	22	17	12	23	19	13
(g x 10³)	M	25	23	19	27	25	20
Bacteria	C	209	145	121	212	115	92
(g x 10³)	M	140	123	81	135	95	45
Actinomycetes	C	49	66	43	54	65	61
(g x 10³)	M	79	42	45	59	39	40

Following mancozeb treatment, the high dose appeared to be toxic; about 25% suppression in nodulation was recorded for sowing period A and 20% for sowing period B. This proved that the difference in sowing influences pesticide activity to some extent.

Results of a quantitative estimation of Mn indicated greater accumulation at 2 FR in all plant parts with higher accumulation in plants sown 7 days after mancozeb application. Shoots reached a maximum concentration of Mn (*i.e.* 53%) which was three times higher than found in shoots from sowing period A (20%) (Table 2). This difference is believed to arise from the fact that up to seven days mancozeb is subjected mainly to microorganisms which appear to play a major role in determining the soil levels of reduced Mn which is rapidly absorbed by plants; this is one of the major pathways by which toxic metals enter the food chain.

The microbial assessment of soils revealed that treatments induced a reduction in the total microbial population (Table 3). Bacteria and actinomycetes were found to be more responsive than fungi. Significant differences in the two sowing period are evident from the results for bacterial counts: at 2 FR the population declined by 42% in sowing period A and by 67% in period B (Table 3).

The data suggest that nodulation and microbial population changes provide good evidence of the toxicity of heavy metals present in the pesticides. It further establishes that the sowing time can influence the toxicity and growth performance of the crop in question. These findings are certainly important for tropical conditions since in many temperate situations the responses have been reported to be otherwise.

5.   Acknowledgements

I am grateful to the Head of the School of Studies in Botany, Vikram University, Ujjain (M.P) for laboratory facilities and to the University Grants Commission, New Delhi for financial support.

6.   References

Arnon, D.J (1949) Copper Enzyme in Isolated Chloroplast, *Plant Physio.* 24: 1-25.

Blaschke, H (1977) Influence of Increased Copper Supply on Root Growth of Some Cultivated Plants. Z. Acker-planzenbau 144, 222, 229, in: Nriagu, J.O. (ed.) *Copper in the Environment, Part I: Ecological Cycling,* John Wiley and Sons Inc., New York.

Domsch, K.H (1980) Interpretation and evaluation of data. J. 'Recommended Tests for Assessing the Side Effects of Pesticides on the Soil Microflora', ARC WRO *Technical Report* 59: 6-8.

Dubey, P.S., Mahendru, P. & Sikka, J. (1988) Agroecosystem Studies - Review of Research at Vikram University with Reference to Pesticides and Cultivar Response, *Progress in Ecology* X: 43-53, Symp. Adv. Crops Mon. Env. Today and Tomorrow's Printers and Publishers, New Delhi.

Dubey, P.S., Rao, M.V. & Shrotriya, L. (1989) Soil Pollution Studies at Vikram University - A Research Review, in: Mishra, P.C. (ed.) *Soil Pollution and Microorganisms,* Ashish Publ., New Delhi, pp. 255-265.

Dubey, P.S. & Mishra M. (1991) Review of Heavy Metal Research in India. Proc. 8th Int. Conf. Heavy Metals in the Environment, Edinburgh 16-20 Sept., 1991.

Duxbury, A.C. & Yentsch, C.S. (1956) Plankton Pigments Nomographs, *J. Marine Res.* 15: 92-101.

Gettier, S.W., Martens, D.C. & Donohue, S.J. (1985) Soybean Yield Response Prediction from Soil Test and Tissue Manganese Levels, *Agron. J.* 77: 63-67.

Greaves, M.P., Cooper, S.L., Davies, H.A., Marsh, J.A.P. & Wingfield, G.J. (1976) Methods of Analysis for Determining the Effect of Herbicide on Soil Microorganisms and Their Activities, ARC WRO *Tech. Report* 45: 1-55.

Heckman, J.R., Angle, J.S. & Chaney, R.L. (1987) Residual Effect of Sewage Sludge on Soybean. I - Accumulation of Heavy Metals, *J. Environ. Qual.* 16: 113-117.

Jadhav, S.N. & Singh, N.P. (1991) Influence of Sowing Date, Insect Pest Control Measure and Irrigation on Growth and Yield of Mustrad, *Agric. Univ.* 16: 183-186.

Johnson, L.F & Curl, E.A. (1972) *Methods for Research on the Ecology of Soil Borne Plant Pathogens,* Burgees Publishing Company, Minneapolis, Minnesota.

Lowry, O.H., Rosebrough, N.J., Farr, A.L. & Randell, R.S. (1951) Protein Measurement with the Folin Phenol Reagent, *J. Biol. Chem.* 193: 2655-2275.

Miller, W.P., Martens, D.C & Zelezny, L.W. (1986) Effect of Sequence of Extraction of Trace Metals from Soils, *Soil Sci. Soc. Am. J.* 50: 598-601.

Miller, W.P., Martens, D.C. & Zelezny, L.W. (1987) Short Term Transformations of Copper in Copper Amended Soils, *J. Environ. Qual.* 16: 176-180.

Mishra, M. (1991) *Evaluation of Toxicity of a Few Pesticides and Activity of Antidote,* Ph.D. Thesis, Vikram University, Ujjain (M.P) India.

Rao, A.N. & Dubey, P.S. (1980) Pollution of Agroecosystems-Assessment of a Few Herbicides for Their Pollution Potential with Special Reference to the Crop

Rotational Practices, *Progress in Ecol.* 4: 103-116, Today Tomorrow Publishers, New Delhi.

Shrivastava, A. & Dubey, P.S. (1983) Pigment and Nucleic Acid Response of Green Gram Varieties against Three Organophosphate Insecticides, *Pesticides* 27: 32-33.

Sikka, J. & Dubey. P.S (1984) Pesticides in Agroecosystems Herbicides and Wheat Cultivars (RNA response). Nat. Seminar on Environ. Management. EPCO, Bhopal, 101: 59.

Vigue, G.T., Pepper, I.L. & Bezdicek, D.F. (1981) The Effect of Cadmium on Nodulation and Nitrogen Fixation by Dry Bean, *J. Environ. Qual.* 10: 87-90.

3.3

Selection of aluminium-tolerant varieties from several pure lines generated by the hybridization of Dempo x Wilis soybean varieties

Sunarto

Abstract

One of the ways to meet the increased national need for soybeans is to extend the area under cultivation of this crop. Most of Indonesia's land outside Java belongs to the Red Yellow Podzolic soil type which has an aluminium toxicity problem. To overcome this problem we have to produce soybean varieties that can tolerate acid soil or aluminium toxicity. The experiments reported in this paper aimed at understanding the appearances of several pure lines generated from Dempo x Wilis cross-breeding compared with both parents at two levels of Al-saturation of Red-Yellow Podzolic soil and to obtain pure lines that tolerate Al-toxicity and have high yield capacity. This experiment used the split-plot design based on a completely randomized block design. The main plot was Al-saturation and the subplot was varieties of pure lines. There were 15 lines and 2 parental varieties i.e. Wilis and Dempo. The result showed that many lines appeared healthier compared to their parents. The pure lines, namely T_{33}, R_{22} and S_2, were very tolerant of acid soil and had a high yield under higher Al-toxicity conditions.

1. Introduction

Soybeans are a nutritious food, a 100 g of soybeans contains 35 g of protein, 18 g of carbohydrate, 8 g of water and 330 calories of energy (Rifai 1990). As the demand for and consumption of soybeans in Indonesia increases, more intensive farming methods and an extension of the area farmed becomes inevitable. In this way, Indonesia will most probably become self-sufficient in soybeans (Baharsjah 1990).

Extending soybean production to areas outside Java is a very good alternative. However, most of the land has a Red Yellow Podzolic Soil (ultisol). The ultisol outside Java covers over 43 million hectares (Mulyadi & Supraptoharjo 1975). It is not a good soil for crop production. This type of soil is acid, it has a very low mineral content, a high aluminium toxicity and a large population of nitrogen reducing bacteria. Fay *et al.* (1969) reported that aluminium toxicity damages the roots of the plant, so water and minerals cannot be absorbed efficiently. Wallace & Anderson (1984) also showed that aluminium inhibits the synthesis of DNA, so there is no cell development.

Acid soil, especially Al toxicity, can be overcome by liming or by using soybean varieties that are tolerant of aluminium. Cross-breeding between Wilis and Dempo varieties was done to find soybean varieties that are tolerant of acid soil and aluminium. Wilis was chosen as a parent because it has a high yield capacity and Dempo x Wilis cross-breeds are superior in agronomic characteristics and may develop as Al tolerant varieties (Sunarto 1989).

2.   Materials and methods

The experiment was conducted on the acid soil of Gunung Tugel, Purwokerto, at about 125 m above sea level on a Red Yellow Podzolic soil (ultisol). It lasted from November 1990 until June 1991.

A completely randomized block design was used in this experiment. The main plot was Al-saturation namely: Al-saturation 5% (Al1) and Al-saturation 25% (Al2). The sub-plot was varieties/lines of soybean. There were 15 lines and two parental varieties (V_1 ... V_{17}), so there were 34 treatment combinations. NPK basalt fertilizer was applied at dosages of 50 kg of urea, 100 kg of TSP, and 50 kg of KCl per hectare, and the plant spacing was 40 cm x 15 cm.

3.   Results and discussion

Measurements on plant characteristics for the two soil types are shown in Table 1. It shows that Al toxicity significantly affects the number of leaves, the fresh biomass and the number of pods per plant, but it does not affect other variables. The number of leaves, the fresh biomass and the number of pods of the plants grown in high Al-saturation soil are smaller than those grown in the low Al-saturation soil. The results show that Al toxicity reduces the three variables mentioned earlier. This situation indicated that soils with an Al-saturation of 25% were toxic for soybean plants. In accordance with Da Silva (1976), the limit level for soybean stress by Al toxicity is 20% of the saturation value.

The table also shows that there are significant differences among varieties (lines) that have been evaluated for most variables except leaf width. Some pure lines are better than their parents for most variables especially seed weight per effective plot.

Table 2 shows that S_{33}, T_{22}, R_9, S_{33} and S_{14} are greatly stressed by Al toxicity. This is not the case for the other lines. The table also shows that in the soil with a high level of Al-saturation T_{33} gives the best yield, followed by R_{22} and S_4. Thus, T_{33}, R_{22} and S_4 are three lines that are very tolerant of aluminium, and T_{33} is significantly higher than Dempo. The yielding capacity of T_{33} is 2.3 t/ha. It is next highest to the Rinjani variety that is known to be tolerant of acid soil. The average yield of Rinjani is 5.7 t/ha (Manwan *et al.* 1990).

Table 1 *Mean biomass of vegetative and generative components of soybean varieties tested on soil with two different levels of aluminium saturation*

	Plant height (cm)	Number of leaves	Leaf area (cm²)	Wet weight (g)	Root weight (g)	Number of pods	Seed weight per plant (g)	Seed weight per effective plot (g)
25% Al-sat	56.1	48.3 y*	48.0	44.3 y	2.7	116.9 y	23.2	1249
5% Al-sat	62.7	62.9 x	48.7	60.5 x	3.0	159.7 x	32.9	1867
S_3	49.7 de	50.7 bcde	45.1	47.7 bcd	2.7 bcde	128.4 bcdef	24.7 cd	2034 ab
T_{22}	69.7 bc	58.1 abc	46.5	55.2 abcd	2.5 bcde	157.7 abcd	31.6 abc	1957 abc
T_4	74.9 ab	64.1 ab	49.3	58.0 abc	2.6 bcde	166.6 ab	31.9 abc	1657 bcd
R_{18}	53.5 d	50.0 bcde	45.0	49.5 bcd	2.9 bcde	142.1 abcdef	27.4 bcd	1462 cde
R_9	64.6 c	60.2 ab	50.2	48.3 bcd	2.5 bcde	125.9 cdef	27.7 bcd	1463 cde
T_{20}	39.4 f	44.5 cde	53.5	65.4 a	5.4 a	118.9 def	33.2 ab	1504 cde
S_{10}	79.0 a	70.7 a	46.5	52.5 abcd	2.1 e	151.8 abcde	26.7 bcd	1266 de
T_{32}	78.3 a	69.1 a	44.9	61.2 ab	2.9 bcde	168.9 a	31.5 abc	1227 de
T_{33}	78.3 a	68.0 a	51.0	61.7 ab	2.9 bcde	155.7 abcd	37.2 a	1925 abc
S_{22}	54.3 d	52.0 bcde	42.4	50.7 bcd	3.0 bcd	133.9 abcdef	27.6 bcd	1067 e
S_{24}	41.5 ef	42.2 de	46.8	46.4 cd	3.0 bcd	125.3 cdef	25.2 bcd	1360 de
S_{33}	47.7 def	55.7 abcd	46.7	55.7 abcd	3.3 b	158.4 abc	27.6 bcd	2216 a
R_{22}	45.5 def	40.2 e	50.2	49.5 bcd	3.1 bc	136.3 abcdef	26.7 bcd	1601 bcd
S_{14}	46.0 def	43.6 cde	46.8	43.3 d	2.8 bcde	113.1 ef	22.1 d	1251 de
S_4	78.2 a	63.4 ab	57.9	46.1 cd	2.2 de	127.0 cdef	22.9 d	1457 cde
Wilis	68.2 bc	56.4 abcd	54.2	59.9 abcd	2.7 bcde	134.6 abcdef	31.4 abc	1587 bcde
Dempo	62.8 d	56.8 abcd	45.5	42.9 d	2.4 cde	106.7 f	22.2 d	1453 cde

* Differences between two means in the same column followed by the same letter are not significant at the 5% level

Table 2 *Interaction between Al-saturation and soybean seed weight per effective plot*

Variety	5% Al-saturation	25% Al-saturation
S_3	2706 x*	1363 y
T_{22}	2473 x	1441 y
T_4	1835 x	1478 x
R_{18}	1741 x	1182 x
R_9	1904 x	1022 y
T_{20}	1718 x	1291 x
S_{10}	1490 x	1042 x
T_{32}	1428 x	1026 x
T_{33}	1993 x	1857 x
S_{22}	1277 x	857 x
S_{24}	1516 x	1205 x
S_{33}	3071 x	1361 y
R_{22}	1685 x	1571 x
S_{14}	1696 x	806 y
S_4	1409 x	1506 x
Wilis	1947 x	1228 x
Dempo	1846 x	1060 x

* Differences between two means in the same row followed by the same letter are not significant at the 5% level

Table 2 also shows that at a low level of Al-saturation (non-acid soil), S_{33} is the best, followed by S_3 and T_{22}. Thus S_{13}, S_3 and T_{22} are three high yield lines in non-acid soil. Their respective yields are S_{33} = 3.8 t/ha, S_3 = 3.4 t/ha and T_{22} = 3.1 t/ha.

Lines which have a high seed weight per effective plot such as T_{22}, T_{33}, and T_4, also have a high number of pods. This is in agreement with Rifai (1990) who stated that the number of pods and seed weight are closely related with a correlation coefficient of about 90%.

4. Conclusions

1. Soybean cultivars S_{33}, T_{22}, R_9, S_{33} and S_{14} are lines which are susceptible to aluminium toxicity.
2. Soybean cultivars T_{33}, R_{22} and S_4 are lines that are very tolerant of aluminium. The yielding capacity of T_{33} in acid soil (high level of Al-saturation) is 2.3 t/ha.

3. Cultivars S_{33}, S_3 and T_{22} although they are susceptible to Al, in a low level of Al-saturation, have very high-yielding capacity. Their yields are S_{33} = 3.8 t/ha, S_3 = 3.4 t/ha T_{22} = 3.1 t/ha.

This experiment was conducted on land that has conditions similar to the land outside Java. However, a multilocation trial over several seasons will be needed before the selected lines can be used for commercial production.

5.   References

Baharsjah, S. (1990) *The Production Efforts and Marketing of Soybean to Achieve the State of Self Sufficiency at the Era of National 'Take off'* (in Indonesian), Agricultural High School, Tanjungsari, West Java.

Da Silva, A.R. (1976) Application of Genetic Approach to Wheat Culture in Brazil, in: Wright, M.J. (ed.) *Plant Adaptation to Mineral Stress in Problem Soils*, Cornell University Press, New York.

Fay, C.D., Fleming, A.L. & Arminger, H.W. (1969) Aluminum Tolerance of Soybean Varieties in Relation to Calcium Nutrition, *Agron. J.* 61: 505-511.

Manwan, I., Sumarno, Karama, A.S. & Fagi, A.M. (1990) *Advance Soybean Production Technology* (in Indonesian), Center of Research and Development of Food Crops, Bogor.

Mulyadi & Supraptoharjo (1975) Data and Facts on Problem Soils. Symposium of Problem Soils Rehabilitation in Relation to Area Development, Jakarta.

Rifai, I.A. (1990) *Test of Fourth Generation of Cross-breeding between Dempo and Wilis Soybean Varieties*, Faculty of Agriculture, Jendral Soedirman University, Purwokerto.

Sunarto (1989) Dempo is a Tolerant to Acid Soil Soybean Variety, in: Sunarto, Sunaryo, C.H., Hidayat, P. & Hartanto, T.A.D. (eds.) *Proc. Seminar of Upland Management and Cultivation*, Jendral Soedirman University, Purwokerto, pp. 27-37.

Wallace, S.U. & Anderson, I.C. (1984) Aluminum Toxicity and DNA Synthesis in Wheat Roots, *Agron. J.* 76: 5-8.

3.4

Heavy metal contamination in Malaysian rice field snails

A. ISMAIL, H. WAHIDAH & J.H. ALI

Abstract

A study of heavy metal burden in fresh water snails from rice fields in Negeri Sembilan, Malaysia was carried out. The results indicate that the levels of heavy metals Pb, Cu, Zn and Cd are low and within the permissible limit of the Malaysian Food Regulation. The results can serve as background data for further reference. It is concluded that more study is needed to develop snails as bioindicators for heavy metals in Malaysia.

1. Introduction

Freshwater molluscs (snails and bivalves) have been used frequently as bioindicators for toxic chemicals. Reports on gastropods and molluscs that can be used as bioindicators for heavy metals contamination have been summarized by Elder & Collins (1991). However, studies on heavy metal contamination in gastropod molluscs in Malaysia are lacking. So far, some ecological studies on freshwater snails have been conducted in Malaysia (Berry 1963, Tweedie 1974, Palmieri et al. 1978, Palmieri et al. 1980). Recently, we have concluded a thorough study of the biology and ecology of freshwater gastropods in Peninsular Malaysia. Since fresh water snails in Malaysia are widely distributed, even though some species are very localized depending on their microhabitats, the study of heavy metals in snails is important for assessing their potential as bioindicators for heavy metal contamination and to provide background data.

This paper presents the results of a preliminary study of heavy metal contamination in six species of freshwater snails collected from rice fields in Negeri Sembilan, Malaysia.

2. Study site

The sampling sites chosen were rice fields near Kuala Klawang in Jelebu District, Negeri Sembilan. Most of the rice fields in Negeri Sembilan are operated on a small scale. At the time of sampling, the paddies were about one month old.

The rice fields chosen were Kampung Larung, Kampung Sarin, Kampung Triang and Kampung Batu Serambai. All fields receive water from Batang Penar River (a tributary of Linggi River). The river water is considered free from any major metal pollution since there are no human activities upstream. Most industrial and other human activities are located on Linggi River which is downstream of the Batang Penar river (Nather Khan 1990) The only possible source of contamination in the river due to anthropogenic activities are the fertilizers and pesticides used in the rice fields, domestic-derived pollutants and transport activities near the rice fields.

3.   Materials and methods

Six samples of sediment (top 5 cm) were collected at random from each site in the rice fields using a plastic spade. Samples were then air-dried in the laboratory. About 0.5 g of the dried sample was digested in 10 mL of a mixture of concentrated nitric and perchloric acid (4:1 v/v) at 140°C. Samples of snails of equal size from each species were collected from rice fields and brought back to the laboratory where they were kept overnight to empty the digestive tract. Flesh of the snails was removed from the shell and digested as described for sediment. All equipments for sample handling were acid-washed and rinsed with double-distilled water to minimize external metal contamination. Heavy metals were analyzed using flame and flameless AAS (Model 1100B Perkin Elmer).

4.   Results and discussion

Table 1 shows the concentrations of heavy metals in sediment and various species of snails from rice fields. All metal concentration levels were within the range of other findings for the Linggi River basin (Nather Khan 1990) which are 35-135 μg/g for Zn, 33-92 μg/g for Pb and 13-74 μg/g for Cu. These levels are relatively low compared with those from North American and European rivers as reported by Nelson & Nather Khan (1985). No other data are available from similar habitats to compare our result with.

Our finding of high levels of heavy metals in sediments from the rice field areas cannot be attributed to environmental contamination until further analysis is done. Table 1 also shows higher levels of Zn and Pb in sediments collected from paddy fields compared to sediments collected from Malaysian National Parks which are assumed to be free from contamination. It is suggested that heavy metals in the paddy fields could be derived from the fertilizers and pesticides used. Agrochemicals are known to contain Zn, Cu, Pb and Cd.

Table 1 *Heavy metal contamination of sediments (µg/g dry weight) and flesh of freshwater snails (µg/g wet weight) from rice fields. Values expressed as means and range in brackets (n=6)*

	Metals			
	Pb	Cu	Cd	Zn
Sediment:				
This study	86.9 (61.9-97.8)	2.7 (2.4-2.9)	2.0 (1.9-2.4)	80.4 (55.4-107.7)
National parks (Ramlan *et al.* 1992)	54	13	2.2	10
Snails:				
Pila scutata	1.2 (0.1-1.3)	1.3 (1.1-1.4)	1.1 (0.7-1.6)	20.3 (9.8-42.8)
Filopaludina martensi	1.2 (0.7-1.4)	1.3 (0.7-1.7)	0.9 (0.4-1.1)	26.5 (11.5-37.9)
Melanoides tuberculata	0.9 (0.6-1.3)	1.0 (0.7-1.4)	1.2 (0.9-1.3)	13.6 (7.0-26.3)
Lymnaea rubiginosa	1.4 (1.1-1.7)	0.9 (0.6-1.1)	0.9 (0.7-1.3)	16.7 (10.0-28.6)
Indoplanorbis exustus	0.9 (0.7-1.3)	1.1 (0.5-1.6)	0.9 (0.7-1.2)	14.4 (12.3-18.7)
Physa acuta	1.2 (1.0-1.4)	0.8 (0.6-1.0)	0.9 (0.7-1.2)	23.8 (20.8-25.6)
Permissible limit	2.0	30	1.0	100

The values of heavy metal concentration in snails (Table 1) are below permissible limits as recommended by the Malaysian Food Act 1983 and the Malaysian Food Regulation 1985 (Amendments 1990). Since some of the snails like *Pila* and *Filopaludina* are eaten by people, the content of heavy metals should be compared with government guidelines. The snails tested appear safe for human consumption relative to government limits, however, further study on bioaccumulation is needed. Except for Cd, all metals analyzed are also within the levels for those found in fish caught in National Parks in Malaysia (Ramlan *et al.* 1992). Cadmium levels are however, at the upper range of the permissible limit, 1.0 µg/g. Since Cd is very toxic, its level at the upper range of the permissible limit is considered potentially hazardous.

The ability of snails to accumulate heavy metals indicates that they are tolerant to these elements. Earlier studies had shown that snails, especially adults, are tolerant to elevation of heavy metals such as Zn and Cu (Watton & Hawkes 1984, Munzinger & Guarducci 1988).

Since Malaysia is gearing up to become an industrialized country, these data could be used as background reference levels for some heavy metals in snails. Further study is, however, needed before being able to recommend snails as bioindicators for metal pollution in Malaysia.

5. References

Berry, A.J. (1963) An Introduction to the Nonmarine Molluscs of Malaya, *The Malayan Nature J.* 17: 1-17.

Elder, J.F. & Collins, J.J. (1991) Freshwater Molluscs as Indicator of Bioavailability and Toxicity of Metals in Surface Water Systems, *Environ. Contam. Toxicol.* 122: 37-79.

Munzinger, A. & Guardacci, M.L. (1988) The Effect of Low Zinc Concentrations on Some Demographic Parameters of *Biomphalaria glabrata* Say (Mollusca: Gastropoda), *Aquat. Toxicol.* 12: 51-62.

Nather Khan, I.S.A. (1990) The Mineralogy and Trace Element Constituents of Suspended Stream Sediments of the Linggi River Basin, Malaysia, *J. South East Asian Earth Sci.* 4: 133-139.

Nelson, B.W. & Nather Khan, I.S.A. (1985) *Trace Metals Sources in Two Malaysian Estuaries*, Geol. Soc. America (GSA), Boulder, Colorado.

Palmieri, M.D., Palmieri, J.R. & Sullivan, J.T. (1978) The Natural Diet of Three Malaysian Freshwater Pulmonate Snails, *The Malayan Nature J.* 31: 173-180.

Palmieri, M.D., Palmieri, J.R. & Sullivan, J.T. (1980) A Chemical Analysis of the Habitat of Nine Commonly Occurring Malaysian Freshwater Snails, *The Malayan Nature J.* 34: 39-45.

Ramlan, M.N., Ismail, A., Ahmad, I. & Badri, M.A. (1992) The Background Levels of Heavy Metals in Sediments and Fishes from the National Park, Malaysia, *Proc. 1st Symposium Natural Resources*, Kota Kinabalu, Sabah.

Tweedie, M.W.F. (1974) The Mollusca of the Malayan Limestone Hills, *The Malayan Nature J.* 2: 33-37.

Watton, A.J. & Hawkes, H.A. (1984) The Acute Toxicity of Ammonia and Copper to the Gastropod *Potamopyrgus jenkinsi*, *Environ. Pollut.* (Ser. A) 36: 17-30.

3.5

Lead content of vegetables grown in fields adjacent to highways in Java, Indonesia

S. Luwihana

Abstract

In Indonesia many vegetables are cultivated in fields adjacent to highways, where they are contaminated by exhaust gases from vehicles using leaded fuel (tetraethyl-lead). Tomatoes, Lycopersicon lycopersicum (L.) Karsten, representing a fruit crop, carrots, Daucus carota L., representing a root/tuber crop, and cabbage, Brassica oleracea L., representing a leaf crop were sampled at three locations in West, Central and East Java with traffic volumes of 12,000-16,000, less than 5,000 and 6,000-10,000 vehicles per 24 hours respectively. The distances of the sampling sites from the road axis were, respectively, 10, 25 and 55 metres. Vegetables were washed as commonly done before cooking prior to analysis of lead by using an Atomic Absorption Spectrophotometric method. The results showed that average lead contents for tomatoes, cabbage and carrots were 5.37, 4.90 and 4.83 mg/kg, respectively. In Indonesia, there is no information as yet regarding the threshold limit value of lead, but the permissible concentration of lead in the diet for a healthy individual in the United Kingdom (70 kg body weight, adult) is approximately 0.4 mg/kg. If this threshold limit value is assumed, from the regression equation it can be estimated that a distance of 253 meters from the roadside verge may be considered as safe for cultivation of vegetables, either in Central, East or in West Java.

1. Introduction

The toxicity of lead is well known, especially in relation to exposure of children. It is well established that acute or subacute ingestion of lead by children results in encephalopathy and convulsions, while chronic ingestion may cause mental retardation (Munro & Charbonneau 1981). Although acute lead poisoning is not a common phenomenon nowadays, subclinical lead toxicity due to long term exposure is still possible.

Lead is a naturally occurring trace element in plants and animals and low background levels are present in the biosphere. Many studies have recently been conducted on environmental emissions of tetraethyl-lead used as an anti-knock agent in gasoline. At the high operating temperatures of the internal combustion engine, the lead salts are volatilized and expelled with the exhaust gases.

In crop production areas of Java, vegetables are cultivated in fields adjacent to highways, where they are contaminated by exhaust gases from vehicles using leaded fuels.

The aim of this study was to assess the lead content of these vegetables, and ultimately to estimate the distance from the pollution source to cultivated crops, which may be considered safe for vegetable consumption.

2. Materials and methods

2.1 Sampling of vegetables

Vegetables consist commonly of three types: fruits, tubers/roots and leaves. Samples of tomatoes, *Lycopersicon lycopersicum* (L.) Karsten, carrots, *Daucus carota* L. and cabbage, *Brassica oleracea* L. were selected for this study to represent these three types, all types were sampled from West, Central and East Java.

Considering that the lead content of vegetables is mostly due to vehicle exhaust gases, vegetables were sampled from fields adjacent to three highways with a traffic volume of 12,000-16,000 vehicles/24 hours in West Java between Ciawi and Cianjur (JICA 1989), a normal traffic volume of less than 5,000 vehicles/24 hours in Central Java (Ambarawa-Bandungan), and a moderately traffic volume of 6,000-10,000 vehicles/24 hours in East Java (Batu-Selorejo). The traffic volume at the sites in Central and East Java were estimated locally by the author.

Sampling was carried out during June-September 1990, when there was no rain, thus avoiding the washing of the contaminant from the vegetables. Fortunately, in crop production areas, vegetables are grown all the year around.

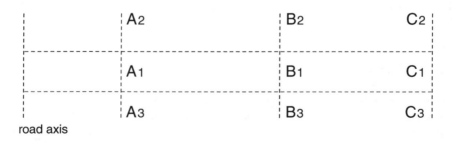

Figure 1 *Lay-out of the sampling points at 5 m (series A), 15 m (series B) and 55 m (series C) away from the road axis*

2.2 Pollution source distance

Sampling distances from the pollution source were chosen in fields that were part of an extensive vegetable-growing area; samples were taken at 10 m (A), 15 m (B) and 55 m (C) from the road axis. Three replicates of each distance were made at about 5 m on both sides of each central point, *i.e.* A, B and C (Figure 1).

2.3   Lead analysis

Samples of vegetables were washed as is commonly done before cooking, prior to analyzing the lead content using an Atomic Absorption Spectrophotometer (AAS) model Nippon Jarrel Ash. 782 in 3 replicates. Lead analysis was done according to Cantle (1982), with modifications as described below.

a. Ten g of each sample were dried in an oven at 60°C for 4 hours: thereafter the temperature was increased gradually to 105°C for 1-2 hours. The dried material was crushed, and 0.25 g was put into a teflon tube, to which 7.5 mL concentrated nitric acid and 2.5 mL concentrated perchloric acid were added; this was then put in a waterbath of 90°C for 3 hours. The digested samples were diluted with aquabidest until 100 mL, pH was 0.5.
b. To 20 mL of the diluted samples a amount of NaOH 3 N was added to increase the pH to 3. Thereafter 0.5 ml 2% APDC (ammonium pyrolidine dithiocarbamate) was added and the mixture was shaken for about 2 minutes. The mixture was extracted with 4 mL MIBK (methyl isobutyl ketone). About 2.5 mL of the supernatant of the MIBK extract was separated for the analysis of Pb by AAS. Both the APDC and MIBK are certified standard solution-free from traces of Pb. The results were calibrated using standard solutions of 0.01, 0.05, 0.1, 0.3 and 0.6 $\mu g/mL$.
c. Calculation of the Pb content of the vegetables was done as follows:

$$C = \frac{V \frac{Asp}{Ast} Cst}{W}$$

where
C   = Pb concentration in vegetable ($\mu g/g$)
V   = volume of the extract (mL)
Asp = absorption of the sample solution
Ast = absorption of standard solution
Cst = concentration of Pb in the standard ($\mu g/mL$)
W   = dissolved dried sample weight (g)

2.4   Analysis of data

Data processing was done by multiple comparisons of the means, in relation to traffic volume, type of vegetable and distance from the road, based on a randomized factorial design.

2.5 Safe distance for vegetable cultivation

There is no information as yet regarding the threshold limit value for lead content in food in Indonesia. Based on the maximum acceptable daily intake for a normal healthy individual in the United Kingdom (70 kg body weight, adult), the maximum permissible level in the diet is 0.4 mg/kg (The UK Ministry of Food 1954, Monier-Williams (nd) after Pearson 1970). A regression equation was fitted with $y = ax^2 + bx + c$; if y is set equal to 0.4, the distance of x can be evaluated.

3. Results and discussion

Results of the analyses are shown in Table 1. From a comparison of the three locations, it may be concluded that the higher the traffic volume, the higher the lead content in the vegetables. From a comparison of the vegetables, it may be seen that among the three types of vegetables, tomatoes have the highest lead content, while carrot have the lowest. As many lead compounds are not soluble in water, they can not be easily translocated from the root to other parts of the plant. The highest lead content of the tomatoes may be due to the direct contamination by lead deposited from the air. According to Casarett & Doull (1975), 50% of the contamination can be washed from the vegetables. According to a study by Sutardi & Sudarmanto (1991) of ten types of vegetables, including tomatoes and cabbage grown along a road between Yogyakarta and Solo in Central Java, the lead contents were decreased by 1-100% after washing.

Table 1 *The average lead content (mg/kg) of vegetables based on the locations and traffic volume (I), type of vegetable (II) and distance from pollution source (III)*

		Lead content (mg/kg)	Remark
I	*Location* (vehicles/24 hrs)		
	Central Java (< 5,000)	1.19[a]	lowest
	East Java (5,000-10,000)	5.91[b]	
	West Java (12,000-16,000)	7.99[c]	highest
II	*Vegetable*		
	Carrot (root)	4.83[k]	lowest
	Cabbage (leaf)	4.89[k]	
	Tomato (fruit)	5.36[l]	highest
III	*Distance from the road axis*		
	10 m	4.82[m]	lowest
	25 m	5.02[mn]	
	55 m	5.24[n]	highest

Note: values followed by the same superscript are not significantly different (p < 0.05)

The regression equation based on the results of lead content by multiple comparisons of main factors is $y = 4.651 + 0.0186 x - 0.00014 x^2$, where y = lead content (mg/kg) and x = distance from the road axis (m). From the equation, the maximum lead content of vegetables will be reached 66.40 m away from the road axis. If y is set equal to 0.4, then $x = 253$. Thus a distance of 253 m from the roadside edge may be considered as safe for the cultivation of vegetables.

In this study the influence of lead in the soil on the lead content of vegetables was not considered. According to Casarett & Doull (1975), the average soil lead content in general is 16 mg/kg; the lead content drastically decreased with increasing depth.

It is difficult to conclude whether the high level of lead content in tomato in this study can be considered as safe or not for consumption. The amount of lead absorbed by humans will depend on diet, state of health, and genetic make-up, as well as on other factors. The pathological effects and the doses required to cause poisoning are extremely varied and complex, depending on many factors that can modify the uptake of metal as well as those which control its subsequent metabolism.

4.   References

Cantle, J.E. (1982) *Atomic Absorption Spectrophotometry*, Elsevier Scientific Publishing Company, Amsterdam.

Casarett, L.J. & Doull, J. (1975) *The Basic Science of Poisons*, MacMillan Publ. Co. Inc., New York.

JICA (1989) *Official Methods of Analytical Study on Bogor-Bandung Road Project*, Interim Report (I), The Republic of Indonesia, Directorate General of Highway, Ministry of Public Works, Jakarta.

Munro, J.C. & Charbonneau, S.M. (1981) Environmental Contaminants, in: Roberts, H.P. (ed.) *Food Safety*.

Pearson, D. (1970) *The Chemical Analysis*, J. & A. Churchill, London.

Sutardi, H. & Sudarmanto (1991) *Study on Metal Lead (Pb) Pollution from Exhausted Gasses of Transportation Vehicles to Horticultural Commodities Cultivated around Highways (in Indonesian)*, Pusat Antar Universitas Pangan dan Gizi, UGM, Yogyakarta.

The United Kingdom Ministry of Food (1954) *Food Standards Committee Report on Lead*, London, H.M.S.O., pp. 1-11.

3.6

Effects of metals on the size of terrestrial isopods in an industrially polluted area

D.T. JONES & S.P. HOPKIN

Abstract

The effects of metals on field populations of the terrestrial isopod Porcellio scaber *have been investigated. Populations were sampled from six sites in the vicinity of a primary zinc, lead and cadmium smelter near Bristol, England, each with a different level of metal contamination. The head-width of individuals was measured and the size distribution at each site compared. The mean size of isopods was significantly smaller at sites close to the smelter in comparison with uncontaminated areas. At the more polluted sites no individuals were present in the larger size classes. The alteration in the size distribution was considered to be due to the combined effects of increased mortality and reduced growth rates.*

1. Introduction

Many natural stress factors can affect terrestrial isopods (woodlice) in the field. For example, Sutton (1968) found that growth rate and fecundity of *Trichoniscus pusillus* were severely reduced by drought conditions. The additional stress due to pollution may combine with natural stresses to lower an animal's performance and increase its probability of death (Hopkin 1990a). The cost of detoxifying high levels of metals in the diet, thus enabling an individual to survive, may be expensive in energetic terms. Such an animal would then have less resources available for growth or reproduction. Deleterious effects of metals on woodlice have been reviewed by Hopkin (1989).

To monitor the effects of metals on organisms it is necessary to identify parameters which show measurable alterations when exposed to differing levels of metals. Therefore, evidence is required of specific effects taking place within populations living in contaminated environments. This paper describes an investigation into the size of woodlice from different populations collected in an area affected to varying degrees by the release of metals from an industrial source.

2. Study area

The world's largest primary zinc, lead and cadmium smelter is located at Avonmouth on the Severn Estuary, South West England. Numerous studies have centred on this area as it is heavily polluted with metals (see Hopkin 1989). Severe disruptions have occurred to local ecosystems as result of the accumulation of particulate metals from the smelter. In woodlands within a few kilometres of the smelter the leaf litter contains concentrations of zinc, cadmium, lead and copper at least an order of magnitude higher than in similar but uncontaminated woodlands (Coughtrey *et al.* 1979). The standing crop of leaf litter at some of these polluted woodlands is considerably greater than at uncontaminated sites and represents the equivalent of approximately 25 years build-up of litter fall. Studies of the macro-invertebrate fauna have revealed the absence of two families of common millipedes, four species of earthworm and one woodlouse species, all of which occur in similar but uncontaminated neighbouring woodlands (Hopkin *et al.* 1985). The diapause of the commonest ground beetle is lost in the most heavily polluted woodlands, Read *et al.* (1987) suggesting this is due to low prey availability caused by the reduction in the abundance of micro-invertebrates.

3. Materials and methods

Six roadside grassland/scrub sites around Avonmouth (Figure 1) were sampled on the same day (13-6-1990). It was known from previous research (see Jones & Hopkin 1994) that, between them, these sites exhibit a wide range of levels of metals, including zinc, cadmium, lead and copper, in the surface soils, nettle leaves and invertebrates. The sites are numbered in ascending order of concentration of metals in nettle leaves collected at each site. At site 1 concentrations approach 'background' levels, while site 6 is the most polluted.

Porcellio scaber were sampled at each site by hand-searching under rocks and stones, and crevices in the substrate. All observed individuals of the species were collected. Woodlice from each site were stored separately at 5°C overnight, and then separated into males and females before measuring. Because of the difficulty of separating small non-gravid females from immatures, and since only male genitalia can be distinguished readily from immature pleopods, all immature animals were included in the female group.

The width of the head capsule was adopted as the most suitable measure of an individual's size. In woodlice the head capsule is a single rigid structure and is therefore a more reliable size parameter than body length, which can vary greatly depending on the degree of contraction of the body (Sutton 1968). Head-width was defined as the greatest width of the head in horizontal plane, when measured at the level of the eyes, and including the eyes.

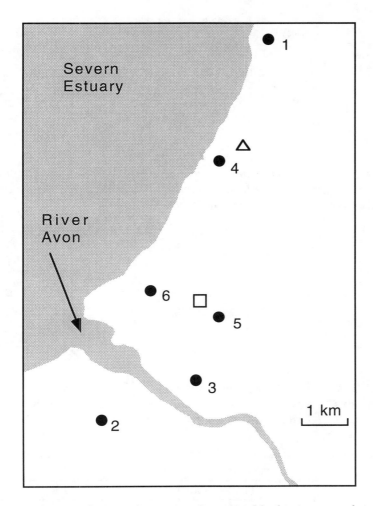

Figure 1 *Study area showing the six sampling sites (•), the Avonmouth smelting works (□), and the chemical factory (△)*

4.   Results

Head-width kite diagrams (size histograms with each class aligned centrally along a vertical axis) of male and female *Porcellio scaber* from each site are given in Figures 2 and 3 respectively. The number of individuals in each size class is shown as the percentage of the total number of males or females collected at that site. Mean and maximum head-width of each population are given in Table 1.

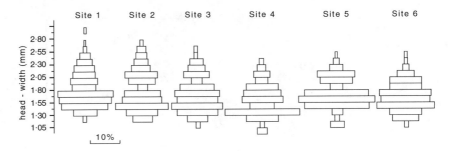

Figure 2 *Size (head-width, mm) distribution of male* Porcellio scaber *collected from the six sites shown in Figure 1. The number of individuals in each class is given as the percentage of the total number of males collected at each site*

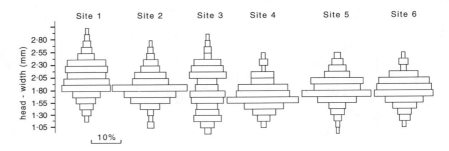

Figure 3 *Size (head-width, mm) distribution of female* Porcellio scaber *collected from the six sites shown in Figure 1. The number of individuals in each class is given as the percentage of the total number of females collected at each site*

Table 1 *Mean and maximum head-width of male and female* Porcellio scaber *collected from the six sites shown in Figure 1*

	Head-width (mm)					
	Site 1	Site 2	Site 3	Site 4	Site 5	Site 6
Males mean	1.80	1.75	1.71	1.57	1.72	1.66
(standard error)	(0.02)	(0.04)	(0.03)	(0.04)	(0.03)	(0.02)
Maximum	2.94	2.72	2.59	2.31	2.53	2.50
Females mean	2.03	1.85	1.79	1.69	1.83	1.80
(standard error)	(0.01)	(0.03)	(0.02)	(0.02)	(0.02)	(0.01)
Maximum	2.97	2.59	2.81	2.50	2.47	2.50
Number (male + female)	808	185	520	286	245	525

One-way ANOVA performed on the head-width of *P. scaber* gave a significant difference between the males (F = 6.91; df = 5, 728; p < 0.01) and the females

($F = 52.3$; df = 5, 1839; $p < 0.01$). Ranking the mean head-width from each site in descending order gives the following pattern:

Males: site $1_a > 2_{ab} > 5_{ab} > 3_{ab} > 6_b > 4$
Females: site $1 > 2_c > 5_c > 6_c > 3_c > 4$

The mean size of males or females is not significantly different ($p > 0.05$) at sites with the same subscript.

When considering the size range at each site, males at site 1 occupied five size classes beyond the upper size limit of the males at site 4, while males from the four largest classes which were represented at site 1 were absent at sites 5 and 6 (see Figure 2 and Table 1). Females from sites 4, 5 and 6 were not present in the four largest classes which were represented at site 1 (see Figure 3 and Table 1).

5.   Discussion

Differences have been observed in the size of woodlice from the study sites in the Avonmouth area. There is a significant reduction in the mean size of both male and female *P. scaber* between sites 1 and 4, as well as the absence of larger individuals from sites 4, 5 and 6. The order of decreasing mean size, and maximum size, recorded at the six sites is not entirely consistent with the order of increasing concentrations of metals in nettle leaves from those sites. However, the largest mean and maximum size occurs at the least contaminated site, whilst the populations with the smallest mean and maximum size occur at sites 4, 5 and 6, which are heavily polluted with metals. One possible cause for the smallest mean size occurring at site 4 is the presence of other pollutants. Site 4 is only 0.5 km from a chemical factory. Release of pollutants from this factory could accentuate the deleterious effects of the metals, however, there is no published data on any release of toxins from this factory.

The reduction in the mean size may be due to two factors:

1. a reduction in the rate of growth of individuals in the population, resulting in a lowering of the mean size;
2. if the rate of mortality increased with age then an increasing proportion of animals would be lost from the larger size classes, thereby causing a reduction in the mean size. If mortality increased rapidly enough it may eventually cause the elimination of all individuals in the top size classes, and thus, also bring about a reduction in the maximum size.

Hopkin (1990b) has shown that individual *P. scaber* with a concentration of zinc in the hepatopancreas exceeding 25 mg/g (equivalent to about 2500 μg/g in the whole body) become moribund and die. Early mortality was attributed to zinc toxicity caused by the detoxification capacity of the hepatopancreas being exceeded (Hopkin 1990a). The population of *P. scaber* at sites 5 and 6 contain individuals with levels of zinc above the critical concentration of 2500 $\mu g/g$ (Jones 1991). Therefore, at these two sites individual woodlice are dying as a result of metal toxicity (either directly or because they become moribund and therefore less able to avoid predation or desiccation).

This may partially account for the reduction in the number of larger animals, and the significant decline in mean size observed at sites 5 and 6. However, any effect of increased mortality upon mean size may be exacerbated by a reduction in growth rate. The work of Joosse *et al.* (1981, 1983) suggests that growth rates in *P. scaber* (measured as weight increase) can decline with increasing levels of zinc in the diet. A reduction in growth rate may not be a consequence of zinc toxicity, but simply a result of lower consumption by the animal because the food is less palatable due to the high metal content. Hopkin *et al.* (1985) recorded significantly lower rates of ingestion by the millipede *Glomeris marginata* when fed on highly contaminated leaf litter from the Avonmouth area.

We can conclude that the reduction in mean and maximum size is due, in part at least, to increased mortality. It is likely that some populations also experience a reduced growth rate. The high levels of metal pollution occuring in the vicinity of the Avonmouth smelter is having a detrimental effect upon the size of *P. scaber* and its population structure.

6. Acknowledgement

This research was conducted while DTJ was in receipt of SERC studentship. The authors would like to thenk NERC for grant support.

7. References

Coughtrey, P.J., Jones, C.H., Martin, M.H. & Shales, S.W. (1979) Litter Accumulation in Woodlands Contaminated by Pb, Zn, Cd and Cu, *Oecologia* 39: 51-60.

Hopkin, S.P. (1989) *Ecophysiology of Metals in Terrestrial Invertebrates*, Elsevier Applied Science, London.

Hopkin, S.P. (1990a) Critical Concentrations, Pathways of Detoxification and Cellular Ecotoxicology of Metals in Terrestrial Isopods, *Funct. Ecol.* 4: 321-327.

Hopkin, S.P. (1990b) Species-specific Differences in the Net Assimilation of Zn, Cd, Pb, Cu and Fe by the Terrestrial Isopods *Oniscus asellus* and *Porcellio scaber*, *J. Appl. Ecol.* 27: 460-474.

Hopkin, S.P., Watson, K., Martin, M.H. & Mould, M.L. (1985) The Assimilation of Heavy Metals by *Lithobius variegatus* and *Glomeris marginata* (Chilopoda; Diplopoda), *Bijdragen tot de Dierkunde* 55: 88-94.

Jones, D.T. (1991) *Biological Monitoring of Metal Polution in Terrestrial Ecosystems*, Ph.D. thesis (Unpublished), University of Reading, United Kingdom.

Jones, D.T. & Hopkin, S.P. (1994) Monitoring the Accumulation of Cadmium Released from Industrial Sources, in: Widianarko, B., Vink, K. & Van Straalen, N.M. (eds.)

Environmental Toxicology in South East Asia, VU University Press, Amsterdam, pp. 315-321.

Joosse, E.N.G., Van Capelleveen, H.E., Van Dalen, L.H. & Van Diggelen, J. (1983) Effects of Zinc, Iron and Manganese on Soil Arthropods Associated with Decomposition Processes, in: *Proc. Int. Conf. Heavy Metals in the Environment*, Vol. 1, pp. 467-470, Heidelberg, CEP Consultants, Edinburgh.

Joosse, E.N.G., Wulffraat, K.J. & Glas, H.P. (1981) Tolerance and Acclimation to Zinc of the Isopod *Porcellio scaber* Latr., in: *Int. Conf. Heavy Metals in the Environment*, pp. 425-428, Amsterdam, CEP Consultants, Edinburgh.

Read, H.D., Wheater, C.P. & Martin, M.H. (1987) Aspects of the Ecology of Carabidae (Coleoptera) from Woodlands Polluted by Heavy Metals, *Environ. Pollut.* 48: 61-76.

Sutton, S.L. (1968) The Population Dynamics of *Trichoniscus pusillus* and *Philoscia muscorum* (Crustacea, Oniscoidae) in Limestone Grassland, *J. Anim. Ecol.* 37: 425-444.

3.7

Arrhenius activation energy of three *Porcellio scaber* (Isopoda) populations: An evaluation of cadmium effects

B. WIDIANARKO, M.H. DONKER &
N.M. VAN STRAALEN

Abstract

Organisms living in cadmium contaminated sites are subjected to a selection pressure for resistance, if cadmium concentrations exceed the effect threshold of the organism. In this work a comparative study of three terrestrial isopod (Porcellio scaber) populations, from mine, smelter and reference areas, has been conducted by employing two types of food (cadmium contaminated and uncontaminated) and four levels of temperature (5°C, 14°C, 23°C and 32°C). In each condition the individual growth of the isopods, measured in body length, was fitted to the Von Bertallanffy growth model. The Arrhenius function was used to describe the temperature-growth rate relationship, from which the activation energy can be derived. The growth rate differentiations were observed among treatments (population, cadmium and temperature). Significant growth rate differences between populations detected at the reference temperature 17°C (290 K), i.e. smelter > reference > mine. The derivation and comparison of the activation energy can only be properly done using the Arrhenius (growth rate-temperature) relation, in uncontaminated conditions. In terms of activation energy, reference animals were observed to have a higher energetic barrier to grow than mine and smelter isopods.

1.   Introduction

The effects of cadmium as a toxic metal have been thoroughly studied in various biological systems. Organisms living in cadmium contaminated sites are subjected to a selective pressure for resistance, if cadmium exposure exceeds the effect threshold of the organism. Donker & Bogert (1991) showed that in terms of growth and food consumption, three populations (reference, mine, and smelter) of the isopod *Porcellio scaber* reacted differently to cadmium contaminated food. These differences could not be explained either by food assimilation or by the body cadmium content of the isopods. In an earlier study (Donker *et al.* 1990), it was reported that the distribution of metals (*i.e.* Cd, Cu and Zn) over protein fractions of haemolymph and hepatopancreas in three populations of *Porcellio scaber* were similar. From this evidence, it can be deduced that adaptation in the mine population is probably based on an increased detoxification capacity (Donker & Bogert 1991).

In the present work a comparative growth study on three isopod populations (reference, mine and smelter) was conducted, to understand the population differentiations in growth caused by adaptation to cadmium in their natural habitat. To have a more detailed picture of the growth process, four levels of temperature (5°C, 14°C, 23°C and 32°C) and two types of food treatments (uncontaminated and Cd contaminated) were used used in the experiment. It was expected that under metal stress the differences between populations would be more pronounced.

The first attempt to fit the growth data of individual *Porcellio scaber* to a growth equation (*i.e.* the logistic model) was made by Brereton, in 1957, cited in Hubbell (1971). Wieser (1965), using growth data for *Porcellio scaber*, measured by Matsakis, showed that the Von Bertallanffy model provided a better fit. Van der Hoeven (1989) also showed that the Von Bertallanffy model gives a good fit for surface area and body weight data of individual *Porcellio scaber*. In this study, we used body length data as a measure for growth.

The relationship between the rate of a particular biological process and temperature can be described by the Arrhenius relation, which was theoretically derived from Van't Hoff's theory of chemical reactions. The main reason for the preferred use of the Arrhenius relation is the theoretical framework developed by Arrhenius which assumes that biological processes behave kinetically as simple reactions and can be profitably interpreted as such. One of the parameters in the Arrhenius equation, T_A (Arrhenius temperature) has a biochemical interpretation; if we multiply this temperature by the gas constant R, we arrive at the so-called activation energy, which is specific for any chemical reaction (Kooijman 1988).

2. Materials and methods

2.1 Animals

Field animals collected from three sites were used in this work. The sampling of the animals was undertaken from the end of September until the middle of October 1990. The three sites were an ancient Roman zinc-lead mining area (Plombières, Belgium), a zinc smelter area (near Budel, the Netherlands), and a reference area (Spanderswoud, near Hilversum, the Netherlands). The isopods were collected under birch stands, birch and poplar stands, and poplar wood, at Plombières, Budel and Spanderswoud respectively. According to the list of site-specific metal concentrations presented by Van Straalen *et al.* (1987), the cadmium concentrations in the litter layer (A_0-A_{000} combined) were 0.525 μmol/g, 0.037 μmol/g and < 0.005 μmol/g on dry weight basis, for Plombières, Budel and Spanderswoud respectively.

In the laboratory all animals were kept in litter from their site of origin. Animals were maintained in terraria in a climate room with a temperature of 17°C and 80% relative humidity. The laboratory rearing period was about 3 months prior to the start of the experiment.

For the experiment, animals within a body weight range of 30 mg to 42 mg were selected. From these selected animals, 64 individuals were randomly chosen to represent each population, with a sex ratio of 1:3 (female:male).

2.2 Food

Food was prepared from dried ground poplar leaves supplemented with 20% DOKO (commercial dog food). Cadmium was added to the food as a $Cd(NO_3)_2$ solution. This mixture was dried and moistened again to contain 25% dry weight when it was offered to the isopods. The nominal Cd-concentration in contaminated food was 0.2 μmol/g dry weight. The concentration was chosen based on the result of previous work (Donker & Bogert 1991) from which growth differences of animals from three populations were observed. The actual concentrations after metal analysis, using acid digestion and AAS, were 0.333 μmol/g and 0.019 μmol/g in contaminated food and uncontaminated food respectively. The food was supplied to the animals in ad libitum level. Fresh food was offered twice a week with a new dish.

2.3 Experimental conditions

Four levels of temperature (5°C, 14°C, 23°C and 32°C) and two types of food (uncontaminated and Cd-contaminated) were used, making up eight treatments assigned to each population. In total 192 individuals were involved in this experiment, 8 replicate individuals from each population per treatment group.

One week prior to the experiment individual isopods were acclimatized in four incubators, according to the temperature levels described above. For all incubators the light/dark regime was 12/12 h. The air humidity in the incubators was 80%, 60%, 40% and 40% for the temperature treatments of 5°C, 14°C, 23°C and 32°C respectively. A thermo-hygrograph was placed in each incubator to record the temperature and the relative humidity.

Animals were kept individually in polystyrene boxes (diameter 5 cm), with a perforated lid. Each box was filled with purified sand, to approximately 1 cm depth. A moistened fired clay ball was put in the box, to provide a humid shelter for the isopod. Food was offered in polyethylene dishes (diameter = 9 mm, depth = 3 mm), containing approximately 100 mg fresh food. Pots were placed in plastic containers with the dimension of 33 cm x 33 cm x 14 cm (length x width x depth). Plain sand was put inside these containers to form a layer of about 1.5 cm depth. Twelve pots were placed randomly in each container. To maintain the humidity of the sand layer in pots and containers, water was added every 3 days. In addition wet filter paper was used to cover the containers.

2.4 Measurements

Individual isopod body length was regularly measured every 7 days for a period of 35 days. Body length was determined by measuring the photocopy image of an animal's body, using a stereo microscope, with a built-in micrometer. Length was taken as the distance between the end of the telson and the front of the head, excluding the antennas.

The actual concentrations of cadmium in the food were measured using a graphite furnace atomic absorption spectrophotometer (Perkin Elmer 3030), following the procedure described by Van Straalen & Van Wensem (1986).

2.5 Data analysis

Growth data of each treatment combination (population, temperature and cadmium contamination) measured in body length were fitted to the Von Bertallanffy growth equation (equation 1). It is assumed that the ultimate length of isopods will be independent of temperature but dependent on cadmium:

(1) $L_t = L_u - (L_u - L_b) e^{-\gamma t}$

where
L_t, L_u and L_b are length at time t, ultimate length and initial length respectively and γ is the Von Bertallanffy growth rate.

Growth rate-temperature relationships were expressed in Arrhenius plots for all populations (contaminated and uncontaminated food). The Arrhenius equation is given in equation (2).

(2)
$$\ln \gamma(T) = \ln \gamma_{290} + T_A \left[\frac{1}{290} - \frac{1}{T} \right]$$

with γ_{290} = growth rate at 290 K (17°C, reference) and T_A = the Arrhenius temperature.

Parameter estimates for equations (1) and (2) have been obtained using subroutines programmed in APL developed at the Department of Theoretical Biology, Vrije Universiteit, Amsterdam. To test differences between Arrhenius regression lines, a generalized likelihood ratio-test according to Mood et al. (1974) was performed (equation 3).

(3) $LR = 2 (\ln L_{H1} - \ln L_{H0})$

where LR = likelihood ratio statistic, $\ln L_{H1}$ and $\ln L_{H0}$ = natural logarithm of the maximum likelihood function under the alternative and the null hypothesis respectively.

The value of LR was compared to the tabulated value of the Chi-square distribution, with degrees of freedom equal to the difference in the number of parameters between the two compared models. An APL subroutine for this test has been developed by the authors.

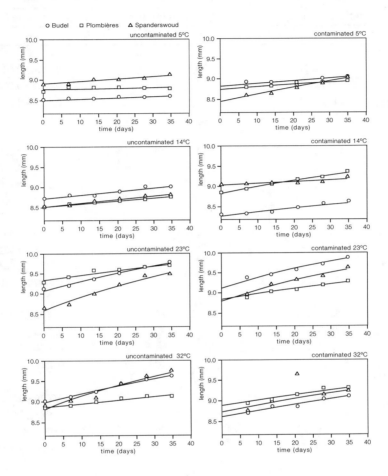

Figure 1 *Growth curves of isopods* (Porcellio scaber) *at four different experimental temperatures (5, 14, 23 and 32°C), exposed to clean food (left) and cadmium-contaminated food (right). Data are shown for isopods from three different populations: Budel (location close to zinc factory), Plombières (lead/zinc mine) and Spanderswoud (reference area). The lines represent the fitted Von Bertalanffy growth curves*

Table 1 *Parameter estimates for the Von Bertallanffy growth model (maximum likelihood point estimates with their standard errors). The ultimate length (L_u) was estimated for all temperatures jointly within a treatment group*

Group	Initial length (mm) L_b	Ultimate length (mm) L_u	Growth rate (day^{-1}) γ
SU			
5°C	8.51±0.019	10.86±0.81	0.0016±0.0007
14°C	8.73±0.019		0.0052±0.0022
23°C	9.10±0.022		0.0129±0.0073
32°C	9.00±0.021		0.0114±0.0060
PU			
5°C	8.77±0.021	11.18±0.16	0.0010±0.0004
14°C	8.53±0.021		0.0035±0.0004
23°C	9.35±0.021		0.0061±*
32°C	8.88±0.021		0.0036±0.0005
BU			
5°C	8.90±0.036	10.62±0.76	0.0043±0.0023
14°C	8.53±0.036		0.0055±0.0024
23°C	8.61±0.041		0.0164±0.0082
32°C	8.85±0.042		0.0182±0.0106
SC			
5°C	8.82±0.021	10.88±0.85	0.0030±0.0014
14°C	8.28±0.022		0.0036±0.0095
23°C	9.15±0.027		0.0150±0.0095
32°C	8.63±0.022		0.0066±0.0028
PC			
5°C	8.76±0.020	10.65±1.81	0.0026±0.0026
14°C	8.86±0.023		0.0085±0.0099
23°C	8.87±0.022		0.0071±0.0082
32°C	8.91±0.022		0.0072±0.0085
BC			
5°C	8.46±0.029	10.22±0.50	0.0103±0.0036
14°C	9.04±0.028		0.0032±0.0018
23°C	8.83±0.034		0.0219±0.0113
32°C	8.75±0.029		0.0116±0.0049

SU = Spanderswoud-Uncontaminated, PU = Plombières-Uncontaminated, BU = Budel-Uncontaminated, SC = Spanderswoud-Contaminated, PC = Plombières-Contaminated, BC = Budel-Contaminated; * = standard error could not be estimated (non-convergence iteration).

3. Results and discussion

3.1 Growth

The isopod body length data are well described by the Von Bertallanffy model (Figure 1). The variation expressed as the standard deviation of the estimates is low for initial length (L_b), and ultimate length (L_u), but relatively high for growth rate, γ (see Table 1).

The growth rate of uncontaminated animals from all populations increased with the increase of temperature from 5°C to 23°C, and then decreased at 32°C, except for the smelter animals which still increased upto 32°C. This growth enhancement may be due to the shortening of the intermoult period (Cossins & Bowler 1987, Nugedoda & Rainbow 1987). Cadmium seemed to disturb the temperature-induced growth enhancement in isopods.

In all treatments smelter animals demonstrated the highest growth rate, followed by the reference isopods. The mine isopods showed the lowest growth rate, except at 14°C on cadmium contaminated food; at this temperature the growth of mine isopods exceeded the growth of the other two populations.

In the mine animals, it seemed that cadmium increased the growth rate, but this was not the case for animals from other populations which had no clear pattern. Independent of cadmium, low temperature (5°C) reduced the growth of isopods with the exception of smelter animals which have a relatively high growth rate, particularly when cadmium is present in their food. This growth reduction may be caused by the inhibition of the neurosecretory system that controls the moulting process, which is rather common in crustaceans at low temperatures (Cossins & Bowler 1987).

3.2 Temperature responses

A trial to fit the Arrhenius equations for growth rates (body length) in the temperature range of 5°C to 32°C (278 to 305 K) for individuals of all populations either contaminated or not, resulted in bad fits, particularly in the presence of cadmium. The data indicated that as soon as cadmium is involved the Arrhenius equation can not properly describe the relationship between growth rate and temperature. This may infer that a conventional model such as the Arrhenius equation, which was intended to describe physiological responses under 'clean conditions', cannot be used directly under contaminated conditions. It seems that for uncontaminated isopods, the Arrhenius relation is only obeyed within the temperature range of 5°C to 23°C or 278 K to 296 K (see Figure 2).

Parameter estimates for the Arrhenius model depicted in Figure 2 are listed in Table 2. The reference population showed the best fit, followed by the mine and smelter populations respectively.

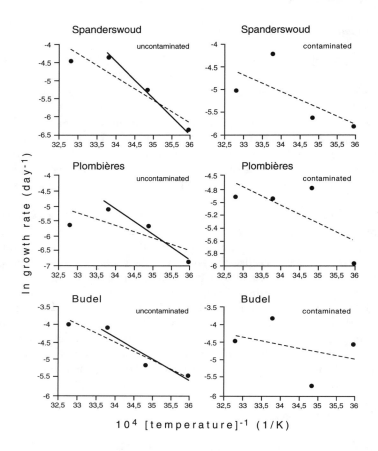

Figure 2 *Arrhenius plots showing the relationship between the Von Bertalanffy growth parameter for length increase and the inverse Kelvin temperature, for isopods cultured on clean food (left) and on cadmium-contaminated food (right). Data are shown for three different populations (see also legend to Figure 1). Dashed lines represent linear regressions for all data points; for the solid lines (left graphs only) the highest temperature has been deleted*

Table 2 *Parameter estimates for the Arrhenius equations (5°C to 23°C)*

No.	Group	T_A (K)	Activation energy (kJ/mol)	Growth rate at 17°C (day^{-1})
1	SU	9395 ± 282	78.146	0.0069 ± 0.00004
2	PU	8333 ± 927	69.306	0.0038 ± 0.00006
3	BU	6113 ± 1305	50.848	0.0093 ± 0.00026

SU: Spanderswoud-Uncontaminated, PU: Plombieres-Uncontaminated, BU: Budel-Uncontaminated; Activation Energy estimated from T_A and the gas constant per mole (R).

Based on the generalized likelihood ratio test, Arrhenius lines of the three populations are significantly different (Table 3). In terms of slope (T_A, the Arrhenius temperature), from which the activation energy is derived, animals from the reference population differ significantly from both mine and smelter populations, but there is no significant difference between mine and smelter animals.

Table 3 *Generalized likelihood ratio tests of Arrhenius equations fitted to different experimental groups*

No.	Group	Test	df	LR-statistic
1	SU vs PU	Invariance for both intercept and slope	2	12.41***
		Invariance for intercept	1	12.12***
		Invariance for slope	1	2.76*
2	SU vs BU	Invariance for both intercept and slope	2	8.42**
		Invariance for intercept	1	3.71*
		Invariance for slope	1	4.18*
3	PU vs BU	Invariance for both intercept and slope	2	13.17***
		Invariance for intercept	1	11.12***
		Invariance for slope	1	1.67[ns]

SU: Spanderswoud-Uncontaminated, PU: Plombieres-Uncontaminated, BU: Budel-Uncontaminated; df = degrees of freedom, LR-statistic = Likelihood Ratio Statistic, *** = significant with $p < 0.005$, ** = significant with $p < 0.025$, * = significant with $p < 0.100$, ns = not significant.

In terms of the activation energy, isopods from the reference population have the lowest intrinsic capability to grow, followed by animals from the mine population and the smelter population respectively. This evidence may be related to the life strategy of the populations in relation to the pollution history of their habitat. Smelter animals, which have experienced a shorter time span of pollution compared to mine animals, may be developing a high growth strategy when faced with heavy contamination. The mine population may already be well adapted due to the longer pollution history and so exhibit an intermediate growth capacity.

4. Acknowledgments

The authors are indebted to the Vrije Universiteit, Amsterdam for providing the first author with a Master degree fellowship which made it possible to conduct the experiments described here. Prof.Dr. S.A.L.M. Kooijman (Theoretical Biology, VU) laid the theoretical basis for this work and provided stimulation throughout. Dr. C. Zonneveld kindly helped with computer programming.

5. References

Cossins, A.R. & Bowler, K. (1987) *Temperature Biology of Animals*, Chapman & Hall, London.

Donker, M.H., Koevoets, P., Verkleij, J.A.C & Van Straalen, N.M. (1990) Metal Binding Compounds in Hepatopancreas and Haemolymph of *Porcellio scaber* (Isopoda) from Contaminated and Reference Areas, *Comp. Biochem. Physiol.* 97C: 119-126.

Donker, M.H. & Bogert, C.G. (1991) Adaptation to Cadmium in Three Populations of the Isopod *Porcellio scaber*, *Comp. Biochem. Physiol* 100C: 143-146.

Hubbel, S.P. (1971) Of Sowbugs and Systems: The Ecological Bioenergetics of a Terrestrial Isopods, in: Patten, B.C. (ed.) *Systems Analysis and Simulation in Ecology*, Vol. I, Academic Press, London, pp. 269-324.

Kooijman, S.A.L.M. (1988) The Von Bertallanffy Growth Rate as a Function of Physiological Parameters - A Comparative Analysis, in: Hallam, T.G., Gross, L.J. & Levin, S.A. (eds.) *Mathematical Ecology*, World Scientific Publisher, Singapore.

Mood, A.M., Graybill, F.A. & Boes, D.C. (1974) *Introduction to Theoretical Statistics*, McGraw Hill, Singapore.

Nugedoda, D. & Rainbow, P.S. (1987) The Effect of Temperature on Zinc Regulation by the Decapod Crustacean *Palaemon elegans* Rathke, *Ophelia* 27: 17-30.

Van der Hoeven, N. (1989) *Groei en overleving van afzonderlijk gehouden Porcellio scaber (Pissebed)*, TNO-rapport, Delft.

Van Straalen, N.M. & Van Wensem, J. (1986) Heavy Metal Content of Forest Litter Arthropods as Related to Body Size and Trophic Level, *Environ. Pollut.* (A) 42: 209-221.

Van Straalen, N.M., Burghouts, T.B.A., Doornhof, M.J., Groot, G.M., Janssen, M.P.M., Joosse, E.N.G., Van Meerendonk, J.H., Theeuwen, J.P.J.J., Verhoef, H.A. & Zoomer, H.R. (1987) Efficiency of Lead and Cadmium Excretion in Populations of *Orchesella cincta* (Collembola) from Various Contaminated Forest Soils, *J. Appl. Ecol.* 24: 953-968.

Wieser, W. (1965) Untersuchungen über die Ernährung und den Gesamtstoffwechsel von *Porcellio scaber* (Crustacea: Isopoda), *Pedobiologia* 5: 304-331.

3.8

Dietary intake of toxic trace elements from seafood consumption in Malaysia

S. Sarmani & A.A. Majid

Abstract

The daily dietary intake data of some toxic trace elements, arsenic, cadmium, lead, mercury, selenium and zinc, via fish consumption were estimated from the analysis of these elements in commercial sea fish normally consumed in large quantities by the general population. The concentrations of arsenic, mercury and selenium in fish muscle were determined by neutron activation analysis, while the concentrations of cadmium and lead were determined by anodic stripping voltametry. High intakes of arsenic and mercury were recorded. The levels were within the recommended daily intake (RDI) for lead, cadmium, selenium and zinc.

1.   Introduction

Elements such as arsenic, mercury, selenium, lead, cadmium and zinc have been given special attention in environmental monitoring studies, especially in biological organisms. These elements may accumulate in humans via food chains. Non-occupational groups are primarily exposed to environmental toxic elements via their diet. Fish have been reported to contain high amounts of toxic as well as essential elements compared to other food items.

Fishing is one of the most important industries in Malaysia, providing people with employment and supplying them with protein. In recent years industrialisation and urbanisation have encroached onto many coastal fishing villages, and have in many cases caused water pollution. As a result, coastal fish are being contaminated. Being a coastal state, fish and fish products supply about 75% of the protein requirements of the population in Malaysia. Although the average per capita consumption of fish is about 100 g/day/person, some population groups may consume five times more. Daily dietary intake of trace elements via fish consumption is therefore very significant. It is thus important to establish the daily dietary intake of essential as well as toxic elements from seafood. The aim of this study was to estimate the daily dietary intake of arsenic, mercury, selenium, lead, cadmium and zinc due to fish consumption.

2. Materials and methods

2.1 Sample preparation

Fish samples were bought from coastal fishermen at landing jetties along the west coast of the Malay Peninsula as shown in Figure 1. The samples were kept refrigerated and brought to the laboratory. The samples were then cleaned with distilled water. Only body muscle was used in the analysis. The cleaned samples were kept at -50°C and then dried in a freeze-dryer. Samples were then blended and homogenised in a clean blender with stainless stell blades. The homogenised samples were kept in plastic bottles for analysis.

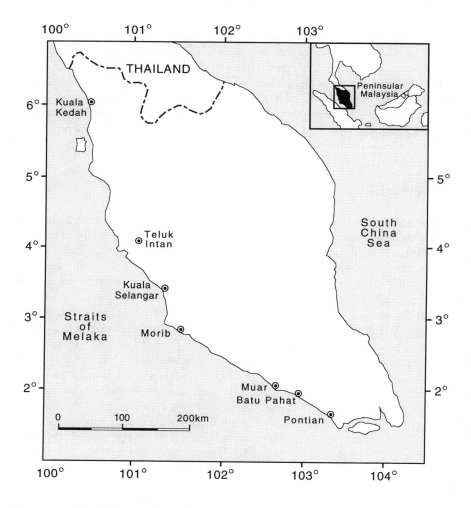

Figure 1 *Map of Peninsular Malaysia showing the location of sampling sites*

2.2 *Anodic stripping voltametry*

Lead and cadmium were analysed by anodic stripping voltametry as described by Sarmani *et al.* (1989). A sample of about 200 mg was placed in a platinum crucible and 10 mL concentrated nitric acid was added. The crucible was heated on a hot-plate to near dryness. About 10 mL of a solution of potassium nitrate and sodium nitrate was added and the crucible was then heated in a furnace at 400°C for 30 minutes. Then, a few drops of concentrated nitric acid were added and the cru-cible was heated until dry. Acetate buffer solution was added into the crucible to dissolve the sample which had become ash. The sample was transferred into a 25 mL volumetric flask, the pH was adjusted to 4 and the sample was made to vol-ume by adding buffer solution. The voltametric analysis was carried out on a Chemtronics Voltameter Model PDV 2000.

2.3 *Neutron activation analysis*

Arsenic, mercury, selenium and zinc were determined by neutron activation analysis. About 200 mg of each sample was put into a precleaned quartz vial. Standards were prepared from standard chemical solutions applied as drops to ashless filter paper and then packed into quartz vials. After drying samples and standard, both were irradiated for 8-36 hours at a neutron flux of 2.3 x 10^{12} n $cm^{-2}s^{-1}$.

The gamma ray activities of the samples were measured by a high resolution gamma spectrometer consisting of an ORTEC Hyper Pure Germanium detector with a resolution of 1.8 keV at 1322 keV and a relative efficiency of 20%. The detector was connected to an ORTEC 472A Spectroscopy Amplifier and a Nuclear Data ND66 Multichannel Analyser calibrated at 0.5 keV per channel. Peak identi-fication and quantitation were carried out by a dedicated PDP-11 Combus Com-puter connected to the system.

Arsenic was analysed using the 559.2 keV photopeak of As-76, while mercury was analysed via the 279.1 keV photopeak of Hg-203. Selenium was determined using the 279.6 keV photopeak of Se-75. Correction was made for the contribu-tion from the 279.1 keV of Hg-203. Zinc was determined using the 1115.4 keV photopeak of Zn-65.

3. Results and discussion

Accuracy and precision of the analytical techniques used were evaluated by ana-lysing MAA-2 fish muscle (IAEA) standard reference material. The accuracy and precision of the methods were found to be satisfactory.

In Malaysia the most popular sea foods consumed in large quantities by the general population are squid (*Loligo sp.*), shrimp (*Peneaus sp.*), Indian mackerel (*Rastrelliger kanagurata*), Spanish mackerel (*Scomberomorus commersoni*), and cockles (*Anadara sp.*). Table 1 provides the estimates for daily dietary intake of trace elements via fish consumption, for Malaysia and for other countries in the region. The estimates were based on previously published data (Sarmani *et al.* 1989, 1991), and the data for other countries were estimated from figures published in recent studies organised by the International Atomic Energy Agency (IAEA 1990).

Table 1 *Dietary intake of trace elements in µg/day/person*

Element	Malaysia	Australia	Indonesia	Japan	Thailand	China
As	90-400	2-15	24-180	185	664	55
Cd	5-50	13-42	8-40	1	15	43
Hg	5-40	4-29	2-7	14	20	12
Pb	3-30	4-10	4-61	19	no data	64
Se	40-120	22-78	9-220	56	74	95
Zn	40-2000	600-3500	176-718	460	1261	7970

The measured dietary intake of arsenic in the range of 90-400 µg per person per day in Malaysia is relatively high compared to other regions but is similar to Thailand. This is understandable, as the two countries consume fish from the same source (Malaysia imports fish from Thailand and vice versa). Some population groups in Malaysia which consumed five times the daily per capita value for fish may have ingested arsenic up to 2.5 mg/person/day. The high concentration of arsenic in fish may originate from terrestrial activities. Previous studies have shown that 50% of river water samples contained arsenic (As) in a concentration exceeding the prescribed standard of 0.44 mg/L (Anonymous 1990). Arsenic may also come from the weathering of peat soil (Pace & DiGiulio 1987); much of coastal Malaysia is covered with peat.

Selenium is an essential element, vital in human physiology for the synthesis of certain selenoenzymes and selenoproteins. It has been suggested that for healthy adults a daily intake of 50 to 200 µg Se represents a safe and adequate range (USFNB 1980). The average daily dietary intake of Se via fish was estimated to be 70 µg Se, which is still within the recommended daily intake. In Canada, the estimated daily dietary intake of Se was 95 µg with 46% derived from meat and eggs (McDowell *et al.* 1987), while in Japan 45% of the 56 µg intake was derived from fish and shellfish (IAEA 1990).

The daily dietary intake of mercury at 5-40 µg in Malaysia is rather high compared to figures from other countries in the region. In some cases the levels may exceed the tolerable recommended weekly intake (PTWI) set by WHO and FAO at 200 µg. About 75% of the mercury intake can be contributed by fish consumption. Mercury is mainly in the organic form and at very low concentration levels in most foodstuffs. The exceptions are fish and fish products, which are usually the dominant source of methylmercury in the diet (IAEA 1990).

The effects of methylmercury on the adult differ both qualitatively and quantitatively from the effects seen with prenatal and possibly early postnatal exposure. Clinical and epidemiological evidence indicates that prenatal life is more sensitive to the toxic effects of methylmercury than postnatal life. Recent epidemiological studies have shown effects on early childhood development and the mental ability of children whose mothers were exposed during pregnancy to 3-4 times the PTWI (IAEA 1991).

4.   Conclusions

This study has shown that seafood is a significant source of trace elements in Malaysian diets. Some of these toxic elements pose a potential health risk to consumers and further systematic evaluation and assessment of the exposure of selected population groups is needed. In particular, levels of potentially hazardous elements and chemical compounds, such as mercury and methyl mercury, need to be monitored.

5.   References

Anonymous (1990) *Malaysia, Environmental Quality Report*, Kuala Lumpur, 235 p.

IAEA (International Atomic Energy Agency) (1990) *Co-ordinated Research Programme on Nuclear Techniques for Toxic Elements in Foodstuffs*, NAHRES-3, Vienna, 1990.

IAEA (International Atomic Energy Agency) (1991) *Co-ordinated Research Programme on Assessment of Environmental Exposure to Mercury in Selected Human Populations as studied by Nuclear and Other Techniques*, NAHRES-7, Vienna, 1991.

McDowell, L.S., Giffen, P.R. & Chatt, A (1987) Determination of Selenium in Individual Food Items Using the Short-lived Nuclide Se-77m, *J. Radioanal. Nucl. Chem.* 110: 519-530.

Pace, C.B & DiGiulio, R.T. (1987) Lead Concentration in Soil, Sediment and Clam Samples from Pungo River Peatland Area of North Carolina, USA, *Env. Pollut.* 43: 301-311.

Sarmani, S., Ng, S.M., Wood, A.K. & Hamzah, Z. (1989) Analysis of As, Cd, Pb and Hg in Squid Muscle from Peninsular Malaysia, Paper presented at the 3rd Asian Chemical Congress, Brisbane, Australia, 28 August-2 September.

Sarmani, S., Wood, A.K., Hamzah, Z. & Majid, A.A. (1991) Analysis of Trace Toxic Elements in Seafood Samples by Neutron Activation, Paper presented at 8th Int. Conf. Modern Trends in Activation Analysis, Vienna, Austria, 16-20 September 1991.

USFNB (U.S. Food and Nutrition Board) (1980) *Recommended Dietary Allowances*, National Academy of Sciences, Washington, D.C.

3.9

Mercury binding to the plasma membrane of rat erythrocytes

S. Bose, S. Chaudhury, P. Ghosh, S. Ghosh &
S. Bhattacharya

Abstract

Mercury poisoning in mammals has assumed great importance as a result of rapid industrialization. In the case of any xenobiotic stress, blood is one of the vital tissues to show immediate effects, as yet there are only fragmentary reports on any heavy metal binding to erythrocyte membranes. The present study attempts to see if there is any significant binding of inorganic mercury to rat erythrocyte membranes. Binding data demonstrate that even at a concentration of 3.02 μmol Hg per incubation the pellet does not reach maximum saturation and Scatchard analysis indicates cooperative binding of the ligand to the membrane. It may be suggested from the present experiments that there are multiple binding sites for mercury in the plasma membrane and secondly, in the presence of cadmium non-specific binding of mercury is further enhanced.

1.   Introduction

Mercury, one of the most hazardous environmental contaminants is known to cause severe damage to living systems. The cytotoxic effect of mercury is well known; it includes cytoskeletal perturbation (Imura *et al.* 1980), DNA breakage (Cantoni *et al.* 1984) and mitochondrial dysfunction (Southard *et al.* 1974). Although the basic intrinsic mechanism involved in the mercury-mediated biochemical responses is not well known, the role of the plasma membrane in transducing the signal raised through biochemical alteration due to mercury binding can not be ignored. The Hg-sensitive thiol groups involved in various types of membrane transport systems are located at the inner surface of the membrane or at least are not readily accessible from the outside, *e.g.* neuronal Na-K-ATPase: Patzelt-Wenczler *et al.* (1975), renal sodium transport: Ullrich *et al.* (1973), erythrocyte nucleoside transport: Tse *et al.* (1985).

In the present investigation an attempt has been made to study the binding pattern of mercury to rat erythrocyte plasma membrane. Erythrocyte ghosts were used as a model, which can be treated as a primary tool in evaluating the mercury mediated alterations of biochemical processes.

2. Materials and methods

2.1 Animals

Male Sprague-Dawley rats (100 ± 10 g body weight) were purchased from an animal breeding centre at Calcutta, India. They were acclimatized for at least 10 days before the experiments in an air-conditioned animal house. Water and food were made available to them *ad libitum*.

2.2 Chemicals

Sucrose, bovine serum albumin, bovine γ-globulin and polyethylene glycol (PEG) used were of analytical grade. [^{203}Hg] mercuric nitrate (specific activity 15 GBq/g) was supplied by Bhabha Atomic Research Centre, Bombay, India.

2.3 Erythrocyte ghost preparation

The blood was collected in a heparinized syringe directly from the heart of anaesthetized rats. The ghost membranes were prepared following the method of Steck & Kant (1974). The protein contents of the membrane was measured according to the method of Lowry *et al.* (1951).

2.4 Membrane binding assay of mercury

The method for mercury binding assay was based on the principle of protein-ligand interaction in which conditions of binding were standardized with respect to membrane protein and mercury (hot versus cold) concentration. The incubation medium for the present study contained 5 mM $MgCl_2$, 0.1 M sucrose, 0.1% BSA in 0.01 M phosphate buffer (pH 8.0) in a final volume of 700 μL. Two mg of erythrocyte membrane protein was incubated with different concentrations of hot mercury in the absence (total binding) or presence of 1000 fold excess of cold mercury or cadmium to measure non-specific binding. The tubes were incubated at 30°C for 2 h in a shaking water bath; incubation was terminated by the addition of 1 mL ice-cold washing medium containing 0.1% bovine γ-globulin and 0.1 M NaCl dissolved in 0.01 M phosphate buffer pH 8.0. The tubes were stirred thoroughly and 1 mL of 20% PEG (w/v) was added to each tube under ice followed by another thorough stirring. The tubes were then allowed to stand on ice for 20 minutes and subsequently centrifuged at 10,000 rpm for 10 minutes. The supernatant was discarded by careful aspiration. The pellet was resuspended in 1 mL of ice-cold washing medium followed by the addition of 1 ml of 20% PEG. The tubes were centrifuged as above and the supernatant was aspirated out. The radioactivity of the pellet was measured in a gamma counter (1282 Compu Gamma Cs, LKB Wallac) having 20% efficiency for mercury. Specific binding was calculated by substracting non-specific binding from total binding.

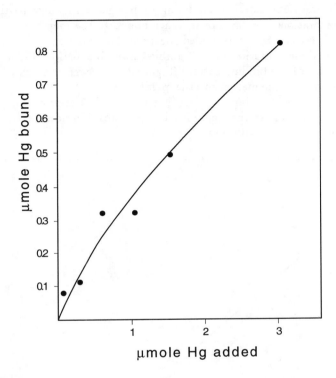

Figure 1 *Binding profile of inorganic mercury to rat erythrocyte membrane*

Table 1 *Binding characteristics of Hg to rat erythrocyte plasma membrane in the presence of 1000 fold excess cadmium*

[203]Hg added (μM)	[203]Hg bound (μM)	
	Total binding	Non-specific binding
0.85	0.285	0.40
1.42	0.257	1.24
2.42	0.410	2.24
3.42	0.599	2.29
4.14	0.585	3.22
5.28	1.990	4.39

3. Results

The present study demonstrated a binding of inorganic mercury to the ghost membrane preparation. The level of mercury bound to the membrane increased with increasing concentration of added mercury, but did not reach maximum saturation upto a concentration of 3.02 μmole Hg per incubation (Figure 1). The Scatchard analysis of the binding pattern (Figure 2), however, is as expected for a cooperative binding of the mercury to the membrane.

Table 1 shows the ^{203}Hg-binding data in a 1:1000 fold excess cadmium in the incubation. It clearly shows that there is a linear increase in non-specific binding of ^{203}Hg in the presence of cadmium.

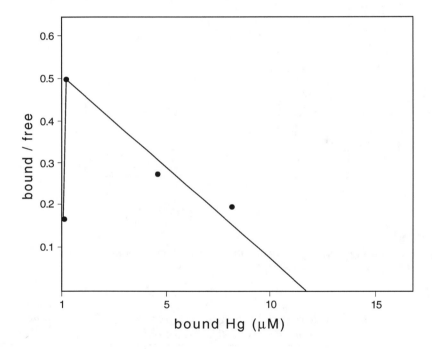

Figure 2 *Scatchard analysis of mercury binding to erythrocyte membrane*

4. Discussion

In biological systems, heavy metals are capable of binding to ligands containing O, N and S donor atoms. Based on stability constants of metal complexes, preferred metal ion binding sites can be identified (Denizeau *et al.* 1990). Mercury is known to bind avidly with -SH containing biomolecules and high sulphur binding strength of mercury has been observed in a metal cytotoxicity study (Denizeau *et al.* 1990). The involvement of -SH groups may explain the high binding capacity of mercury to the membrane. It may be suggested from the present investigations that there are multiple binding sites for mercury, functioning in a cooperative manner and secondly, in the presence of cadmium the non-specific binding of mercury is further enhanced.

5.   Acknowledgments

S. Bose is grateful to the Department of Atomic Energy, Bombay for a Dr. K.S. Krishnan Fellowship. S. Chaudhury, P. Ghosh and S. Ghosh gratefully acknowledge CSIR, New Delhi for a Pool Officership and Senior Research Fellowship respectively. S. Bhattacharya is thankful to Visva-Bharati University for financial assistance. The authors also gratefully acknowledge Mr. A.K. Majumder for typing the manuscript.

6.   References

Cantoni, O., Christie, N.T., Swann, A., Drath, D.B. & Costa, M (1984) Mechanism of HgCl$_2$ Cytotoxicity in Cultured Mammalian Cells, *Molec. Pharmacol.* 26: 360-368.

Denizeau, F., Marion, M., Chtaib, M. & Schmit, J.P. (1990) Toxicity of Heavy Metals in Cultured Hepatocytes, *Environ. Toxicol. Chem.* 9: 737-743.

Imura, N., Miura, K., Inokawa, M. & Nakada, S (1980) Mechanisms of Methylmercury Cytotoxicity: By Biochemical and Morphological Experiments Using Cultured Cells, *Toxicology* 17: 241-254.

Lowry, O.H., Rosebrough, N.J., Farr, A.L. & Randall, R.J. (1951) Protein Measurement with Folin Phenol Reagent, *J. Biol. Chem.* 193: 265-275.

Patzelt-Wenczler, R., Pauls, H., Erdmann, E. & Schoner, W. (1975) Evidences for a Sulfhydryl Group in the ATP-binding Site of (Na$^+$ + K$^+$)-activated ATPase, *Eur. J. Biochem.* 53: 301-311.

Southard, J., Nitisewojo, P. & Green, D.E. (1974) Mercurial Toxicity and the Perturbation of the Mitochondrial Control System, *Fed. Proc.* 33: 2147-2153.

Steck, T.L. & Kant, J.A. (1974) Preparation of Impermeable Ghosts and Inside-out Vesicles from Human Erythrocyte Membranes, in: Fleischer, S. & Packer, L. (eds.) *Methods in Enzymology*, Vol. 31, Academic Press, New York, pp. 172-180.

Tse, C.M., Wu, J.S.R. & Young, J.D. (1985) Evidence for the Asymmetrical Binding of p-Chloromercuriphenyl Sulfonate to the Human Erythrocyte Nucleoside Transporter, *Biochem. Biophys. Acta.* 818: 316-324.

Ullrich, K.J., Fasold, H., Klöss, S., Rumrich, G., Satzer, M., Sato, K., Simon, B. & De Vries, J.X. (1973) Effect of SH-, NH$_2$- and COOH-site Group Reagents on the Transport Processes in the Proximal Convolution of the Rat Kidney, *Pflüger's Arch.* 344: 51-68.

Part 4

Toxicity tests

4.1

A laboratory method to test side-effects of pesticides on tropical litter decomposition

K. VINK

Abstract

A laboratory method was developed to measure side-effects of pesticides on the decomposition of leaf litter and non-target saprotrophic invertebrates. The litter used in this research was Pinus mercusii *needles and a mixture of carrot, cabbage and bean leaves obtained as left-overs from agricultural fields. The decomposition process was simulated in micro-ecosystems in which the isopod* Porcellio scaber *was used as a representative of the soil fauna in forest floors and compost heaps. Pesticides are commonly used in agriculture to protect crops against pest organisms, residues of the pesticides used may have an effect on the decomposition process or on the soil fauna species involved. The aim of this research was the implementation of a method in which side-effects of pesticides can be studied on the components of or interactions between components of an ecosystem, and on processes which are important for the system in general, with special attention to the decomposition process. CO_2 production and changes in soluble nutrient concentrations were used as decomposition parameters. The CO_2 produced in the micro-ecosystem was measured using the KOH method, while soluble ammonium and nitrate were measured using colorimetric methods. The results of the presented experiments illustrate that the microcosms are a useful tool to evaluate several types of treatments. In the system it is possible (a) to separate the CO_2 produced by microorganisms and CO_2 produced by* P. scaber, *and (b) to measure an effect of microbial inoculation on CO_2 production and nitrogen mineralization. By comparing the results for the two litter types it was concluded that the efficiency of the system and its sensitivity to effects of treatments will depend on the type of litter used.*

1. Introduction

To investigate the effects of pollutants on ecosystems, interaction between organisms have to be taken into account, as well as effects on processes such as decomposition and mineralization, Moreover, it is necessary to have efficient, practical, reproducible and easy to use systems for assessing effects.

Microcosms and mesocosms are often used in aquatic ecology and ecotoxicology when testing for effects of pesticides (Kersting 1991, Liber *et al.* 1992, Webber *et al.* 1992). These systems are also beginning to be more commonly used in terrestrial ecology, for example, in decomposition research (Baath *et al.* 1981, Buldgen 1982, Taylor & Parkinson 1987a, 1987b) and also in ecotoxicological research (Gillet 1988, Van Wensem 1989). In this last field it seems to be a promising approach to validate environmental quality standards in relation to single species tests. Microcosms allow the researcher to observe processes or interactions between the components of an ecosystem, and this is why they are appropriate for ecotoxicological (and ecological) research (Levin *et al.* 1989).

For terrestrial ecosystems decomposition is often studied by using microcosms (Baath *et al.* 1978, Taylor & Parkinson 1987b, Taylor *et al.* 1989). It is an important process because it leads to the release of nutrients bound in dead organic matter. Since microflora is very important for decomposition in the tropics (Swift *et al.* 1979) CO_2 production is an important parameter and it can be measured using several methods (Macfadyen 1970). The decomposition process is a complex of reactions by which dead organic material is degraded to simple compounds such as CO_2, several nutrients such as ammonium, and water. Parts of the process can be relatively easily studied in laboratory experiments (Swift *et al.* 1979) and effects of chemicals on this process can be demonstrated within a short time when using microcosms.

The aim of this research was to design a microcosm method in which the effects of (potential) pollutants on the decomposition process can be measured, with special attention to pesticides. The system must be suitable for tropical countries, thus restricting the substrates which can be used. Effects of some important modifying factors are documented, such as microbial inoculation and soil fauna.

2. Material and methods

2.1 The microcosm

The microcosm (MES) used in the experiments described here, was designed to measure several parameters of the decomposition processes in laboratory studies. The system can be used for measurements of CO_2 production and the mineralization processes of microflora in the litter. The system is basically the same as the one used by Van Wensem (1989). It consists of a perspex cylinder (11 cm height, 7 cm diameter), of which the bottom is closed with gauze. The MES was filled with 120 gram dry sand (sea sand extra pure) and wetted by adding 0.240 mL distilled water per gram of sand. In the sand a small plastic pole was placed carrying a polythene dish to which 5 mL KOH could be applied. Twenty gram fresh litter was placed on top of the sand. Litter and sand were separated by a nylon gauze. A lid with a gauze was placed on the microcosm to provide free air exchange. During the CO_2 measurement the lid was replaced by a closed type to prevent air exchange. The microcosms were incubated within an enclosure (1 m^3) box to reduce the temperature and humidity fluctuations during the experiment. Ambient temperature was 28°C on the average.

2.2   *Carbon dioxide measurement and mineral nitrogen analyses*

The CO_2 production of the MES was measured according to the method described in Macfayden (1970) and Anderson (1973) which is based on the absorption of carbon dioxide to a 1 N KOH solution. The amount of CO_2 absorbed was determined by titration with 0.1 N HCl with phenolphthalein and thymolphthalein as indicators. The time during which KOH was present in the MES (exposure time) was between 24 and 48 hours for pine litter, while for crop litter the exposure time changed during the experiment from 3 hours in the first days until 24 hours after adding isopods. The exposure times chosen in the experiments were based on pilot experiments, conducted with each litter type, which are not presented here.

The nutrients measured in the litter samples were ammonium and nitrate. Ten gram of fresh litter was shaken in 100 mL distilled water for 2 hours at 75 rpm. After filtration through Whatman GFB 1 μm filters and Whatman 0.45 μm filters samples were stored at 4°C for one or two days before nutrients were measured. The nutrient analysis were done using colorimetric methods based on routine analysis of waste water samples (Mackereth 1978). For ammonium the Nessler method was used and for nitrate cadmium was used as a reductor. The absorption of the reagent was measured at 425 nm for NH_4 and at 540 nm for NO_3. Concentrations of NH_4 and NO_3 were expressed per gram dry weight of the litter from which the nutrients had been extracted.

2.3   *Litter preparation*

Pine litter was collected from a pine forest at Mount Ungaran, near Gintungan in Central Java. The litter was air-dried after collection for at least two weeks and stored at room temperature (about 25°C) before using it. Before putting the litter in the microcosm it was re-wetted for 4 hours to obtain a moisture content of ca. 75% of the fresh weight.

Agricultural litter, a mixture of carrot, Chinese cabbage and bean leaves, was collected from an agricultural area at Kopeng, Central Java. After collection the litter was air-dried for one week. Hard parts such as twigs and the heads of Chinese cabbage were removed. Before putting the litter in the microcosm the three types were mixed in a ratio of 1 : 1 : 1, based on the dry weight, and the mix was re-wetted for 24 hours to obtain a moisture content of 50%.

2.4   *Soil fauna*

The isopod *Porcellio scaber* (Crustacea) was obtained from Dieng Plateau, Central Java (ca. 2000 m above sea level) and kept in a terrarium in the laboratory at room temperature for several months, on leaves collected from a domestic garden. Animals with a fresh weight varying between 35 and 45 mg were used.

2.5 Soil microflora

Fusarium sp. was isolated from pine litter to represent the microflora in experiment 1a and cultured on agar plates which contained an extract of pine litter. A spore suspension was made ($2.7 \cdot 10^6$ spores per mL) and 1 mL of this was added per 20 g fresh litter.

2.6 Experimental design

Table 1 shows the experimental design for each experiment. Each experiment contained 5 replicates per treatment including a blank which contained only sand to allow a correction for the CO_2 available in the MES at the moment the dish with KOH was put in the MES. In experiment 1a, the effect of the inoculum on the CO_2 production and mineralization of the microflora of pine litter was examined. The litter was not sterilized before using it. For the determination of mineral nitrogen five MES per treatment were added for each time these measurements were done.

Table 1 *Overview of the experiments*

Exp. nr.	Litter type	Treatment	Parameter	Exposure time
1a	*Pinus merkusii*	*Fusarium* inoculum	CO_2 NH_4; NO_3	24 h
1b	*Pinus merkusii*	*Porcellio scaber* (after 26 days)	CO_2	42 h
2a	Crop (carrot, cabbage, bean)	*Porcellio scaber* (after 14 days)	CO_2	3-24 h
2b	Crop (carrot, cabbage, bean)	benomyl *Porcellio scaber* (after 16 days)	CO_2	3-24 h

In experiments 1b and 2a isopods were added after some time to investigate the effect of soil fauna on CO_2 production of the litter microflora.

The last experiment, 2b, was designed to determine the effect of the fungicide benomyl (concentration 1000 μg/g dry litter) on the CO_2 production of the litter microflora and the interaction with soil fauna.

2.7 Statistical analysis

All data were analyzed using one way analysis of variance (ANOVA) as described by Sokal & Rohlf (1981) to examine the effect of the treatment. Assumptions for homogeneity of variances and normality were taken into account by logarithmic transformations if necessary.

3.   Results

The results of experiment 1 are summarized in Figure 1. This demonstrates that CO_2 production first increased then gradually decreased in the course of the experiment. There was a significant effect ($p < 0.001$) of the inoculum added to the litter on carbon dioxide production during the first 14 days. The existing microflora population developed in both treatments as well as the added *Fusarium* sp. population. After the first 14 days the effect was no longer significant, perhaps due to competition between the added microflora and the existing microflora in the litter; the more or less stable CO_2 production as found in other experiments (Figures 3, 4) was not reached. This was because the experiment was not completed over the 30 days. In Figure 3 the stable situation is reached after about 20 days, the same as in Figure 1.

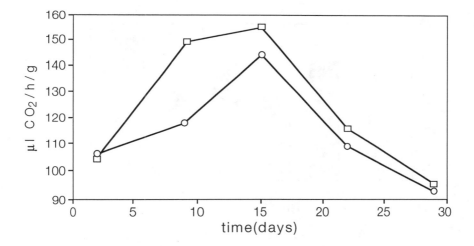

Figure 1 *Respiration rate of micro-ecosystems containing pine litter with the natural microflora (o), and an extra inoculum of fungi* (Fusarium sp.) (□)

Figure 2 shows the results for the ammonium and nitrate changes in the litter, in experiment 1a. The nitrate concentrations differed significantly between the two treatments and the difference became greater in the course of time, from $0.01 < p \ll 0.05$ at 7 days up to $p < 0.01$ at 21 days. This may be a result of nitrification which may be inhibited by the *Fusarium* sp. inoculum. Differences were also found in the ammonium concentration but these are not significant, although the F-values found at day 7 and day 14 were 4.71 and 4.91 respectively. The inoculum seems to stimulate the ammonification process. No significant differences were found for the total mineral nitrogen concentrations (Figure 2).

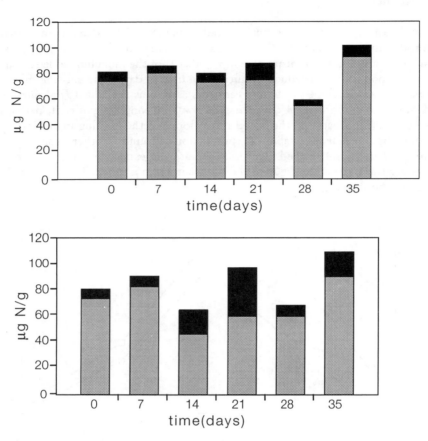

Figure 2 *Concentrations of mineral nitrogen in micro-ecosystems containing pine litter, at various times in the course of the incubation, either with the natural micro-flora only (lower figure), or with an extra inoculum of Fusarium (upper figure). The total mineral N concentration is the sum of NH_4-N (lower, grey, part of each bar) and NO_3-N (upper, black, part of each bar)*

The effect of adding eight isopods to the system after a more or less stable situation is reached is shown in Figure 3. When isopods were added to the system after 26 days CO_2 production increased significantly ($0.01 < p < 0.05$ to $0.001 < p < 0.01$) and remained significant until day 42. At the end of the experiment it turned out that about 40% of the isopods had died. Because of this, there was no significant effect for CO_2 production at the last measurement. CO_2 produced by one isopod was about 20 μL/h, which corresponds to about 440 μL/g/h, based on an average fresh weight of the isopods of 45 mg. In experiment 2a the CO_2 measured was significantly affected by the isopods ($0.01 < p < 0.05$ at day 16 and 21). After 24 days the difference was not significant due to increasing variance (Figure 4). At day 19 a one-way ANOVA with unequal sample size was applied. After day 24 the effect was too small because of mortality among the isopods (nearly 40%). Although the isopods used in experiment 1b also died during the experiment an effect was still measurable, the CO_2 produced without isopods was 200-300 μL $CO_2/g/h$. The CO_2 produced without isopods in experiment 2a was 5-10 mL/h which makes it difficult to detect the small amount produced by the isopods (150-200 $\mu L/g/h$ for eight individuals).

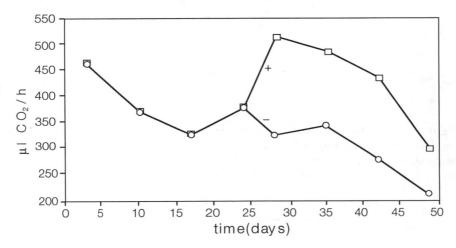

Figure 3 *Respiration changes in micro-ecosystems containing pine litter. After 24 days isopods were added to one group of units (indicated with +) while the other units were further incubated without isopods (indicated as -). For the period before day 24, the mean respiration of all units is given*

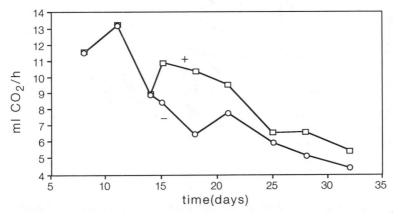

Figure 4 *Respiration changes in micro-ecosystems containing a mixture of crop litter. After 14 days, half of the units were supplemented with isopods (+), while the other units were incubated without isopods (-)*

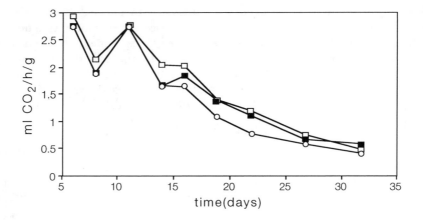

Figure 5 *Respiration in micro-ecosystems containing a mixture of crop litter. Means are shown for three treatment groups: -□-: without benomyl, no isopods; -o- : with benomyl, no isopods; -■- : with benomyl, plus isopods (from day 14 onwards). Respiration on the first five days was extremely high and is not represented in the figure*

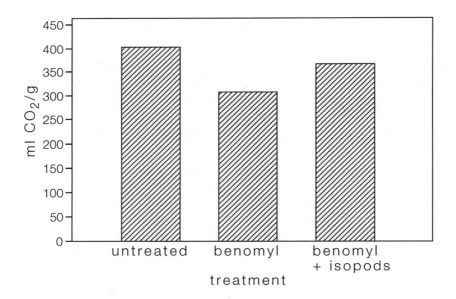

Figure 6 *Integrated carbon dioxide production over a 26 days incubation period (day 6 to 32) in micro-ecosystems containing a mixture of crop litter. The means for three groups are shown: untreated, treated with benomyl, and treated with benomyl plus isopods added*

When litter was treated with benomyl, no significant effect was found before day 14 (Figure 5). After day 14 there was a significant difference found between litter treated with and without benomyl, and for litter treated with benomyl and with isopods. Carbon dioxide production was integrated over the period during which isopods were present (day 6 to day 32). These data, displayed in Figure 6, show that benomyl decreased CO_2 production slightly, but the effect can only be seen in MES without isopods.

4.   Discussion

To assess the ecotoxicological impact of chemical substances such as pesticides and heavy metals, on a level above that of organisms, microcosms provide promising opportunities. Microcosms can be seen as the lowest level of ecological organization while still allowing for the observation of ecosystem processes as well as interactions between components of the ecosystem. However, not all ecological processes can be studied using this system. They are very appropriate for studies on chemical fate and effects of pollutants on species interactions and processes (Sheehan 1984, Levin et al. 1989). Processes which can be observed in microcosms are decomposition processes, such as nutrient mineralization and soil respiration, in which microorganisms are involved. Inter-species interactions such as interactions between microflora and specific soil fauna activity, can also be studied in these systems (Sheehan 1984, Levin et al. 1989, Eijsackers 1991). To assess the impact of toxic pollutants at an ecosystem level by way of ecological processes, the decomposition of litter material is a very suitable process to study because: (1) it is a common and important process within ecosystems (Swift et al. 1979, Sheehan 1984), (2) it is a process which is sensitive to stress factors such as pollutants (Sheehan et al. 1984, Eijsackers 1991), (3) decomposition parameters are indicative of the condition of the system, (4) responses of the parameters are comparable for a variety of ecosystems and (5) the parameters are easy to measure and give reliable results (Sheehan et al. 1984).

Microorganisms have an important role in the recycling of nutrients due to mineralization and in the conservation of nutrients. Recycling of essential elements, particularly that of nitrogen, can be inhibited by toxic substances (Sheehan et al. 1984, Van Wensem et al. 1991). Disruption of these nutrient cycling processes can illustrate the impact of long term disturbances in ecosystem functions. Although such information is based on short term laboratory experiments such observations should be made to asses the environmental impact of the substance (Sheehan et al. 1984, Eijsackers 1991).

It is clear that the parameters chosen for microcosm studies, which can be used to define soil quality standards, should reflect the responses of populations as well as changes in the overall structure and function of an ecosystem. This implies that responses to chemical substances should not only be studied on the level of the individual (single species tests) but also on a higher, more complex, ecosystem level (Sheehan et al. 1984). Potential toxic effects of chemicals in the field can be detected at an early stage using laboratory experiments. Ammonium, nitrate and carbon dioxide are measures of decomposition activity (Van Wensem 1989, Van Wensem *et al.* 1991). If these processes are disturbed by pollutants, estimations of the possible impact can be made before visible impacts actually occur.

Considering the increase in environmental pollution, ecotoxicological impact assessment procedures for soil contamination should be developed further. The microcosm method as described here is not yet complete. According to the results of the first experiment, the effect of introduced microorganisms can be measured. To avoid high variation between the replicates and to be able to observe processes in a better way, the litter should be sterilized before the microflora is introduced. However sterilization could have a greater influence on nutrient availability than the introduction of microorganisms (Van Wensem 1989).

Isopods were used as representatives of the soil fauna group responsible for comminution of the litter. Litter fragmentation is a first step in the recycling of organic matter, as a result of this process the surface area is increased which could affect microbial activity (Eijsackers 1991). Although it should be possible to detect this effect in this system (Van Wensem 1989) the results presented in this paper do not show such an effect, maybe because the litter type used is not suitable. The relatively high percentage of dead isopods after 3 weeks, indicates that pine litter is not suitable as a standard substrate. Pine litter contains lignin and phenolic components (Blascke 1979, Berg *et al.* 1981) which are probably disliked by *P. scaber*. The isopod species is not found in pine forest around Central Java (Vink, unpublished). Although *P. scaber* is found is compost heaps in Central Java, crop litter as used in these experiments is also not suitable. This litter decomposes too fast which makes it rather pulpy within a short time. The litter condition present in the microcosms used is not suitable for the survival of *P. scaber*. The high decomposition rate is reflected in the amount of carbon dioxide produced in these microcosms (expressed in mL). The isopods produce 160-200 μL CO_2 per 8 individuals, which corresponds to 400 μL CO_2 per gram body weight. The amount of CO_2 produced by these isopods corresponds with results found by Wieser & Oberhauser (1984), taking the high ambient temperature into account. If the litter type used in these experiments produces a high level of carbon dioxide it will be very difficult to detect the amount produced by the isopods.

A more appropriate litter to use might be a mixture of three to five deciduous tree species. These litter types should preferably be obtained from trees that are common in tropical countries, shedding their leaves either within a short period, or at a steady rate throughout the year. The litter should not decompose as fast as crop litter but also not as slow as pine litter, that is why foliage litter will be a good alternative. Further experiments are planned to finalize the protocol for the MES test for side-effects of pesticides.

5. References

Anderson, J.M. (1973) Carbon Dioxide Evolution from Two Temperate, Deciduous Woodland Soils, *J. Appl. Ecol.* 10: 316-378.

Baath, E., Lohm, U., Lundgren, B., Rosswall, T., Soderstrom, B., Sohlenius, B. & Wiren, A. (1978) The Effect of Nitrogen and Carbon Supply on the Development of Soil Organism Populations and Pine Seedlings: A Microcosm Experiment, *Oikos* 31: 153-163.

Baath, E., Lohm, U., Lundgren, B., Rosswal. T., Soderstrom, B. & Sohlenius, B. (1981) Impact of Microbial-feeding Animals on Total Soil Activity and Nitrogen Dynamics: A Soil Microcosm Experiment, *Oikos* 37: 257-264.

Berg, B., Hannus, K., Popoff, T. & Theander, O. (1981) Changes in Organic Chemical Components of Needle Litter During Decomposition. Long Term Decomposition in a Scots Pine Forest I., *Can. J. Bot.* 60: 1310-1319.

Blaschke, H. (1979) Leaching of Water-soluble Organic Substances from Coniferous Needle Litter, *Soil Biol. Biochem.* 11: 581-584.

Buldgen, P. (1982) Features of Nutrient Leaching from Organic Soil Layer Microcosms of Beach and Spruce Forests: Effects of Temperature and Rainfall, *Oikos* 38: 99-107.

Eijsackers, H. (1991) Litter Fragmentation by Isopods as Affected by Herbicide Application, *Neth. J. Zool.* 41: 277-303.

Gillet, J.W. (1989) The Role of Terrestrial Microcosms and Mesocosms in Ecotoxicological Research, in: Levin, S.A., Harwell, M.A., Kelly, J. R. & Kimball, K.D. (eds.) *Ecotoxicology: Problems and Approaches*, Springer Verlag, New York, pp. 367-410.

Kersting, K. (1991) Microecosystem State and Its Response to the Introduction of Pesticide, *Verh. Internat. Verein. Limnol.* 24: 2309-2312.

Levin, S.A., Harwell, M.A., Kelly, J.R. & Kimball, K.D. (1989) *Ecotoxicology: Problems and Approaches*, Springer Verlag, New York.

Liber, K., Kaushik, N.K., Solomon, K.R. & Carey, J.H. (1992) Experimental Designs for Aquatic Mesocosm Studies: A Comparison of the 'ANOVA' and 'Regression' Design for Assessing the Impact of Tetrachlorophenol on Zooplankton Populations in Limnocorrals, *Environ. Toxicol. Chem.* 11: 49-59.

Macfayden, A. (1970) Simple Methods for Measuring and Maintaining the Proportion of Carbon Dioxide in Air, for Use in Ecological Studies of Soil Respiration, *Soil Biol. Biochem.* 2: 9-18.

Mackereth (1978) *Standard Methods for the Examination of Water and Waste Water*, 16th edition, Am. Health Assoc. Inc., New York.

Sheehan, P.J., Miller, D.R., Butler, G.C. & Bourdeau, P. (1984) *Effects of Pollutants at the Ecosystem Level*, Scope 22, John Wiley and Sons, Chichester.

Sokal, R.R. & Rohlf, F.J. (1981) *Biometry*, 2nd edition, W.H. Freeman and Company.

Swift, M.J., Heal, O.W. & Anderson, J.M. (1979) Decomposition in Terrestrial Ecosystems, *Studies in Ecology*, Vol. 5, Blackwell Scientific Publications, Oxford.

Taylor, B. & Parkinson, D. (1987a) A New Microcosm Approach to Litter Decomposition Studies, *Can. J. Bot.* 66: 1933-1939.

Taylor, B. & Parkinson, D. (1987b) Respiration and Mass Loss Rates of Aspen and Pine Leaf Litter Decomposing in Laboratory Microcosms, *Can. J. Bot.* 66: 1948-1959.

Taylor, B., Parkinson, D. & Parsons, W.F.J. (1989) Nitrogen and Lignin Content as Predictors of Litter Decay Rates: A Microcosm Test, *Ecology* 70: 97-104.

Van Wensem, J. (1989) A Terrestrial Micro-ecosystem for Measuring Effects of Pollutants of Isopod-mediated Litter Decomposition, *Hydrobiologia* 188/189: 507-516.

Van Wensem, J., Jagers op Akkerhuis, G.A.J.M. & Van Straalen, N.M. (1991) Effects of the Fungicide Triphenyltin Hydroxide on Soil Fauna Mediated Litter Decomposition, *Pestic. Sci.* 32: 307-316.

Webber, E.C., Deutsch, W.G., Bayne, D.R. & Seesock, W.C. (1992) Ecosystem Level Testing of a Synthetic Pyrethroid Insecticide in Aquatic Mesocosms, *Environ. Toxicol. Chem.* 11: 87-105.

Wieser, W. & Oberhauser, C. (1984) Ammonia Production and Oxygen Consumption During the Life Cycle of *Porcellio scaber* (Isopoda, Crustacea), *Pedobiologia* 26: 415-419.

4.2

The use of soil invertebrates as test organisms in bioassays

ADIANTO

Abstract

A technique is described for estimating the biological effects of low and high levels of insecticides on the rate of reproduction of the protozoans Colpoda cucullus *and* Oxytricha sp. *(Ciliata),* Stenostomum sphagnetorum *(Turbellaria) and* Caenorhabditis elegans *(Nematoda). The aim of the research was to introduce soil invertebrates i.e.* C. cucullus, Oxytricha sp., C. elegans *and* S. sphagnetorum *as test organisms for bioassays. The animals were collected, identified and cultured in a synthetic medium at room temperature. Preliminary experiments showed that the rate of reproduction of* C. cucullus *was significantly inhibited by levels of 10 µg/mL of the insecticide Bayrusil 25 EC (quinalphos); the cells showed lysis at levels of 30 µg/mL of either Bayrusil 25 EC or Bayrusyl 52.3%. Using the other ciliate* Oxytricha sp., *the rate of reproduction was inhibited by levels of 5 µg/mL of the insectide Basudin 60 EC (diazinon), and the cells showed lysis at levels of 30 µg/mL. Using the turbellaran* S. sphagnetorum, *the rate of reproduction was inhibited by levels of 5 µg/mL of the insecticide Ambush 2 EC (permethrin), while* C. elegans *was inhibited by levels of 25 µg/mL Basudin 60 EC. The results showed that there were differences between the organisms with respect to different kinds of insecticides in different concentrations. A control mechanism in* C. elegans *appeared to counteract the inhibitory effect of the insecticide, restoring growth to that of controls after about 9 days. The results indicated that the soil invertebrates that were tested appeared to have a good prospective value for use in bioassays.*

1. Introduction

It has become the rule to use pesticides in intensive agricultural and horticultural situations. Economic plant production at a high yield level is now difficult to imagine without the use of herbicides, fungicides, insecticides and growth regulators. We therefore need to have an accurate knowledge of the effectiveness of these substances, but we also have to determine the side-effects of the various active substances on other organisms. It is desirable for ecological and also for economic reasons to know as much as possible about the effects of pesticides on non-target soil animals, especially those which take part in the decomposition process in the soil. Soil Protozoa, for instance, are important in the decomposition process. As Protozoa control the bacteria population by consuming it, one-third of bacterial N will be incorporated into protozoan biomass, one-third will be excreted as bacterial cell walls and one-third as NH_4^+. Ammonium is released very close to roots and is taken up by the roots (Clarholm 1985).

Although some people noted that indirect or long-term effects of some pollutants in higher Metazoa do not occur in Protozoa (Dive & Persoone 1984), in many cases Protozoa have been used for bioassay testing (Persoone & Uytterspot 1975).

The protozoan *Uronema marinum* was used for testing the toxic effects of heavy metals (Parker 1979) and *Tetrahymena pyriformis* was used for a toxicity bioassay in water (Carter & Cameron 1973, Slabbert & Morgan 1982). Another protozoan, *Euplotes crassus* was used for testing mercury (Dini 1981).

This paper deals with the side-effects of pesticides on the reproduction rate of the invertebrates *Colpoda cucullus* and *Oxytricha sp.* (Ciliata), *Stenostomum shagnetorum* (Turbellaria) and *Caenorhabditis elegans* (Nematoda).

2.   Materials and methods

2.1   Test organisms

Colpoda cucullus, *Oxytricha sp.*, and *C. elegans* used in the test were isolated from the garden soil at ITB, Bandung, whereas *Stenostomum sphagnetorum* were isolated from a pine forest soil at Lembang, Bandung, West Java.

2.2   Feeding

C. cucullus was cultured on a medium developed for *Pseudomonas fluorescens* (Adianto 1980). The composition of the medium is as follows, pH being adjusted to 6.3. Per liter: 0.05 g $(NH_4)_2PO_4$, 0.08 g $Na_2HPO_4 \cdot 7H_2O$, 0.02 g K_2HPO_4, 0.01 g $MgSO_4 \cdot 7H_2O$, 0.02 g $CaCl_2$, 0.01 g $CaCO_3$, 0.02 mannitol, 5 mL trace elements (after Drews 1968, with little modification).

Oxytricha sp. was cultured on hay infusion and fed with *Aerobacter aeruginosa*. *S. sphagnetorum* was fed with *Tetrahymena pyriformis* and cultured on the same medium as *C. cucullus*. *C. elegans* was fed with *Escherichia coli* and cultured on a NGM medium consisting of the following ingredients: 1.5 g NaCl, 2.0 g pepton, 2.0 g agar, 0.5 mL $CaCl_2 \cdot 2H_2O$ 1 M, 0.5 mL 5 mg cholesterol/100 mL ethanol, 0.5 mL $MgSO_4 \cdot 7H_2O$ 1 M, 4.15 mL $K_2HPO_4 \cdot 3H_2O$ 1.5 M, 800 mL aquadest (Dusenbery *et al.* 1975). Cultures were kept at an ambient temperature of 23-27°C on the laboratory bench.

2.3   Insecticides

Bayrusil 25 EC, Bayrusil 52.3% (active ingredient: quinalphos), Basudin 60 EC (active ingredient: diazinon) and Ambush 2 EC (active ingredient: permethrin) were used. Since none of these substance are easily soluble in water, they were first dissolved in acetone as a 'carrier'.

2.4   Toxicity tests

2.4.1   Colpoda cucullus
Twenty individuals of the test organism were taken from the stock culture using a micropipette and transferred to a 100 mL suspension of bacteria *P. fluorescens* and insecticide Bayrusil 25 EC or 25% active ingredient in an Erlenmeyer flask. The insecticide concentrations for each flask were 5, 10, 15, 20, 25, 30 μg/mL with a control. This was repeated for the insecticide Bayrusil 52.3%. For each concentration of the insecticide tested, 10 replications were inoculated. The highest number of individuals during observation were counted and plotted against the exposure concentration.

2.4.2   Oxytricha sp.
Twenty individuals of the test organism were taken from the stock culture using a micropipette and transferred to 100 mL of a suspension of the bacteria *Aerobacter aeruginosa* and the insecticide Basudin 60 EC or 60% active ingredient in an Erlenmeyer flask. The insecticide concentrations of each flask were 10, 50, 100, 200, 500 μg/mL with a control. The influence of insecticide concentrations on the population growth of the protozoans were counted using a microscope after 3, 6, 9, 12, and 24 hours per mL and replicated 3 times. For each dilution the average number of generations in the 10 replications was calculated and compared with the average number of generations in the control. The ratio of these two figures, expressed in % and substracted from 100, gives the procentual inhibition. Mathematically:

$$\% \; inhibition \; = \; 100 \; \frac{(average \; number \; generations \; + \; pollutant)}{(average \; number \; of \; generations \; control)} \; \times \; 100$$

2.4.3   Stenostomum sphagnetorum
Twenty individuals of these animals were taken from the stock culture using a micropipette and transferred to a 20 mL suspension of *Tetrahymena pyriformis* and the insecticide Ambush 2 EC in a petridish. The insecticide concentrations of each petridish were 5, 10, 15, 20 μg/mL with a control. For each concentration of the insecticide tested, 10 replications were inoculated. Changes in the number of individuals were counted daily for 12 days.

2.4.4   Caenorhabditis elegans
Ten individuals of these animals were inoculated on a NGM medium spread with the live bacteria *E. coli* and then counted each day using a microscope. The concentrations of the insecticide Basudin 60 EC were applied by droplet. For the acute test the concentrations of insecticide were 10, 25, 50, 100, 200, 400 μg/mL with a control. Duration of the observations were 6, 12, 24, and 48 hours. Calculation of the procentual inhibition was done as given above. The sublethal effects

of the insecticide is to depress the intrinsic rate of increase (r), which is calculated from:

$$r = \frac{\ln N_t - \ln N_o}{t}$$

where N_o is the number of organisms on the first day (t=0) and N_t the number after t days.

For each dilution the average value for r for the 10 replicates was calculated and compared with the average r-value of the control. The duration of the experiment was nine days.

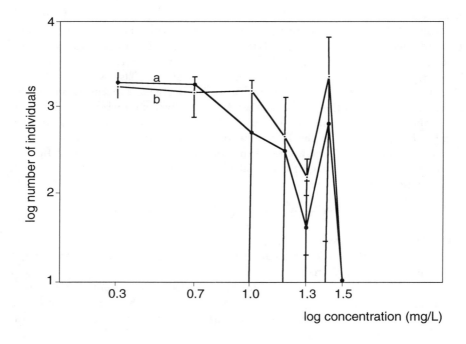

Figure 1 *Concentration-response relationship for the effect of quinalphos, in formulations Bayrusil 25 EC (line a) and Bayrusil 52.3% (line b) on the population of ciliates,* Colpoda cucullus, *developed during a 48h observational period. Means are given with standard deviations based on 10 replicates*

3. Results

3.1 Bayrusil 25 EC (Colpoda cucullus)

Up to 5 μg/mL no influence was detected. At 10 μg/mL inhibition of reproduction occurred and some animals died. At 20 μg/mL inhibition of reproduction was more significant, and at 30 μg/mL all the test organisms died. No significant difference was found between the effects of Bayrusil 25 EC and Bayrusil 52.3% (Figure 1).

3.2 Ambush 2 EC (Stenostomum sphagnetorum)

At 5 μg/mL, 50% inhibition occurred after 48 hours and at concentrations of 5-20 μg/mL, almost all turbellarians died after 12 days (Figure 2).

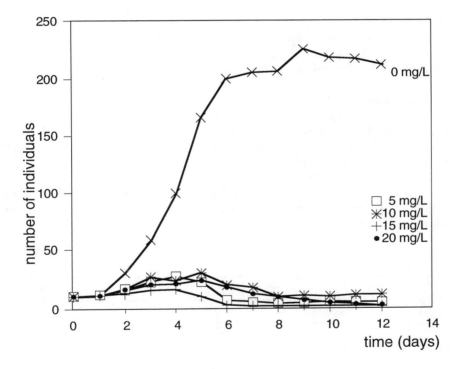

Figure 2 *Changes in the number of individuals of the turbellarian flatworm,* Stenostomum sphagnetorum, *maintained in a range of Ambush 2 EC (permethrin) concentrations*

Table 1 *Responses of population size of the ciliate,* Oxytricha *sp. to the insecticide* Basudin 60 EC (diazinon) under laboratory conditions at room temperature

Insecticide concentration (μg/ml)	% of inhibition				
	Exposure time (h)				
	3	6	9	12	24
0	0	0	0	0	0
5	3	17	15	40	43
10	12	4	30	41	48
15	21	25	38	47	49
20	30	37	45	51	62
25	57	83	90	95	96
30	100	100	100	100	100

3.3 Basudin 60 EC

3.3.1 Oxytricha sp.
At 5 μg/mL, inhibition of reproduction was 3% after 3 hours, 17% after 6 hours, and 40% after 12 hours. At 25 μg/mL more than 50% inhibition occurred after 3 hours and at 30 μg/mL all ciliates died after 3 hours (Table 1).

3.3.2 Caenorhabditis elegans
Up to 50 μg/mL no influence was detected after 6 hours exposure, but there was 5% inhibition after 12 hours. At 200 μg/mL all nematodes died after 48 hours (Table 2). The concentration-response curve (Figure 3) is derived from the mean rate of increase (r) for an entire nine days experiment. Changes in values of r during the experiment show that the rate of reproduction oscillates after exposure to the insecticide. At concentrations of 5-50 μg/mL, r was restored to that of the controls in nine days, but at 100 μg/mL r-levels remained at significantly lower rate than the controls.

Table 2 *Percentage inhibition of nematode populations* (Coenorhabditis elegans) after exposure to various concentrations of Basudin 60 EC (diazinon)

Insecticide concentration (μg/mL)	No. of replicates	Exposure time (h)			
		6	12	24	48
400	10	70	75	90	100
200	10	45	50	65	100
100	10	20	30	35	45
50	10	0	5	5	5
25	10	0	0	5	5
10	10	0	0	0	0
0	10	0	0	0	0

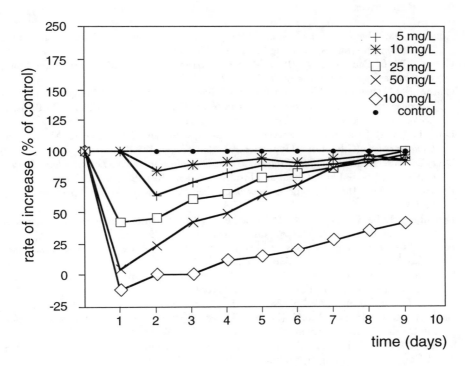

Figure 3 *Curves showing the effect of Basudin 60 EC (diazinon), in various concentrations, on the intrinsic rate of population increase of the nematode* Coenorhabditis elegans, *calculated for different exposure times, relative to the rate of increase in the control*

4.   Discussion

We found that the inhibitory effect of the insecticide Basudin 60 EC on the growth rate of *Oxytricha sp.* was greater than on the growth of nematodes. *Caenorhabditis* appeared to be capable of neutralizing the potentially inhibitory effects of low levels of insecticide. At a concentration of 5 μg/mL and above, the capacity of *Stenostomum* to completely counteract the effect of the insecticide was exceeded so that the rate of reproduction declined with the concentration. Stebbing & Pomroy (1978) suggested that this could be characteristic of the action of a control mechanism and that the rate of reproduction could be regulated, as observed on *Hydra littoralis* exposed to 0.5-2.5 mg/L Cu^{2+}. The results showed that there were differences in organism response to different kind of insecticides and indicated that the soil invertebrates tested appear to have a good prospective value for bioassays in future studies.

5. References

Adianto (1980) *The Influence of Natural Organic Material and Insecticides on the Soil Fauna Population*, Disertation, Bandung Institute of Technology.

Carter, J.W. & Cameron, I.L. (1973) Toxicity Bioassay of Heavy Metals in Water Using *Tetrahymena pyriformis*, *Water Res.* 7: 951-961.

Clarholm, M. (1985) Possibles Roles for Roots, Bacteria, Protozoa and Fungi in Supplying Nitrogen to Plants, in: Fitter, A.H., Atkinson, D., Read, D.J. & Usher, M.B. (eds.) *Ecological Interactions in Soil*, Blackwell Sci. Pub., pp. 355-365.

Dini, F. (1981) Relationship between Breeding Systems and Resistance to Mercury in *Euplotes crassus* (Ciliophora: Hypotrichida), *Mar. Ecol.* 4: 195-202.

Dive, D. & Persoone, G. (1984) *Protozoa as Test Organisms in Marine Ecotoxicology: Luxury or Necessity?*, State Univ. Ghent and Inst. Mar. Scient. Res., Bredene, Belgium.

Drews, G. (1968) *Mikrobiologisches Praktikum fuer Naturwissenschaftler*, Springer-Verlag, Berlin.

Dusenbery, D.B., Sheridan, R.W. & Russel, R.L. (1975) Chemotaxis Defective Mutants of the Nematode *Caenorhabditis elegans*, *Genetics* 80: 297-309.

Parker, J.G. (1979) Toxic Effects of Heavy Metals upon Cultures of *Uronema marinum* (Ciliophora: Uronematidae), *Mar. Biol.* 54: 17-24.

Persoone, G. & Uyttersprot, G. (1975) The Influence of Inorganic and Organic Pollutants on the Rate of Reproduction of a Marine Hypotrichous ciliate: *Euplotes vannus* Muller, *Rev. Intern. Oceanogr. Med.* 37/38: 125-151.

Slabbert, J.L. & Morgan, W.S.G. (1982) A Bioassay Technique Using *Tetrahymena pyriformis* for the Rapid Assessment of Toxicants in Water, *Water Res.* 16: 517-523.

Stebbing, A.R.D. & Pomroy, A.J. (1978) A Sublethal Technique for Assessing the Effects of Contaminants Using *Hydra littoralis*, *Water Res.* 12: 631-635.

4.3

The application of biological toxicity tests to assess the environmental impact of mining in tropical Northern Australia

G.D. Rippon, R.V. Hyne & S.M. Hunt

Abstract

To ensure adequate protection of the aquatic environment from mine waste water discharge, Biological Toxicity Tests (BTTs) were developed to determine environmental 'safe' dilutions for the release of effluent into streams. Testing within a National Park precluded the use of introduced species and necessitated the search for suitable local species. It was also desirable to use local species to ensure relevance to the local ecosystem. Following a survey of nineteen local species for their suitability as potential test organisms, the Office of the Supervising Scientist has developed both acute and chronic BTTs which use both lethal and sub-lethal end-points for eight local species. Four species are use routinely; two Hydra (Hydra viridissima and H. vulgaris), a water flea (Moinodaphnia macleayi), and a gudgeon fish (Mogurnda mogurnda). These tests and their application to a particular mine waste water are described.

1.   Introduction

The Alligator Rivers Region (ARR) was identified as a region rich in natural and cultural resources but a region where conflict might arise from the desire to mine uranium, conserve species, and protect the cultural interests of the indigenous traditional landowners (Fox 1977). This has been reflected by most of the region being set aside as Kakadu National Park (about 20,000 km^2). The park is a World Heritage area with its wetlands entered in the Convention of Wetlands of International Importance. The ARR was specifically identified in legislation to further protect the wetlands and river catchments of the West, South and East Alligator Rivers (Figure 1) from the impact of uranium mining. This legislation was later modified to enable protection against general mining in the head waters of the South Alligator River.

The highly seasonal rainfall of northern tropical Australia, which has a typical wet/dry seasonal cycle with virtually all the rainfall occuring between October and May, can place severe constraints on mine waste water management practices (Holdway 1992). The principal methods adopted to dispose of excess water that accumulates during the wet season are direct release of water into surface streams during the wet season and land application during the dry season. The release of waste water into local surface streams is regulated by a state authority, the Department of Mines and Energy of the Northern Territory Government, while a federal authority, the Office of the Supervising Scientist (OSS), makes recommendations for the control regime.

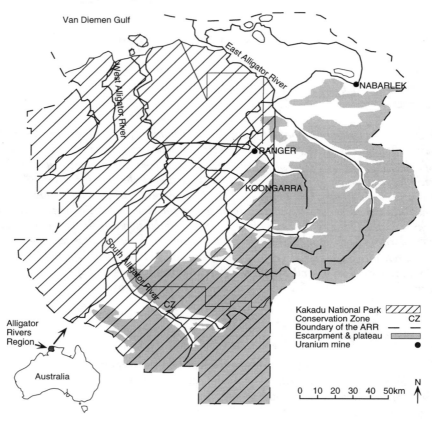

Figure 1 *Map of the Alligators Rivers Region in Northern Australia*

The control regime proposed by the OSS (1989) to ensure the protection of the aquatic ecosystems from the impact of mine waste water release has three components: long-term post-release monitoring, creek-side monitoring during release, and pre-release biological toxicity testing to establish dilution rates.

Long-term post-release monitoring involves considerable effort in collection, sorting and identification of macrobenthic species and fish surveys. This monitoring is essential for detecting subtle environmental impacts and therefore needs good base-line data sets (Humphrey *et al.* 1990). Creek-side monitoring during release involves drawing water upstream of the release point to give control water, and downstream of the release point to give water considered to be adequately diluted. These waters are pumped to header tanks at the top of the creek bank and then through test containers holding the test animals. Currently, a snail fecundity and juvenile survival test and a larval fish test are used to monitor any effects during a release. These tests provide an assessment of the adequacy of the dilution rate. The BACI design and associated statistical tests will be used for both these types of biological monitoring (Faith *et al.* 1991). The last strategy in our control regime and the one which is the focus of this paper, is the pre-release assessment of mine waste waters using biological toxicity tests.

Biological toxicity test (BTTs) are becoming increasingly prominent in regulating the discharge of waste waters. This contrasts with previous reliance on chemical standards that cannot, even when based on toxicity tests, take into acount the synergistic and antagonistic effects that occur when large numbers of potentially toxic chemicals are mixed in a given receiving water. This is particularly important when assessing the potential impact arising from the release of complex mixtures such as mine waste waters. In these circumstances, the most reliable method is to test the effect, on local aquatic species, of mixing the actual water to be released with receiving waters (Brown 1986).

To overcome the inherent lack of environmental complexity in single species tests, several of the tests can be used as a *battery of tests* (Blanck 1984). Further these tests should then use species from dissimilar taxa and trophic level, and use sublethal or lethal endpoints with chronic or sub-chronic exposure periods. BTTs to be used in the enforcement of legislation should, however, be standard, reliable, precise, inexpensive, reasonably sensitive, and produce unequivocal responses (Mackay *et al.* 1989, Robinson 1989), although probably not all of these conditions will be met in any one test.

The OSS uses four tests using local aquatic species and recommends their use in the pre-release screening of mine waste waters to set dilution rates (Johnston 1991). These tests were developed at the ARR Research Institute by Allison *et al.* (1991), Holdway *et al.* (1991), Hyne *et al.* (1991), and McBride *et al.* (1991), and are registered with the National Association of Testing Authorities, a quality control and assurance organisation run by member registrants. This is the first such registration in Australia.

2.   Biological toxicity test methods

The water flea, *Moinodaphnia macleayi*, is used in two tests, a survival test and a reproduction test. It has a typical parthenogenic life cycle under optimal conditions and will have its first brood within 48 hours, with a subsequent brood every 24h. The brood size typically increases from about 8 young for the first brood to 16 for the third brood. The diet of the water flea includes a vitamin enriched fermented food and a local algae. The water flea survival test specifically uses survival as an endpoint commencing with 10 animals per replicate, 3 replicates per treatment with 6 treatments. The water flea reproduction test specifically uses reproduction as an endpoint but information is also gained on water flea survival; 10 animals are used per treatment, with 6 treatments in total. The test duration for both test is nominally 5 days. However, the reproduction test requires a minimum of three broods and is continued until this number of broods is produced.

The *Hydra* test can be used for either of the two known local *Hydra* species, *H. vulgaris* (pink *Hydra*) and *H. viridissima* (green *Hydra*). *Hydra* has an asexual life cycle under optimal conditions. The animals are fed daily with newly hatched brine shrimp. Observation are made on the degree of contraction of *Hydra* tentacles which can indicate effects of stress, or the early effects of some toxicants. The degree of tentacle contraction is, however, imprecise and therefore population growth is used as the major endpoint for this test. The duration of the test is 6 days.

The gudgeon, *Mogurnda mogurnda*, is used in a United States Environment Protection Agency based fish embryo/larval survival test with two endpoints, hatchability and survival. The duration of the test is nominally 8 days with the test animals requiring no feeding. The larval fish will normally hatch after 4-5 days and the test is then continued for a further 4 days.

The OSS has made recommendations on the use of the above biological toxicity tests in the authorisation of waste water release into surface streams of the ARR. The basic recommendations are:

- The results of at least three biological toxicity tests must be made available to the regulatory authority prior to release.
- The tests used must be approved by the regulatory authority and should use three species of quite different phylogeny (*e.g.* fish, *Hydra*, Cladocera)
- The dilution ratio (d) for the release should be given by

$$d \geq F / \sqrt{LOEC \times NOEC}$$

where LOEC and NOEC are the lowest-observed-effect-concentration and no-observed-effect-concentration obtained in the tests for the most sensitive species tested and F is a safety factor taken to be greater than or equal to 10.

A full discussion on the need for a safety factor is given in Johnston (1991).

3. Mine waste water assessment using biological toxicity tests

Results obtained from the testing of waters at the Nabarlek uranium mine (Figure 1) are presented as an example of the application of biological toxicity testing to mine waste water assessment.

The Nabarlek mine is being prepared for decommissioning and, as part of the decommissioning process, disposal of water remaining in one of its evaporation ponds (EP1) is necessary. A number of options for disposal, including release to the nearby Cooper Creek, were considered by the company. OSS carried out preliminary biological toxicity tests in 1989 and 1991 to asses the viability of the release option. On the basis of the results obtained, the company applied for approval to release and this approval was granted by the regulatory authority subject to the provision, by the company, of suitable toxicity testing data immediately prior to release. The OSS assisted in this process by providing toxicity data, complementary to operating company, prior to the scheduled date of release. The results of the OSS testing program from 1989 to 1992 are given in Table 1.

Table 1 *Biological toxicity test results for EP1 water at Nabarlek*

Date	End-point	LOEC (%)	NOEC (%)
Mogurnda mogurnda			
30/10/89	4-d larval mortality	10	3.2
10/1/92	4-d larval mortality	32	10
24/1/92	4-d larval mortality	32	10
Moinodaphnia macleayi			
30/10/89	3-d adult mortality	10	3.2
16/7/91	5-d adult mortality	10	3.2
10/1/92	5-d adult mortality	10	3.2
24/1/92	5-d adult mortality	10	3.2
Hydra viridissima			
30/10/89	6-d population growth	1.0	0.3
9/7/91	6-d population growth	1.0	0.3
16/7/91	6-d population growth	0.3	< 0.3
10/1/92	6-d population growth	1.0	0.3
24/1/92	6-d population growth	1.0	0.3

The results for the gudgeon fish show that it is the least sensitive of the three species with a LOEC of 32% and a NOEC of 10% EP1 water. The water flea is more sensitive than the gudgeon fish with a LOEC and NOEC of 10% and 3.2% EP1 water, respectively, using survival as the endpoint. The results of the *Hydra* test showed agreement between tests with the LOEC and NOEC of 1% and 0.3% EP1 water, respectively. The *Hydra* LOEC and NOEC were recommended for use in setting the dilution rate for EP1 water release. On the basis of these results, a dilution of about 1800:1 would have been requires to achieve 'safe' conditions in the receiving water of Cooper Creek. Eventually, however, approval of the release was rescinded by the NT Government following objections by the Aboriginal traditional landowners.

EP1 water is greatly enriched in ammonia and sulphate relative to Cooper Creek receiving water with a total concentration of 1650 mg NH_4^+/L and 11000 mg SO_4^{2-}/L. The LOEC of 10% for the gudgeon thus gives an ammonia concentration of 165 mg NH_4^+/L. Under conditions of the test, about 0.23% of the total ammonia would be un-ionised, giving a total of 380 μg NH_3/L (*i.e.* 0.23% x 165 mg/L). In another study (Rippon & Hyne 1992), it was demonstrated with ammonium sulphate that the LOEC for ammonia was 200 μg NH_3/L. This suggests that ammonia is likely to be a major contributor to the toxicity of the water with differences in ionic strength and pH explaining the slightly lower toxicity of EP1 water.

4.   Acknowledgments

The authors thank Ms. J. Summerton and Mrs. Megan Bailey for their technical assistance in the testing of EP1 waste water and Dr. A. Johnston for his comments on the paper.

5.   References

Allison, H.E., Holdway, D.A., Hyne, R.V. & Rippon, G.D. (1991) OSS *Procedures for the Biological Testing of Waste Waters for Release into Magela Creek*, XII. *Hydra* test (*Hydra viridissima* and *Hydra vulgaris*). Open File Record No. 72, Office of the Supervising Scientist, Sydney.

Blanck, H. (1984) Species Dependent Variation among Aquatic Organisms in Their Sensitivity to Chemicals, *Ecol. Bull.* 36: 107-119.

Brown, V.M. (1986) Development of Water Quality Criteria from Toxicological Data, in: Hart, B.T. (ed.) *Water Quality Management: Freshwater Ecotoxicity in Australia*, Water Studies Centre, Chisholm Institute of Technology, Melbourne.

Faith, D.P., Humprey, C.L. & Dostine, P.L. (1991) Statistical Power and BACI Designs in Biological Monitoring: Comparative Evaluation of Measures of Community Dissimilarity Based on Benthic Macroinvertebrate Communities in Rockhole Mine Creek, Northern Territory, Australia, *Austr. J. Mar. Freshw. Res.* 42: 589-602.

Fox, R.W. (1977) *Ranger Uranium Environmental Inquiry*, 2nd Report, Australian Government Publishing Service, Canberra.

Holdway, D.A. (1992) Control of Metal Pollution in Tropical Rivers of Australia, in: Connell, D.W. & Hawker, D.W. (eds.) *Pollution in Tropical Aquatic Systems*, CRC Press, Boca Raton.

Holdway, D.A., Wiecek, M.M., Hyne, R.V. & Rippon, G.D. (1991) OSS *Procedures for the Biological Testing of Waste Waters into Magela Creek*, I. Embryo Gudgeon Test (*Mogurnda mogurnda*). Open File Record No. 69, Office of the Supervising Scientist, Sydney.

Humphrey, C.L., Bishop, K.A. & Brown, V.M. (1990) Use of Biological Monitoring in the Assessment of Effects of Mining Wastes on Aquatic Ecosystems of the Alligator Rivers Region, Tropical Northern Australia, *Environ. Monit. Ass.* 14: 139-181.

Hyne, R.V., Miller, K., Hunt, S. & Mannion, M.M. (1991) OSS *Procedures for the Biological Testing of Waste Waters into Magela Creek*, XI. Cladoceran Survival Test (*Pseudosida bidentata* or *Moinodaphnia macleayi*), Open File Record No. 71, Office of the Supervising Scientist, Sydney.

Johnston, A. (1991) Water Management in the Alligator Rivers Region - A Research Review, in: Hyne, R.V. (ed.) *Proceedings of the 29th Congress of the Australian Society of Limnology*, Jabiru NT 1990. Australian Government Publishing Service, Canberra.

Mackay, D.W., Holmes, P.J. & Redshaw, C.J. (1989) The Application of Bioassays in the Resolution of Environmental Problems - The United Kingdom Experience, *Hydrobiologia* 188/189: 77-87.

McBride, P., Allison, H.E., Hyne, R.V. & Rippon, G.D. (1991) *OSS Procedures for the Biological Testing of Waste Water into Magela Creek*, X. Cladoceran Reproduction Test (*Moinodaphnia macleayi*), Open File Record No. 70, Office of the Supervising Scientist, Sydney.

OSS (1989) *Supervising Scientist for the Alligator Rivers Region Annual Report 1988-1989*, Australian Government Publishing Service, Canberra.

Rippon, G.D. & Hyne, R.V. (1992) Purple Spotted Gudgeon: Its Use as a Toxicity Test Animal in Tropical Northern Australia, *Bull. Environ. Contam. Toxicol.* 49: 471-476.

Robinson, R.M. (1989) Environmental Impact Assessment: The Growing Importance of Science in Government Decision Making, *Hydrobiologia* 188/189: 137-142.

4.4

Ecotoxicology of soil Protozoa

M.P.M. JANSSEN

Abstract

Only a few organisms have been proposed as test organisms for soil ecotoxicology tests until now. Soil Protozoa have not been included in such tests yet. In this study the importance of soil Protozoa both in numbers and functioning of the soil ecosystem is indicated. Methods and data on ecotoxicity tests with protozoans will be given indicating the possibilities for standardization of Protozoa toxicity tests. Finally, recommendations on the species and experimental conditions will be given.

1.   Introduction

Soil Protozoa play an important role in the soil ecosystem, however, they are often neglected in toxicity tests and risk assessment. Mohr already stated in 1952 that Protozoa may be useful in the detection of toxicants, but recognized that there was a negligible amount of data and that other invertebrates seemed to be more popular as laboratory test animals. Prescott & Olson (1972) made a similar remark on the number of tests in which Protozoa are included as test organisms.

We may question why Protozoa have been used in a small number of tests considering their abundance and importance in the soil ecosystem. This probably has to do with a lack of knowledge among most biologists on this group. Their importance seems only to be recognized by specialists. We shall first consider some fundamental aspects of Protozoa; the number of protozoan species, their place in evolution and their design. Then we shall focus on their numbers in soils and their importance on the functioning of the soil ecosystem. This importance should be reflected in toxicity tests. Finally, recommendations on how to use soil Protozoa in toxicity tests will be given.

2.   Evolution of Protozoa

Member species of the Protozoa have been considered representatives of both the animal and the plant kingdoms. Some species clearly show animal characteristics (*e.g.* locomotion) while other species clearly show plant-like characteristics (*e.g.*

chlorophyll). Using the old division in plants and animals, some of the species can even change from one kingdom to another during their lifetime.

Nowadays Protozoa are considered to be members of the Protista. This kingdom is related to the Monera (bacteria and blue algae) on one side, and to Plantae, Fungi and Animalia on the other (Figure 1). Protista does not only contain Protozoa, but also different groups of algae (*e.g.* red algae, brown algae). Protista species have evolved from the Monera. The Protista kingdom comprises different branches of evolution, and, as a result, diversity within Protista is relatively high (Anderson 1987, Barnes *et al.* 1988, Sleigh 1989). The other three kingdoms, Plantae, Animalia and Fungi, are monophylitic. This article will focus mainly on Protozoa.

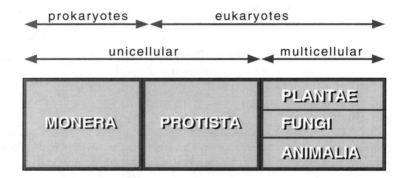

Figure 1 *Showing the position of the Protista kingdom*

3.   Anatomic design

Organisms can be divided into prokaryotes and eukaryotes. All Protista belong to the eukaryotes, as they contain eukaryotic ribosomal RNA, endoplasmatic membranes and eukaryotic organelles such as mitochondria, chloroplasts and flagelles. In this respect they are similar to representatives of the Plantae, Animalia and Fungi. Along with the Monera, Protista share the character of unicellularity (Hausmann 1985).

Protozoa may grow in colonies or appear as separate entities. In contrast to eukaryotes all cells in such colonies are similar. As a consequence, there is no differentiation of function. A large variation in size and shape may be observed among the species. The smallest Protozoa (some flagellates) are smaller than the largest prokaryotes (a few mm), whereas in the largest species cells may reach a few cm in size. In the latter case, one organism often contains more nuclei. The small species are often round or cylindric; the bigger ones are often flattened.

Individual Protozoa can be compared to a single cell of the multicellular organisms on the one hand, and to multicellular organisms as a whole on the other.

They have combined the functional aspect (one cell) and the selective unit (one organism) in one cell. Protozoa give us the opportunity to study toxicity using individual cells which can multiply or reproduce (Apostel 1973).

4. Number of species

Since the 1970s Protozoa have been divided into seven phyla of which the Sarco-mastigophora and the Ciliophora are most important, considering the number of species. The total number of species described has been estimated to be 30,000 - 40,000 of which ca. 25,000 belong to the Sargomastigophora and 7,500 to the Ciliophora (Hausmann 1985, Wheeler 1990). These two phyla contain most free-living species.

The number of protozoan species is still increasing, partly because new species are being discovered using modern techniques, and partly because new species are being found among earlier described species complexes. The ciliate *Paramecium caudatum* consists of 14 sibling species, for *Tetrahymena pyriformis* 17 different types have been described (Fenchel 1987, Foissner 1988). Both species are often used in toxicity tests (see Table 1).

Table 1 *Number of species described for different major taxa*

Bacteria & blue green algae	4760	Molluscs	50000
Fungi	47000	Echinodermata	6100
Algae	26900	Insects	751000
Plants	248000	Non-insect-arthropods	123000
Protozoa	30800	Fish	19100
Sponges	5000	Amphibians	4180
Coelenterata	9000	Reptiles	6300
Flatworms	12200	Birds	9040
Nematodes	12000	Mammals	4000
Annelida	12000		

After Wheeler (1990).

5. Soil Protozoa

The number of free-living soil Protozoa is rather small in comparison to the total number of Protozoa. The number of soil flagellates has been estimated at 260, the number of soil amoebae is probably less than 250. The testaceans or testate amoebae are a relatively important group with 310 species described for the soil ecosystem, 250 ciliate species have been isolated (Foissner 1987, 1991). A summary of the data is given in Table 2.

Table 2 *Number of protozoan species and number of species in the soil ecosystem based on Hausmann (1985), Foissner (1987) and Foissner (1991)*

Flagellates		260
Amoebae	25000	
Free-living amoebae		< 250
Testate amoebae		310
Ciliates	7500	250

A large number of the soil inhabiting species can also be found in aquatic environments, while only a limited number of species are confined to terrestrial ecosystems. Common species in the soil ecosystem are members of the flagellate genera *Oikomonas*, *Cercomonas*, and *Heteromita*, members of the ciliate genus *Colpoda* and amoeban genera *Hartmanella*, *Acanthamoeba* and *Naegleria*. Common soil Testacea genera are *Centropyxis*, *Nebela*, *Difflugia*, *Phryganella* and *Euglypha* (Bamforth 1980, Sleigh 1989).

Protozoa are abundant in different soil types, although the numbers in forest soils are often much higher than the numbers in soils of meadows and arable land. Numbers decrease with depth, which can be attributed to the decline in the amount of available nutrients and aeration. Table 3 shows the amount of soil Protozoa in comparison with numbers of other soil organisms. It stresses their importance in the soil ecosystem.

Table 3 *Number of organisms in a pine forest soil in the Netherlands throughout a one-year period (in number per m²)*

Bacteria	$2 \cdot 10^{11} - 3 \cdot 10^{11}$
Protozoa	$10^9 - 10^{11}$
Nematoda	$1 \cdot 10^8 - 5 \cdot 10^8$
Enchytraeidae	10,000 - 50,000
Arthropoda	50,000 - 130,000

Data from Berg *et al.* (1994).

The relative turnover time of Protozoa is high in comparison to other organisms (Fenchel 1974, Schoener 1983). In most laboratory studies generation times of less than one day have been found. It should, however, be stressed that generation times under field circumstances may be much longer. This is partly due to lower temperatures, and partly to encystment under unfavorable circumstances (*e.g.* dryness). Stout (1981) estimated 16-17 generations per year for testaceans in the field. Foissner (1987) summarized literature data and found 8-90 generations for testaceans and about 15 generations for naked amoebae. It is generally accepted that flagellates, naked amoebae and ciliates grow and reproduce rapidly, whereas in testate amoebae regeneration is relatively slow (Bamforth 1980, 1984, Lousier

& Bamforth 1990). The impact of soil Protozoa on nutrient cycling is considered to be high.

6.   Culturing Protozoa

There are a lot of media available for culturing Protozoa. These range from relatively natural media, prepared from soil or litter, to completely artificial media. The media can be used for rearing axenic strains (without endobacteria), monoxenic strains (with one bacteria species) or strains isolated from nature (Thompson et al. 1988).

The number of strains which are available from different culture collections is relatively large but not evenly distributed over the different Protozoa groups. The numbers reflect roughly the number of species in each group. However, the number of testate amoebae which can be ordered as a certified strain at the CCAP is remarkable low. Only three species can be ordered as non-axenic strains (Thompson et al. 1988).

The number of axenic Protozoa strains is limited and most of them belong to the genera *Euglena*, *Acanthamoeba* and *Tetrahymena* (see Table 4). The limited number of axenic strains may be explained by the fact that some of the species cannot be reared without endobacteria, in other species the endobacteria are hard to remove from the Protozoa (Moravcova 1976, Pons & Pussard 1980). Experiments with axenic strains may enable us to distinguish between uptake via the surrounding medium and uptake via food. Such experiments have not been carried out yet.

Table 4 *Number of axenic and non-axenic protozoan species in the CCAP catalogue of strains 1988**

Main group	Non-axenic	Axenic	Genus
Flagellates	64	10	*Euglena* (5)
Amoebae	108	3	*Acanthamoeba* (3)
Ciliates	40	17	*Tetrahymena* (17)

Source: Thompson et al. (1988).
* The main axenic genus per main group is given with the number of axenic strains between brackets.

7.   Toxicokinetics

The value of Protozoa as indicators of organic pollution has been recognized since the beginning of the 20th century. Toxicity experiments executed during this period had a purely scientific background, dealing with questions such as at what concentrations the species would die, and in particular, what are the underlying processes of death (Gause 1933). A number of these processes still remain unclear.

Protozoa depend on water for their locomotion and feeding. Toxicants may be assimilated via food uptake or directly from the surrounding medium. It is not yet clear which of these two is most important in microorganisms, as the limited amount of studies on this subject are contradictory (Houba & Remacle 1982, Doelman *et al.* 1984).

There are only a few studies on uptake kinetics of pollutants and duration of the uptake phase in Protozoa. These studies show a relatively short uptake phase. The species *Amoeba proteus* reached an equilibrium cadmium concentration within a few days of exposure (Al-Atia 1980). In the ciliate *Tetrahymena pyriformis* such an equilibrium was reached within ca. 6 hours (Berhin *et al.* 1984). In metal uptake by bacteria a rapid and slow uptake phase has been distinguished. The first one, taking less than half an hour, is thought to represent binding to the cell wall, whereas the second phase, representing uptake in the cell often takes a few hours to one day. The relatively short uptake phase in microorganisms, including Protozoa, enables us to establish a realistic dose-effect relationship based on equilibrium concentrations. Unfortunately in higher organisms toxicity experiments are often finished before an equilibrium is reached within the organism.

Table 5 *The use of Protozoa in toxicity tests and bioassays. The number of studies confined to a certain genus are shown**

Genus	No. studies	Environment	Genus	No. studies	Environment
Flagellates			**Ciliates**		
Entosiphon	1	F	*Tetrahymena*	13	F
Prorocentrum	1	M	*Paranophrys*	1	M
Chilomonas	1	F	*Miamiensis*	1	M
Amphidinium	1	F	*Colpidium*	2	F
Euglena	3	F	*Colpoda*	2	S
Oikomonas	1	S	*Paramecium*	5	F
Amoebae			*Blepharisma*	1	S
Amoeba	3	F	*Euplotes*	1	M
Acanthamoeba	1	S/F			

* The data are derived from 34 studies.
F = freshwater, M = marine and S = soil.

8.   Toxicity experiments with Protozoa

Various protozoan species have been used in toxicity experiments (Table 5). The large number of experiments executed using the ciliate genera *Tetrahymena* and *Paramecium* is striking. Most of these experiments deal with axenic cultures. Ciliates have the advantage of being larger than most other Protozoa, they are relatively well known and easier to identify than flagellates and amoebae. A good review of the use of ciliates in toxicity experiments is given by Persoone & Dive (1978). The number of studies carried out with soil Protozoa is limited (see Table 5).

In many toxicity experiments with Protozoa, population growth has been used as the endpoint (Bringmann & Kühn 1980, Huber *et al.* 1991, Moravcova 1976). In such experiments the increase in the number of individuals at a certain treatment is compared with the increase in the control during a number of days. The advantage of Protozoa is that results on population characteristics can be obtained within a few days, in contrast to experiments with larger organisms which often take at least several weeks. In a number of studies changes in morphology (Jeanne-Levain 1974, Moravcova 1976), protein content (Silberstein & Hooper 1972) and chemotaxis (Bergquist & Bovee 1973, Berk *et al.* 1985, Roberts & Berk 1990) have been used as the endpoint. Such measurements may be used as biomarkers, although the advantages compared to population growth used as endpoint are limited.

Rearing of Protozoa can be carried out in Erlenmeyer flasks or in microtiter-plates with a small amount of culture medium (*e.g.* 200 μL). The numbers can be counted either electronically, *e.g.* using a Coulter counter, or by eye using a microscope. In this latter the Protozoa are often killed and stained (*e.g.* by aniline blue or fuchsine).

9.   Effects on cellular level

The sequence of effects of pollutants on Protozoa are comparable to those described for higher organisms (Weinstein & Birk 1989).The effects on Protozoa are described thoroughly by Apostel (1973) and Moravcova (1976) for the ciliates *Paramecium* and *Tetrahymena*. In the first stages effects on locomotion and morphological changes can be observed. The body shape changes to a more cylindrical one, according to Apostel (1973) to optimize the surface-content ratio. Under heavier stress, changes in endoplasm and ectoplasm and increase of the contractile vacuole can be observed. In the last stage, plasmolysis occurs resulting in cell lysis. Protozoa can protect themselves by excluding the toxicant or by storage and excretion of the toxicant (Pons & Pussard 1980, Nilsson 1992). The mechanisms used by Protozoa for regulating their internal heavy metal concentration are relatively well known. These mechanisms are more or less similar to those in other invertebrates. Protozoa may contain metal binding proteins, so called metallo-thioneines, and organic granules in which metals are stored. Such granules are often composed of calcium and phosphate, but also contain micronutrients and heavy metals *e.g.* lead and cadmium (Nilsson 1978, Taylor & Simkiss 1984). The concentration in other body compartments may be kept within tolerable limits by binding heavy metals into granules. It is assumed that the granules can be excreted through the food vacuole (Nilsson 1992). The heavy metals are probably transported to the granules via metallothioneins. These compounds have a shorter turnover time than the granules.

10. Variation in toxicity

One of the main aims in ecotoxicological research is to answer questions on the effects of toxic compounds and variation in sensitivity among organisms. Are Protozoa more or less sensitive to toxicants than other organisms? It is often assumed that Protozoa will be affected more easily by toxicants because they are unicellular and have fewer mechanisms to prevent exposure via the surrounding medium. However resistance mechanisms could have been developed more rapidly because of the short generation time and their longer evolutionary development.

A comparison of different studies on variation in sensitivity to toxic substances among organisms shows contradictory results. Bringmann & Kühn (1980) compared the sensitivity of the prokaryote *Pseudomonas putida*, the alga *Scenedesmus quadricauda* and the protozoan *Entosiphon sulcatum* for 150 different compounds. *Entosiphon* proved to be most sensitive to 43 compounds *e.g.* cations of different metals, halogenids, alcohols, aldehydes and amides. Devillers *et al.* (1990) compared the toxicity of p-benzoquinone for different organisms; yeasts and Protozoa proved to be relatively insensitive in comparison to bacteria, crustaceans and fish.

In Protozoa a large variation in sensitivity to toxic substances has been observed. Among the Protozoa studied by Slooff *et al.* (1983) overall toxicity decreased along the sequence *Entosiphon*, *Chilomonas* and *Uronema*. For some compounds a 50 fold difference in sensitivity was observed. Among amoebae a large difference was found in the toxicity of herbicides (Pons & Pussard 1980). According to Pons & Pussard (1980) the use of herbicides may thus affect population composition under field circumstances. There are indications that some species may be less sensitive than others, *e.g. Euglena* species (Jeanne-Levain 1974, Ruthven & Cairns 1973). As a consequence, it can be concluded that Protozoa are relatively sensitive to a number of compounds, but also that there is a large variation in sensitivity among Protozoa. Selection of test organisms cannot be based only on these data, as sensitivity strongly depends upon the compound.

11. Standardization and future research

Toxicity experiments using Protozoa have been carried out on different species, using different media and at different temperatures. In some cases, even within one study, different media and different temperatures have been used (Jeanne-Levain 1974, Devillers *et al.* 1990). Considering the large diversity among Protozoa, rearing on one specific medium is probably unrealistic. In most cases however, conclusions on relative toxicity can be reliably drawn. Examples of the toxicity of different metals for different protozoan genera are summarized in Table 6. Mercury was the most toxic compound in most studies, followed by cadmium and lead. Copper had intermediate toxicity,whereas zinc was least toxic.

Advantages and disadvantages of toxicity tests with Protozoa have already been mentioned throughout the text, but are summarized below. One of the most evident advantages is that experiments can be carried out with many replicates and relatively simple equipment. Results on population parameters can be obtained within a relatively short time. The disadvantages are difficulties with identification and the fact that manual counting is laborious. For further soil ecotoxicological tests with Protozoa, standardization of some experimental conditions such as temperature and media, is necessary.

Table 6 *Toxicity of different metals (in moles) measured by different endpoints*

Species	Sequence of toxicity	Reference
Acanthamoeba	Hg > Pb > Cu > Zn	Prescott *et al.* (1977)
Paramecium	Hg,Pb > Ag > Cu,Cd > Ni,Co > Mn > Zn	Nieboer & Richardson (1980)
Tetrahymena	Hg,Cd > Se > Cu > Mn,Zn > Ca,Mg	Yamaguchi *et al.* (1973)
Tetrahymena	Hg > Cd > Pb	Huber *et al.* (1990)
Colpidum	Hg > Cd > Pb > Cu > Zn	Dive & Leclerc (1977)
Colpoda	Cd > Pb > Cu > Zn	Van Capelleveen *et al.*, unpubl.
Colpoda	Cd > Pb > Cu > Zn	Janssen *et al.* (1992)

Data obtained from different sources.

The flagellate genus *Cercomonas*, the amoebae genus *Acanthamoeba* and the ciliate genus *Colpoda* are the most favorable test organisms as they all contain common soil species. The advantages of ciliates have been discussed above; they are relatively large, can be observed by eye and are more easy to identify than the other Protozoa. *Colpoda* is an ubiquitous genus and species belonging to this genus have been used in different countries, *e.g.* Denmark, Indonesia, (Adianto 1994) as test organisms. The use of certified strains obtainable from CCAP or ASTM is recommended as this facilitates the comparison of test results.

12.   Acknowledgements

The author appreciates the comments on earlier drafts of this manuscript made by G.J.S.M. Heijmans, A.C.C. Plette and H.J.P.A. Verkaar.

13. References

Adianto, (1994) The Use of Soil Invertebrates as Test Organisms in Bioassays, in: Widia-narko, B., Vink, K. & Van Straalen, N.M. (eds.) *Environmental Toxicology in South East Asia*, VU University Press, Amsterdam, pp. 235-242.

Al-Atia, G.R. (1980) Toxicity of Cadmium to *Amoeba proteus*: A Biochemical Approach, *J. Protozool.* 27: 128-132.

Anderson, O.R. (1987) *Comparative Protozoology. Ecology, Physiology, Life history*, Springer Verlag, Berlin.

Apostel, S. (1973) A Bioassay of Toxicity Using Protozoa in the Study of Aquatic Environment Pollution and Its Prevention, *Environ. Res.* 6: 356-372.

Bamforth, S.S. (1980) Terrestrial Protozoa, *J. Protozool.* 27: 33-36.

Bamforth, S.S. (1984) Ecology of Protozoa, in: Lee, J.J., Hutner, S.H. & Bovee, E.C. (eds.) *An Illustrated Guide to the Protozoa*, Soc. of Protozoologists, Lawrence, Kansas, USA, pp. 8-15.

Barnes, R.S.K., Calow, P. & Olive, P.J.W. (1988) *The Invertebrates. A New Synthesis*, Blackwell Scientific Publication, London.

Berg, M., Didden, W., Van Esbroek, M., De Fluiter, R., Heijmans, G., Janssen, M.P.M., Kniese, P., Masselink, N., Schouten, T. & Verhoef, H.A. (1994) The Role of Soil Biota in Nutrient Dynamics of Forest Ecosystems: Population Dynamics, *Acta Zool. Fenn.* (in press).

Bergquist, B.L. & Bovee, E.L. (1973) Some Adverse Effects of Cadmium on Growth and Locomotion of *Tetrahymena pyriformis*, *J. Protozool.* 20: 497.

Berhin, F., Houba, C. & Remacle, J. (1984) Cadmium Toxicity and Accumulation by *Tetrahymena pyriformis* in Contaminated River Waters, *Environ. Pollut.* (Ser. A) 35: 315-329.

Berk, S.G., Gunderson, J.H. & Derk, L.A. (1985) Effects of Cadmium and Copper on Chemotaxis of Marine and Freshwater Ciliates, *Bull. Environ. Contam. Toxicol.* 34: 897-903.

Bringmann, G. & Kühn, R. (1980) Comparison of the Toxicity Thresholds of Water Pollutants to Bacteria, Algae and Protozoa in the Cell Multiplication Inhibition Test, *Water Res.* 14: 231-241.

Devillers, J., Steiman, R., Seigle-Murandi, F., Prevot, P., André, C. & Benoit-Guyod, J.L. (1990) Combination of Single-species Laboratory Tests for the Assessment of the Ecotoxicity of p-Benzoquinone, *Tox. Assess.* 5: 405-416.

Dive, D. & Leclerc, H. (1977) Standardized Tests Method Using Protozoa for Measuring Water Pollutant Toxicity, *Progr. Water Technol.* 7: 67-72.

Doelman, P., Nieboer, G., Schrooten, J. & Visser, M. (1984) Antagonistic and Synergistic Toxic Effects of Pb and Cd in a Simple Food Chain: Nematodes Feeding on Bacteria and Fungi, *Bull. Environ. Contam. Toxicol.* 32: 717-723.

Fenchel, T. (1974) Intrinsic Rate of Natural Increase: The Relationship with Body Size, *Oecologia* (Berl.) 14: 317-325.

Fenchel, T. (1987) *Ecology of Protozoa*, Science Techn. Publ., Madison, Wisconsin.

Foissner, W. (1987) Soil Protozoa: Fundamental Problems, Ecological Significance, Adaptations in Ciliates and Testaceans, Bioindicators, and Guide to the Literature, in: Corliss, J.O. & Patterson, D.J. (eds.) *Progress in Protistology*, Vol. 2, Biopress Ltd., Bristol, pp. 69-212.

Foissner, W. (1988) Taxonomic and Nomenclatural Revison of Sladeceks List of Ciliates (Protozoa: Ciliophora) as Indicators of Water Quality, *Hydrobiologia* 166: 1-64.

Foissner, W. (1991) Diversity and Ecology of Soil Flagellates, in: Patterson, D.J. & Larsen, J. (eds.) *The Biology of Free-living Heterotrophic Flagellates*, Clarendon Press, Oxford, pp. 93-112.

Gause, G.F. (1933) Certain Properties of the Curves of Toxicity, *Protoplasma* 17: 543-553.

Hausmann, K. (1985) *Protozoologie*, Thieme, Stuttgart.

Houba, C. & Remacle, J. (1982) Factors Influencing Toxicity of Cadmium to *Tetrahymena pyriformis*: Particulate or Soluble Form and Degree of Complexation, *Environ. Pollut.* (Ser. A) 28: 35-43.

Huber, H.C., Huber, W. & Ritter, U. (1991) Ein Einfaches in vitro-Prufsystem zur Toxizitätsbestimmung von Umweltchemikalien mit monoxenischen Mikrokulturen von *Tetrahymena pyriformis*, *Z. Wasser-Abwasser-Forsch.* 24: 109-112.

Janssen, M.P.M., Oosterhoff, C. & Heijmans, G.J.S.M. (1992) The Effect of Heavy Metal Salts on the Population Growth of *Colpoda cucullus*, *Proc. 1st Eur. Congress Protozool*, Reading, UK, p. 22.

Jeanne-Levain, N. (1974) Étude des effets du lindane sur la croissance et le developpement de quelques organismes unicellulaires, *Bull. Soc. Zool. France* 99: 105-109.

Lousier, J.D. & Bamforth, S.S. (1990) Soil Protozoa, in: Dindal, D.L. (ed.) *Soil Biology Guide*, Wiley & Sons, New York, pp. 97-136.

Mohr, J.L. (1952) Protozoa as Indicators of Pollution, *Sci. Mon. N.Y.* 74: 7-9.

Moravcova, V. (1976) Axenic Cultures of *Tetrahymena pyriformis* as Toxicological Tools, *Acta Hydrochim. Hydrobiol.* 4 (1): 83-94.

Nieboer, E. & Richardson, D.H.S. (1980) The Replacement of the Nondescript Term 'Heavy Metals' by a Biologically and Chemically Significant Classification of Metal Ions, *Environ. Pollut.* (ser. B) 1: 3-26.

Nilsson, J.R. (1978) Retention of Lead Within the Digestive Vacuole in *Tetrahymena*, *Protoplasma* 95: 163-173.

Nilsson, J.R. (1992) On the Response of *Tetrahymena pyriformis* to External Agents, *Proc. 1st Eur. Congress Protozool*, Reading, UK, p. 16.

Persoone, G. & Dive, D. (1978) Toxicity Tests on Ciliates. A Short Review, *Ecotoxicol. Environ. Saf.* 2: 105-114.

Pons, R. & Pussard, M. (1980) Action des herbicides sur les Ambes libres (Rhizopoda, Protozoa). Etude preliminaire, *Acta Oecol.* 1: 15-20.

Prescott, L.M. & Olson, D.L. (1972) The Effects of Pesticides on the Soil Amoebae *Acanthamoebae castellani* (Neff), *Proc. S.D. Acad. Sci.* 51: 136-141.

Prescott, L.M., Kubovec, M.K. & Tryggestad, D. (1977) The Effects of Pesticides, Polychlorinated Biphenyls and metals on the growth and reproduction of *Acanthamoeba castellani*, *Bull. Environ. Contam. Toxicol.* 18: 29-34.

Roberts, R.O. & Berk, S.G. (1990) Development of Protozoan Chemoattraction Bioassay for Evaluating Toxicity of Aquatic Pollutants, *Tox. Assess.* 5: 279-292.

Ruthven, J.A. & Cairns, J. (1973) Response of Fresh-water Protozoan Artificial Communities to Metals, *J. Protozool.* 20 (1): 127-135.

Schoener, T.W. (1983) Rate of Species Turnover Decreases from Lower to Higher Organisms: A Review of the Data, *Oikos* 41: 372-377.

Silberstein, G.B. & Hooper, A.B. (1972) Herbicide (2, 4, 5T) Effect on *Tetrahymena pyriformis*, *J. Protozool* 19: 28-29.

Sleigh, M. (1989) *Protozoa and Other Protists*, Cambridge Univ. Press, Cambridge.

Slooff, W., Canton, J.H. & Hermens, J.L.M. (1983) Comparison of the Suspectibility Freshwater Species to 15 Chemical Compounds, *Aquat. Toxicol.* 4: 113-128.

Stout, J.D. (1981) The Role of Protozoa in Nutrient Cycling and Energy Flow, in: Alexander, M. (ed.) *Advances in Microbial Ecology*, Plenum Press, New York, Vol. 4, pp. 1-50.

Taylor, M.G. & Simkiss, K. (1984) Inorganic Deposits in Invertebrate Tissues, *Environ. Chem.* 3: 102-138.

Thompson, A.S., Rhodes, J.C. & Pettman, I. (1988) *Culture Collection of Algae and Protozoa. Catalogue of Strains. Culture Collection of Algae and Protozoa*, Ambleside, UK.

Weinstein, D.A. & Birk, E.M. (1989) The Effect of Chemicals on the Structure of Terrestrial Ecosystems: Mechanisms and Pattern of Change, in: Levin, S.A., Harwell, M.A., Kelley, J.R. & Kimball, K.D. (eds.) *Ecotoxicology: Problems and Approaches*, Springer, New York, pp. 181-209.

Wheeler, Q.D. (1990) Insect Diversity and Cladistic Constraints, *Ann. Entom. Soc. Am.* 83: 1031-1047.

Yamaguchi, N., Wada, O., Ono, T., Yazaki, K. & Toykawa, K. (1973) Detection of Heavy Metal Toxicity by *Tetrahymena pyriformis* Culture Method, *Ind. Health* 11: 27-31.

4.5

The importance of extended post-exposure observation in acute toxicity tests with aquatic snails

J.H. ALI

Abstract

This paper describes a study to determine the toxicity of carbofuran to the freshwater snails, Filopaludina sumatrensis *and* Lymnaea rubiginosa. *An exposure of 24 h in the test solutions killed only 0-20% of the snails, however, the remaining snails which were transferred to recovery tanks continued to die. A recovery time of seven days was found to be sufficient for the extended observation period in these acute toxicity tests. LC_{50} values for* F. sumatrensis *and* L. rubiginosa *(exposed for 24 h) computed from pooled mortality rates (from both exposures and recovery times) were 200 mg/L and 447 mg/L respectively. It was found that the LC_{50} values could not be computed when based only on mortality data of the 24 h exposure. Based on pooled mortality data the LC_{50}s from 96 h exposure period were 68 mg/L for* F. sumatrensis *and 151 mg/L for* L. rubiginosa. *These values were lower than the values calculated from the number of snails that died during actual exposure only.*

1.   Introduction

Snails are commonly found in aquatic ecosystems. Being constantly exposed to toxic chemicals, whether agrochemicals or other pollutants, snails may not escape the detrimental effects of these chemicals. As a result, snails have been studied as indicators for certain heavy metals, pesticides and radioactive material since the 1960s. Analysis of gastropods living in biotopes exposed to pollutants can provide a quantitative indication of the amounts of the existing pollutants (Harman 1974).

The application of some systemic pesticides (by direct casting) such as carbofuran to wet paddy fields, can pose a threat to non-target organisms including freshwater snails. It has been observed (unpublished data) that paddy fields, where agrochemicals are applied extensively, carry fewer freshwater snails, measured both in terms of diversity and abundance. Snails such as *Biomphalaria* and *Bulinus* may be the target for some pesticides because they act as intermediate hosts of human schistosomes while others such as *Pomacea*, are considered to be paddy pests (Adalla & Morallo-Rejesus 1989).

In experiments carried out by Robertson & Mazella (1989) on the freshwater snail, *Gillia altilis* using an organophosphorus insecticide diazinon, it was found that the snails died beyond the exposure time, and the value of LC_{50} was computed based on the pooled number of snails which died between exposure time and recovery time. The present study was undertaken to find out if freshwater snails are also susceptible to carbofuran and if so, whether the response is similar to that for diazinon.

2. Materials and methods

Carbofuran (technical grade 75% a.i.) was used. The insecticide powder was dissolved in acetone to improve its solubility before being serially diluted with conditioned tap water. For all experiments, the snails were collected from a disused pond close to the laboratory at Universiti Pertanian Malaysia. They were collected by hand and transported to the laboratory in a 1.5 L pail. Upon arrival the snails were placed in continuously aerated holding tanks. The snails were acclimated to the laboratory conditions for at least 3 days before any experiments were carried out. Water characteristics were as follows:

Temperature:	25.7 (25.5-26) °C
pH:	6.7 (5.8-7.4)
Hardness $CaCO_3$:	2.9 (2.8-3.4) mg/L
Dissolved oxygen:	2.96 (2.9-3.0) mg/L
Nitrogen:	1.1 (1.0-1.2) mg/L
Phosphate:	0.27 (0.2-0.3) mg/L
Conductivity:	90.3 (87-94) μS/cm

Freshwater snails, *Filopaludina sumatrensis* (Prosobranchia) were divided into five size groups. Snails in size-class 1 were about 8 mm in shell length, size 2 about 10 mm, size 3 about 13 mm, size 4 about 15 mm and size 5 (adult) about 19 mm. All exposures to carbofuran were carried out in 1 L rectangular plastic aquaria which were aerated continuously. The water used in all experiments was dechlorinated tap water left standing for at least 7 days. Preliminary trial exposures were conducted to determine the concentration of carbofuran that killed between 20% to 80% of snails to satisfy the requirement of the probit analysis, used to determine the LC_{50}. For each size group, ten snails of approximately equal size in five replicates were exposed to various concentrations. Snails that died during the 24 h exposure were removed and the remaining snails were taken out from the tanks and rinsed under running tap water to remove any residual carbofuran from the shell. The snails were then placed for 7 days in a recovery system which consisted 1 L aquaria filled with 750 mL of conditioned water, aerated continously. The water in the recovery aquaria was changed daily. During this 7 days period, dead snails were removed and counted every 24 hours.

A 96 h static renewal bioassay was also performed in which the carbofuran solutions were changed every 24 h. At each 24 h interval, the snails were removed from the tanks and rinsed with conditioned water to remove the residual carbofuran from the snails. The water tanks were then refilled with fresh solution of carbofuran and the snails were replaced. At the end of 96 h, snails were transferred to recovery tanks for further observation. Adult *Lymnaea rubiginosa* (Pulmonata) of 10 mm in shell length were also exposed for 24 h and 96 h as described above. Control tanks in all experiments contained 1 L of conditioned water. Since the carbofuran was dissolved in acetone, snails were also exposed to the highest doses of acetone used for 24 h and 96 h exposures. Death was established by the failure of a snail to respond when its foot was prodded with a blunt needle.

3.   Results and discussion

The acetone used to improve the solubility of carbofuran apparently had no significant effect on the snails. The highest mortality recorded in acetone was 12% which is within the allowed percentage in the probit analysis.

Generally, in the first 24 h exposure, there was no apparent effect on the adult snails (size group 5). The mortality of snails exposed to the test concentrations at this stage ranged from 0 to 20% as shown in Figures 1, 2 and 3. The mortality rates, especially for those exposed to the higher concentrations, increased dramatically on the first day in the recovery tank. The rate then stabilized quickly until the end of the recovery time. The mortality rates at the lower concentrations, however, increased gradually as shown by Figure 1.

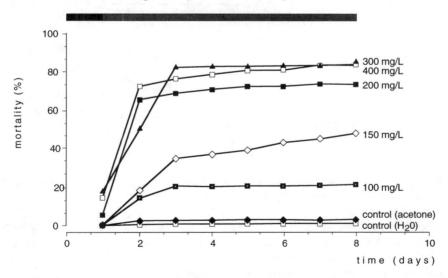

Figure 1 *Mortality rate of* Filopaludina sumatrensis, *exposed for 24 h to various concentrations of carbofuran, during exposure (black bar) and recovery (grey bar)*

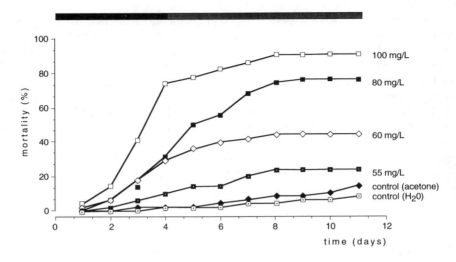

Figure 2 *Mortality rate of adult* Filopaludina sumatrensis *exposed for 96 h to various concentrations of carbofuran, during exposure (black bar) and recovery (grey bar)*

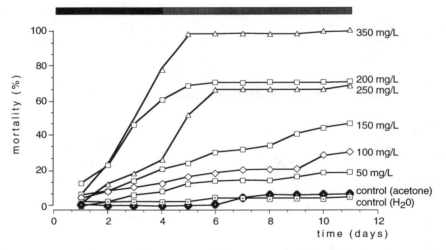

Figure 3 *Mortality rate of* Lymnaea rubiginosa, *exposed for 96 h to various concentrations of carbofuran, during exposure (black bar) and recovery (grey bar)*

A similar pattern of mortality was also demonstrated by snails exposed for 96 h. In the first 24 h the mortality rate was only about 15%, then it increased gradually until the end of the exposure time. The remaining snails, however, continued to die in the recovery tanks as shown in Figures 2 and 3.

As the mortality rates during the exposure times were too low to meet the requirements for probit analysis, LC_{50} values could not be computed for *F. suma-*

trensis and *L. rubiginosa* exposed for 24 h to carbofuran (Table 1). LC_{50} values could only be computed when the data for numbers of snail deaths during exposure and during recovery were pooled. LC_{50} values for *F. sumatrensis* and *L. rubiginosa* exposed for 24 h to carbofuran were 200 mg/L and 447 mg/L respectively (Table 1).

For the longer exposure (96 h), LC_{50} could be calculated based on the number of snails which died during exposure. The LC_{50} values for *F. sumatrensis* and *L. rubiginosa* were 84 mg/L and 249 mg/L respectively. As the snails continued to die during recovery time, the values of LC_{50} were reduced to 68 mg/L and 151 mg/L respectively (Table 1), showing that the snails were more susceptible to carbofuran than initially appeared.

Table 1 *The values of LC_{50} of adult snails exposed to carbofuran, based on mortality during exposure time and pooled for both exposure and recovery times*

Species	LC_{50} (mg/L)	
	Exposure time	Pooled
F. sumatrensis		
24 h	NC	200
96 h	84	68
L. rubiginosa		
24 h	NC	447
96 h	249	151

NC = not computable; Pooled = combined data from exposure time and recovery time.

Table 2 *The values of LC_{50} for* F. sumatrensis *of various size groups exposed for 24 h to carbofuran*

Snail size group	LC_{50} (mg/L)	
	Exposure time	Pooled
1	NC	119
2	NC	158
3	NC	154
4	NC	186

NC = not computable; Pooled = combined data from exposure time and recovery time.

Although carbofuran is formulated as an insecticide and is used widely in Malaysia to control plant hoppers in paddy fields, the result of the study showed that it is quite toxic to freshwater snails. The operculated *F. sumatrensis* was found to be more sensitive than the pulmonate, *L. rubiginosa* as shown by both 24 h and 96 h exposures.

Similar patterns for mortality were also shown by younger *F. sumatrensis* (size classes 1, 2, 3 and 4) exposed for 24 h to carbofuran. Because of this, the LC_{50} value could only be calculated from pooled data as described above and the LC_{50} values for the four groups were 119 mg/L, 158 mg/L, 154 mg/L and 186 mg/L respectively. These lower figures, compared with the adult snails, show that the younger snails are more sensitive to carbofuran.

The first reaction of *Filopaludina* to carbofuran was to withdraw its body into the shell and tightly close the aperture with its operculum. A few hours later the foot emerged from the shell and the foot muscle became stiff and curled, facing upward. In this position, the foot was unable to grip the surface of the aquarium. Mucus was found surrounding the body. Mucus secretion is one of the first reactions of molluscs to chemical irritation from molluscicidal poisoning (Godan 1979). Ultrastructural studies have shown that carbamates cause deformation of the mucus-producing system while the molluscicide, metaldehyde, induces total destruction of the mucus-producing system of the slug, *Deroceras reticulatum*, leading to its death (Triebskorn & Ebert 1989).

Due to the snail's slow response, it is very important to observe carefully the immobilized animals which have been exposed to some chemicals to determine death. It is also very important to keep the snails in the recovery tanks after exposing them to pesticides, especially those which are not designed to kill molluscs, as an extended observation period is necessary to observe the full response.

4. References

Adalla, C.B. & Morello-Rejesus, B. (1989) The Golden Apple Snail *Pomacea* sp., a Serious Pest Lowland Rice in the Philippines, *Proc. British Crop Protection Council* 41: 417-422.

Godan, D. (1979) *Schadschnecken*, Ulmer Verlag, Stuttgart.

Harman, W.N. (1974) Snails (Mollusca: Gastropoda), in: Hart, C.W. & Fuller, S.L.H. (eds.) *Pollution Ecology of Freshwater Invertebrates*, Academic Press, New York.

Robertson, J.B. & Mazella, C. (1989) Acute Toxicity of the Pesticide Diazinon to the Freshwater snail *Gillia altilis*, *Bull. Environ. Contam. Toxicol.* 43: 320-324.

Triebskorn, R. & Ebert, D. (1989) The Importance of Mucus Production in Slugs Reaction to Molluscicides and the Impact of Molluscicides on the Mucus Producing System, *Proc. British Crop Protection Council* 41: 373-378.

4.6

Early warning indicators in aquatic systems, with reference to the production of stress proteins

N.R. NGANRO & S. SASTRODIHARDJO

Abstract

In terms of environmental monitoring, the production of stress proteins in response to environmental insults is a recently studied phenomenon. Many workers have suggested that stress proteins could be initiated by a wide range of stressors such as chemical agents, many of which are increasingly present in polluted areas. The inducibility and ease of detection of these proteins has led to considering the use of stress proteins as an indicator of environmental pollution. In the present study, the possibility of using stress proteins as an early indicator of pollution in marine coelenterates was investigated. The animal studied was the temperate anemone Anemonia viridis which possesses symbiotic algae (zooxanthellae) that are similar to almost all tropical coelenterates as builder organisms of coral reefs. In this study the anemone A. viridis, exposed to different regimes of heat shocks and/or copper treatments, showed the expression of at least six enhanced/induced proteins with molecular weights 30, 31, 35, 39, 69 and 127 kD. In future studies, the use of such techniques could be extended to early warning bioassay development for assessing the health of reef corals in particular and other aquatic organisms in general.

1.   Introduction

The aim of ecotoxicological study is to assess the risk to ecosystems of exposure to environmental stressors, including pollution. Abel & Axiak (1991) comment that although data on environmental factors (chemical and physical factors) are important components of risk assessment, ultimately it is the data on biological responses to stressors or pollutants that will help to determine the degree of biologically harmful effects which may be expected.

According to Bayne *et al.* (1985), indices of biological responses for measurements of water quality may span a wide level of biological organization, *i.e.* at molecular, cellular, individual, population and community levels. Some of these biological approaches have been successfully applied in the clonal hydroid *Campa-*

nularia (Stebbing 1976, 1979), the scope for growth of *Mytilus* (Widdows *et al.* 1978, 1982) and community effects (Warwick *et al.* 1986).

Biological indices measured in the temperate coelenterates *Anemonia viridis* after copper exposure (Nganro 1992) included assays at the molecular, cellular and organism levels.

In the present study, the molecular marker selected in the temperate *Anemonia* was the production of stress proteins. These proteins are induced in a wide range of living cells, from prokaryotes to eukaryotes, in response to environmental stressors (Atkinson & Walden 1985).

In terms of environmental monitoring, the production of stress proteins in response to environmental insults is a recently studied phenomenon. According to Anderson (1989), stress proteins can be initiated by a wide variety of chemical agents (around 30 in all) such as arsenate, arsenite, heavy metal ions and oxidizing agents (Welch 1985, Caltabiano *et al.* 1986), many of which are increasingly present in polluted waters.

2. Materials and methods

Anemonia viridis (Forskal) were maintained in tanks of aerated artificial seawater (S=35‰) at two temperate regimes, $15 \pm 1°C$ and $20 \pm 1°C$. The anemones were fed with fresh *Mytilus* (about 1 g/anemone) once a week. Daily illumination was established to give a 12 h light and 12 h dark cycle. The anemones were maintained at selected temperatures for five weeks before experimental use. Other anemones were maintained for 5 months at $20 \pm 1°C$.

Fifteen anemones (size 30-35 basal disc) were used for heat shock and copper exposures. The experimental exposure was as follows:

Heat shock:
    15°C   28°C (2 h)   15°C (0 h, 1 h, 4 h recovery)
    20°C   32°C (2 h)   20°C (0 h, 1 h, 4 h recovery)

Copper exposure:
    15°C Cu^{2+} (6 h)   15°C (4 h recovery)

The whole anemone was cut into small pieces and homogenized in a sample buffer (Miller 1988) for electrophoresis assays. The homogenate was kept at -20°C. A defrosted sample was centrifuged at 5000 rpm, 45 min at 4°C. The supernatant was then centrifuged at 13000 rpm, 1 h, at 4°C. The high speed supernatant was dialyzed against 62.5 mM Tris-HCl buffer pH 6.8, 18h at 10°C. A protein assay was carried out using Bradford's method (1976). The rest of the sample was concentrated using a mini-concentrator (Amicon product). The sample was denatured in a sample buffer. A one-dimensional SDS-PAGE (sodium dodecylsulphate polyacrylamide gel-electrophoresis) was prepared for BIO-RAD mini gel using Laemmli's method (1970). The sample was then subjected to electrophoresis using 15% polyacrylamide slab gels.

3. Results

Examination of the CBB (Comassie Brilliant Blue) stained gels with an ultrascanning laser densitometer showed changes in the protein composition in all experimental anemones, *Anemonia viridis*. The relative molecular weight of new proteins (enhanced stress proteins) were scanned and calibrated using protein markers on the same stained gels. The proteins extracted from the anemone and loaded onto the gels were assumed to be mainly from the host (not from the symbiont algae or zooxanthellae). The algae were removed from the homogenate by differential centrifugation. The final supernatants were observed under the light microscope to check for the presence of algae, prior to use for SDS-PAGE.

Table 1 *Appearance of heat shock proteins in Anemonia viridis following various treatments*

	Induced/enhanced proteins (kD)					
	30	31	35	39	69	127
Heat shock exposure:						
C-15°C	--+	--+	-++	---	---	---
HS-28°C, 2h	-++	--+	-++	---	---	--+
R-15°C, 1h	-++	--+	+++	--+	---	--+
R-15°C, 2h	+++	-++	+++	-++	--+	-++
R-15°C, 4h	-++	+++	-++	-++	-++	-++
C-20°C	-++	+++	+++	-++	-++	--+
HS-32°C, 2h & R-20°C, 4h	-++	+++	+++	-++	-++	--+
Copper exposure:						
Cu^{2+}, 6h at 15°C & R-15°C, 4h	--+	--+	+++	+++	+++	--+

Notes: C-15 = anemone maintained at 15°C; HS-28 = anemone maintained at 15°C, sampled after heat shock at 28°C; R-15, 1 h, 2 h, 4 h = anemone maintained at 15°C, sampled after 1 h, 2 h, 4 h recovery at 15°C following a 2 h heat shock at 28°C; C-20 = anemone maintained at 20°C; HS-32 = anemone maintained at 20°C, sampled after 4 h recovery at 20°C following a 2 h heat shock at 32°C; copper = anemone maintained at 15°C, sampled after 4 h recovery at 15°C following a 6 h exposure to 0.1 mg/L copper chloride; --- = no protein present or induced/enhanced; --+ = protein present or induced/enhanced; -++ = protein more enhanced; +++ = protein highly induced/enhanced.

The anemones exposed to different regimes of heat shock or copper treatment showed the expression of at least six enhanced or induced proteins; *i.e.* 30, 31, 35, 39, 69 and 127 kD. The full identity of these proteins is not yet clear. Western immunoblotting using monoclonal antihuman Abs of the sample gels was unsuccessful. The same Abs did recognize the hsp90 and hsp70 of human cells (Miller, pers. comm.). The relative expression of heat shock and copper induced proteins in *Anemonia* is presented in Table 1.

4. Discussion

Organisms as diverse as bacteria, plants, invertebrates and vertebrates respond to environmental stress by synthesizing a small number of highly conserved heat shock proteins or stress proteins (Morimoto *et al.* 1990). In this study, the marine coelenterate *Anemonia viridis* appeared to synthesize these proteins. The maintenance of anemones at two temperature regimes produced different patterns of protein synthesis. However, both heat shock and copper exposure induced/enhanced similar expressions of proteins with molecular weights at 35, 39, 69 and 127 kD. Proteins of 30 kD and 31 kD were enhanced only by heat stress.

Protein synthesis by the anemone at 35 kD and 39 kD was induced/enhanced by both copper and increased temperature shock. These proteins are probably specific stress proteins produced by the anemone. Work by Caltabiano *et al.* (1986) on human and murine cells exposed to heavy metals or sulphydryl reactive agents, has demonstrated synthesis of 32 kD and 34 kD stress proteins. Other workers have found that the exposure of human leukemic cells to cadmium chloride (1.8 $\mu g/L$) for 8h leads to an increase of the enzyme heme-oxygenase (34 kD) (Taketani *et al.* 1990).

Since 30-35 kD proteins appear to be ubiquitously induced by heat shock, heavy metals and other sulphydryl agents in diverse cell types, it has been suggested that these proteins might play a role in detoxification (Caltabiano *et al.* 1986, 1988). Several detoxification enzymes with a similar range of lower molecular weights have been identified; they include methyltransferase (28 kD), acetyltransferase (32 kD), and sulphurtransferase (33 kD) (Jakoby 1980). Production of heme-oxygenase in mouse cells exposed to heavy metals (Taketani *et al.* 1990) is also thought to have a detoxification role; the function of the enzyme being similar to that of metallothionein.

The induced/enhanced proteins exhibited by *Anemonia* in the present study have similar molecular weights to actin-binding proteins (Craig & Pollard 1982) which may be involved in inducing cellular contraction in *Anemonia*, ultimately resulting in the loss of zooxanthellae (Nganro 1992).

In conclusion, there is clearly considerable scope for the use of early warning bioassays in future studies on the bleaching response of reef corals in particular and for monitoring water quality in aquatic systems in general.

5. References

Abel, P.D. & Axiak, V. (1991) *Ecotoxicology and the Marine Environment*, Ellis Horwood Ltd., 269 p.

Anderson, R. (1989) Early Warnings of Stress, *New Scientist* 122: 50-52.

Atkinson, B.G. & Walden, D.B. (1985) *Changes in Eukaryotic Gene Expression in Response to Environmental Stress*, Academic Press, New York, 379 p.

Bayne, B.L., Brown, D.A., Burns, K., Dixon, D.R., Ivanovici, A., Livingstone, D.R., Lowe, D.M., Moore, M.N., Stebbing, A.R.D. & Widdows, J. (1985) *The Effects of Stress and Pollution on Marine Animals*, Praeger, 384 p.

Bradford, M.M. (1976) A Rapid and Sensitive Method for the Quantification of Microgram Quantities of Protein Utilizing the Principle of Protein-dye Binding, *Anal. Biochem.* 72: 248-254.

Caltabiano, M.M., Koestler, T.P., Poste, G. & Greig, R.G. (1986) Induction of 32- and 34-kDa Stress Proteins by Sodium Arsenite, Heavy Metals and Thiol-reactive Agents, *J. Biol. Chem.* 261: 13381-13386.

Caltabiano, M.M., Poste, G. & Greig, R.G. (1988) Isolation and Immunological Characterization of the Mammalian 32/34 kDa Stress Protein, *Exp. Cell Res.* 178: 41-50.

Craig, S.W. & Pollard, T.W. (1982) Actin-binding Proteins, *Trends Biochem. Sci. (TIBS)* 7: 88-92.

Jakoby, W.B. (1980) *Enzymatic Basis of Detoxication*, Academic Press. New York, 2 vols, 784 p.

Laemmli, U.K. (1970) Cleavage of Structural Proteins During the Assembly of the Head of Bacteriophage T4, *Nature* 227: 680-685.

Miller, D. (1988) The Heat Shock Response of the Cryptobiotic Brine Shrimp *Artemia*-I. A Comparison of the Thermotolerance of Cysts and Lavae, *J. Therm. Biol.* 13: 119-123.

Morimoto, R., Tissres, A. & Georgopoulos, C. (1990) *Stress Proteins in Biology and Medicine*, Cold Spring Harbor Lab. Press, 450 p.

Nganro, N.R. (1992) *Development of a Tropical Marine Water Quality Bioassay Using Symbiotic Coelenterates*, Ph.D. Dissertation, Univ. of Newcastle upon Tyne, U.K., 225 p.

Stebbing, A.R.D. (1976) The Effects of Low Metal Levels on a Clonal Hydroid, *J. Mar. Biol. Ass.* (UK) 56: 977-994.

Stebbing, A.R.D. (1979) An Experimental Approach to Determinants of Biological Water Quality, *Phil. Trans. Roy. Soc. Lond.* 286: 465-481.

Taketani, S., Kohno, H., Yoshinaga, T., Tokunaga, R., Ishii, T. & Bannai, S. (1990) Induction in Mouse Peritoneal Macrophages of 34 kDa Stress Protein and Heme Oxygenase by Sulphydryl Reactive Agents, *J. Biochem.* 108: 28-32.

Warwick, R.M. (1986) A New Method for Detecting Pollution Effects on Marine Macrobenthic Communities, *Mar. Biol.* 92: 557-562.

Welch, W.J. (1985) Phorbol Ester, Calcium Ionophore, or Serum Added to Quiescent Rat Embryo Fibroblast Cells, All Result in the Elevated Phosphorilation of Two 28000 Dalton Mammalian Stress Proteins, *J. Biol. Chem.* 260: 3058-3062.

Widdows, J. (1978) Physiological Indices of Stress in *Mytilus edulis*, *J. Mar. Biol. Ass.* (UK) 58: 125-142.

Widdows, J., Bakke, T., Bayne, B.L., Donkin, P., Livingstone, D.R., Lowe, D.M., More, M.N., Evan, S.V. & Moore, S.L. (1982) Responses of *Mytilus edulis* on Exposure to Water Accommodated Fractions of North Sea Oil, *Mar. Biol.* 67: 15-31.

Part 5

Environmental assessments

5.1

Preliminary study on the environmental pollution in the Citarum river basin, West Java, Indonesia

N. DJUANGSIH & H. SALIM

Abstract

An analysis was made of environmental impacts following construction of three water reservoirs (for irrigation and electricity) in the Citarum river basin. The increase of water supply for irrigation and electricity has provided favourable conditions for agricultural and industrial development in the area, and consequently, some environmental problems, such as water pollution by agricultural and industrial activities have increased considerably. These environmental problems are described in this paper, particularly with regard to the characteristics of the pollution sources. Strategies and mitigations implemented to manage the problems are outlined.

1. Introduction

The environmental quality of the Citarum river basin, a multipurpose reservoir for irrigation water, fishery, electricity, agri-aquaculture, drinking water supply and tourism, has become more important since the construction of a hydroelectric power plant.

The Citarum river basin is one of the largest river basins in the Province of West Java, and land use in the Citarum river basin is dominated by agriculture. The river originates at the foot of Mount Wayang in the agricultural area, about 40 km south of Bandung City, and runs northward for about 225 km, ending in the Java Sea. The watershed covers several ecosystems of riverain agricultural land, rural and urban areas. The topographic conditions of the river basin and its surrounding area make the river a potential site for the construction of a series of hydroelectric power plants (HEPP). There are already three large HEPPs, the most downstream of which is the Juanda HEPP. Its major function is to provide a reservoir for irrigation, but it also produces electricity with an installed capacity of 150 MW. The Saguling HEPP and the Cirata HEPP are located above the Juanda HEPP. Their main functions are to produce electricity with respectives capacities of 700 MW and 500 MW.

The main problems of environmental pollution in the Citarum river basin can be outlined as follows:

- There is a high risk of aquatic problems along the river and in the reservoir of Saguling and Cirata, especially due to the fast growth of some aquatic weed species, *i.e. Eichornia crassipes* (the water hyacinth), *Salvinia molesta* and *Hydrilla verticillata* (IOE 1979, 1980, in Djuangsih 1993).
- There is a high risk of water pollution especially by hazardous and toxic chemicals (metals and pesticides).

The problems identified above are complicated because the sources of water pollution are settlement, industrial, agricultural and estate areas. However, the local government now is trying to mitigate the environmental pollution in various ways such as the implementation of law enforcement, the clean river program, the development of toxic and hazardous waste management, and the application of life-cycle analysis ('from cradle to grave').

2. Characteristics of the Citarum river basin

The area of the Citarum river basin is 45,232 ha, consisting of 6,409 ha (14,2%) of forest, 35,466 ha (78.4%) of agricultural land, 855 ha (1.9%) of land settlement area, 860 ha (1.9%) of estates and 1,612 ha (3.6%) of bareland. The largest area in the upstream region of the Citarum basin and its surroundings is dominated by agricultural use (mixed garden, rice field and dryland crop) and estates. Fertilizers and pesticides are used very intensively.

The Citarum discharges water at an average of 220 m³/second; the minimum and maximum values respectively are about 30 m³/second and 1200 m³/second. This river flows from south to north with an estimated flow of 5.0 billion m³/year. The Citarum is used as a source of drinking water supply, for irrigation, for industry and for the daily need of the inhabitants living along the river bank.

The population in the Citarum river basin is estimated to be 9 million people, with a density of between 215 to 5,048 inhabitants/km² in the upper basin. They work mostly as farmers, government workers, traders and laborers. The education of the people ranges from elementary school up to university level. The most densely populated area is Bandung City, whose surroundings are dominated by textile factories. The other cities are Cianjur, Purwakarta, Cikampek, Karawang, and Bekasi. Those settlements are surrounded by rice fields with the largest rice field area at Cikampek (96,000 ha), Karawang (80,000 ha), and Bekasi (84,000 ha). The area is known as 'daerah lumbung padi Jawa Barat' or 'paddy stock area of West Java'. This rice field area is irrigated regularly by the Juanda multi purpose dam.

There are two other big dams in the upper Juanda reservoir, namely Saguling and Cirata with electricity generations of 700 MW and 500 MW, respectively. In the Saguling and Cirata reservoirs aquaculture has been very intensively developed.

Industrial development in the Citarum river basin has increased tremendously since 1975 and has stimulated the economy of the country. Most of the industry in this area is textile, with approximately 458 textile factories. The others are leather, paper, paint, chemical, pharmaceutical, machinery and metals, with a total of 490 industrial units (Table 1). The water supply for industrial needs comes from ground water, the Citarum river and its tributaries, while at the same time effluent is discharged into the rivers. Most of those industries are located in the upper Citarum river basin, so the industrial waste will affect the water quality of the Saguling reservoir.

Table 1 *Type of industries in the Citarum river basin and their production rates*

No.	Type of industries	Number of companies	Capacity (production/year)
1.	Textile industries	458	
	a. Synthetic rayon		46,600
	b. Thread		75,423
	c. Weaving		391,357,696
	d. Knitting		13,564
	e. Dyeing		
	- Cloth		69,475
	- Thread		4,007
	f. Finishing		101,093
	g. Printing		143,486,840
2.	Leather industry	10	5,691,500
3.	Paper industry	3	40,200
4.	Paint industry	2	6,650
5.	Chemical industry	6	26,330
6.	Machinery and metal	11	7,000

Source: Brotoisworo (1990).

3. The Citarum river basin problems

The problems which have arisen in the Citarum river basin are due to several activities concentrated in the basin itself, namely agricultural practices, disposal of domestic and industrial waste, shortages in domestic water supply and the socio-economic aspects of the community. These problems contribute to the environmental pollution in the Citarum river basin, especially of the water. If the present conditions continue, it will have a negative impact on the HEPP development within the Citarum river basin.

3.1 Agricultural practices

The problem which arise from agricultural practice are caused by intensive land exploitation including planting in marginal land and increasing the use of pesticides, fertilizers, and organic compost. Use of those materials has increased tremendously in the past 9 years. The enhancement of pesticides and fertilizer use is 300% per ha and 56% per ha respectively (Table 2).

Table 2 *The increasing rates of pesticides and fertilizer usage in West Java (kg/ha)*

Year	Pesticide	Fertilizer		
		Urea	TSP	Others
1979	1.2	144.4	38.8	0.61
1980	1.7	180.5	73.8	0.42
1981	1.9	198.6	83.6	0.65
1982	2.4	200.4	85.7	2.76
1983	2.9	210.2	94.6	2.16
1984	3.3	218.8	105.9	3.14
1985	3.8	211.4	100.3	3.10
1986	4.4	207.0	106.0	-
1987	3.8	200.2	112.3	9.97

Source: Statistic Centre Bureau.

The run-off from agricultural land and forest areas brings a number of chemical compounds such as pesticides, fertilizer, organic compost and soil into the river. During the wet season the Citarum river and its tributaries become brownish due to the many suspended solids. According to a study conducted by the Institute of Ecology, the erosion rate of the Citarum river basin is in the range of 1.82 - 5.20 mm/ha with an average of 3.35 mm/year. The erosion problem could cause sedimentation of lakes and rivers, and could promote flooding in the plain areas. The study showed that during the application of the fertilizers in rice field approximately 20% of the fertilizer will be leached, while for pesticides leaching is about 5% (Brotoisworo 1990). Therefore, the extent of the load of those compounds which may cause eutrophication problems in the river and reservoir can be calculated. An excessive amount of nitrogen and phosphorus compounds may cause fast growth of aquatic weeds or 'blooming', especially for *Eichornia crassipes* (the water hyacinth), and *Hydrilla verciculata* in the Saguling reservoir.

The adverse effects of water hyacinths are high evapotranspiration, growth of floating islands, silting up of the lakes, provision of a habitat for vector diseases, and a decrease in fish yield.

Residues of organochlorine and organophosphate pesticides were found in the Citarum river Basin. Detectable amounts were found for fenitrothion, supricide, dichlorvos and propoxur. All concentrations were very low, falling in the range of undetectable to 0.338 μg/L, usually less than the National Water Quality Standard of 0.1 μg/L for the raw water supply of drinking water (Anonymous 1988).

However, two kinds of organochlorine pesticide residues were found with concentration ranges from 37.2 to 56.2 μg/L for HCB and from undetectable to 14.4 μg/L for DDT. Pesticide residues of DDT in the water were less than The National Water Quality Standard for the raw drinking water supply. There is no value for the concentration of HCB in the water in the National Water Quality Standard. However there is an indication that the organochlorine pesticides are more persistent in the environment than the organophosphorus and carbamate pesticides.

Organochlorine pesticide residues were found in fish (liver and meat) from three different places in Bandung, the biggest city at the Citarum river basin. It was shown that DDT and its derivates, dieldrin, endrin and lindane, were found in the organochlorine pesticide residues in the liver and meat respectively, with the range of undetectable to 1.314 μg/kg net weight and undetectable to 1.658 μg/kg (Djuangsih 1993). However, based on the previous monitoring, organochlorine pesticide residues in the Citarum River were not detected (IOE 1991).

3.2 Domestic water supply and its waste

The average amount of domestic water needed for rural and urban people is 60 L/cap and 100 L/cap, respectively. Although these amounts are much lower than those needed by people in the developed countries (150-200 L/cap), the drinking water supply is still insufficient. As an example, in urban areas, less than 50% of households drinking water needs are met by the drinking water source of the drinking water agency. The rest are still using shallow ground water sources and sub-ground water obtained by the use of pumps.

Rural people have no access to purified drinking water, therefore they use surface water (lake, river and pond) and shallow ground water for their daily needs. People who use this kind of water are very vulnerable to illnesses caused by the low quality of drinking water and bad sanitation systems. In Indonesia more than 3.5 million children under 3 years of age suffer from gastroenteritis and 105,000 of these children (3%) die anually.

The above problems are very closely related to improper sanitation systems in rural and urban areas. A study conducted by the Department of Public Work show that only 14.9% of households have a septic tank, and most domestic waste is discharged directly into the river without adequate treatment. Concerning the domestic waste load per capita of Indonesia, it can be predicted that water pollution will occur because of the high concentrations of BOD, COD, nitrite, ammonia, detergent and faecal coli (Table 3) and the potential load of pollutants, mostly originating from domestic waste water in the upper Citarum river basin and the basin as a whole (Table 4).

Table 3 *Composition and pollution load of domestic waste*

Parameter	Units	Pollution load
BOD	gram/capita/day	25
COD	gram/capita/day	57
Nitrogen		
NH_4-N	gram/capita/day	1.83
NO_2-N	gram/capita/day	0.006
NO_3-N	gram/capita/day	0.97
Organic-N	gram/capita/day	8.3
Total-N	gram/capita/day	11.1
Phosphorus		
Ortho-P	gram/capita/day	-
Total-P	gram/capita/day	1.1
Detergents (as MBAS)	gram/capita/day	0.63
Phenol	gram/capita/day	0.006
Faecal coli	total/capita/day	14×10^{12}

Source: Badrudin (1987).

Table 4 *Potential pollution load of domestic waste*

Parameters (ton/day)	Citarum river basin	Upper Citarum river basin (Saguling)
BOD	87.07	47.02
COD	198.51	107.21
Total-N	38.66	20.88
Total-P	3.83	2.07
Detergents (MBAS)	2.19	1.18
Phenol	0.021	0.011

Source: Badrudin (1987)

In addition, solid domestic waste may contribute to the water pollution, because in the Bandung area 5,000 - 6,000 m^3 of garbage is produced each day, see Table 5. This garbage comes mostly from markets, shopping centers and city dwellings. About 80% is treated in a landfill, while 20% is handled improperly. During landfill, decomposition of the solid waste takes place and produces a leachate with a high concentration of chemical substances as shown in Table 6. This leachate is discharged directly into the surface water without any treatment at all, causing both surface water pollution and decreasing ground water quality.

Table 5 *Composition of domestic waste in the Bandung area*

Composition	Percentage
Organic materials (leaves)	73.35
Paper	9.74
Plastics	8.56
Metals	0.54
Rubber	-
Woods	-
Cotton	1.32
Glass	0.43
Others	6.14

Source: Anonymous (1989).

Table 6 *Physical and chemical characteristics of leachate from landfill in the Bandung area*

No.	Parameter	Unit	Concentration
I.	**Physical**		
	Temperature	°C	25
	Electrical conductivity	μS/cm	7000
	Salinity	$^0/_{00}$	4
II.	**Chemical**		
	pH	mg/L	8.5
	DO	mg/L	0
	BOD	mg/L	299
	COD	mg/L	622.04
	NO_2	mg/L	10.46
	NO_3	mg/L	14.56
	NH_3	mg/L	17.46
	N-total	mg/L	284.07
	SO_4	mg/L	47.40
	SiO_2	mg/L	90.12
	Cl^-	mg/L	3.0
	PO_4	mg/L	1.754
III.	**Heavy metals**		
	Fe	mg/L	15.70
	Mn	mg/L	0.25
	Cu	mg/L	0.07
	Cr	mg/L	0.12
	Pb	mg/L	0.91
	Ni	mg/L	0.64
	Zn	mg/L	0.84
	Cd	mg/L	0.06
	Hg	mg/L	0.0042

Source: IOE (1991).

A study on ground water resources and contamination problems in the Bandung basin (Wagner 1990) concluded that the main sources of possible ground water contamination are:

- Unsewered sanitation from urban and rural areas
- Intensive agriculture practices
- Solid waste disposal
- Industrial waste water

The pollutants from the above sources may infiltrate the ground water. For example, ammonia and nitrite levels have increased above the permissible limit set for water quality standards with ranges of 0.05 to 0.2 mg/L. Although no data is available yet on pathogenic bacteria and viruses in ground water, their impact should be considered because waste water derived from domestic waste, organic fertilizer (manure), and hospital and clinical waste provides a good habitat for the propagation of pathogens.

3.3   Industrial waste

The characteristics of industrial waste are very much dependent on the type of industry and the process used, there are however two major groups, organic and inorganic waste.

The industrial zone is mostly located in the upper Citarum river basin. About 93% of the zone is dominated by the textile industry, a 'greedy water user' because one ton of product needs about 580 m^3 of water. The raw water used comes from the river or the deep ground water.

The BOD and COD loads entering the Citarum river basin are 332 ton/day and 498.5 ton/day, while for the upper Citarum river the load are 292 ton/day and 438 ton/day, respectively. Other pollutants that enter the Citarum river are heavy metals such as Cr, Cd, Pb, Ni, Cu, Zn and dye stuffs many of which are known to be toxic chemicals.

A study of the fate of mercury in the aquatic ecosystem demonstrated that the highest concentration of mercury is found in the sediment in a range of 30.0-84.0 mg/kg, and the next highest in the water (1.00-7.40 mg/L), in fish (10.24-17.53 mg/kg) and in rice (1.10-2.20 mg/kg).

Although the government mandated the clean river program (Prokasih) for eight rivers in Indonesia, including the Citarum river, this program faces many constraints. The program set out by the government obliges industries to install waste water treatment plants, but in reality the program does not work properly. This is caused by many factors. There are, at least, five types of waste water treatment by industry, namely:

1. Factories with perfect waste water treatment plants which are operated according to standard operational procedures.

2. Factories with waste water treatment plants that are not operated according to normal procedures.
3. Factories with waste water treatment plants which cannot treat their own waste water generated; in other words, the capacity of the installation is too low to treat all of the waste.
4. Factories with waste water treatment plants which are too simple; therefore the quality of the discharged effluent is still above the permitted standard.
5. Factories without waste water treatment plants.

According to the above list, type no. 1 seems to be the best technique for waste treatment, but the results are hardly better than the others, because it produces sludge which is frequently discharged into the environment without being controlled. Sludge is disposed in landfill and on agricultural land, and sometimes it is also found on the river banks. Some of the factories cannot keep their waste in their storage or in their backyard because it can affect the owners and workers, who are valuable.

3.4 Surface and ground water problems

The most critical area in the Citarum river basin is upstream of the Saguling area, due to high population pressure on the agricultural land and forest area, untreated domestic and industrial waste, high population density, erosion and sedimentation. All these problems will affect the sustainability of the existing Saguling reservoir in many ways, such as for drinking water, fishery, tourism, health and sanitation and the hydroelectric power plant.

At present, the water of the Saguling reservoir is already polluted and very eutrophic. This can be seen from the oxygen depletion below a depth of 2 meters which cannot support fish life. This is due to the heavy pollutant load from domestic, agriculture and industrial waste. Consequently aquatic weed and algal bloom occur throughout the year, H_2S, NH_3 and NO_2 are increasing and the deoxygenation layer of the lake is becoming wider. The worst situation may be observed in the transitional period from the dry to the wet season (September-November). During this period, water turnover, as a natural phenomenon, takes place and the combination of a high organic load and oxygen depletion causes fish kill. Table 7 shows the fish killed since 1986-1991. There has been an increase from year to year with irregular periods of fish death.

The quality of the Citarum river water influences the condition of the Saguling lake, because of heavy pollution, the slight slope of the river gradient, and closeness to the source of pollutants. Therefore, there is little impact from the oxygen diffusion from the air to the river water to support natural self-purification. On the other hand, the contribution to the pollutant load is quite high from fishery activities at Saguling. There has been development of the floating net culture, with about 1856 units producing up to 3500 tons of fish in 1991. The progressive development of aquaculture should be considered seriously as a source of pollutants to the Saguling lake. The fish farmers feed the fish using pellets, as much as 3-4% of fish weight per day. The load of pollutant released by the fishery sector is presented in Table 8.

Table 7 *Incidents of fish kills in Saguling lake from 1986 to 1990*

Month/Year	Total (kg)
1986 January	2,000
1987 November/December	14,750
1988 June/July/August/September/October	14,000
1989 October/October	20,000
1990 January/January/July/October	226,000
1991	354,000

Source: Saguling Fishery Sector.

Table 8 *Composition and pollution load from the aquaculture sector*

Parameter	Load (mg/kg fish/day)
BOD	1000
NH_4	125
N-total	230
P-total	30
Suspended solid	1528

Well water discharge also decreased from 1982-1984-1988, with 32.6, 29.6 and 18.1 L/sec respectively. This means that the recharge area has become smaller and the surface runoff has become higher due to many development activities such as real estate, industrial building, road buildings, etc., which is then followed by 'over exploitation' of ground water for domestic and industrial needs. As a consequence, these activities have depleted the ground water level in the Bandung basin.

4. Adaptive strategies and mitigation of environmental impact

The problems which have arisen in the Citarum basin are very complicated, because many institutions are actively involved in the area such as agriculture, forestry, industry, local government, public works, tourism, the Ministry of Population and Environment, etc. Although much effort and financial support has been given the problems still continue. One of the reasons, may be because mitigation of environmental impacts has not been conducted in an integrated way. Problems have been solved in terms of needs of sectors and there has not been a holistic approach. Therefore, expenditures have become higher, but still remain insufficient to improve the quality of the environment. On the other hand, exploitation of the natural resources of the rural areas is not equal to the inputs of energy, technology, materials, education and skills from the urban areas. That means the rural areas are exploited by the urban areas, while the energy and materials flowing from the urban area to the rural area are minimal. Therefore, the rural people are left behind in most development processes.

Nowadays, to fullfil their daily needs the marginal land and forests are exploited by villagers, and sometimes these engage in agricultural practices without paying attention to soil conservation.

The landless people in the village become farm laborers or move to the city looking for jobs although they lack the necessary skills and education. Often these unfortunate people remain jobless and become a burden to the city, so the problem is merely transferred from rural to urban areas. Therefore, the problems in the Citarum river basin are not only the problems of technical knowledge or skills of the rural people, it is also a social problem. The important question is how to create jobs, so that rural people can fullfil their daily needs. To develop the concept of diversification, off-farm activities such as rural industries based on rural resources and farm activities based on smaller areas of land with higher productivity should be studied in the Citarum river basin.

A reduction in the leaching of fertilizers may be made by the application of granular fertilizer to the subsoil surface. This method has been introduced in the last few years but only within a limited area. In addition, to reduce the population pressure on the marginal land, the farmers should choose high yielding crop varieties which are directed to the agricultural industry.

To eliminate surface water pollution and ground water contamination caused by domestic and industrial waste water, the government has to take the initiative to create integrated domestic waste water plants, especially in the densely populated urban areas, while in rural areas the installation of septic tanks should be obligatory for houseowners, either singly or cooperatively.

The clean river program and relevant regulations must be enhanced by a tightening of supervision, and polluters should be taken to court as stated in the Basic Provision of Environmental Management Act of 1992.

In addition, the methods for life-cycle analysis, also known as 'from cradle to grave' analysis of hazardous waste management should be applied and the development of a toxic and hazardous waste management center should be built soon due to the fact that one of the largest industrial estates in Indonesia continues to expand in west Java. Water quality monitoring of the Citarum river and its tributaries should be conducted by an appointed authority to provide beneficial input to minimize the impact of water quality on the surface and ground water. The other benefits are that the number of fish killed and the excessive growth rate of aquatic weeds may be reduced.

The domestic and industrial water supplies for rural and urban areas should be enhanced by building a reservoir with a larger capacity. This is important to avoid lowering the ground water level.

From the Citarum river basin management point of view, it seems that a responsible independent authority is needed to manage the overall impact in the basin. This authority must maintain a harmonious relationship with related institutions. The management of the Citarum river basin should be based on more effective and efficient activity from financial, institutional, regulatory, and research institutions. The benefits are that the natural resources integrated controlling system will be more efficient, so that a higher economic benefit could be achieved and the project development activities in the Citarum river basin would become environmentally sound and sustainable.

5. References

Anonymous (1988) *The National Water Quality Standard*, The Secretariat Ministry of Population and Environment, Jakarta.

Anonymous (1989) *Environmental Statistic of Indonesia*, Statistic Center Bureau, Jakarta.

Badrudin, N. (1987) *Mitigation of Air Pollution at the Citarum River Basin* (in Indonesian), Congress of Alumni Association ITB, Bandung.

Brotoisworo, I. (1990) *Country Experience in River/Lake Basin Management Focused on Water Quality*, Institute of Ecology, Padjadjaran University, Bandung.

Djuangsih, N. (1993) Understanding the State of River Basin Management from an Environmental Toxicology Perspective: An Example from Water Pollution at Citarum River Basin, West Java, Indonesia, in: Slooff, W. & De Kruijf, H. (eds.) *Proc. 2nd. European Conf. Ecotoxicology. Sci. Total Environ.*, Suppl. 1993: 283-292.

IOE (Institute of Ecology) (1991) *Leachate Water Management at the Center of Garbage Treatment of Pasir Impun* (in Indonesian), Padjadjaran University, Bandung.

Wagner, W. (1990) *Ground Water Resources and Ground Water Contamination Problems in the Bandung Basin* (interim), Project CTA 108.

5.2

Estimating ecological risks of pesticides by combined assessment of toxicity and persistence in soil

J.P. VAN RIJN, M. HERMANS, C.A.M. VAN GESTEL & N.M. VAN STRAALEN

Abstract

Chemical pesticides are used with success to control agricultural pests and diseases. Adverse effects of this practice, have however, become evident. To prevent unacceptable side-effects most countries have developed procedures for evaluation of environmental risks following the use of pesticides. Risk assessments generally include the toxicity of pesticides and their degradation products, their persistence in the environment, and their mobility in water and soil. Environmental risks of pesticides are often evaluated according to more or less arbitrary classification systems. A method for integrated ecological risk assessment was developed to estimate the hazard for soil communities. This method makes it possible to calculate the Hazardous Concentration for 5% of the organisms (HC_5) in a certain community. The HC_5 indicates the level of contamination at which at least 95% of the species are exposed to a concentration level below their NOEC-value. The calculation is based on individual NOEC-values for several species. When the HC_5 is combined with the degradation rate of a pesticide the impact of pesticides on communities can be described more clearly. Shortly after application in most cases the pesticide concentration will exceed the HC_5. It is possible to calculate the time needed to reach the relatively 'safe' level of the HC_5. This Chemical Recovery Time (R) determines the time-weighted risk to the ecological community, consisting of many species. Literature on side-effects of the fungicide benomyl and the insecticide carbofuran to soil invertebrates was reviewed. HC_5-values and Chemical Recovery Times for both pesticides were calculated. The results show that R-values for carbofuran will vary from 1.4-7.3 years, while R for benomyl ranges from 2.6 to 5.7 years. Both pesticides can be classified as 'high risk - pesticides' based on the proposed classification of Chemical Recovery Times.

1. Introduction

Chemical pesticides are widely used to control agricultural pests and diseases. During the last decades, however, adverse environmental effects of this practice have become evident. Many pesticides appear to be toxic to non-target organisms. Some have been found to degrade very slowly and residues and degradation products have been found in deeper soil layers, ground water and surface waters.

To prevent unwanted effects, most countries of the world have adopted certain methods to evaluate environmental risks as part of the registration procedure. These evaluations generally include the toxicity of pesticides and their degradation products, their persistence in the environment, and their mobility in water and soil. Information gathered in a series of experiments on the pesticide is evaluated according to a more or less arbitrary classification system (Jepson *et al.* 1990, IOBC/WPRS 1985, Bostrom & Lofs-Holmin 1982, Martin 1986).

Similar systems are common in classical toxicology to predict or avoid damage caused by toxic chemicals, for example to calculate maximum acceptable exposure of humans. When it comes to estimating ecological risks, however, these systems may not be applicable.

Most methods for estimating risks of pesticides are based on single species mortality tests, which means that variations in sensitivity between species and sublethal toxicity of pesticides are not taken into account. It is, in addition, impossible to predict indirect effects, such as the disturbance of prey - predator interactions caused by the application of pesticides.

In most assessment methods, toxicity and degradation of pesticides are evaluated by separate criteria, and it is not possible to combine several pesticidal qualities and give an integrated view of the impact of pesticides. Most methods require little scientific data. The amount of available data does not influence the final judgement, although it would seem plausible that the reliability of an evaluation increases with increasing data.

In this paper a risk assessment method is presented that to some extent meets these deficiencies. It explores the possibilities for combined evaluation of toxicity and persistence of a pesticide. Numerical examples are given for the effects of the fungicide benomyl and the insecticide carbofuran on soil invertebrate fauna.

2. Hazardous concentration

The probability that a species is exposed to a pesticide concentration exceeding the no observed effect concentration (NOEC) for that species has been estimated by Van Straalen & Denneman (1989). They assumed that the distribution of sensitivities to a certain pesticide in a large community follows a log - logistic distribution. Based on available NOEC-data for several species, it is possible to derive a Hazardous Concentration for 5% of the species. This concentration indicates the level at which at least 95% of the species are exposed below their NOEC.

HC_5 can be calculated using the following formula:

(1)
$$HC_5 = \exp[x_m - s_m k_m]$$

where:

m = sample size, number of species tested

x_m = mean of m NOEC data transformed to natural logarithms

s_m = standard deviation of ln (NOEC) data

k_m = a safety factor depending on m, given in a Table by Aldenberg & Slob (1991)

3.   Chemical recovery

The Hazardous Concentration for pesticides indicates the concentration level above which lethal and sublethal effects can be expected for a given percentage of the animal species in the soil community. In reality, the environmental concentration of a pesticide is seldom constant. Van Straalen *et al.* (1992) proposed that in the case of a chemical that is emitted at intervals and degrades quickly, the ecological damage is often transient. One would like to base an assessment of the ecological risk not only on effects immediately after application, but also on the potential for ecological recovery following degradation of the pesticide. By combining the above mentioned Hazardous Concentration with the degradation rate, it is possible to obtain an integrated picture of the impact of pesticides on animal communities.

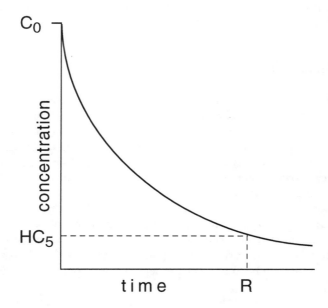

Figure 1 *Model for the concentration decrease of a pesticide in soil after application at time zero with initial concentration C_0, illustrating that HC_5 is reached after time R*

Figure 1 shows the degradation of an imaginary pesticide in soil, assuming first order degradation kinetics. After application the concentration in the soil declines according to this exponential curve. The rate of degradation can be characterized by a constant half - life (DT_{50}). We can derive the Chemical Recovery Time (R), *i.e.* the time needed for the pesticide concentration to drop below the level of the HC_5. We assume that when the HC_5 has been reached, ecological recovery of the system will be possible. At time zero, immediately after application, the pesticide concentration equals C_0. Assuming simple exponential decay of pesticides we can write the following equation:

(2)
$$C(t) = C_0 \exp \left[- \frac{\ln 2}{DT_{50}} t \right]$$

When t = R, C(t) = HC_5, and we can calculate R:

(3)
$$R = \frac{DT_{50}}{365 \ln 2} \ln \{ \frac{C_0}{HC_5} \}$$

The quantities C_0 and HC_5 are measured in the same units (*e.g.* $\mu g/kg$), DT_{50} is measured in days and R is measured in years. From formula 3 it can be seen that the time for chemical recovery (R) will last longer with longer half lives (DT_{50}), higher application rates (C_0) and/or a higher toxicity (*i.e.* lower HC_5) of the pesticidal compound.

4. Example: effects of benomyl and carbofuran

We used the concept described above to estimate the environmental risks following the application of two commonly used pesticides. The first is the insecticide carbofuran *(2,3-dihydro-2,2-dimethyl-2-benzofuran-7-yl-methylcarbamate)*. This carbamate blocks the activity of the enzyme acetylcholinesterase in the nervous system. Because all animals possess this enzyme, the activity spectrum of carbofuran is very broad. In agriculture the chemical is used to kill a wide variety of insects, nematodes and mites.

The second pesticide to be considered is benomyl [*methyl-1-1 (butycarbamoyl) benzimidazol-2-ylcarbamate*], a fungicide with a benzimidazole structure. It is used to suppress ascomycetes in fruit, vegetables and rice. Directly after application benomyl converts into carbendazim *(methylbenzimidazole-2-ylcarbamate)*. This compound, more than benomyl, is considered to be responsible for the fungicidal activity.

There is a considerable amount of literature on the persistence and mobility of carbofuran in soils. Degradation generally starts a few days after application. Pretreatment of soils with carbofuran and other carbamates is shown to enhance degradation (Achik & Schiavon 1989, Camper *et al.* 1987, Dzantor & Felsot 1990, Harris *et al.* 1988, Rajagopal *et al.* 1986). Degradation rates are highly dependent on temperature and microbial activity in the soil (Sahoo *et al.* 1990, Ou *et al.* 1982). Soil pH and other characteristics such as organic matter content, cation exchange capacity and water holding capacity also seem to influence degradation (Getzin 1973, Ou *et al.* 1982), although some authors consider this influence to be very small (Ahmad *et al.* 1979, Chapman & Cole 1982). DT_{50}-values for carbofuran range between 35 and 188 days (Worthing & Hance 1991). According to these data and the classification of persistence given below (Table 1), we may characterize carbofuran as moderately degradable to persistent in soil.

Table 1 *Classification for persistence in soil*

DT_{50}	Classification
< 2 days	highly degradable
2-15 days	readily degradable
15-60 days	moderately degradable
60-180 days	persistent
> 180 days	highly persistent

Carbofuran is found to incorporate readily in soils, and mobility is not very high (Achik & Schiavon 1989, Harris *et al.* 1988, Kumari *et al.* 1988, Nicosia *et al.* 1991). Adsorption and mobility are reported to depend on soil characteristics (Kumari *et al.* 1988, Somasundaram *et al.* 1991). According to data from the Dutch Commission for the Authorization of Pesticides (Canton *et al.* 1990) carbofuran is classified as slightly mobile to mobile in soil.

Information on the behavior of benomyl in soil is less abundant. Li & Nelson (1985) mention that benomyl converts into carbendazim immediately after application. Carbendazim is much more stable and remains active in the soil for a period of 3 months to more than 2 years, depending on soil type, temperature and soil moisture content. Highest concentrations are found in the upper soil layer from 0-15 cm depth. The Dutch Commission for the Authorization of pesticides (Canton *et al.* 1990) characterizes benomyl as slightly mobile in soil. The Pesticide Manual (Worthing & Hance 1991) reports DT_{50}-values between 180 and 365 days for benomyl/carbendazim, and we may classify this chemical as highly persistent.

Given the relatively high persistence and the relatively low mobility of both pesticides, we may expect that after application, carbofuran and benomyl will remain active for some time in the upper soil layer. Various authors have described the toxicity of benomyl and carbofuran to soil animals. Tables 2 and 3 show a compilation of quantitative literature data on the toxicity of both pesticides.

Table 2 *Summary of literature on lethal and sublethal effects of carbofuran for soil organisms*

Species	Para-meter	Value in standard soil (mg/kg dry soil)	Reference
Lumbricus terrestris	LC_{50}	4.7	Haque & Ebing (1983)
Eisenia fetida	LC_{50}	28	Haque & Ebing (1983)
Eisenia fetida	LC_{50}	> 64*	Stenersen (1979a)
Aporrectodea caliginosa	LC_{50}	< 4*	Stenersen (1979a)
Aporrectodea chlorotica	LC_{50}	< 4*	Stenersen (1979a)
Lumbricus rubellus	LC_{50}	< 4*	Stenersen (1979a)
Eisenia fetida	LC_{50}	5-10	Heimbach (1985)
Eisenia fetida	NOEC	0.25	Bouwman & Reinecke (1987)
Aporrectodea caliginosa	NOEC	0.25	Martin (1986)
Folsomia candida	NOLC	0.05	Tomlin (1975a)
Hypogastrura armata	NOLC	0.5	Tomlin (1975a)
Onychiurus justi porteri	NOLC	2.5	Tomlin (1975a)
Pterostischus melanarius	NOLC	0.25	Tomlin (1975b)

* Data have not been normalized for standard soil.

Both lethal and sublethal effects are presented, expressed by $NOLC/LC_{50}$ and NOEC values respectively. All data have been normalized to a standard soil (organic matter content of 10%) by applying the following formula:

$$\left\{ \begin{array}{c} NOEC \\ NOLC \\ LC_{50} \end{array} \right\} \text{ standard soil } = \left\{ \begin{array}{c} NOEC \\ NOLC \\ LC_{50} \end{array} \right\} \left\{ \frac{\text{organic matter content standard soil(10\%)}}{\text{organic matter content experimental soil}} \right\}$$

The data from Stenersen (1979a) on carbofuran toxicity could not be normalized because information about the organic matter content of the soil used was not given.

Being an acetylcholinesterase inhibiting insecticide, carbofuran is lethal for a broad spectrum of soil animals. Several data are available on lethal effects for springtails, carabid beetles and earthworms (Floate *et al.* 1989, Heimbach 1985, Martin 1978, 1980, 1986, Tomlin 1975a, 1975b, Stenersen 1979a, 1979b). Sublethal effects on earthworms include weight loss, suppression of cocoon production, swellings of the body, and decreased activity (Haque & Ebing 1983, Martin 1980, 1986, Stenersen 1979a, 1979b, Bouwman & Reinecke 1987). Soil type seems to affect the toxicity of carbofuran (Achik & Schiavon 1989).

Generally, No Observed Effect Concentrations (measuring mortality or reproduction) appear to be more sensitive than LC_{50}'s. LC_{50}-values very between < 4 - > 64 mg/kg (standard deviation = 23). Less variation is found in NOEC and

NOLC data (standard deviation = 0.8). Differences in test protocols and conditions in the experiments may explain the high variation in LC_{50} - values (Bouwman & Reinecke 1987, Bostrom & Lofs-Holmin 1982). Differences in the metabolic system between species of earthworms may also be responsible (Gilman & Vardanis 1974). The data on Collembola all originate from one author (Tomlin 1975a, 1975b); from these results we can see that *Folsomia candida* is much more sensitive than other species of Collembola. Although benomyl is applied as a fungicide, many papers report effects on non-target organisms (Haque & Ebing 1983, Roark & Dale 1979, Stringer & Wright 1975, Tomlin 1977, Zoran *et al.* 1985). Apparently soil type affects toxicity (Krogh 1991, Lofs-Holmin 1982). As shown in Table 3 we found reports on lethal and sublethal effects for springtails and earthworms. Again, NOEC and NOLC data showed less variation than LC_{50} values (standard deviation 2.1 and 9 respectively). No differences have been found in sensitivity for species of Collembola. Although a few authors specify the toxic compound as carbendazim, toxicity data on carbendazim and benomyl have been used together in the calculations of R and HC_5.

Table 3 *Summary of literature on lethal and sublethal effects of benomyl/carbendazim for soil organisms*

Species	Parameter	Value in standard soil (mg/kg dry soil)	Reference
Lumbricus terrestris	LC_{50}	2.3	Karnak & Hamelink 1982
Lumbricus terrestris	LC_{50}	3.5	Haque & Ebing 1983
Eisenia fetida	LC_{50}	27	Haque & Ebing 1983
Eisenia fetida	LC_{50}	19	Heimbach 1985
Eisenia andrei	LC_{50}	6.0	Van Gestel *et al.* 1992
Eisenia andrei	LC_{50} (carbendazim)	5.7	Van Gestel *et al.* 1992
Eisenia andrei	NOEC	1.0	Van Gestel *et al.* 1992
Eisenia andrei	NOEC (carbendazim)	1.9	Van Gestel *et al.* 1992
Eisenia fetida	NOEC (carbendazim)	1.6	Vonk *et al.* 1986
Eisenia fetida	NOLC (carbendazim)	4.8	Vonk *et al.* 1986
Eisenia fetida	LC_{50} (carbendazim)	9.3	Vonk *et al.* 1986
Aporrectodea caliginosa	NOEC	0.25	Lofs-Holmin 1982
Folsomia candida	NOLC	5	Tomlin 1977
Hypogastrura armata	NOLC	5	Tomlin 1977
Onychiurus justi porteri	NOLC	5	Tomlin 1977

Using the NOEC and NOLC data and the given DT_{50}-values (Worthing & Hance 1991) calculations of HC_5 and R were made for both pesticides. The results are shown in Table 4. The prescribed dosage for benomyl ranges from 140-550 g a.i./ ha, and for carbofuran 6-10 kg a.i./ha (Worthing & Hance 1991). Soil density was estimated for a soil with 10% organic matter, using the formula given by Lexmond & Edelman (1986); this yielded 1061 kg/m^3.

Assuming a uniform distribution of the chemical in the top 2.5 cm of the soil and an organic matter content of 10%, environmental concentrations at t = 0 (C_0, mg/kg) were estimated:

(5)
$$C_0 = \frac{applied\ dosage\ (mg/m^2)}{soil\ density\ (kg/m^3) * sampling\ depth(m)}$$

We calculated a range for R, based on the available range of DT_{50} data. For both pesticides the estimated environmental concentrations exceeded the calculated Hazardous Concentration for soil organisms. The Chemical Recovery Time for benomyl ranges from two to five years. Although carbofuran is less persistent, the estimated Recovery Time is longer, due to its high toxicity and the high application rate.

Table 4 *Summary of calculations*

	Carbofuran			Benomyl/Carbendazim	
Parameter	Value	Calculation	Parameter	Value	Calculation
m	6	table 2	m	7	table 2
x_m	-1.16	table 2	x_m	0.63	table 2
s_m	1.27	table 2	s_m	1.10	table 2
k_m	3.93	Aldenberg & Slob 1991	k_m	3.59	Aldenberg & Slob 1991
$C_{0(max)}$	37680 µg/kg	equation 5	$C_{0(max)}$	2071 µg/kg	equation 5
HC_5	2.13 µg/kg	equation 1	HC_5	36.2 µg/kg	equation 1
R	1.4-7.3 years	equation 3	R	2.9-5.7 years	equation 3

5.   Discussion

Persistence and toxicity determine the risk of pesticides to the soil animal community. This paper provides an assessment method which integrates these two elements. The Chemical Recovery Time (R) is based on data on sublethal effects, represented by the HC_5, and information about degradation rates, represented by DT_{50}.

Various factors seem to influence the toxicity and the degradation rate of chemicals. Calculations could therefore be more accurate when specific data about toxicity and degradation in certain soil types were introduced. In the examples given here, the effects for soil animals only were studied. To get a more general idea about the impact of pesticides, data covering other trophic levels could be introduced.

According to the calculations presented above we may expect that the application of benomyl and carbofuran implies a certain risk for soil animals. As stated by Van Straalen et al. (1992) the disappearance of the pesticide is a necessary condition for the recovery of the ecosystem. Consequently, in the case of benomyl, ecological recovery may only be possible two to five years after a single treatment. For carbofuran, recovery lags at least seven years behind application.

Not much is known about long term effects of benomyl and carbofuran. Krogh (1991) described a decrease in the population of the hemiedaphic collembolan *Folsomia nano* and in representatives of Brachychthonoidea (Acarina: Cryptostigmata) for more than 3 years after a single application of benomyl (2.5 kg a.i./ha). Other species of Acarina and Collembola remained relatively unaffected by the fungicide. Broadbent & Tomlin (1982) found that regular rates of carbofuran (1.1 kg a.i./ha) applied in a corn field had no long term effects on microarthropods. Several short term effects, up to 18-22 weeks, could be observed however. A high mortality rate shortly after application and a rapid decline of toxicity within a few weeks thereafter was observed in field studies with carabid beetles (Floate et al. 1989) and earthworms (Martin 1976).

All these papers, however, concerned field experiments in which mortality is measured, whereas we calculated Chemical Recovery Times based on No Effects Concentrations observed in laboratory tests. Although acute toxicity testing in the laboratory generally can give a good indication of acute effects to be expected in the field (Van Gestel 1992, Heimbach 1992), this relationship is not clear for long term effects. In field situations, many complex factors influence both the degradation rate and the mobility of pesticides and population sizes of soil animals. Hence, long term effects may be hard to recognize.

By expressing the chemical recovery time of a chemical (R) in terms of risks to soil organisms, this factor may be used in authorization procedures for pesticides. Van Straalen et al. (1992) suggest that a Recovery Time of one year is maximally acceptable. Based on this proposal a classification could be constructed like that given in Table 5. In this example, a recovery time longer than one year accounts for a high risk to the soil community, It would be interesting to adjust the classification proposed here to scientific field data on recovery processes and generation times within soil communities.

Table 5 *Proposed classification of R in terms of risks to soil organisms*

R	Classification
< 0.02 year	negligible risk
0.02-0.25 year	moderate risk
0.25-1 year	significant risk
> 1 year	high risk

6. References

Achik, J. & Schiavon, M. (1989) Persistence of Biological Activity of Four Insecticides in Two Soil Types under Field and Laboratory Conditions, *J. Econ. Entomol.* 82: 1572-1575.

Ahmad, N., Walgenbach, D.D. & Sutter G.R. (1979) Degradation Rates of Technical Carbofuran and a Granular Formulation in Four Soils with Known Insecticide Use History, *Bull. Environ. Contam. Toxicol.* 23: 572-574.

Aldenberg, T. & Slob, W. (1991) *Confidence Limits for Hazardous Concentrations Based on Logistically Distributed NOEC Toxicity Data*, RIVM-report 719102002, Bilthoven.

Bostrom, U. & Lofs-Holmin, A. (1982) *Testing Side-effects of Pesticides on Soil Fauna - A Critical Literature Review*, Institutionen for Ekologi och Miljovard. Report 12, Swedish University of Agricultural Sciences.

Bouwman, H. & Reinecke, A.J. (1987) Effects of Carbofuran on the Earthworm, *Eisenia foetida* Using a Defined Medium, *Bull. Environ. Contam. Toxicol.* 38: 171-178.

Broadbent & Tomlin (1982) Comparison of Two Methods for Assessing the Effects of Carbofuran on Soil Animal Decomposers in Cornfields, *Environ. Entomol.* 11: 1036-1042.

Camper, N.D., Fleming, M.M. & Skipper, H.D. (1987) Biodegradation of Carbofuran in Pretreated and Non-pretreated Soils, *Bull. Environ. Contam. Toxicol.* 39: 571-578.

Canton, J.H., Linders, J.B.H.J., Luttik, R., Mensink, B.J.W.G., Panman, E., Van de Plassche, E.J., Sparenburg, P.M. & Tuinstra, J. (1991) *Catch-up Operation on Old Pesticides: An Integration*, RIVM-report 678801002, Bilthoven.

Chapman, R.A. & Cole, C.M. (1982) Observation on the Influence of Water and Soil pH on the Persistence of Insecticides, *J. Environ. Sci. Health* B17: 487-504.

Dzantor, E.K. & Felsot, A.S. (1990) Soil Differences in the Biodegradation of Carbofuran and Trimethacarb Following Pretreatment with These Insecticides, *Bull. Environ. Contam. Toxicol.* 45: 531-537.

Floate K., Elliot, R.H., Doane, J.F. & Gillott, C. (1989) Field Bioassay to Evaluate Contact and Residual Toxicities of Insecticides to Carabid Beetles (Coleoptera: Carabidae), *J. Econ. Entomol.* 82: 1543-1547.

Getzin, L.W. (1973) Persistence and Degradation of Carbofuran in Soil, *Environ. Entomol.* 2: 461-467.

Gilman, A.P. & Vardanis, A. (1974) Comparative Toxicity and Metabolism in the Worms *Lumbricus terrestris* and *Eisenia foetida*, *S.J. Agr. Food Chem.* 22: 625-628.

Haque, A. & Ebing, W. (1983) Toxicity Determination of Pesticides to Earthworms in the Soil Substrate, *Z. Pflanzenkr. Pfanzenschutz* 90: 395-408.

Harris, C.R., Chapman, R.A., Tolman, J.H., Moy, P., Henning, K. & Harris, C. (1988) A Comparison of the Persistence in a Clay Loam of Single and Repeated Annual Application of Seven Granular Insecticides Used for Corn Rootworm Control, *J. Environ. Sci. Health* B23: 1-32.

Heimbach, F. (1985) Comparison of Laboratory Methods, Using *Eisenia foetida* and *Lumbricus terrestris*, for the Assessment of the Hazard of Chemicals to Earthworms, *Z. Pfanzenkr. Pflanzenschutz.* 92: 186-193.

Heimbach F. (1992) Effects of Pesticides on Earthworm Populations: Comparison of Results from Laboratory and Field Tests, in: Greig-Smith, P.W., Becker, H., Edwards, P.J., Heimbach, F. (eds.) *Ecotoxicology of Earthworms*, Intercept, Andover, pp. 100-106.

IOBC/WPRS Working group 'Pesticides and Beneficial Organisms' (1985) Standard Methods to Test the Side-effects of Pesticides on Natural Enemies of Insects and Mites (Hassan, S.A., ed.), *OEPP/EPPO Bull.* 15: 214-255.

Jepson, P.C, Duffield, S.J., Thacker, J.R.M., Thomas, C.F.G. & Wiles, J.A. (1990) *Predicting the Side-effects of Pesticides on Beneficial Invertebrates*, Brighton Crop Protecting Conference - Pest and Diseases, pp. 957-962.

Karnak, R.E. & Hamelink, J.L. (1982) A Standardized Method for Determining the Acute Toxicity of Chemicals to Earthworms, *Ecotox. Environ. Saf.* 6: 216-222.

Krogh, P.H. (1991) Perturbation of the Soil Microarthropod Community with the Pesticides Benomyl and Isofenphos, *Pedobiologia* 35: 71-88.

Kumari, K., Singh, R.P. & Saxena, K. (1988) Movement of Carbofuran in Soil Columns, *Ecotox. Environ. Saf.* 16: 36-44.

Lexmond, T.M., Edelman, T. & Van Driel, W. (1986) Voorlopige referentiewaarden en huidige achtergrondgehalten voor een aantal zware metalen en arseen in bovengrond van natuurterreinen en landbouwgronden, in: *Advies bodemkwaliteit*, VTCB-advies A86/02, Leidschendam.

Li, Ching, Y. & Nelson Earl, E. (1985) Persistence of Benomyl and Captan and Their Effects on Microbial Activity in Field Soils, *Bull. Environ. Contam. Toxicol.* 34: 533-540.

Lofs-Holmin (1982) Measuring Cocoon Production of the Earthworm *Allolobophora caliginosa* (Sav) as a Method of Testing Sublethal Toxicity of Pesticides, *Swedish J. Agric. Res.* 10: 25-33.

Martin, N.A. (1976) Effects of Four Insecticides on the Pasture Ecosystem V: Earthworm (Olichogaeta: Lumbricidae) and Arthropoda Extracted by Wet Sieving and Salt Flotation, *N.Z.J. Agr.* 19: 111-115.

Martin, N.A. (1978) Effect of Four Insecticides on the Pasture Ecosystem VI: Arthropoda Dry Heat-extracted from Small Soil Cores, and Conclusions, *N.Z.J. Agr.* 21: 307-319.

Martin, N.A. (1980) Earthworm (Olichochaeta: Lumbricidae) Populations and Late Summer Pasture Renovation, *N.Z.J. Agr. Res.* 23: 417-419.

Martin, N.A. (1986) Toxicity of Pesticides to *Allolobophora caliginosa* (Oligochaeta: Lumbricidae), *N.Z.J. Agr. Res.* 29: 699-706.

Nicosia, S., Carr, N., Gonzales, D.A. & Orr, M.K. (1991) Off - Field Movement and Dissipation of Soil-incorporated Carbofuran from Three Commercial Rice Fields, *J. Environ. Qual.* 20: 532-539.

Ou, L.T., Gancarz, D.H., Wheeler, W.B., Rao, P.S.C. & Davidson, J.M. (1982) Influence of Soil Temperature and Soil Moisture on Degradation and Metabolism of Carbofuran in Soils, *J. Environ. Qual.* 11: 293-302.

Rajagopal, B.S., Panda Soudamini & Sethunathan, N. (1986) Accelerated Degradation of Carbaryl and Carbofuran in a Flooded Soil Pretreated with Hydrolysis Products, 1-naphthol and Carbofuran Phenol, *Bull. Environ. Contam. Toxicol.* 36: 827-832.

Roark, J.H. & Dale, J.L. (1979) The Effect of Turf Fungicides on Earthworms, *Arkansas Academy of Science Proceedings* 35: 71-74.

Sahoo, A., Sahu, S.K., Sharmita, M. & Sethunathan, N. (1990) Persistence of Carbamate Insecticides, Carbosulfan and Carbofuran in Soils as Influenced by Temperature and Microbial Activity, *Bull. Environ. Contam. Toxicol.* 44: 948-954.

Somasundaram, L., Coats, J.R. & Racke, K.D. (1991) Mobility of Pesticides and Their Hydrolysis Metabolites in Soil, *Environ. Toxicol. Chem.* 10: 185-194.

Stenersen, J. (1979a) Action of Pesticides on Earthworms. Part 1: The Toxicity of Cholinesterase Inhibiting Insecticides to Earthworms as Evaluated by Laboratory Tests, *Pestic Sci.* 10: 66-74.

Stenersen, J. (1979b) Action of Pesticides on Earthworms. Part III: Inhibition and Reactivation of Cholinesterases in *Eisenia foetida* (Savingny) after Treatment with Chlolinesterase Inhibiting Insecticides, *Pestic. Sci.* 10: 113-122.

Stringer, A. & Wright, M.A. (1975) Toxicity of Benomyl and Some Related 2-substituted Benzimidazoles to the Earthworm *Lumbricus terrestris, Pestic. Sci.* 7: 459-464.

Tomlin, A.D. (1975a) Toxicity of Soil Application of Insecticides to Three Species of Springtails (Collembola) under Laboratory Conditions, *Can. Entomol.* 107: 767-774.

Tomlin, A.D. (1975b) The Toxicity of Insecticides by Contact and Soil Treatment to Two Species of Ground Beetles (Coleoptera: Carabidae), *Can. Entomol.* 107: 592-532.

Tomlin, A.D. (1977) Toxicity of Soil Application of the Fungicide Benomyl and Two Analogues to Three Species of Collembola, *Can. Entomol.* 109: 1619-1620.

Van Gestel, C.A.M. (1992) Validation of Earthworm Toxicity Tests by Comparison with Field Studies: A Review on Benomyl, Carbendazim, Carbofuran and Carbaryl, *Ecotox. Environ. Saf.* 23: 221-236.

Van Gestel, C.A.M., Dirven-van Breemen, E.M., Baerselman, R., Emans, H.J.B., Jansen, J.A.M., Postuma, R. & Van Vliet, P.J.M. (1992) Comparison of Sublethal and Lethal Criteria for Nine Different Chemicals in Standardized Toxicity Test Using the Earthworm *Eisenia andrei, Ecotox. Environ. Saf.* 23: 206-220.

Van Straalen, N.M. & Denneman, C.A.J. (1989) Ecotoxicological Evaluation of Soil Quality Criteria, *Ecotox. Environ. Saf.* 18: 241-251.

Van Straalen, N.M., Schobben, J.H.M. & Traas, T.P. (1992) The Use of Ecotoxicological Risk Assessment in Deriving Maximum Acceptable Half-lives of Pesticides, *Pestic. Sci.* 34: 227-231.

Vonk, J.W., Adema, D.M.M. & Barug, D. (1986) Comparison of the Effect of Several Chemicals on Microorganisms, Higher Plants and Earthworms, In: Assink, J.W. & Van den Brink, W.J. (eds.) *Contaminated Soil*, Martinus Nijhoff Publishers, Dordrecht, The Netherlands. pp. 191-202.

Worthing, C.R. & Hance, R. (eds.) *The Pesticides Manual 1991*, British Crop Protection Council.

Zoran, M.J., Heppner, T.J. & Drewes, C.D. (1985) Teratogenic Effects of the Fungicide Benomyl on Posterior Segmental Regeneration in the Earthworm, *Eisenia fetida*, *Pestic. Sci.* 17: 641-652.

5.3

The impact of a textile factory in Salatiga on the Ledok river system, Central Java

F. GOELTENBOTH

Abstract

The daily discharge of chemical wastewater into the Ledok River by a textile factory in Salatiga, Central Java, is a striking example of the gross misuse of the environment. Using chemical and physical screening methods in combination with an investigation of the macroinvertebrates of this river system, this research revealed the following facts: Water temperatures have risen up to 31°C, pH to 10.4, the oxygen saturation has declined more than 30%, and all macrofauna and flora over a stretch of more than 3 km have been lost. The data indicate possible health hazards to the people living in the vicinity of the river who use it for drinking and bathing water supplies not more than 10 m away from the highly polluted water.

1. Introduction

In Salatiga, a textile factory has been operating since 1961 with a printing unit in operation since 1965 and a dyeing unit since 1970. The waste water of the cotton printing and dyeing unit was, until recently, released into adjacent paddy fields, while the waste water from the dyeing and printing unit for non-cotton materials was released, untreated, into the Ledok River.

2. Material and methods

During April-May 1992, eight stations were randomly sampled for water quality. The sample area and sites are shown in Figure 1.

2.1 Water temperature

Water temperature was measured using an electronically operated OXI-Meter OXI 96 of WTW, Germany. Three duplicate runs for each measurement were performed.

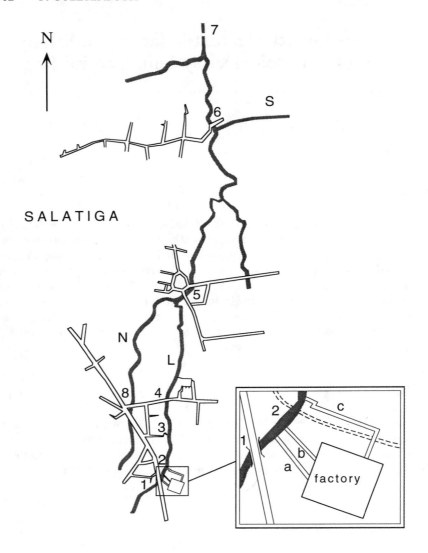

Figure 1 *Map of the Ledok river system around Salatiga, Central Java, showing the location of sampling sites (1 to 8). L = Ledok river; N = Ngaglik river; S = Senjoyo river; a = old discharge channel from the dye unit; b = old discharge channel from the print unit; c = new discharge channel for the DAMATEX textile factory*

2.2 Hydrogen ion concentration (pH)

The pH was measured with a battery operated PHEP transportable meter from Hanna Inc., USA. The calibrated instrument was used at the single stations and each measurement repeated three times, rinsing the contact with distilled water after each measurement.

2.3   Dissolved oxygen (DO)

Oxygen was measured by means of the OXI-Meter OXI 96, WTW. The calibrations were performed using the Oxical R-S tube. Three duplicate runs for each measurement were performed rinsing the membrane of the EOT 190 electrode after each measurement. Due to the current velocity of the river water no specific stirring device was needed to guarantee an adequate current velocity for the DO measurement.

2.4   Oxygen saturation

Measurement of the oxygen saturation was carried out using the OXI-meter OXI 96, WTW, as described above.

2.5   Collection and identification of macroinvertebrates

At three stations macroinvertebrates were collected using the Kicking-method and a macro-fauna net. The macroinvertebrates of an area of 25 x 25 cm were collected using the net firmly held on the substratum with its open end facing upstream. Then the river bed was disturbed upstream just in front of the net by rolling over stones and grubbing through the gravel. The macro-fauna floated with the current into the net. Three diagonally positioned sampling sites at each point of investigation were used. The identification of the formalin-fixed specimens was performed in the laboratory using a stereomicroscope to classify the specimens and to obtain the total number of individuals per order for each community. The percentage of the total community for each order was calculated.

3.   Results

The water temperature under natural conditions at station 1 on the Ledok River and station 8 on the Ngaglik River oscillated between 23.1 and 26.2°C. Station 7, about 8 km from the effluent site of the Damatex Factory, showed the parameters of mixed water from Ledok, Ngaglik, Gandu, and Senjoyo, with a temperature range of 26.1 to 28.1°C. In the heavily polluted part of Ledok the temperature fluctuated between 26.7 and 31.4°C (Table 1). The pH-values, under unpolluted conditions, were in the range between 7.0-7.4. The affected river water showed values between 6.4-10.4, often exceeding the officially allowed maximum for waste water (OACWW), grade IV from textile industries with a pH range of 6-9 (Keputan Menteri Negara KLH 1991).

Table 1 *Chemical and physical parameters of the water of River Ledok, Ngaglik and Senjoyo during April-May 1992*
(see Figure 1 for the locations of the sampling stations)

Parameter		Station number							
		1	2	3	4	5	6	7	8
Temperature (°C)	Max.	23.1 ± 0.3	24.6 ± 0.7	28.0 ± 0.7	28.2 ± 0.3	27.6 ± 0.1	28.0 ± 0.1	28.1 ± 0.1	26.2 ± 0.1
	Min.	25.9 ± 0.1	24.1 ± 1.9	23.6 ± 0.1	31.4 ± 0.1	26.9 ± 0.1	26.7 ± 0.1	26.1 ± 0.1	24.2 ± 0.1
Colour		clear	grey	variation of black, blue, yellow, grey, red				grey	clear
Smell		none	none	phenol-like smell				none	none
pH	Max.	8.3 ± 0.1	7.4 ± 0.1	10.2 ± 0.1	10.4 ± 0.1	9.3 ± 0.1	8.9 ± 0.1	8.5 ± 0.1	7.3 ± 0.1
	Min.	7.0 ± 0.3	7.5 ± 0.1	6.9 ± 0.2	10.0 ± 0.1	8.8 ± 0.1	7.4 ± 0.1	7.5 ± 0.1	7.1 ± 0.1
DO (mg/L)	Max.	8.8 ± 0.1	8.9 ± 0.2	8.4 ± 0.2	7.2 ± 0.3	6.4 ± 0.2	8.8 ± 0.1	7.7 ± 0.3	9.5 ± 0.3
	Min.	7.6 ± 0.3	7.5 ± 0.3	6.4 ± 0.2	5.6 ± 0.2	5.1 ± 0.2	7.5 ± 0.1	7.4 ± 0.2	7.4 ± 0.1
DO-saturation (%)	Max.	119	120	105	106	88	119	105	125
	Min.	100	107	88	67	71	102	99	102

Note: DO = dissolved oxygen.

Oxygen saturation as a percentage rather than the DO in mg/L is of importance for the interpretation of the status of a water body. Oxygen depletion with saturation values around 67.3% were recorded at stations 3-6. On 14.4.92 the temperature at station 4 was the highest recorded, being 31.4 °C, while the control station 1 showed 23.1 °C. The pH gave a maximum at station 3 of 10.1 compared to 7.5 at the control station and the DO saturation values were lowest at station 3 with 88.0% compared to 101.3% for the control station (Figure 2). Collection of macroinvertebrates at the control station on the Ledok, about 200 m upstream from the effluent site at station 8 on the unpolluted Ngaglik, and at station 7, about 8 km downstream, revealed that Diptera form the most important group in the macroinvertebrate community with 46.6% (Ledok), 63.38% (Ngaglik) and 78.31% (Senjoyo). Oligochaeta were found with 12.04% only in the Senjoyo, indicating, together with the abundant Chironomidae (larvae), the α-mesosaprobic status of the Senjoyo water (Liebmann 1962). The water quality of the control station of the Ledok and Ngaglik can be classified as β-mesosaprobic according to the bioindicator organisms found. All attempts to find at least one macroinvertebrate in the heavily polluted stretch between the effluent site and station 5 were in vain (Table 2).

Table 2 *Composition of the macroinvertebrate fauna from River Ledok, Ngaglik and Senjoyo* (see Figure 1 for the locations of the sampling stations)

Order	River Ledok: Station 1 Status: β-mesosaprobic				River Ngaglik: Station 8 Status: β-mesosaprobic				River Senjoy: Station 7 Status: α-mesosaprobic			
	L	P	I	%TC	L	P	I	%TC	L	P	I	%TC
Oligochaeta	-	-	-	-	-	-	-	-	-	-	10	12.04
Arachnida	-	-	-	-	-	-	-	-	-	-	1	1.20
Plecoptera	-	-	-	-	7	-	-	26.92	2	-	-	2.40
Neuroptera	-	-	-	-	1	1	-	7.69	-	-	-	-
Trichoptera	5	-	-	33.3	-	-	-	-	3	-	-	3.61
Ephemeroptera	3	-	-	20.0	-	-	-	-	2	-	-	2.40
Diptera	7	-	-	46.6	17	-	-	65.38	41	22	2	78.31
Total number of individuals	15	-	-		25	1	-		48	22	13	

L = Larvae, P = Pupae, I = Imagines, TC = Total Community.

4. Discussion

The data collected on the impact of the effluent, released untreated from the textile factory show clearly the deleterious effects on the living organisms in a stretch of about 5 km. Even after dilution of the wastewater by three tributaries the harmful effect of the effluent is visible and measureable.

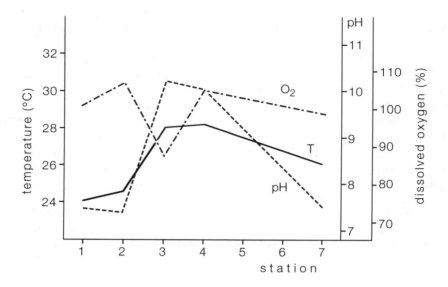

Figure 2 *Comparison of temperature, pH, and dissolved oxygen of the water of the Ledok river system on April 14th, 1992. 1: control station; 2: previously polluted area; 3 to 7: presently polluted areas 5: station after confluence of rivers Ledok and Ngaglik; 6: station after confluence of rivers Ledok/Ngaglik with Gandu and Senjoyo; 7: mixed water of all rivers about 8 km from the source*

Tests on acute toxicity of the waste water performed with two fish species revealed that at concentrations of 12.25% and 12.0% in less than 48 hours the LC_{50} was reached for *Oreochromis niloticus* fingerlings of 5-8 cm length at 25-28°C and for *Lebistes reticulatus* of 1-3 cm length (Nirarita *et al.* 1988). The effect of this chemical suspension on the mitotic activity of the meristematic root tip cells of *Allium cepa* showed a highly cytotoxic effect. At a concentration of 40% no mitotic activity, as measured by the mitotic index, could be revealed (Julianto 1986).

BOD values have been recorded with up to 2056 mg/L by the Balai Penelitian Kimia, Semarang, exceeding the OACWW of 85 mg/L by 2400%. COD values up to 7691 mg/L exceed the OACWW of February 1991 by 3076%. Even phenol was recorded with 1.89 mg/L. The phenol-like odour is a hazard for the people living along the Ledok River causing headaches, running noses and irritated eyes to mention only the minor nuisances.

The use of naphthol, most probably as 2-hydroxy-naphthalene for the treatment of the textiles before the dyeing process with dyestuffs such as AnthrasolR, Remazol, Levafix, and Immedia in previous years and most recently Dispersol from ICI and Sumarol from Japan, is an environmental and health hazard. Due to the water solubility of 866 ± 31 μg/mL, absorption to soil will occur and bioaccumulation is possible (Ney 1990). The octanol-water partition coefficient (K_{OW}) of 780 ± 62 supports the bioaccumulation possibilities of naphthol. The absorption coefficient (K_{OC}) of 522 indicates absorption by soil. This data strongly support the evidence that this chemical will biodegrade but may also bioaccumulate (Ney 1990).

At present available data give rise to fears that not only is the run-off water of the Ledok a hazard, but that the sediment and adjacent soil layers are already contaminated. The use of this polluted water for the irrigation of paddies, some kilometers downstream from the source, gives rise to fears of an even wider spread of contaminated material via the food chain.

The low level of oxygen on most days throughout the year clearly shows that the innocuous gas nitrogen is released during the anoxic phase due to the action of bacteria which start to obtain oxygen from dissolved nitrates and nitrities if the oxygen content drops to about 5% of the saturation value. If the bacteria start to obtain oxygen from sulphate, under anaerobic conditions, the resultant sulphids are toxic to any aquatic life (Moriarty 1990).

Using the extended saprobity system (Sladecek 1965) the water of the polluted Ledok can be decribed as ultrasaprobic or antisaprobic or as an azoic to toxic zone. Firm and immediate steps to clean the waste-water of Damatex Textile Factory are a must.

5.   Acknowledgement

I would like to thank the following students for their substantial support in collecting the data and their stimulating and steady interest: Putu S. Permanasari, Peggy O.A. Ratulangi, Paulus W. Nugroho, Letansia, Jung Hok, Dedy Kurniadhie and Untung S. Widjaja.

6.   References

Julianto, J. (1986) *The Effect of Two Kinds of Damatex Textile Factory Effluents on the Root Tip Mitosis of Onion (Allium cepa L. var. aggregatum G. Don)*, Thesis Fac. Biol. Satya Wacana Christian University, Salatiga, 26 p.

Keputusan Menteri Negara KLH (1991) *Baku mutu limbah cair bagi kegiatan yang sudah beroperasi*, No.: KEP - 03/MENKLH/II/1991/Lampiran X, p. 10. dan Lampiran XV p. 15.

Liebmann, H. (1962) *Handbuch der Frischwasser- und Abwasserbiologie*, Vol. I, 2nd edition, Oldenbourg, Germany, 588 p.

Moriarty, F. (1990) *Ecotoxicology*, 2nd edition, Acad. Press, London, 289 p.

Nirarita, C.E., Ong Tjoen Bing, Samanya, R. (1988) *The Toxicity of Damatex Textile Factory Effluent to Oreochromis niloticus and Lebistes reticulatus*, Seksi Pen. Senat Mahasiswa Satya Wacana Christian University, Salatiga, 24 p.

Ney, E. (1990) *Where Did That Chemical Go?*, Van Nostrand, New York, 138 p.

Sladecek, V. (1965) The Future of the Saprobity System, *Hydrobiologia* 25: 518-533.

5.4

Cosmetics may contribute to mercury contamination of hair in the Surabaya population

W. Susetyo

Abstract

Human hair samples were used as bioindicators for mercury contamination in the metropolitan area of Surabaya. Four hundred scalp hair samples were collected from people living in four different areas: Kenjeran, Nyamplungan, Rungkut, and Darmo. The first three areas are fishing villages with a relatively low socioeconomic status. Darmo is an 'elite' area with a much higher socioeconomic status. To establish a 'normal' value for Java Island, Yogyakarta was chosen as the comparative reference area. The mercury concentration of the samples was determined by a neutron activation technique. The results of measurements (arithmetic mean ± standard deviation) were as follows: Yogyakarta 6.1 ± 7.9 µg/g, Rungkut 6.4 ± 6.7 µg/g, Nyamplungan 9.7 ± 15.2 µg/g, Kenjeran 10.1 ± 20.4 µg/g and Darmo 17.3 ± 30.5 µg/g. The mean value for the metropolitan area of Surabaya was 10.8 ± 20.2 µg/g. These data indicate, that compared with Yogyakarta, residents of Surabaya area are slightly more contaminated with mercury. The Darmo population had the highest mercury concentration of all, almost three times higher than that of Yogyakarta. The difference between mercury concentrations of males and females living in Darmo was also significant: 12.5 ± 11.5 µg/g versus 22.6 ± 42.1 µg/g. The male-female difference was insignificant in the other areas including Yogyakarta. It is suspected that the high mercury concentrations in women with a high socioeconomic status comes from cosmetics. Further investigations still need to be done to confirm this.

1. Introduction

Natural and anthropogenic inorganic mercury in the environment is readily methylated to become methylmercury which is much more toxic than its inorganic predecessor (Lu *et al.* 1972). Mercury species in industrial waste water or in rain water are transformed by microorganisms. Mercury contamination is biomagnified in food chains, extending to fish, shells, mussels, etc. and finally to mammals including human beings.

Many researchers have monitored or assessed the level of mercury contamination in Jakarta (Yatim 1985). Similar to the Jakarta situation, the Surabaya Metropolitan area is also heavily industrialized, however, details of the level of mercury contamination in Surabaya are scarce. A number of major industries have developed in Surabaya which use mercury in their process and products such as mercury lamps; dry cells, soda paint, cosmetics, etc. The use of mercury in large quantities places the population at some risk of mercury contamination. A notorious example is the mercury contamination at the Minamata bay in Japan several decades ago.

For this study, human scalp hair was selected as bioindicator in assessing the level of mercury contamination of the Surabaya population. One way for the human body to 'excrete' mercury (and any other metals) is by disposing it of to the hair. Unlike excretion via urine, faeces, and transpiration, mercury excretion via skinpores to hair is accumulative. Due to this cumulative process, the concentration of metals (mercury included) in hair is relatively high. Mercury concentrations between 1-10 $\mu g/g$ are common in hair while the mercury concentration in blood is 250 times lower than that in the hair of the same individual (WHO 1976).

Originally, the aim of the study was to assess the extent of mercury contamination in Surabaya's population. This was done by comparing mercury concentrations in hair samples collected in Surabaya with those collected from residents of Yogyakarta which were assumed to have no industrial source of anthropogenic mercury contamination.

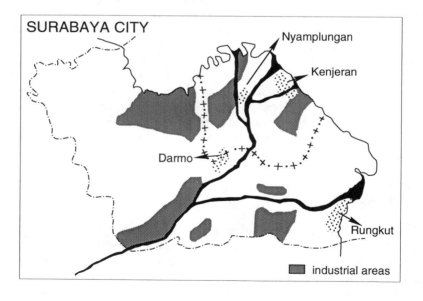

Figure 1 *Map of greater Surabaya, East Java, showing the location of the districts Nyamplungan, Kenjaran, Rungkut and Darmo where hair samples were obtained*

2.   Materials and methods

2.1   Sampling areas

Four hundred and fifty scalp hair samples were collected from four different locations in the Surabaya area: Kenjeran, Rungkut, Nyamplungan, and Darmo, and from Yogyakarta (the reference area). Hair samples were cut using new stainless steel scissors from several sites and as close as possible to the scalp in an amount which corresponded to about 0.5 gram. The volunteers were found in public places such as hospitals, hair cutting salons, etc. Only adults (> 20 years old) were asked to be volunteers. Figure 1 depicts the location of sampling areas in the greater Surabaya. Kenjeran, Rungkut, and Nyamplungan are fishing villages with a relatively low socioeconomic status. Darmo is the only 'elite' area (*i.e.* high economic status). The distribution of the samples based on area and sex is shown in the Table 1.

Table 1 *Summary of mercury concentration levels in hair samples*

Area	No. of samples	Sex*	Minimum (μg/g)	Maximum (μg/g)	Median (μg/g)	Arithmetic mean (μg/g)	Geometric mean (μg/g)
Kenjeran	89	m + f	0.6	144.6	4.6	10.1 ± 20.4	5.1
	43	m	0.6	99.1	4.9	11.0 ± 19.2	6.0
	46	f	1.3	144.6	3.7	9.2 ± 21,7	4.5
Rungkut	96	m + f	0.5	39.7	4.5	6.4 ± 6.7	4.3
	49	m	0.6	39.7	4.8	7.5 ± 8.5	4.8
	47	f	0.5	17.9	4.2	5.2 ± 4.0	4.0
Nyamplungan	99	m + f	0.5	116.2	4.6	9.7 ± 15.2	4.9
	51	m	1.0	55.2	4.6	8.3 ± 11.0	4.9
	48	f	0.5	116.2	4.3	11.1 ± 18,7	5.0
Darmo	90	m + f	1.0	197.9	8.7	17.3 ± 30.5	9.0
	47	m	1.3	63.9	9.1	12.5 ± 11.5	8.9
	43	f	1.0	197.9	8.4	22.6 ± 42.1	9.0
Surabaya (total)	374	m + f	0.5	197.9	4.9	10.8 ± 20.2	5.5
	190	m	0.6	99.1	5.5	9.7 ± 13.0	5.8
	184	f	0.5	197.9	4.5	11.8 ± 25.6	5.2
Yogyakarta (Reference area)	50	m + f	0.2	46.2	3.5	6.1 ± 7.9	3.6
	28	m	0.2	46.2	3.2	6.1 ± 9.0	3.3
	22	f	0.9	29.2	3.6	6.2 ± 6.4	4.1

m = male, f = female.

2.2   Sample preparation

Each hair sample (0.5 g) was washed using acetone and rinsed three times using demineralized water and finally washed with acetone again. The samples were shaken manually for 10 minutes between each of the above steps. The samples were then dried at room temperature. Once the sample was dry, it was weighed (dry weight ranged from 0.1 to 0.4 g) and put into polyethylene vials. The mercury standard solution was made by dissolving HgO in 1 L 0.05 N HNO_3 (supra-pure) to get the final concentration of 1.5671 μg/ml. Five microliter aliquots of the standard solution were pipetted into polyethylene vials similar to the ones used for the samples.

2.3 Mercury measurement

The sample and standard vials were irradiated for 6 hours in a TRIGA swimming-pool-type reactor. The estimated thermal flux neutron was 5 x 10^{12} cm^{-2} s^{-1}. The samples and the standards were cooled down for a few days to let the short lived radionuclides decay. This allows instrumental determination of mercury without any chemical separation. The standards and the samples were then counted for 4000 seconds, 30 cm above a Ge(Li) detector of a gamma spectrometer. The activity of mercury in standards and samples were determined by the combined areas of the 69 and 77.3 keV peaks of ^{197}Hg (Guinn 1972).

3. Results and discussion

3.1 Mean values

Table 1 summarizes the mean values of the mercury measurements in the hair samples. The arithmetic mean of mercury concentration of the reference area, Yogyakarta, was found to be 6.1 ± 7.9 μg/g. This value is assumed to represent a 'normal' value for Java Island. Samples from Rungkut with a mercury concentration of 6.4 ± 6.7 μg/g were not significantly different from those of Yogyakarta. Significant differences were, however, observed for samples from Kenjeran (10.1 ± 20.4 μg/g) and Darmo (17.3 ± 30.5 μg/g).

3.2 Level of contamination

The data mentioned in Table 1 indicate that a slight mercury contamination is present in the population of the Surabaya metropolitan area. WHO and FAO have established a Provisional Tolerable Weekly Intake (PTWI) of mercury of 0.2 mg Hg/week (as methyl mercury). Long term mercury intake as high as the PTWI value corresponds to a mercury concentration in hair of 5-6 μg/g (IAEA 1991). Table 1 shows that Yogyakarta (and Rungkut) have mercury concentrations which are quite close to this range. This confirms the assumption that the reference area (i.e. Yogyakarta) has no significant mercury contamination. Long term daily intake of methyl mercury between 3 and 7 μg/kg body weight has been shown to lead to a hair concentration of approximately 50-125 μg/g. It turns out that none of the investigated individuals of Yogyakarta and Rungkut has a mercury concentration greater than 50 μg/g. On the contrary 6.7% of the investigated individuals of Darmo, 2% of Nyamplungan, and 3.4% of Kenjeran have mercury concentration above 50µg/g.

3.3   The cosmetic factor

As noted above, Darmo is the only elite residential area. This implies that Darmo's women can afford modern cosmetics (such as bleaching cream, make-up, etc.) while females from the other investigated and reference areas cannot. The later usually put on traditional cosmetics which do not contain mercury. From Table 1 it is clear that hair samples of the women from Darmo contain the highest mercury concentrations of all groups sampled, i.e. 22.6 ± 42.1 µg/g. It is safe to assume that no males in Surabaya use cosmetics. The other investigated and reference areas have no significant difference in the mercury content between males and females. Therefore, it can be inferred that the high mercury content in the females of Darmo does not come from food, drinking water, or atmospheric sources. It is suggested that this difference in mercury contamination levels between males and females, is due to the use of cosmetics. Further studies still have to be done to confirm this suggestion.

4.   Conclusions

1. Relative to Yogyakarta, residents of some parts of the Surabaya Metropolitan Area (Kenjeran and Nyamplungan) show a slight increase in mercury levels in their scalp hair.
2. High mercury concentration in females of Darmo, the only high socioeconomic status suburb among the four investigated areas, is believed to be due to the use of cosmetics containing mercury substances, rather than to ingestion of mercury from food, drinking water, or atmospheric sources.

5.   Acknowledgements

The scalp hair samples from Surabaya were collected by staff of the School of Medicine in the Airlangga University. The scalp hair samples from Yogyakarta were collected by staff of the School of Dentistry of Gadjah Mada University. The irradiation was done in the Bandung Atomic Reactor Center. The induced radioactivity of mercury in the samples was measured by the gamma spectrometer at the Yogyakarta Nuclear Research Center. The author gratefully acknowledges all the assistance that was given to him by the above institutes during the investigation.

6. References

Guinn, V.P. (1972) Determination of Mercury by Instrumental Neutron Activation Analysis, *The International Atomic Energy Agency Technical Reports Series*, No. 137, IAEA, Vienna, pp. 87-98.

IAEA (International Atomic Energy Agency) (1991) Report on the First Research Coordination Meeting of Coordinated Research Programme on Assessment of Environmental Exposure to Mercury in Selected Human Population as Studied by Nuclear and Other Techniques, IAEA-NAHRES-7, Vienna, pp. 7-10.

Lu, F.C., Berteau, P.E. & Clegg, D.J. (1972) The Toxicity of Mercury in Man and Animals, *The International Atomic Energy Agency Technical Reports Series*, No. 137, IAEA, Vienna, pp. 67-86.

WHO (World Health Organization) (1976) *Environmental Health Criteria 1: Mercury*, WHO, Geneva.

Yatim, S. (1985) A Study of Trace Element Concentrations in Human Hair of the Inhabitants of the Jakarta City, *The International Atomic Energy Agency IAEA-TECDOC-330*, IAEA, Vienna, pp. 219-228.

5.5

Monitoring the accumulation of cadmium released from industrial sources

D.T. JONES & S.P. HOPKIN

Abstract

The accumulation of metals from two major industrial sources in south west England was investigated. Surface soils, nettle leaves, two species of isopods and three species of gastropods were collected from 88 sites in the region and analysed for cadmium content. Correlations between concentrations of cadmium in the different sample types revealed that in all cases woodlice gave more accurate predictions of the bioavailability of cadmium in the other species of invertebrates than was given by the soils, nettles or snails.

1. Introduction

Man's industrial activities have greatly increased rates of mobilization of many metals, including cadmium. Concern has been raised over the public health implications of increased exposure to metals (Nriagu 1988), while much research has also been conducted into the effects of metal pollutants on natural and semi-natural ecosystems (for example, see Hopkin 1989, Tyler *et al.* 1989). Reliable methods of monitoring the accumulation of metals in terrestrial habitats, and detecting and quantiflying detrimental effects upon the biota caused by these pollutants, are still at an early stage of development. Recent advances in the theory and practice of using invertebrates as biological monitors of pollution have been reviewed by Hopkin (1993).

This present paper details some of the results of an investigation into monitoring the dispersal of metals from two industrial sources, and their accumulation by invertebrates (Jones 1991). One of the aims was to ascertain whether the amount of metal in an invertebrate could be predicted accurately from levels in soils, plants or other species of invertebrate.

2. Study site

The study area was defined as the land to the south of the Severn Estuary depicted on the British Ordnance Survey 1:50,000 map sheet 172. Two major sources of cadmium exist in this area, one at Avonmouth, north west of Bristol, the other at Shipham in the Mendip Hills, south of Bristol (Figure 1).

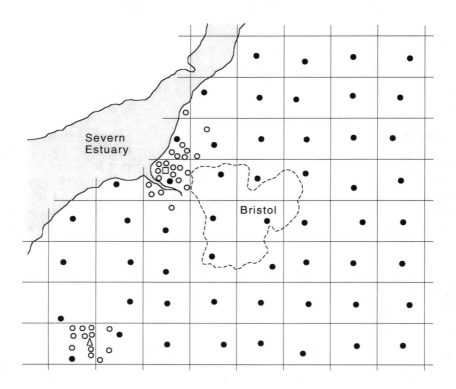

Figure 1 *Study area showing positions of sampling sites (5 km resolution sites: •; 1 km resolution sites: ○), the Avonmouth smelting works (□), and the Shipham mine (△). The grid lines are 5 km apart*

The world's largest primary zinc, lead and cadmium smelter, located at Avonmouth, emits 3.5 tonne Cd yr^{-1}, 53 tonne Zn yr^{-1} and 35 tonne Pb yr^{-1} to the atmosphere (Coy 1984). Severe disruptions have occurred to local ecosystems as a result of the accumulation of particulate metals (for descriptions see Jones & Hopkin 1994). The Mendip Hills, including the rich lead and zinc deposits at Shipham, have a long history of mineral exploitation. As a result of early mining methods the surface soils near the Shipman mine have very high concentrations of cadmium, a frequent guest element in zinc ores (Khan & Frankland 1983).

3.   Material and methods

The study area was divided into a regular grid consisting of 54 squares each 5 x 5 km. A roadside grassland/scrub site was selected as close to the centre of each square as public access would allow. A further 34 sites, positioned within a 1 km grid were selected, 22 in the vicinity of the Avonmouth smelter, and 12 in the vicinity of the Shipham mine (Figure 1).

From each of the 88 sites six samples of the top 2 cm of mineral soils, and the top 20 cm of shoot from six individual nettle plants (*Urtica dioica*) were collected. Specimens of the woodlice *Oniscus asellus* and *Porcellio scaber*, and the pulmonate snails *Helix aspersa*, *Cepaea hortensis* and *Monacha cantiana* were gathered. Where possible, 14 adult woodlice and 8 adult snails of each species were collected at each site. Sampling was conducted between 2 m and 4 m from the edge of the road.

All animals were starved for 24 hours before analysis to allow the gut contents to be voided. Soils, nettles and woodlice were prepared and analysed for cadmium content using flame and flameless AAS, as described by Hopkin *et al.* (1986). Snails were first removed from their shells before being subjected to the same treatment as the woodlice. Standard reference materials were prepared and analysed in a similar manner, as recommended by Ihnat (1988). Derived values were within 5% of the certified concentrations.

Two dimensional isoline maps were produced using the computer graphics system Unimap. The computer interpolated between the recorded concentrations of cadmium in the samples collected from the 88 sites to produce concentration values for every 1 km grid square in the study area.

4.   Results

The spatial distribution of the concentration of cadmium in surface soils is shown in Figure 2. The highest concentrations were recorded at the site 0.5 km north of the smelter (212 μg g^{-1}), and at the Shipham mine (238 μg g^{-1}). The upper limit of concentrations of cadmium in uncontaminated soils in lowland southern England is about 1.0 μg g^{-1} (Jones *et al.* 1987). Within 2 km of the Shipham mine levels of cadmium in the surface soil return to 'background' levels. In contrast, the area of elevated concentrations around the Avonmouth smelter is far more extensive. Concentrations of cadmium in surface soils above 'background' levels were detected up to 25 km from the smelter.

The correlation coefficient between the [10]log concentration of cadmium in pairs of variables collected from as many of the 88 sites in the study area where they were found, is given in Table 1. The concentration of cadmium in *Porcellio scaber* at any site can be predicted more accurately from levels of cadmium in *Oniscus asellus* (Figure 3a) than from levels in either surface soils (Figure 3b) or nettle leaves (Figure 3c). Similarly, concentrations of cadmium in the three species of snail are more highly correlated with the concentration of cadmium in either

P. scaber or *O. asellus* (for example Figure 3d) than with levels in either soils or nettles.

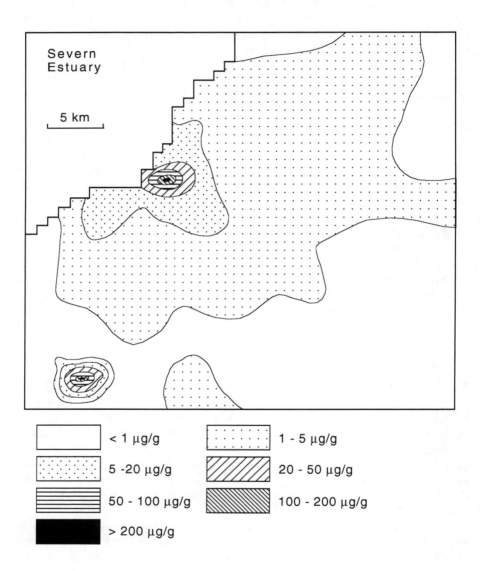

Figure 2 *Isoline map of study area showing the spatial distribution of concentrations of cadmium (µg/g dry weight) in pooled samples of surface soils collected from the 88 sites shown in Figure 1*

Table 1 *Correlation coefficients (r) between the [10]log concentrations of cadmium in surface soil, nettle leaves and invertebrates collected from the sites shown in Figure 1. All values are significant (p < 0.002)*

	Oniscus	Porcellio	Helix	Cepaea	Monacha
Soil	0.813	0.892	0.808	0.769	0.836
Nettles	0.808	0.766	0.707	0.773	0.857
Oniscus		0.955	0.906	0.900	0.887
Porcellio			0.915	0.851	0.951

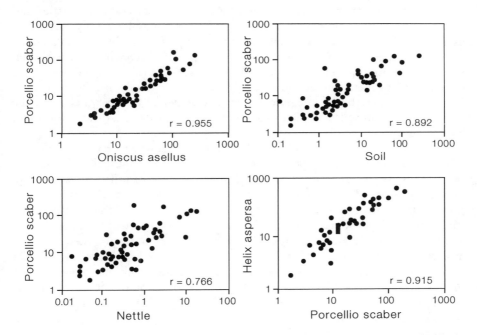

Figure 3 *Scatter diagrams relating concentrations of cadmium (μg/g dw) in pooled samples of isopods* (Porcellio scaber, Oniscus asellus), *snails* (Helix aspersa), *nettle leaves* (Urtica dioica), *and soil collected from the sites shown in Figure 1*

5.   Discussion

The general pattern of spatial distribution of cadmium in surface soils, with 'hot-spots' at Avonmouth and Shipham, is similar to that produced by Hopkin et al. (1986) in their survey of the same area. When concentrations were mapped using only the 54 sites in the 5 km grid (Jones & Hopkin 1991) the contamination at Shipham was not detected. The highest concentration recorded in the study area was only 19.3 μg g⁻¹, from soils collected at a site 3 km north of the smelter.

However, when a finer resolution of collecting sites around the known sources of metals was incorporated into the sampling network, the full extent of the contamination was revealed (Figure 2) and a more detailed view of the spatial distribution of cadmium is given. The influence of the wind in causing greater dispersal of airborne cadmium from the smelter is seen clearly, in contrast to the more limited distance the cadmium is transported from the ground level source at the Shipham mine.

The relatively poor correlation between concentrations in soils and concentrations in the invertebrates reflects the fact that soil properties such as pH, cation exchange capacity and organic matter content affect the availability of cadmium to organisms. Further, the relationship between concentrations in nettles and invertebrates is not a simple one because nettle leaves may form only part of the invertebrate's diet, while the metal content in samples of leaf litter from any one location can be very heterogeneous. Hopkin et al. (1986) concluded that knowledge of concentrations of metals in both surface soil and leaf litter did not enable the amounts of metals in woodlice to be predicted accurately at individual sites. By contrast, invertebrates integrate all the environmental factors which cause the levels of metals in soils and plants to fluctuate, and thus give a direct measure of bioavailability.

A biological monitor should have the ability to predict accurately the concentration of a pollutant in a range of other species, thereby eliminating the need to collect those species and thus saving much time and effort. In the context of monitoring levels of cadmium in invertebrates in the Bristol region *Oniscus asellus* is a suitable candidate as a biological monitor (it occurred in 82 of the 88 sites in the study area, and was found in at least 32% more sites than any of the other invertebrate species). In a global context, *Porcellio scaber* has been suggested as a biomonitor of metals because it is now widely distributed (Hopkin et al. 1993). If concentrations of metals in invertebrates can be related to deleterious effects on those species in the wild, it will then be possible to use biomonitors to map the geographical extent of known effects on populations, rather than simply mapping concentrations. Ultimately, it is only by monitoring the effects of pollution on organisms in the field that the effectiveness of pollution control can be measured.

6. Acknowledgements

This research was conducted while DTJ was in receipt of a Science and Engineering Research Council studentship. The authors would like to thank the Natural Environment Research Council for grant support.

7. References

Coy, C.M. (1984) Control of Dust and Fume at a Primary Zinc and Lead Smelter, *Chemistry in Britain*, May: 418-420.

Hopkin, S.P. (1989) *Ecophysiology of Metals in Terrestrial Invertebrates*, Elsevier Applied Science, London.

Hopkin, S.P. (1993) In Situ Biological Monitoring of Pollution in Terrestrial and Aquatic Ecosystems, in: Calow, P. (ed.) *Handbook of Ecotoxicology*, Vol. 1, Blackwell, Oxford, pp. 397-427.

Hopkin, S.P., Hardisty, G.N. & Martin, M.H. (1986) The Woodlouse *Porcellio scaber* as a 'Biological Indicator' of Zinc, Cadmium, Lead and Copper Pollution, *Environ. Pollut.* 11B: 271-290.

Hopkin, S.P., Jones, D.T & Dietrich, D. (1993) The Terrestrial Isopod *Porcellio scaber* as a Monitor of the Bioavailability of Metals: Towards a Global 'Woodlouse Watch' Scheme, in: Slooff, W. & De Kruijf, H. (eds.) *Proc. 2nd European Conf. Ecotoxicology. Sci. Total Environ.*, Suppl 1993: 357-365.

Ihnat, M. (1988) Pick a Number - Analytical Data Reliability and Biological Reference Materials, *Sci. Total Environ.* 71: 39-51.

Jones, D.T. (1991) *Biological Monitoring of Metals Pollution in Terrestrial Ecosystems*, Unpublished Ph.D. thesis, University of Reading.

Jones, D.T. & Hopkin, S.P. (1991) Biological Monitoring of Metal Pollution in Terrestrial Ecosystems, in: Ravera, O. (ed.) *Terrestrial and Aquatic Ecosystems. Perturbation and Recovery*, Ellis Horwood, London, pp. 148-152.

Jones, D.T. & Hopkin, S.P. (1994) Effects of Metals on the Size of Terrestrial Isopods in an Industrially Polluted Area, in: Widianarko, B., Vink, K. & Van Straalen, N.M. (eds.) *Environmental Toxicology in South East Asia*, VU University Press, Amsterdam, pp. 191-197.

Jones, K.C., Symon, C.J. & Johnston, A.E. (1987) Retrospective Analysis of an Archived Soil Collection. 2. Cadmium, *Sci. Total Environ.* 67: 75-89.

Khan, D.H. & Frankland, B. (1983) Chemical Forms of Cd and Pb in Some Contaminated Soils, *Environ. Pollut.* 6B: 15-31.

Nriagu, J.O. (1988) A Silent Epidemic of Environmental Metal Poisoning?, *Environ. Pollut.* 50: 139-161.

Tyler, G., Balsberg Pahlsson, A.M., Bengtsson, G., Baath, E. & Tranvik, L. (1989) Heavy-metal Ecology of Terrestrial Plants, Microorganisms and Invertebrates. A Review, *Water Air Soil Pollut.* 47: 189-215.

5.6

Health status of small ruminants foraging in the Cimulang rubber plantation, West Java

T.B. Murdiati, D. Priyanto & A. Suparyanto

Abstract

Livestock can be integrated with rubber plantation, since the undergrowth vegetation is palatable and nutritious as animal feed. Farmers in the villages area near Cimulang rubber plantation, Sempak, Bogor - West Java have been using the undergrowth as foraging pasture for their sheep and goats. Animal health problems have been reported from the village where sheep and goats were allowed to graze under the rubber trees. Pesticides intoxication was implicated as the main health problem. The survey revealed that intoxication was due to pesticide residues which were applied regularly in the plantation.

1.   Introduction

Various crops planted in the interspace between rows of rubber trees could provide additional income for rubber plantations. However, most intercrops cannot be grown when the rubber canopy closes at about three years, and consequently the inter-row spaces are infested by weeds. Since the weeds compete with the rubber trees, they have to be controlled, which is usually done by herbicide application.

Regular application of pesticides should be handled properly, because animals may graze on the undergrowth which causes pesticide poisoning to the animals. Such problems were reported from the village near the Cimulang rubber plantation.

Weeds and other undergrowth species are usually quite palatable and nutritious as animal feed, and livestock such as sheep and goat can be integrated into plantation production systems (Vanselow 1982, Amir *et al.* 1986). Tajuddin (1986) suggested using sheep and goats as a means of biological weed control, as sheep or goats can consume up to 70% of weed species.

2.   Materials and methods

This report originated from a study on traditional veterinary health care for animal ruminants, which was conducted in the village of Pasir Gaok, Bogor (Mathias-Mundy *et al.* 1992) The study was conducted using rural rapid appraisal (RRA), which combines the use of secondary data, observations and interviews (Beebe 1985).

The village administration was consulted about village structure, crops grown and general information on animal husbandry. The rubber estate administration was consulted for history and management of the plantation including pesticide application. Farmers were interviewed about animal diseases, and other relevant information such as practices of veterinary health care. The interviews were undertaken using a written interview guide. An inspection was also made of some 50 barns, in which observations of disease and animal condition were made.

3.   Results and discussion

The village of Pasir Gaok, Samplak is located about 18 km north of Bogor. One third of the village in the southern part is covered by rice fields, while most of the northern part belongs to a rubber estate (PTP XI Cimulang) planted with rubber trees (Mathias-Mundy *et al.* 1992).

Table 1 *Type of management in keeping small ruminants at Pasir Gaok*

	Southern part (Rice field)	Northern part (Rubber estate)
Kept in barn	73.3%	38.7%
Grazing	26.7%	61.3%

In the southern part of the village, most sheep and goats are kept in barns, built on stilts with slatted floors (Table 1). The animals are fed at least once a day with fodder collected by the family members at the sides of roads or from harvested fields, forests and plantations, this is a common way of keeping small ruminants in West Java. Farmers in this area indicated that they usually do not send their animals to graze, but sometimes towards the end of the dry season when finding fodder is difficult, they send their animals to graze around the rice field or on the side of the road, in addition to the regular cut and carry feeding.

Most sheep or goats were grazed daily, usually between noon and 4 or 5 p.m. The rubber estate indicated that it is only since 1965 that animals from the neighbourhood villages have been allowed to enter the plantation and graze the undergrowth species.

In general, more disease problems in small ruminants were reported from the northern part of the village (Table 2), where most sheep and goat graze under the rubber trees every day. It was noted during the field study that grazed animals were thinner than those kept confined in a barn, and more animals with diarrhoea were observed.

Table 2 *Diseases observed by the team and reported by respondents in the village of Pasir Gaok*

Disease	Observed cases		Reported cases	
	South	North	South	North
Bloat	-	-	3	4
Broken leg	-	-	-	1
Coughing	-	-	-	3
Diarrhoea	1	13	9	5
Early death	-	-	1	3
Myasis	-	2	6	7
Paralysis	-	-	2	2
Pink eye	3	2	5	12
Poisoning	-	-	5	12
Ringworm	-	-	-	1
Scabies	-	-	-	7
Thinness	1	6	-	-

More poisoning was reported from the northern part of Pasir Gaok. Twelve cases of poisoning were reported from the northern area. These were claimed to be due to pesticide residues under the rubber trees. Since animals graze the undergrowth in the rubber plantation which could be newly sprayed with pesticides, poisoning cases may occur. Most farmers in the northern part of the villages relied solely on the undergrowth species for their small ruminants. Their sheep and goats grazed daily under the rubber tree with no supplemental fodder. One farmer reported a case of poisoning caused by fertilizer applied to the rubber trees.

In comparison, five cases of poisoning were reported from the southern part of the village, where most sheep and goat were kept in barns. Furthermore, only one case of poisoning was claimed to be due to grass or weeds, which were collected from the rubber plantation, these grass and weeds were probably contaminated with pesticides. Other poisoning cases from the southern part described by farmers were believed to be caused either by feeding cassava leaves or young rubber leaves. This finding suggests that pesticides residues in weeds and grass under the rubber trees have caused major health problems for animals grazing this undergrowth.

Other causes of poisoning should not be excluded, as there is a possibility of ammonia poisoning from fertilizer, since fertilizer is also applied regularly in addition to pesticides. It is difficult to assess the diagnosis of poisoning from the farmer's reports, however, the symptoms described by the farmers seem to confirm the diagnosis.

Regular application of pesticides has been conducted by the estate, especially herbicides, because weeds compete with the rubber trees (Anonymous 1991). Glyphosate, paraquat and dimethyl-amine have been the main pesticides used. In addition, sulphur dust was also applied as a fungicide during the early stages of rubber plantation establishment.

It is likely that livestock management practices also account for the differences in the animal condition and health. Some farmers in the northern part of the village kept their animals on the ground, making the barns difficult to clean, since the fodder remains and faeces often accumulated on the floor and were removed only every three months or so. This could also contribute to the health problem reported from the northern part of the village; at this method is apparently easier and cheaper than using stilted barns.

Although no faeces examination was performed during the study, Dahan & Hutagalung (1983) suggested that small ruminants in the rubber plantation are often subjected to endoparasites infestation (such as haemonchus).

Pesticides poisoning in the rubber plantation could be avoided by keeping animals away from the grass under the rubber trees which are newly sprayed with pesticides. Notification of the spraying time should be properly given by the estate to the neighbouring villagers. Farmers may not always be aware when spraying is to be done, and it seems that information from the estate is not transmitted properly.

4. References

Amir, P., Knipscheer, H.C., Karo-Karo, S., Reese, A. & De Boer, A.J. (1986) *The Potential of Small Ruminants Livestock on Rubber Plantation Schemes: A Linear Programming Analysis*, Working paper No. 86, Small Ruminants Collaborative Research Support Program - Balai Penelitian Ternak, Pusat Penelitian dan Pengembangan Peternakan, Bogor.

Anonymous (1991) *Pestisida untuk pertanian dan kehutanan*, Penerbit Departemen Pertanian, Jakarta.

Beebe, J. (1985) *Rapid Rural Appraisal: The Critical First Step in a Farming Systems Approach to Research*, Networking Paper No. 5, Farming System Support Project, University of Florida, Gainsville, Florida, USA.

Dahan, M.M. & Hutagalung, R.I. (1983) *Integration of Small Ruminants with Plantation Crops*, Australian National University.

Mathias-Mundy, E., Wahyuni, S., Murdiati, T.B., Suparyanto, A., Priyanto, D., Isbandi, Beriajaya & Sangat-Roemantyo, H. (1992) *Traditional Animal Health Care for Goats and Sheep in West Java: A Comparison of Three Villages*, Small Ruminants Collaborative Research Support Program - Balai Penelitian Ternak, Pusat Penelitian dan Pengembangan Peternakan, Bogor.

Tajuddin, I. (1986) Integration of Animals in Rubber Plantation, *Agroforestry System* 4: 55-66.

Vanselow, B. (1982) Sheep Production in a Commercial Rubber Plantation: A Malaysian Experience, *Trop. Animal Prod.* 7: 50-56.

5.7

Relevance of biochemical parameters in assessing the responses of tropical plants to SO_2

P.S. DUBEY

Abstract

Assessment of plant responses to air pollutants requires our careful attention. In an intensive study of five years at various sites in India with sulphur dioxide air pollution, a preliminary twenty species were selected for screening and later ten species of plants were identified for detailed investigations. The results reveal interesting information on the statistical relationship between sulphate levels and parameters such as leaf area dry weight ratio, enzymes such as superoxide dismutase (SOD), peroxidase (POD), nitrate reductase (NR), amino and ascorbic acid, protein, sugars and chlorophyll content and stomatal conductance. Leaf area dry weight ratio, activities of SOD, POD and to some extent stomatal conductance were correlated with lower (40-50 $\mu g/m^3$) as well as higher (above 100 $\mu g/m^3$) ambient SO_2 loads. At higher levels of SO_2, at a lower level of statistical significance, chances of inclusion of five to seven parameters for assessment of tolerance/susceptibility appeared. However tolerant plants showed correlations with two or three parameters, while in susceptible ones all the parameters were affected indicating significant relationships, for nine or ten. The data so obtained can serve the purpose of bioindication, species-dependent response assessing and the selection of appropriate and relevant parameters in assessment of the tolerance of plants against air pollutants.

1. Introduction

Air pollution and plant responses in temperate regions has seen intensive and extensive research in the field as well as under laboratory conditions (Heck *et al.* 1979, Keller 1983, Bell 1984, Posthumus 1984, Dubey 1991, 1992). This is further illustrated by the remarkable ability of pine needles or lichens to act as bioindicators (Rao & Leblanc 1965, Schubert 1982). In the tropics the problems are more complicated because of sharp seasonal regimes with changes in temperature and rainfall patterns, biodiversity, evergreen and deciduous trees with a shorter period of leaflessness, high light intensity and many other factors. Also in countries like India and other developing countries, as reviewed by Dubey (1990), much of the information generated is for crops and from experiments done in too poorly designed chambers employing too high concentrations of SO_2 (2000-5000 $\mu g/m^3$) which are rarely near to ambient loads. The important centres like BHU, JNU, NBRI etc. in India use in general only one or two and at times three or four parameters of their choice for assessing the plant response against the oxides of sulphur and nitrogen and ozone. Field studies pose a more complex picture, leading to greater difficulties of interpretation, since in many cases the assessment is done with two or three parameters observed on some susceptible species while practically in field situations the mature trees appeared to be fairly tolerant to the ambient SO_2 loads (Rao & Dubey 1990, Dubey & Rao 1991).

The conclusions drawn in this paper are in fact derived from intensive and extensive research from field situations for more than five years as part of the All India Coordinated Program On Air Pollution and Plants (Ministry of Environment and Forests Govt. of India) and later reconfirmed in the Green Belt Development Project of Indian Petrochemical Corporation Limited. The objective of these studies was to establish concrete systems and parameters of assessment which are more universal in application and can be employed for some definite recommendations at field levels (Dubey 1990).

2. Experimental sites and methods

The industrial areas of Dewas, Nagda, Pithampur and Ratlam in the south west part and Neemuch, Kota and Baroda in the western part of India were selected for the studies. Twenty common species from these areas were selected for the initial investigations and ten of these investigated in detail. The accumulation of sulphate in leaves was determined following Patterson (1958). Stomatal conductance was measured with a Steady State Porometer, LI 1600 (USA). The other parameters were analyzed using the following methods: LDR (leaf area dry weight ratio, Rao & Dubey 1990), chlorophylls (Arnon 1949), proteins (Lowry et al. 1951), sugars (Malhotra & Sarkar 1979), amino acids (Rosen 1957), ascorbic acid (Rosen 1954), nitrate reductase (Shrivastava & Mathur 1980), POD (peroxidase, Shannon et al. 1986), and SOD (superoxide dismutase, Keith et al. 1983).

A randomized composite sampling technique was used for sampling of thirty leaves, collected five each from top, middle and bottom of the canopy. Of these, fifteen were thus sun-exposed leaves and fifteen were taken from the shaded part of the tree. In the case of smaller plants this number was twelve to fifteen. The statistical correlations were calculated and the level of significance for 'r' values was taken from the standard tables.

3. Results and discussion

Since sulphur dioxide was the predominant pollutant and sulphite formed from it is converted into sulphate, accumulation of sulphate and its correlation with other parameters may yield relevant information on various aspects of plant responses as well as relevance of the parameters to be selected (Dubey 1990, Dubey 1991, Dubey & Rao 1991).

Table 1 *Number of species (out of 20) with positive correlation with one parameter*

Sulphate & chlorophylls	= 7
Sulphate & sugars	= 8
Sulphate & leaf area dry wt.	= 18
Sulphate & none	= 2

Table 2 *Relationship between sulphate accumulation and the parameters chlorophyll, sugars, and leaf area dry wt. ratio (in twenty species)*

A. Positive with two parameters:

   (a) Leaf Area Dry Wt. Ratio and Sugars:
      Eucalyptus globulus, Ziziphus mauritiana, Phoenix sylvestris

   (b) Leaf Area Dry Wt. Ratio and Chlorophyll:
      Syzygium cuminii, Mangifera indica

   (c) With Chlorophyll and Sugar: None

                                                    Total = 5

B. Positive with all three parameters:

   Azadirechta indica, Bauhinia racemosa, Butea monosperma, Dalbergia sissoo, Xanthium strumarium

                                                    Total = 5

C. Negative with all three parameters:

   Acacia nilotica, Prosopis juliflora

                                                    Total = 2

Initially twenty species were chosen and in eighteen plant species a relationship between sulphate level and change in leaf area/dry weight ratio was found; for chlorophyll and sugars, this number was seven and eight species respectively (Table 1). The reports about sugar metabolism under sulphur dioxide pollution thus gets confirmation, there may be positive or negative changes; however, the case of chlorophyll content which is normally reported to be negatively affected is to be interpreted differently, *i.e.* it cannot be taken as a relevant parameter. A perusal of Table 2 demonstrates that with sulphate the number of species showing a positive relationship with all the three parameters is just five and we may assume that these species as susceptible ones; however among these five a broad range of response exists which may be misleading, for example when *B. racemosa*, the most susceptible species (field derived data with ten parameters) and *A. indica*, a moderately tolerant plant, are compared. Even with two parameters there are only five species out of twenty that show a positive correlation with accumulated sulphate levels, including *P. sylvestris* and *M. indica*. Such problems were demonstrated with many species with contrasting results when more parameters were involved in the assessment. However relationships with two or three parameters could be the initial indicators for classifying plant species in a range of susceptibility to tolerance. Also, the relation between sulphate levels and stomatal conductance offered interesting information (Table 3), since in many species with lower conductance the accumulation was very high (*B. variegata, C. procera, D. sissoo*), while in others (*A. indica, C. siamea, B. monosperma*) conductance was moderate and more sulphate accumulated indicating poor utilization of the sulphate; in several species (*F. benghalensis, F. religiosa,* etc.) conductance was high but sulphate accumulation was very low and subsequently the plant damage was also lower. Analysis of these events needed more parameters and a lower number of species (ten out of the twenty) for detailed investigation.

Table 3 *Stomatal conductance (SC) rate and accumulation of sulphate*

A. Low SC and moderate accumulation:

Acacia nilotica, Azadirechta indica, Melia azedarach, Phoenix sylvestris, Prosopis juliflora, Syzygium cuminii, Ziziphum mauritiana

B. Low SC and high accumulation:

Bauhinia racemosa, Calotropis procera, Dalbergia sissoo

C. Moderate SC and high accumulation:

Butea monosperma, Cassia siamea, Eucalyptus globulus

D. Low SC and low accumulation:

Lantana camara

E. High SC and higher accumulation:

Xanthium strumarium, Ipomea fistulosa

F. Moderate/high SC and low accumulation:

Ficus benghalensis, Ficus religiosa, Ficus sp.

SC: Low = 0.35-0.5 cm s^{-1}, Moderate = 1.0-1.3 cm s^{-1}, High = 1.5-1.9 cm s^{-1}.
Sulphate: Low = 25-30%, Moderate = 50-65%, High = 90-125%.

The statistical data given in Table 4 present some interesting information about these selected ten species. The tolerant species exhibit a significant relationship for two or three parameters only and show a very low degree of impact on the metabolism; most of the parameters change to minimum, rather adjustable levels. In moderate species more parameters show a significant change at some levels and with variations in meteorological and metabolic conditions they survive better in the field. However, as expected, the susceptible species, since the entire metabolism is severely affected, show a significant relationship with even nine or all ten parameters. In chamber experiments even if concentrations of SO$_2$ are brought down to 500 to 1000 $\mu g/m^3$, the impact is severe and positive results are obtained for tolerant species; however in field samples it never happens since the average ambient load in all the experimental sites ranged to 50-60 μg/m^3 to 90-110 μg/m^3 at different stations depending upon the distance from the source. Higher concentrations may be accidental episodes and assessments are to be made in tropics more with assessment of latent injuries since in many cases no symptoms appear on leaves (Dubey 1991).

Table 4 *Number of parameter of certain plants with significant correlation coefficient values at different levels*

Plant species	Significance level	
	95.0 (p < 0.05)	99.0 (p < 0.01)
Tolerant		
F. benghalensis	3	2
C. procera	3	2
C. siamea	3	2
Moderate		
I. fistulosa	5	4
M. indica	6	3
S. cumini	6	3
M. azedarach	6	6
Susceptible		
A. indica	10	5 (6)
B. monosperma	9	6 (7)
D. sissoo	9	6

Values in parentheses indicate the number of parameters when the nearest 'r' value was considered.

The data analysis in Table 5 indicates that for most of the species at any level of significance, leaf area dry weight ratio, activities of peroxidase and superoxide dismutase and to some extent stomatal conductance too can serve as indicators under both lower and higher (above 100 μg/m^3) levels of sulphur dioxide. Obviously these are sensitive parameters suitable for indication of the impact. But in the areas with sulphur dioxide levels of 40-50 μg/m^3 more parameters should be investigated because some of the metabolic functions may not be impaired or disturbed at these levels of sulphur dioxide. In about six or seven species, amino acid contents appear to be useful. These findings lead to the conclusion that the traditional parameters like NR, sugars, chlorophylls, ascorbic acids and protein contents commonly employed may not be of universal significance as biochemical indicators since even at the 95% level in only four or five plant species these parameters show a response. Of course these could be taken as second priority parameters. LDR, POD, SOD, and SC bear a potential for wider application at all ranges of sulphur dioxide and gaseous pollution.

Table 5 *Parameter-wise distribution of number of plant species at different levels of significance*

Levels of significance	Parameters									
	LDR	SOD	POD	Sc	Am A	Pt	Chl	As A	NR	Sg
99.9 (p < 0.01)	6	5	4 (5)	1 (2)	0	2	0	3	0 (1)	1
99.0 (p < 0.01)	10	8 (9)	7	6	1	2 (3)	0	4	1	1
95.0 (p < 0.05)	10	10	9	7 (8)	6 (7)	5	5	4	3 (4)	1
90.0 (p < 0.10)	10	10	10	8	10	5	6	6 (8)	6	6

LDR = Leaf Area Dry Weight Ratio; SOD = Superoxide Dismutase Activity; POD = Peroxidase Activity; Sc = Stomatal Conductance; Am A = Free Amino Acid; Pt = Foliar Protein; Chl = Total Chlorophyll; As A = Ascorbic Acid; NR = Nitrate Reductase Activity; Sg = Total Sugars; Values in parentheses indicate the number of plant species when the nearest 'r' value is considered.

These extensive and intensive investigations establish that one or two or even three parameters are not sufficient to reveal the ecophysiological strategy of the species to tolerate air pollution stress and that it becomes obligatory to adopt many more parameters, of which a few may be relevant in general, while a others may be more species-dependent. For example nitrate reductase activity is not a significant factor for *C. siamea*, and ascorbic acid is not relevant for *F. benghalensis*. In the case of susceptible plant species, such as *B. monosperma* and *D. sissoo*, the sugars and amino acids will stand at a low priority, while the same holds for protein in the case of *A. indica*. These data and analyses can assist us in deciding the priorities of the parameters and even species, so as to make definite recommendations for bioindication (Dubey 1992).

4. Acknowledgements

The author wishes to thank the Ministry of Environment, Govt. of India and Indian Petrochemical Corporation Ltd., Baroda for financial assistance. Thanks are due to Mr. R. Pandya for assisting in statistical treatments on the large volume of data.

5. References

Arnon, D.J. (1949) Copper Enzymes in Isolated Chloroplast, *Plant Physiol.* 24: 1-25.
Bell, J.N.B. (1984) Air Pollution Problems in Western Europe, in: Koziol, M.J. & F.R. Whatley, F.R. (eds.) *Gaseous Air Pollutants and Plant Metabolism*, Butterworths, London, pp. 4-23.
Dubey, P.S. (1990) Sulphur Dioxide and Crop Productivity - Indian Contribution, *Ind. Rev. of Life Sci.* 10: 99-120.

Dubey, P.S. & Rao, M.V. (1991) Plant System: Complex But Reliable for Monitoring Air Pollutants, in: Aery, N.C. & Chaudhary, B.L. (eds.) *Botanical Researches in India*, Himanshu Publications, Udaipur, pp. 333-344.

Dubey, P.S. (1991) Biomonitoring the Environment: Theory, Practice and Problems, *J. Environ. Biol.*, JEB Decade Issue. AEB, Meerut, India, pp. 233-241.

Dubey, P.S. (1992) Evaluation of Existing Plant Species Against Air Pollution in IPCL Area, *Green Belt Development Project Report*, IPCL, Baroda, pp. 1-54.

Heck, W.W., Krupa, S.V. & Linzon (1979) *Methodology for Assessment of Air Pollution Effects on Vegetation. A Handbook*, Air Pollution Control Ass., Pittsburgh.

Keith, H., Voisin, E., Helenc, B. & Anclair, C. (1983) Superoxide Dismutase Activity Using Alkaline Dimethyl Sulphoxide Generating System, *Annal. Biochem.* 135: 280-287.

Keller, T. (1983) Air Pollutant Deposition and Effects of Plants. In: *Effects of Accumulation of Air pollutants in Forest Ecosystems*, D. Reidel Publishing Co. Dordrecht, Holland.

Lowry, O.H., Rosenburgh, N.J., Farr, A.L. & Randell, R.S. (1951) Protein Measurement with Folin Phenol Reagent, *J. Biol. Chem.* 193: 265-275.

Malhotra, S.S. & Sarkar, S.K. (1979) Effects of Sulphur Dioxide on Sugars and Free Amino Acids Content of Pine Seedlings, *Plant Physiol.* 47: 223-238.

Patterson, J. (1958) Colorimetric Analysis of Non Metals, in: *Methods in Biochemical Analysis*, Vol. II., Interscience Publ., New York.

Posthumus, A.C. (1984) Monitoring Levels and Effects of Air Pollutants, in: Treshow, M. (ed.) *Air Pollution and Plant Life*, John Wiley and Sons, New York, pp. 73-96.

Rao, D.N. & Leblanc, B.F. (1965) Effects of SO₂ on the Lichen, Algae with Special Reference to Chlorophyll, *Bryologist* 69: 69-75.

Rao, M.V. & Dubey, P.S. (1990) Explanations for the Different Response of Certain Tropical Plants to SO₂ under Field Conditions, *Water Air Soil Pollut.* 51: 297-305.

Rosen, H. (1954) Chemical Determination of Ascorbic, Dehydroascorbic and Diketogluconic Acids, in: Glick, D. (ed.) *Methods of Biochemical Analysis*, Vol. I, Interscience Publication Inc., New York.

Rosen, H. (1957) A Modified Ninhydrin Colorimetric Analysis for Amino Acids, *Arch. Biochem. Biophy.* 67: 1015.

Schubert, R. (1982) Selected Bioindicators Used to Recognize Air Pollution, in: Streubing, L. & Jager, H.J. (eds.) *Monitoring of Air Pollutants in Plants: Methods and Problems*, Dr. W. Junk Publ., The Hague, pp. 47-51.

Shannon, L.M., Kay, E. & Lew, J.Y. (1966) Peroxidase Isoenzymes from Horse Radish Roots, *J. Biol. Chem.* 241: 2166-2172.

Shrivastava, H.C. & Mathur, K.C. (1980) Nodulation and NR Activity in Nodules and Leaves of Blackgram (*V. mungo*) as Affected by Varying Day Length, *Ind. J. Exp. Biol.* 18: 301-302.

5.8

The 'no effect' of the powerful natural sulphur pollution from Merapi volcano on vegetation

R.G. SIEFFERMAN

Abstract

The input of metals and acidifying elements from volcanoes into the atmosphere is globally weak, compared to that from industrial activity. A volcano permanently active is however a powerful local source of pollution by sulphur, fluorine, zinc, selenium, arsenic, lead and mercury, and represents an ideal place to study the effect of these elements on vegetation and human health. At Merapi (Central Java, Indonesia), we are close to the equator where strong atmospheric disturbances are rare; it rains almost everyday and a large part of the released elements have, for centuries, been washed down by the rain in the immediate vicinity of the volcano. According to volcanologists, Merapi releases 30 to 200 tons of SO_2 into the atmosphere per day of which 20% falls in a radius of 8 to 10 km. Although this seems like a small amount, it means that at least 300 kg of SO_2 has fallen down per hectare per year for centuries. Despite the acid precipitations, the negative effect is not obvious; the vegetation is always very lush with a profusion of lichens, liverworts and mosses on the trees and the forest reaches up to 2,500 m in altitude, as close as 1 km to the crater. In spite of the high input of polluting and acidifying elements, there is no visible evidence of forest perishing outside the fire-destroyed areas. The negative effect of sulphur on vegetation remains to be proved.

1. Introduction

Since 1955 there have been an increasing number of publications concerning the destruction of forests in Europe and changes in the composition of rain water, in particular, increased acidification. The principal cause might be SO_2 and its oxidation to sulphuric acid (Almer *et al.* 1974, Gorham 1955, Hofmann & Rosen 1980, Overrein *et al.* 1980, Paces 1985).

Despite the increasing number of publications, none has actually proved that sulphur is the main element causing destruction. The facts reported in the scientific literature are contradictory: agronomists recommend the use of sulphur as considerable increases in yields have been shown after sulphur fertilization (Cornforth & Sinclair 1986, Fauconnier 1986, Morris 1986).

The literature on active volcanoes shows that all release a large quantity of sulphur in the form of SO_2, hundreds and sometimes even thousands of tons per day (Buat Menard & Arnold 1978, Phelan *et al.* 1982, Symonds 1985). In addition to this, variable quantities of other toxic elements are also released:

- Chlorine, fluorine and bromine up to 100 tons/day
- Zinc and copper up to 3 tons/day
- Selenium, arsenic and lead up to 800 kg/day
- Mercury up to 100 kg/day
- Cadmium up to 30 kg/day

Soil experts and agronomists working in volcanic equatorial areas know very well that outside the zones destroyed either mechanically or thermally by eruptions the vegetation around a volcano is always very lush.

Despite undeniable improvements over the past 20 years in our knowledge of the sulphur cycle and its major fluxes (Brimblecombe 1989, Lein & Ivanov 1989), the negative effect of sulphur on vegetation remains to be proved.

We know well enough the SO_2 content in the atmosphere. In industrialized countries, the concentration varies from 0.2 to 100 ppb (Hidy 1973). The content depends on latitude and shifts from high values of around 3 ppb at 40° North to very low values of 0.1-0.2 ppb in the equatorial zone (Georgii 1970, Cullis & Hirschler 1980, Delmas & Servant 1983, Rodhe & Granat 1984).

The SO_2 content at the equatorial zone is mainly a consequence of the high water vapor content of the atmosphere which plays the powerful role of 'sink', and of the very high chemical reactivity of the gas itself. Therefore, the low SO_2 content cannot be correlated with the volume of discharge of sulphur sources at altitudes below 4,000 m.

Although the input of metals and acidifying elements from volcanoes to the atmosphere is globally weak compared to that of industrial activity (Le Guern 1982, Berresheim & Jaeschke 1983, Moller 1984, Rhode & Granat 1984), it is no less true that a permanently active volcano is a powerful local source of pollution of sulphur, fluorine, zinc, selenium, arsenic, lead and mercury, and it represents an ideal place for a study of the effect of these elements on the vegetation and soil.

In temperate zones with a relatively dry atmosphere, elements released by a volcano can stay for a long time in the atmosphere and, mixed with industrial pollution, can be carried away over hundreds of kilometers. Rhode (1972) estimates, for SO_2, a possible life-span of 30-70 hours under these conditions before its precipitation by rain. Things are different close to a volcano in a humid equatorial zone where the elements are released into an atmosphere containing more than 80% water vapor. In these conditions, they dissolve very quickly and their residence time is only several hours (Scott & Hobbs 1967).

2.   The case of Merapi volcano

At Merapi, a permanently active volcano, we are close to the equator where strong atmospheric disturbances are rare. It rains almost every day and a large part of the released metals and acidifying elements have, for centuries, fallen down with the rain in the immediate vicinity of the volcano.

According to volcanologists (Symonds 1985, Bahar 1986), Merapi releases 30 to 200 tons of SO_2 into the atmosphere per day (Table 1). We can expect, through experimental determinations of SO_4^{2-} in the precipitations, that 25 tons of SO_2 will fall within a radius of 8 to 10 km. This implies 12 to 28 ppm of SO_2 in the rain in that area for a rainfall of 2,500 mm per year. In layman's terms, this means that it has 'rained' 300 to 700 kg of SO_2 per hectare per year in the area in question for centuries.

Table 1 *Transport rates (Jan.-Febr. 1984) of elements into the atmosphere by Merapi volcano*

Elements		Fluxes in kg/day
S	Sulphur	200,000
Cl	Chlorine	30,000
F	Fluorine	1,500
Br	Bromine	140
Zn	Zinc	89
Pb	Lead	7
As	Arsenic	4.6
Cu	Copper	0.8
Sb	Antimony	0.5
Cd	Cadmium	0.2

Source: Symonds (1985).

Despite the acid precipitations, the negative effect is not obvious; the vegetation is always very lush with a profusion of lichens and mosses on the trees and liverworts on the soil, while the forest reaches to 2,500 m in altitude as close as 1 km to the crater. In spite of the high input of heavy metals and acidifying elements, there is no visible evidence of forest perishing outside the fire destroyed areas. The situation on the slope of Merapi volcano is illustrated in Plates 1 to 4.

Following Van Bemmelen (1949), the essential landscape of the present Merapi volcano was created by a paroxymal eruption in the year 1006 AD. Volcanic activity has not changed since then (Kusumadinata 1979), and we can evaluate the amounts of pollutants received by each hectare in the immediate vicinity since this eruption: some tens of tons of fluorine, 2 tons of bromine, 3 tons of zinc, 1 ton of lead, and at least 500 kg of mercury. However, these figures signify little since we have ignored the residence time of these elements in the soils.

Plate 1 *Tree line on the Southern slope of Merapi volcano. Notice the fire and the upper area with rocks*

Plate 2 *Detail of Plate 1. Notice the luxuriant vegetation as close as 500 meter to the crater*

Plate 3 *Western slope of Merapi after the 1992 eruption. Notice the abrupt contact at about 2000 m alt. between forest islets and the fire-destroyed upper area*

Plate 4 *The every day flow of gases down the slopes of Merapi volcano*

3. Conclusion

The Merapi landscape presents 3 exceptional characteristics:

1. An extremely rapid increase in pollutants in about 30 km from the lowest to the highest values in the world.
2. Homogenous Andosols catenas, with allophane type clay minerals, having variable charges, which allow us to expect particularly strong fixation of S, F, Se and As, in anionic form.
3. A forest ecosystem that has functioned for millennia which should allow us to see visual negative effects of these elements on the vegetation.

We can only conclude that despite high inputs of polluting and acidifying elements, there is no clear visible evidence at Merapi volcano of negative effects on the vegetation.

Again we notice the same contradiction: in the zone where acid precipitations seem particularly strong and have affected the environment for centuries, maybe millennia, a negative effect of acidifying elements such as sulphur, chlorine and fluorine on the vegetation is not obvious, and one may even speak of beneficial effects.

It still remains an open question why such a clear discrepancy exists between the effects of acidifying substances on pine forests in the northern hemisphere and the Merapi case. Diverging soil chemical properties, as well as the evolution of SO_2 - tolerant vegetation may be involved.

4. References

Almer, B., Dickson, W., Ekstrom, C., Hornstrom, E. & Miller, U. (1974) Effects of Acidification of Swedish Lakes, *Ambio* 3: 30-36.

Bahar, I. (1986) Volcanic Survey of Indonesia (oral communication).

Berresheim, H. & Jaeschke, W. (1983) The Contribution of Volcanoes to the Global Atmospheric Sulphur Budget, *J. Geophys. Res.* 88 (C6): 3732-3740.

Brimblecombe, P., Hammer, C., Rodhe, H., Ryaboshapko, A. & Boutron, C.F. (1989) Human Influence on the Sulphur Cycle, in: Evolution of the Global Biogeochemical Sulphur Cycle, *Scope* 39: 77-121.

Buat-Menard, P. & Arnold, M. (1978) The Heavy Metal Chemistry of Atmosphere Particulate Matter Emitted by Mount Etna Volcano, *Geoph. Res. Lett.* 5: 245-248.

Cornforth, I.S. & Sinclair, A.G. (1986) Fertilizer Advice for New Zealand Farmers with Particular Reference to Sulphur Requirements, Int. Conf. Management and Fertilization of Upland Soils, *Ac. Sinica Proceedings* 144.

Cullis, C.F. & Hirschler, M.M. (1980) Atmospheric Sulphur: Natural and Man Made Sources, *Atmos. Environ.* 14: 1263-1278.

Delmas, R. & Servant, J. (1983) Atmospheric Balance of Sulphur Above an Equatorial Forest, *Tellus* 35B: 110-120.

Fauconnier, D. (1986) Sulphur Fertilization in Grain Legumes, Int. Conf. Management and Fertilization of Upland Soils, Ac. Sinica Proc. 130.

Georgii, H.W. (1970) Contribution to the Atmosphere Sulphur Budget, J. Geophys. Res. 75: 2365-2371.

Gorham, E. (1955) On the Acidity and Salinity of Rain, Geochim. Cosmochim. Acta 7: 231-239.

Hidy, G.M. (1973) Removal Processes of Gaseous and Particulate Pollutants, in: Rasool, S.I. (ed.) Chemistry of the Lower Atmosphere, Plenum Press, New York.

Hofmann, D.J. & Rosen, J.M. (1980) Stratospheric Sulphuric Acid Layer: Evidence for an Anthropogenic Component, Science 208: 1368-1370.

Kusumadinata, K. (1979) Data dasar gunung api Indonesia, Volcanol. Bull. Special Edit., 834 p. (Catalogue of reference on Indonesian volcanoes with eruptions in historic times), Direktorat Geologi, Bandung.

Le Guern, F. (1982) Les debits de CO_2 et SO_2 volcaniques dans l'atmosphere, Bull. Vulcanol. 45: 197-202.

Lein, A.Y. & Ivanov, M.V. (1989) Contribution of Endogenous Sulphur to the Global Biogeochemical Cycle in the Geological Past, in: Evolution of the Global Biogeochemical Sulphur Cycle, Scope 39: 65-74.

Moller, D. (1984) Estimation of the Global Man-made Sulphur Emission, Atmos. Environ. 18: 19-27.

Morris, J.R. (1986) Sulphur - A Major Nutrient for Field Improvement, Int. Conf. Management and Fertilization of Upland Soils, Ac. Sinica Proc. 17.

Overrein, L., Seip, M.H. & Tollan, A. (1980) Acid Precipitation Effects on Forest and Fish, Final report, Oslo-As., 175 p.

Paces, T. (1985) Sources of Acidification in Central Europe Estimated from Elemental Budgets in Small Basins, Nature 315: 31-36.

Phelan, J.M., Finnegan, D.L., Ballantine, D.S., Zoller, W.H., Hart, M.A. & Moyers, J.L. (1982) Airborne Aerosol Measurements in the Quiscent Plume at Mount St. Helens: September, 1950, Geophys. Res. Lett. 9: 1093-1096.

Rhode, H. (1972) A Study of the Sulphur Budget for the Atmosphere over Northern Europe, Tellus 24: 54-57.

Rhode, H. & Granat, L. (1984) An Evaluation of Sulphate in European Precipitations 1955-1982, Atmos. Environ. 18: 2627-2639.

Scott, W.D. & Hobbs, P.V. (1967) The Formation of Sulphate in Water Droplets, J. Atm. Sci. 24: 54-57.

Symonds, R.B. (1985) Transport and Enrichment of Elements in High Temperature Gases at Merapi Volcano Indonesia, Thesis, Michigan Technology University, 102 p.

Van Bemmelen, R.W. (1949) The Geology of Indonesia, Vol. IA, Martinus Nijhoff, The Hague.

Author index

Hyne, R.V.
(243)

Alligator Rivers Region Research Institute, Office of the Supervising Scientist, PMB 2 Post Office Jabiru, NT 0886, Australia

Ismail, A.
(181)

Department of Biology, Universiti Pertanian Malaysia, 43400 UPM Serdang, Selangor, Malaysia

Janssen, M.P.M.
(251)

IBN-DLO, Department of Ecotoxicology, Kemperberger-weg 67, 6816 RM Arnhem, The Netherlands.
Current address: RIVM-LSO, P.O. Box 1, 3720 BA Biltho-ven, The Netherlands

Jones, D.T.
(191, 315)

Biology Department, Universiti Brunei Darusalam, Bandar Seri Begawan 3186, Brunei Darusalam
Current address: Department of Entomology, Natural History Museum, Cromwell Road, London SW7 5BD, United Kingdom

Liang, O.B.
(131)

Department of Biology, Bandung Institute of Technology, Jl. Ganesha 10, Bandung 40132, Indonesia

Luwihana, S.
(185)

Institute of Science & Technology 'AKPRIND', Jl. Kalisa-hak 28 Kompleks Balapan, P.O. Box 45, Yogyakarta, Indonesia

Magallona, E.D.
(19, 89, 119, 145)

Pesticides Chemistry and Toxicology Laboratory, National Crop Protection Center, University of the Philippines at Los Baños, College, Laguna 4031, Philippines

Magbauna, M.G.
(89)

Pesticides Chemistry and Toxicology Laboratory, National Crop Protection Center, University of the Philippines at Los Baños, College, Laguna 4031, Philippines

Majid, A.A.
(209)

Department of Nuclear Science, National University of Malaysia, 43600 Bangi, Malaysia

Makarim, N.
(3)

Deputy Head for Pollution Control BAPEDAL. Artha Lo-ka Building 11th Floor, Jl. Jend. Sudirman 2, Jakarta, Indonesia

Merlin, G.
(113)

Laboratory of Biology and Biochemistry, Ecole Supe-rieurs d'Ingenieurs en Genie de l'Environment et de la Construction, 73000 Chambery, France

Subject index